INFORMATION PROCESSING
BIASES AND ANXIETY

INFORMATION PROCESSING BIASES AND ANXIETY

A Developmental Perspective

Edited by

Julie A. Hadwin and Andy P. Field

A John Wiley & Sons, Ltd., Publication

This edition first published 2010
© 2010 John Wiley & Sons Ltd.

Wiley-Blackwell is an imprint of John Wiley & Sons, formed by the merger of Wiley's global Scientific, Technical, and Medical business with Blackwell Publishing.

Registered Office
John Wiley & Sons Ltd, The Atrium, Southern Gate, Chichester, West Sussex, PO19 8SQ, UK

Editorial Offices
The Atrium, Southern Gate, Chichester, West Sussex, PO19 8SQ, UK
9600 Garsington Road, Oxford, OX4 2DQ, UK
350 Main Street, Malden, MA 02148-5020, USA

For details of our global editorial offices, for customer services, and for information about how to apply for permission to reuse the copyright material in this book please see our website at www.wiley.com/wiley-blackwell.

The right of the editors to be identified as the author of this work has been asserted in accordance with the UK Copyright, Designs and Patents Act 1988.

Wiley also publishes its books in a variety of electronic formats. Some content that appears in print may not be available in electronic books.

Designations used by companies to distinguish their products are often claimed as trademarks. All brand names and product names used in this book are trade names, service marks, trademarks or registered trademarks of their respective owners. The publisher is not associated with any product or vendor mentioned in this book. This publication is designed to provide accurate and authoritative information in regard to the subject matter covered. It is sold on the understanding that the publisher is not engaged in rendering professional services. If professional advice or other expert assistance is required, the services of a competent professional should be sought.

Library of Congress Cataloging-in-Publication Data
Information processing biases and anxiety : a developmental perspective / edited by Julie A. Hadwin and Andy Field.
        p. cm.
   Includes bibliographical references and index.
   ISBN 978-0-470-99819-9 (cloth)
   1. Anxiety in children. 2. Human information processing in children. I. Hadwin, Julie A.
II. Field, Andy P.
   BF723.A5I54 2010
   155.4'1246 – dc22

                                                                                      2009052147

A catalogue record for this book is available from the British Library.

Typeset in 9.5/11.5pt Minion by Laserwords Private Limited, Chennai, India.
Printed in Singapore by Markono Print Media Pte Ltd.
1 – 2010

Contents

List of Contributors

Yair Bar-Haim
Department of Psychology
Tel Aviv University
Tel Aviv, Israel

Maria J.W. Cowart
Child Study Center
Department of Psychology
Virginia Polytechnic Institute
   and State University
Blacksburg, VA
USA

Cathy Creswell
School of Psychology and Clinical
   Language Studies
University of Reading
Whiteknights
Reading, UK

Peter Cooper
School of Psychology and Clinical
   Language Studies
University of Reading
Whiteknights
Reading, UK

Nick Donnelly
Centre for Visual Cognition
University of Southampton
Southampton, UK

Thalia C. Eley
Social, Genetic and Developmental
   Psychiatry Centre
Institute of Psychiatry
Kings College London
De Crespigny Park
London, UK

Andy P. Field
Department of Psychology
University of Sussex
East Sussex, UK

Nathan A. Fox
Department of Human Development
Child Development Laboratory
University of Maryland
College Park, MD
USA

Matthew Garner
School of Psychology and
Division of Clinical Neuroscience
School of Medicine
University of Southampton
Southampton, UK

Julie A. Hadwin
Developmental Brain-Behaviour
   Laboratory
University of Southampton
Southampton, UK

Jorg Huijding
Institute of Psychology
Erasmus University Rotterdam
Rotterdam, The Netherlands

Sarah M. Helfinstein
Department of Human Development
Child Development Laboratory
University of Maryland
College Park, MD
USA

Tina In-Albon
Clinical Child and Adolescent
    Psychology
University of Basel
Basel, Switzerland

Merel Kindt
Faculty of Social and Behavioural
    Sciences
University of Amsterdam
Amsterdam, The Netherlands

Kathryn J. Lester
Department of Psychology
University of Sussex
East Sussex, UK

Tamaryn Menneer
Centre for Visual Cognition
University of Southampton
Southampton, UK

Lynne Murray
School of Psychology and Clinical
    Language Studies
University of Reading
Whiteknights
Reading, UK

Peter Muris
Institute of Psychology
Erasmus University Rotterdam
Rotterdam
The Netherlands

Thomas H. Ollendick
Child Study Center
Department of Psychology
Virginia Polytechnic Institute
    and State University
Blacksburg VA
USA

Koraly Pérez-Edgar
Department of Psychology
George Mason University
Fairfax, VA
USA

Helen J. Richards
Developmental Brain-Behaviour
    Laboratory
University of Southampton
Southampton, UK

Silvia Schneider
Clinical Child and Adolescent
    Psychology
University of Basel
Basel, Switzerland

Lauren K. White
Department of Human Development
Child Development Laboratory
University of Maryland
College Park, MD
USA

Zoë C. Nightingale
Department of Psychology
University of Sussex
East Sussex, UK

Reinout W. Wiers
Department of Psychology
University of Amsterdam
Amsterdam
The Netherlands

Helena M.S. Zavos
Social, Genetic and Developmental
    Psychiatry Centre
Institute of Psychiatry
Kings College London
London, UK

Preface

When I go upstairs to bed,
I usually give a loud cough.
This is to scare The Monster off.

When I come to my room,
I usually slam the door right back.
This is to squash The Man in Black
Who sometimes hides there.

Nor do I walk to the bed,
But usually run and jump instead.
This is to stop The Hand –
Which is under there all right –
From grabbing my ankles.

Reprinted with premission from Allan Ahlberg, 'Bedtime' from *Please Mrs. Butler*, Puffin Books, London. © Allan Ahlberg 1983.

1

An Introduction to the Study of Information Processing Biases in Childhood Anxiety: Theoretical and Methodological Issues

Julie A. Hadwin and Andy P. Field
Jah7@soton.ac.uk

Why is the Study of Information Processing Biases in Child Anxiety Important?

Anxiety is an emotion that appears early in childhood and follows a typical developmental course. Inborn fears are seen in children younger than 2 years who display transient anxieties and worries associated with separation and strangers (Kagan, Kearsley and Zelazo, 1978). Fears related to the dark and to imaginary creatures typically appear at around 5–6 years of age (Bauer, 1976) and are thought to be a function of cognitive change related to an emerging imaginative capacity (Wellman, 1990). Other fears, such as fear of failure, appear later in childhood (Muris *et al.*, 2000; Schaefer, Watkins and Burnham, 2003) and are more likely to reflect learning processes related to distinctive aspects of a child's environment (Stevenson, Batten and Cherner, 1992). The early occurrence of anxiety in childhood is argued to play an adaptive function that facilitates the detection of threat or danger (Bowlby, 1973) and promotes the development of emotional regulation and coping (Sroufe, 1995). The development of these skills through anxiety displays initially rely on the elicitation of nurturing behaviours (e.g. increased proximity, soothing, verbal reasoning) from caregivers when children are young (Bowlby, 1969; Sroufe, 1995). As children get older, cognitive development leads to an increasing reliance on self-regulation strategies such as attention switching and positive thinking (Fox and Calkins, 2003).

Information Processing Biases and Anxiety: A Developmental Perspective Edited by Julie A. Hadwin and Andy P. Field
© 2010 John Wiley & Sons, Ltd.

Typical and atypical patterns of anxiety share core underlying features related to a distinctive profile of physical change (increased physiological arousal), cognition (worry and rumination) and behaviour (avoidance; Lang, 1985. Clinical levels of anxiety occur in around 2–15% of children and adolescents (review by Rapee, Schniering and Hudson, 2009) and are associated with atypical (i.e. developmentally inappropriate) and maladaptive behaviours (e.g. excessive crying, persistent fears and anxious apprehension) that interfere with daily routines and the development of relationships (American Psychiatric Association, 2000). The emergence of anxiety disorders follows a similar developmental pattern to anxieties seen in typical development, suggesting that children at different ages are at risk for developing specific disorders (Weems, 2008). Concerns with separation, for example, are most commonly seen early in childhood, while specific phobias, social phobia and generalized anxiety disorder occur more frequently in late childhood and early adolescence (Weiss and Last, 2001; Essau *et al.*, 2001). Researchers have found that symptoms associated with clinical or sub-clinical levels of anxiety can be found in children as young as 3 years (Egger and Angold, 2006). Further studies have shown that these symptoms often follow a stable course from childhood through adolescence and into adulthood (Essau, Conradt and Petermann, 2002; Roza *et al.*, 2003; review by Weems, 2008). In addition, anxiety has been found to place children at risk for academic underachievement (Ashcraft, 2002; Crozier and Hostettler, 2003; Owens *et al.*, 2008). It is also associated with social and peer difficulties (Asendorpf, Denissen and van Aken, 2008) and the development of other mental (Lewinsohn *et al.*, 2008; Roza *et al.*, 2003) and physical (Beesdo *et al.*, 2009) health problems.

Given the early occurrence of anxiety disorders and evidence for its chronic course, studies within developmental psychopathology are increasingly pursuing a research agenda that allows researchers and clinicians to understand factors that play a causal role in its development and contribute to its stability over time. Cognitive biases for the detection and processing of threat-related information are a significant feature of adult (review by Bar-Haim *et al.*, 2007) and, increasingly, developmental models of anxiety (review by Muris and Field, 2008). Some early models did not recognize information processing biases as being causally linked to the development of anxiety (e.g. Muris and Merckelbach, 2001). Research has, however, demonstrated through longitudinal (Warren, Emde and Sroufe, 2000) and experimental studies (MacLeod *et al.*, 2002) that they can play a causal role in its onset.

Given the increasing recognition of the importance of understanding information processing biases, we are delighted to be able to bring together a collection of papers to give a comprehensive overview of relevant theory and research related to biases in children and adolescents who experience elevated or clinical levels of anxiety. We are grateful to the contributors who have taken time to summarize the theoretical frameworks they work in and the related empirical research to provide a series of chapters that serve to establish a firm scientific basis for this area of study and to highlight important avenues for further research.

We have structured the book in two broad sections. The first section allows the reader to consider how researchers have adapted and utilized experimental paradigms typically developed for use with adults to younger populations. Its aim is to highlight the rich canvas on which different researchers have explored diverse aspects of information processing (e.g. selective attention, inhibition, interpretation) in anxious children and adolescents through different levels of analysis (behavioural, neurophysiological and neuropsychological). Working through these chapters the reader will start to get some sense of the theoretical and empirical issues that are generic to the broader research programme on information processing biases in childhood anxiety. Section 2 aims to provide readers with an understanding of the role of information processing biases more broadly in the context of developmental psychopathology. It presents a comprehensive series of chapters that explore the origins of information processing biases in development and that draw on the microparadigms utilized in the study of development and psychopathology to consider issues related to heritability, temperament, learning and parenting (Achenbach, 1990; Cicchetti and Cohen, 1995). In addition, this section also provides an overview of the relevance of this research programme for the development of preventive methods and treatment protocols in childhood and adolescent anxiety.

Information Processing Biases in Childhood Anxiety: Theoretical and Research Issues

Chapters in Part One highlight that one challenge for research in information processing biases with children and adolescents is that the majority of the phenomena they test stem from theory and method utilized in adult psychopathology. Several chapters describe the experimental and practical modifications they have used when working with children and adolescents. These chapters suggest that making simple paradigm changes when working with younger populations (e.g. using picture-based stimuli rather than word-based stimuli or reducing the number of experimental trials) has been effective in allowing this area of research to develop. Researchers using the implicit association task (IAT), designed to look at the extent to which individuals automatically associate objects or events and described by Huijding, Wiers and Field (Chapter 7), for example, have made several changes to a task typically used with adults to make it accessible for children. These changes include reducing the number of trials and using specifically designed response pads or a touch screen when working with very young children. Muris (Chapter 2) outlines further modifications to investigate covariation bias (perceptions that two stimuli are consistently associated) and probability bias (increased perceptions of the likelihood of the occurrence of future negative events) in childhood anxiety. It describes a series of studies that have found that the use of emotional faces to depict negative outcomes to investigate covariation bias has been successful in demonstrating that anxious children more readily link negative stimuli to negative outcomes.

Once changes have been made to established paradigms, a further challenge for researchers is to demonstrate that the tasks they are using are reliable and valid.

Very few researchers working either with adults or with children provide details about the psychometric properties of the cognitive tasks they use. Some researchers have explored the extent to which one task that purports to measure attention to threat correlates with similar measures. For example, Chapter 3 (Nightingale, Field and Kindt) summarized recent work showing that in an emotion categorization task, the mis-categorization of faces with low levels of happiness (as angry) was correlated with increased reaction times (i.e. greater interference) to colour name threat versus neutral words in an emotional Stroop task. However, this chapter also highlights earlier work showing that interference of colour naming threat words in a Stroop task was not correlated with selective attention to similar stimuli in a dot-probe task, suggesting that these tasks tap different underlying cognitive mechanisms. Chapter 7 also reports several indices on the validity and reliability of the IAT task, highlighting moderate internal consistency and test–retest reliability. Furthermore, In-Albon and Schneider (Chapter 6) report statistics related to the psychometric properties of eye tracking tasks in children. They outline a number of studies that have found good internal consistency related to anti-saccade errors. In addition, they report good and moderate test–retest reliability for anti-saccade errors and predictive saccades, respectively. However, the general lack of information related to the psychometric properties of the tasks used to explore information processing biases in children and adults should be addressed in future work.

Other researchers raise the issue of the specificity of information biases across different anxiety disorders, and between anxiety and other internalizing (depression) or externalizing difficulties (conduct disorder). Chapter 1, for example, describes results to show that information processing biases for threat have been associated with depression and externalizing disorders. This chapter does, however, note that some progress has been made utilizing social cognitive tasks to understand how biases have been differentially associated with separation anxiety and social anxiety, as well as between anxiety and depression. Chapter 3 highlights that research has failed to demonstrate specificity of Stroop interference in children with separation anxiety disorder, generalized anxiety disorder and specific phobia for anxiety relevant words. It is evident that if researchers want to argue that information processing biases in anxiety represent a core cognitive feature of this disorder, then they need to be able to demonstrate that the bias is universal in children who experience anxiety; that it plays a causal role in its onset and that it is specific to this disorder (Happé, 1994).[1]

---

[1] This approach to 'sensitivity' (the idea that all children with anxiety should display information processing biases) and 'specificity' (that information processing biases for threat are largely limited to anxiety and its subtypes) is consistent with the suggestion that information processing biases can be conceptualized as endophenotypes (see Crosbie *et al.*, 2008, p. 45) and is similar to thinking about core cognitive deficits in pervasive developmental disorders, such as autism. Other approaches to understanding cognitive deficits in psychological disorders and their treatment are quite different. The transdiagnostic approach, for example, aims to understand the extent to which cognitive or behavioural factors represent shared processes that can cause or maintain a range of psychological disorders (Mansell, 2008).

The review of this literature serves to highlight that the majority of studies exploring information processing biases have worked with typically developing children and adolescents who show some variation on self-report measures of trait anxiety or more specific anxieties. If it is accepted that anxiety represents a dimensional construct such that the boundaries between high levels of anxiety within the typical range and sub-clinical or clinical levels of anxiety are 'fluid' (MacLeod, 1991; Rapee, 2001), then research with typically developing children provides an effective vehicle for testing and developing models of anxiety that can be applied to a less accessible clinical population. In support of this approach, the results of studies described across the book have generally found that information processing biases using a range of tasks associated with high versus low anxiety in a typical range show similar findings with children and adolescents who have been diagnosed with an anxiety disorder. In order to support the integrity of theoretical models and research with typical populations, researchers should also be careful to test models of anxiety with clinical groups of children.

Several chapters note that very little research has considered developmental factors in the study of information processing biases, either longitudinally or cross-sectionally. It is unclear, for example, when biases become most evident in childhood anxiety, whether they show a similar developmental pattern to the emergence of anxiety disorders (e.g. do biases related to separation emerge before those linked to social factors?) and whether they follow a stable developmental course. Chapter 3 outlines what is currently the only strictly developmental theory (i.e. it predicts change over time) related to information processing biases and childhood anxiety (see Kindt and van den Hout, 2001). Kindt and van den Hout developed this framework based on research on anxiety and inhibition using the Stroop task. This framework proposes that information processing biases for negative or threat stimuli are a typical feature of development that is evident in middle childhood and that dissipates in early adolescence, except for children with elevated anxiety. The key feature of this theory is not that information processing biases place children at risk for the development of anxiety, rather that the failure to develop an ability to inhibit attention to threat makes children vulnerable. The evidence base for this proposed developmental course is, however, mixed. Chapter 3 highlights that (consistent with Kindt's account) anxiety-related interference of threat relevant material in the Stroop and other inhibitory tasks has been reliably shown in late childhood and early adolescence, with mixed findings before this age. Few studies have, however, been able to empirically demonstrate the proposed developmental course of information processing biases outlined in Kindt and van den Hout's (2001) framework.

Further chapters also describe work to understand links between cognitive development and information processing biases in childhood. Chapter 1, for example, outlines a series of studies which show that cognitive ability (as measured by theory of mind and conservation tasks) is linked to emotional reasoning and interpretation biases associated with physical symptoms, indicating that the emergence of this phenomenon may be linked to specific developmental stages in childhood. It reports further work highlighting that covariation bias is more evident in children aged 12 years and above versus children aged 8–11 years.

The chapter links this finding to a Piagetian change in abstract reasoning in late childhood and argues that some information processing biases may reflect a cognitive developmental shift that occurs at this time. These studies suggest that age represents a risk factor for the development of information processing biases in children and further work is needed to understand links between cognitive development and the emergence of biases across childhood.

Chapter 1 also highlighted other factors that can moderate interpretation biases including children's perception of physical change in emotional situations. It notes that younger children use information about physical symptoms of anxiety in emotional reasoning tasks, an effect that was found to decrease with age. This developmental pattern is used to propose that emotional reasoning might represent a vulnerability factor for the development of anxiety disorders in young children. The inclusion of a physiological aspect of anxiety (either actual physiological change or an individual's sensitivity or perception of change) in the study of information processing is notable, due to its general absence in developmental research. The lack of a systematic programme of research to understand the impact of both state and trait anxiety in the context of information processing biases in childhood and adolescence anxiety is surprising given the prominence of both aspects in adult models of anxiety (e.g. Mogg and Bradley, 1998; Williams *et al.*, 2007). Further work is required to understand the effects of both trait and state aspects of anxiety in the emergence of information processing biases across development.

Linked to Kindt and van den Hout's (2001) aim to understand information processing biases in the context of the development of inhibitory control, recent theoretical models related to adults (Eysenck *et al.*, 2007) and children (Lonigan *et al.*, 2004) propose that associations between anxiety and information processing biases can be potentially moderated by attentional or effortful control. Attentional control is conceptualized as an individual's ability to strategically regulate attention (Derryberry and Reed, 2002). Effortful control is a similar concept and is defined as 'the ability to inhibit a dominant response in order to activate a subdominant response, in order to plan, and to detect errors' (Rothbart, Sheese and Posner, 2007, p. 3). These models of anxiety relate to 'biased competition models of selective attention' (Bishop, 2007, p. 310) and encapsulate the interplay between the proposed automatic capture of attention to threat in anxiety (reflecting activation of the amygdale and related structures) and the more fragile role of top-down processes (related to activation of the pre-frontal cortex).

Some chapters present recent evidence that effortful or attentional control in adults (Derryberry and Reed, 2002; Reinholdt-Dunne, Mogg and Bradley, 2009) and children (Lonigan and Vasey, 2009) moderate the development of information processing biases. In other words, the association between biases for threat and anxiety is most clear when individuals also show poor attentional or effortful control. This programme of research is linked to further work outlined in Chapter 7 based on the dual-processing model of addiction (see Tiffany, 1990). Chapter 7 considers research which has found that links between drug (alcohol and cigarette) use in adolescence and drug-related associations in memory are moderated by working memory capacity. (These associations are clearest when working memory capacity is low.) It contrasts the dual-processing framework with the discussion of top-down and bottom-up processing outlined in attentional control theories in anxiety (Eysenck *et al.*, 2007) to suggest that while anxiety models focus on links between cognition and emotion, the dual process model of addiction considers the relationship between automatic associations in memory and links with behaviour more broadly.

Working within a similar conceptual framework, Donnelly, Meneer (Chapter 5) considered the use of visual search paradigms in adults and children to look at evidence for the automatic capture of threat in anxious individuals. This paradigm is often used to explore selective attention to threat in anxiety and to test the proposition featured in several adult models of anxiety (e.g. Williams *et al.*, 2007) that threat automatically captures attention, where automatic processing is defined as being involuntary and unintentional (vs. strategic and effortful; see Wolfe, 1994). The chapter reviews how the visual search paradigm has been used to investigate the relative role of top-down (using target searches) and bottom-up (using odd one out search) processing. It outlines the basic processes that influence visual search and discusses how research with children and adults supports the proposition that anxiety moderates search either to enhance threat detection for phobic relevant stimuli or threat stimuli or to make decisions about when to terminate search. Consistent with other chapters in the book, it proposes that this influence is likely to be a function of individual vulnerability that interacts with experience and learning, where these combine to adjust template thresholds in the visual search task for threat stimuli in relation to speed and decision-making in anxiety.

The notion of automatic processing in information processing biases is also addressed in Chapter 7. Utilizing the dual-processing framework this chapter describes a series of tasks designed to explore indirect automatic associations for threat in anxiety. The chapter argues that the use of experimental measures including the IAT, the affective priming task (APP) and the extrinsic affective Simon task (EAST) allow an exploration of the extent to which anxiety-related information in memory is automatically activated in individuals who experience anxiety. The EAST has shown some promising results with children in demonstrating how learned associations can lead to automatic (valence-relevant) processing of these stimuli. The use of these indirect measures more generally have, however, provided mixed results with childhood research. Further research is described to demonstrate the utility of this task in exploring automatic associations of rejection in adolescents with low perceived social acceptance or in negative racial attitudes in children and adolescents. This chapter also notes that these tasks can be utilized alongside more strategic tasks to consider whether automatic biases concur with explicit judgements and to tease apart implicit and explicit processing in anxiety.

Following the theme of automatic capture of threat in anxiety, Garner (Chapter 4) outlines research on information processing biases in childhood and adolescence that has used paradigms that allow some consideration of attentional capture or difficulty in disengaging from threat in anxious children. In relation to attentional capture, this chapter specifically considers evidence based on a vigilance-avoidance model of anxiety (Mogg and Bradley, 1998). It describes work with adults to show that the manipulation of stimulus exposure has allowed researchers to demonstrate vigilance for threat in anxiety at short exposures (<500 milliseconds) and avoidance of threat at longer exposures (>1500 milliseconds). Furthermore, it outlines developmental research which has found evidence of both vigilance and avoidance to threat words and pictures across different types of anxiety and for both clinical and non-clinical anxious populations. The chapter also highlights some preliminary evidence which suggests that anxiety-related biases might work differentially between gender, with girls showing increased vigilance and boys showing increased avoidance of threat stimuli. Research related to understanding whether information processing biases operate differently between genders is sparse.

Linked to the notion of vigilance-avoidance in anxiety, Chapter 6 argues that reliance on behavioural indices of attention provide researchers with a 'snapshot' of attentional processing in anxiety. This chapter considers the benefits of using eye tracking methodology in anxiety research and highlights its utility in allowing researchers to record continuous eye movements, as well as other indices of attention (i.e. first fixation, number of fixations and time spent looking at specific stimuli). Consistent with Chapter 4, it reveals some interesting findings in relation to the time course of attentional processing in adult anxiety that are consistent with a vigilance-avoidance model of attention. It describes several studies that support the notion of initial attention to threat followed by a late avoidance of these stimuli (occurring at around 1500 milliseconds after stimulus presentation) in adults. It also outlines some preliminary results to support this attentional pattern in children with separation anxiety disorder. The exploration of attention in anxiety at different levels of analysis serves to validate the methods and findings in this area of research.

Consistent with a research agenda that moves away from a reliance on behavioural indices of attention to investigate information processing biases in anxiety, Chapter 8 (Pèrez-Edgar and Bar-Haim) looks at empirical research that has used neuropsychological techniques. The chapter focuses on the two most commonly used techniques where these allow an exploration of the time course of information processing [using event-related potential (ERP)], as well as methods that give some indication of brain pathways and locations or structures utilized in the processing of threat information [through functional magnetic resonance imaging (fMRI)]. The chapter describes how neuropsychological research using the dot-probe task has been utilized to investigate early ERP components in anxiety. It outlines several papers that have found increased C1 amplitudes (a negative ERP component which occurs at around 60–90 milliseconds after stimulus presentation and which is suggested to reflect the primary visual cortex response to stimuli; Stolarova, Keil and Moratti, 2006) to threatening stimuli in anxiety. The authors use these findings to argue that the occurrence of neural activation during the early processing of threat in anxiety is likely to be mediated by amygdale activity (see also Anderson and Phelps, 2001; Bishop, 2007). This chapter also outlines a number of studies that have used fMRI and which have found associations between adolescents with generalized anxiety disorder and increased amygdala activity when presented with threat stimuli at very brief durations. The chapter discusses these findings in the context of how they complement and extend studies which have relied on behavioural indices of attention. It suggests that while these literatures are largely consistent, there is some evidence to suggest that neuropsychological techniques are more sensitive in the detection of information processing biases in childhood anxiety.

The Origin and Treatment of Information Processing Biases in Childhood Anxiety

Within the challenging context of developing theoretical frameworks and establishing a strong research basis in information processing biases in children and adolescents, Part Two of this book includes chapters related to understanding the origins of these biases and the implications of this broad research programme for the treatment and prevention of anxiety in children. Chapters 9–12 describe research reflecting the contribution of both genes and environment in the emergence of information processing biases and anxiety in childhood. In addition, they outline studies that have focused on identifying specific aspects of the environment that place children at risk.

Eley and Zavos (Chapter 9) consider the role of information processing biases within a genetics framework. This chapter provides an evaluation of studies that have established a genetic basis for anxiety in children and adolescents, as well as a role for the non-shared environment. It outlines further research which has found moderate heritability estimates for interpretation biases in adolescence and highlights the need for further research in this area. In addition, the chapter reviews recent studies that aim to identify whether specific genes are associated with anxiety and information processing biases in children and adults and considers how genes interact with specific aspects of the environment to place children at increased risk (e.g. Fox *et al.*, 2005). Consistent with other researchers (e.g. Lau and Pine, 2008), the chapter suggests that future research should aim to explore links between genes and intermediate phenotypes (or endophenotypes) in anxiety. When trying to understand the role of genes in psychopathology, researchers have argued that associations between genes and dysfunction in biological or cognitive systems associated with a disorder may be easier to determine because these impairments are nearer to gene expression (Crosbie *et al.*, 2008; Canon and Keller, 2006). Following this approach, Chapter 9 proposes two mediated pathways between genes and anxious behaviour via brain structure and function, which include attentional and interpretation information processing biases.

Consistent with the establishment of information processing biases as an endophenotype in anxiety research, Chapter 9 summarizes a number of studies which have found links between individuals who carry the SS or L_G alleles of the serotonin transporter (5-HTTLPR) gene with both anxious states in childhood and with dysfunction in neural circuitry linked to the processing of threatening stimuli. Research to establish information processing biases as a cognitive endophenotype in anxiety is still in its infancy. This research programme does, however, assume an underlying conceptual profile that links to and extends several avenues of research outlined across a number of chapters. For example, at a basic level this research agenda will encourage researchers to explore the extent to which tasks that measure information processing biases are valid and reliable. It will promote research to take forward the idea that these biases represent a vulnerability factor that place children at risk for the development of anxiety disorders, such that they act independently of anxiety and can be seen in the absence of anxiety symptoms. This status will also serve to encourage researchers to explore the time course of biases in childhood, its origins and to understand associated underlying biological structures and pathways (see Crosbie *et al.*, 2008).

Linked to the exploration of the genetic underpinnings of anxiety, Chapter 10 (White, Helfinstein and Fox) explores links between information processing biases and temperament. The chapter focuses on early temperamental origins of information processing biases in children who are defined as behaviourally inhibited. The chapter highlights that these children show distinctive psychological (avoidance and fear when faced with novelty) and biological (e.g. elevated cortisol and increased heart rate) characteristics from an early age. It describes research which has found that behavioural inhibition is associated with an increased risk of developing anxiety disorders later in development. It looks at empirical evidence from studies with behaviourally inhibited children and links this work to animal models of anxiety to consider three pathways that can explain this relationship, including amygdale hyperresponsivity to threat or ambiguity, the overgeneralization of fear learning (from a learned context to other context that share some features), as well as information processing biases to threat. This chapter also discusses why some children who show this temperamental trait early in childhood do not go on to develop anxiety and it looks at the moderating role of inhibitory processes in this development. Exploring themes raised in Part One of the book, Chapter 10 highlights research which has found that inhibitory control moderates attention to threat in anxiety. It also notes that children who demonstrate high levels of inhibitory control can also have increased anxiety levels. This interesting proposition suggests that the development of inhibitory control in childhood functions like an inverted U-shaped curve[2] where very low or high levels can interact with the development of information processing biases to increase anxiety in children.

While Chapter 10 considers factors intrinsic to the child as being significant in understanding the origins of information processing biases in childhood, it also explores the moderating role of the family context in this development. It presents evidence to suggest that the presence of increased negative emotion in mothers or specific types of parenting interact with temperamentally vulnerable children to place them at risk for the development of anxiety disorders, where this relationship may be mediated by information processing biases for threat.

The role of the family in the development of information processing biases is a theme that continues in Chapters 11 (Field and Lester) and 12 (Creswell, Murray

---

[2]This pattern is reminiscent of the Yerke–Dodson Law (Yerkes and Dodson 1908) which suggests that moderate levels of anxiety can facilitate task performance, while low and high levels are associated with lowered performance.

and Cooper). Based on models of childhood anxiety (e.g. Hudson and Rapee, 2008) Chapter 12 focuses specifically on the role of parenting in information processing biases. It argues that specific parenting styles or the presence of parental anxiety are associated with the sharing of negative cognition from parents to their children that fosters a perception of the world as a threatening place and that reduces children's ability to cope with threat. It presents a model which highlights that parental cognition can lead to the development of information processing biases for threat in children via two mediated pathways. The first pathway links parent and child cognition via parental expectations of the child (how well they think their child can cope) and parent behaviour (e.g. over control). The second pathway shows a mediated link via parent behaviour (e.g. transfer of negative information). The chapter provides some support for the different components of this proposed model. It reviews evidence which indicates, for example, that anxious parents demonstrate information processing biases for threat when asked to interpret ambiguous situations and that they expect their child to interpret ambiguity in a similar way to themselves. In addition, it describes a series of studies which have shown that negative information processing biases in children can be modified through parent discussion leading to either the continuity of maladaptive or the emergence of more adaptive cognitive processing styles. Furthermore, it reviews studies which have demonstrated the bidirectional nature of these relationships, where parents' perceptions of their children's vulnerability were found to lead to changes in parenting approaches and specifically to increased parental control.

Chapter 11 also focuses on parenting behaviours to explore potential mechanisms that lead to information processing biases in children. It reviews evidence which indicates that interpretation and attentional biases for threat can be developed or trained in laboratory settings with adults and children, where training individuals to attend to threat or interpret stimuli as threatening has been found to generalize to similar but unseen stimuli, and to increase anxiety levels and emotional responses to stressors. The chapter focuses on understanding the mechanisms underpinning these effects and their relevance to real life settings. It proposes that analogous 'training' processes could occur in families via the transmission of negative information from parents to their children. In order to understand these mechanisms more clearly it embeds this analogy in models of associative learning. Specifically, it suggests that information processing biases develop through associative and habitual learning, where negative associations in memory are largely driven by parental reactions and behaviour in ambiguous situations that serve to direct children's attention to threat and away from other less threatening or neutral cues. Furthermore, the chapter proposes that attentional biases can appear early in development and are underpinned by habitual learning, whereas interpretation biases emerge later in development and are argued to be dependent on the development of language and theory of mind. Furthermore, the chapter proposes that cognitive change that occurs at around 4–7 years of age places children at risk for the development of information processing biases and represents a sensitive period for their development. Taken together, Chapters 11 and 12 outline important avenues for further research to understand the extent to which information processing biases originate in the interactions between parents and their children.

The final chapter in the book provides the main impetus for this area of research. By understanding more clearly what places children at risk for the development of information processing biases and how they link to anxiety allows for the improvement and advancement of effective prevention and treatment methods in childhood anxiety. Increasingly, researchers and clinicians working with children who experience clinical levels of anxiety recognize that a focus on changing attentional processing can form an effective component of treatment (e.g. Legerstee *et al.*, 2009). This approach to treatment is summarized in Chapter 13. The chapter reviews evidence on attention retraining in adults for the treatment of a range of anxiety disorders. It notes that more traditional treatment methods, like cognitive behavioural therapy, aim to challenge maladaptive cognitions associated with anxious thoughts and to replace these with cognitions that more accurately reflect reality. In contrast, attention retraining is suggested to facilitate an individual's ability to strategically control their attention from threat to neutral stimuli (i.e. to selectively attend to neutral stimuli and to switch attention from threat to neutral stimuli in order to regulate their emotion). It highlights several studies which have used either therapy directed attentional training or experimental attentional training paradigms based on the dot-probe or Stroop tasks and that train anxious adults to attend to neutral rather than threat stimuli. The chapter reports findings that have shown some success in reducing attention to threat or facilitating disengagement from threat stimuli and lowering anxious symptoms and describes similar success in preliminary work with children. Chapter 13 links this approach to treatment in children in the context of the development of effortful control. Consistent with themes raised in Part One of the book, it discusses the role of effortful control in development of the regulation of emotion and behaviour and, specifically, conceptualizes information processing in anxiety as reflecting 'under-controlled attentional processes.' It suggests that children who are low in effortful control are specifically at risk for the development of anxiety because they are unable to direct their attention away from sources of threat.

Chapter 13 outlines evidence which has shown that effortful control can be enhanced in children aged between 4 and 6 years using training programmes. It argues that this training should form the basis of attentional control in children because it would allow them to develop strategies to regulate their attention and manage their emotions more effectively. This approach fits well with an emerging literature that has focused on training executive functions (inhibition, working memory) in young children (e.g. Thorell *et al.*, 2009) and in children with attention-deficit hyperactivity disorder (ADHD). Previous research has highlighted significant success in training working memory skills in children with ADHD (Klinberg, Forssberg and Westerberg, 2002; Klinberg *et al.*, 2005) and adults (Jaeggi *et al.*, 2008). Klinberg *et al.* (2005), for example, found that asking children with ADHD between 7 and 12 years of age to complete a relatively short working memory training protocol (25 days of around 30–40 min of training per day over a 6-week period) led to significant improvements in working memory and related tasks (complex reasoning and response inhibition), as well as a reduction in parent report symptoms of ADHD (inattention and hyperactivity or impulsivity).

The proposition that it is possible to train attention strategies to children fits well with a goal of adjusting the proposed imbalance between top-down and bottom-up processing in anxiety (Bishop, 2007). Consistent with this approach, further research has highlighted increased activation in brain regions (frontal and parietal cortices) following working memory training (e.g. Olesen, Westerberg and Klinberg, 2004). Future research should aim to establish whether it is possible that similar effects would be found post training in children and adolescents who experience elevated levels of anxiety and who undergo attention retraining.

Summary

The chapters across Parts One and Two of this book provide a comprehensive overview of information processing biases in children and adolescents. Part One highlights that the pursuit of a research agenda that considers diverse aspects of information processing biases using different levels of analysis has started to allow researchers to develop a picture of cognitive processing in childhood anxiety that is similar to that found in adults (review by Bar-Haim *et al.*, 2007). Importantly, it outlines a number of different avenues of research for developing the theoretical and empirical bias of this area. Along with Part Two, the chapters delineate several mechanisms to indicate why some children develop information processing biases for threat and to consider whether these place them at risk for the development of anxiety disorders. Importantly, links between these mechanisms and the development of prevention and treatment methods are addressed in the concluding chapter.

Acknowledgements

Andy would like to thank his parents and brother for proving that (contrary to what some chapters of this book might imply) it is possible to grow up to be anxious despite an unconditionally supportive, warm, uncontrolling and loving family environment. The authors also thank Kate Lester for commenting on several chapters and to Helen Richards for her help with proof reading. Finally, they would like to express their sincere gratitude for the willingness of all the contributors to share their thoughts and enthusiasm for this research area with them and the readers.

References

Achenbach, T.M. (1990) Conceptualisation of developmental psychopathology, in *Handbook of Developmental Psychopathology* (eds M. Lewis and S.M. Miller), Plenum Press, New York and London.

American Psychiatric Association (2000) *Diagnostic and Statistical Manual of Mental Disorders-IV-TR*, American Psychiatric Association, Washington, DC.

Anderson, A.K. and Phelps, E.A. (2001) Lesions of the human amygdale impair enhanced perception of emotionally salient events. *Nature*, **411**, 305–309.

Ashcraft, M.H. (2002) Math anxiety: personal, educational, and cognitive consequences. *Current Directions in Psychological Science*, **11**, 181–185.

Asendorpf, J.B., Denissen, J.J.A. and van Aken, M.A.G. (2008) Inhibited and aggressive preschool children at 23 years of age: personality and social transitions into adulthood. *Developmental Psychology*, **44**, 997–1011.

Bar-Haim, Y., Lamy, D., Pergamin, L. *et al.* (2007) Threat-related attentional bias in anxious and non-anxious individuals: a meta-analytical study. *Psychological Bulletin*, **133**, 1–24.

Bauer, D.H. (1976) An exploratory study of developmental changes in children's fears. *Journal of Child Psychology and Psychiatry*, **17**, 69–74.

Beesdo, K., Jacobi, F., Hoyer, J. *et al.* (2009) Pain associated with specific anxiety and depressive disorders in a nationally representative population sample. *Social Psychiatry and Psychiatric Epidemiology*. Published online.

Bishop, S.J. (2007) Neurocognitive mechanisms of anxiety: an integrative account. *Trends in Cognitive Science*, **11**, 307–316.

Bowlby, J. (1969) Attachment, in *Twenty Studies that Revolutionised Child Psychology*, vol. 1 (ed. W.E. Dixon (2003)), Basic Books, New York, Prentice Hall, NJ, pp. 127–139.

Bowlby, J. (1973) *Attachment and Loss. Volume 2: Separation Anxiety and Anger*, Hogarth Press, London.

Canon, T.D. and Keller, M.C. (2006) Endophenotypes in the genetic analysis of mental disorders. *Review of Clinical Psychology*, **2**, 267–290.

Cicchetti, D. and Cohen, D.J. (1995) Perspectives on developmental psychopathology, in *Developmental Psychopathology: Theory Method* (eds D. Cicchetti and D.J. Cohen), John Wiley & Sons, New York, pp. 3–20.

Crosbie, J., Pérusse, D., Barr, C.L. and Schachar, R.J. (2008) Validating psychiatric endophenotypes: inhibitory control and attention deficit hyperactivity disorder. *Neuroscience and Biobehavioural Reviews*, **22**, 40–55.

Crozier, W.R. and Hostettler, K. (2003) The influence of shyness on children's test performance. *British Journal of Educational Psychology*, **73**, 317–328.

Derryberry, D. and Reed, M.A. (2002) Anxiety-related attentional biases and their regulation by attentional control. *Journal of Abnormal Psychology*, **111**, 225–236.

Egger, H.L. and Angold, A. (2006) Common emotional and behavioural disorders in preschool children: presentation, nosology and epidemiology. *Journal of Child Psychology and Psychiatry*, **47**, 313–337.

Essau, C.A., Conradt, J. and Petermann, F. (2002) Course and outcome of anxiety disorders in adolescents. *Anxiety Disorders*, **16**, 67–81.

Essau, C.A., Aihara, F., Petermann, F. and Al Wiswasi, S. (2001) Specific phobia, in *Anxiety Disorders in Children and Adolescents* (eds C.A. Essau and F. Petermann), Brunner-Routledge, Guilford.

Eysenck, M.W., Derakshan, N., Santos, R. and Calvo, M.G. (2007) Anxiety and cognitive performance: attentional control theory. *Emotion*, **7**, 336–353.

Fox, N.A., Nichols, K.E., Henderson, H.A. *et al.* (2005) Evidence for a gene-environment interaction in predicting behavioral inhibition in middle childhood. *Psychological Science*, **16**, 921–926.

Fox, N. and Calkins, S.D. (2003) The development of self-control of emotion: intrinsic and extrinsic influences. *Motivation and Emotion*, **27**, 7–26.

Happé, F.G.E. (1994) Annotation: current psychological theories of autism: the theory of mind account and rival theories. *Journal of Child Psychology and Psychiatry*, **35**, 215–229.

Hudson, J.L. and Rapee, R.M. (2008) Familial and social environments in the etiology and maintenance of anxiety disorders, in *Handbook of Anxiety and Anxiety Disorders* (eds A. Martin and M. Stein), Oxford University Press, pp. 173–189.

Jaeggi, S.M., Buschkuehl, M., Jonides, J. and Perrig, W.J. (2008) Improving fluid intelligence with training on working memory. *Proceedings of the National Academy of Sciences*, **105**, 6829–6833.

Kagan, J., Kearsley, R.B. and Zelazo, P.R. (1978) *Infancy: Its Place in Human Development*, Havard University Press, Cambridge, MA.

Kindt, M. and Van Den Hout, M. (2001) Selective attention and anxiety: a perspective on developmental issues and causal status. *Journal of Psychopathology and Behavioural Assessment*, **23**, 193–201.

Klinberg, T., Fernell, E., Olsen, P.J. *et al.* (2005) Computerised training of working memory in children with ADHD – a randomised controlled trial. *Journal of American Academic Child and Adolescent Psychiatry*, **44**(2), 177–186.

Klinberg, T., Forssberg, H. and Westerberg, H. (2002) Training of working memory in children with ADHD. *Journal of Clinical and Experimental Neuropsychology*, **24**, 781–791.

Lang, P.J. (1985) The cognitive psychophysiology of emotion: fear and anxiety, in *Anxiety and the Anxiety Disorders* (eds A.H. Tuma and J.D. Maser), Lawrence Erlbaum Associates Inc., Hillsdale, NJ, pp. 131–170.

Lau, J.Y.F. and Pine, D.S. (2008) Elucidating risk mechanisms of gene-environment interactions on pediatric anxiety: integrating findings from neuroscience. *European Archives of Psychiatry and Clinical Neuroscience*, **258**, 97–106.

Legerstee, J., Tulen, J., Kallen, V. *et al.* (2009) Threat-related selective attention predicts treatment success in childhood anxiety disorders. *Journal of the American Academy of Child and Adolescent Psychiatry*, **48**, 1–10.

Lewinsohn, P.M., Holm-Denoma, J.M., Small, J.W. *et al.* (2008) Separation anxiety disorder in childhood as a risk factor for future mental illness. *Journal of the American Academy of Child and Adolescent Psychiatry*, **47**, 548–555.

Lonigan, C.J. and Vasey, M. (2009) Negative affectivity, effortful control, and attention to threat-relevant stimuli. *Journal of Abnormal Child Psychology*, **37**, 387–399.

Lonigan, C.J., Vasey, M.W., Phillips, B.M. and Hazen, R.A. (2004) Temperament, anxiety, and the processing of threat-relevant stimuli. *Journal of Clinical Child and Adolescent Psychology*, **33**, 8–20.

MacLeod, C. (1991) Clinical anxiety and the selective encoding of threatening information. *International Review of Psychiatry*, **3**, 279–292.

MacLeod, C., Rutherford, E., Campbell, L. *et al.* (2002) Selective attention and emotional vulnerability: assessing the causal basis of their association through the experimental manipulation of attentional bias. *Journal of Abnormal Psychology*, **111**, 107–123.

Mansell, W. (2008) Keep it simple – the transdiagnostic approach to CBT. *International Journal of Cognitive Therapy*, **1**, 179–180.

Mogg, K. and Bradley, B. P. (1998) A cognitive-motivational analysis of anxiety. *Behaviour Research and Therapy*, **36**, 809–848.

Muris, P. and Field, A. (2008) Distorted cognition and pathological anxiety in children and adolescents. *Cognition and Emotion*, **22**, 395–421.

Muris, P. and Merckelbach, H. (2001) The etiology of childhood specific phobia: a multifactorial model, in *The Developmental Psychopathology of Anxiety* (eds M. Vasey and M.R. Dadds), Oxford University Press, Oxford, pp. 355–385.

Muris, P., Merckelbach, H., Gadet, B. and Moulaert V. (2000) Fears, worries, and scary dreams in 4–12-year-old children: their content, developmental pattern, and origins. *Journal of Clinical Child Psychology*, **29**, 43–52.

Olesen, P.J., Westerberg, H. and Klinberg, T. (2004) Increased prefrontal and parietal activity after training of working memory. *Nature Neuroscience*, **7**, 75–79.

Owens, M., Stevenson, J., Norgate, R. and Hadwin, J.A. (2008) Processing efficiency theory in children: working memory as a mediator between trait anxiety and academic performance. *Anxiety Stress and Coping*, **21**, 417–430.

Rapee, R. (2001) The development of generalised anxiety, in *The Developmental Psychopathology of Anxiety* (eds M.W. Vasey and M.R. Dadds), Oxford University Press, Oxford, pp. 481–504.

Rapee, R.M., Schniering, C.A. and Hudson, J.L. (2009) Anxiety disorders during childhood and adolescence: origins and treatment. *Annual Review of Clinical Psychology*, **5**, 311–341.

Reinholdt-Dunne, M.L., Mogg, K. and Bradley, B.P. (2009) Effects of anxiety and attention control on processing pictorial and linguistic emotional information. *Behaviour Research and Therapy*, **47**, 410–417.

Rothbart, M.K., Sheese, B.E. and Posner, M.I. (2007) Executive attention and effortful control: linking temperament, brain networks, and genes. *Child Development Perspectives*, **1**, 2–7.

Roza, S.J., Holstra, M.B., van der Ende, J. and Verhulst, F.C. (2003) Stable prediction of mood and anxiety disorders based on behavioural and emotional problems in childhood: a 14-year follow up during childhood, adolescence and young adulthood. *American Journal of Psychiatry*, **160**, 2116–2121.

Schaefer, B.A. Watkins M.W. and Burnham, J.J. (2003) Empirical fear profiles among American youth. *Behaviour Research and Therapy*, **41**, 1093–1103.

Sroufe, L.A. (1995) *Emotional Development*, Cambridge University Press, Cambridge.

Stevenson, J., Batten, N. and Cherner, M. (1992) Fears and fearfulness in children and adolescents: a genetic analysis of twin data. *Journal of Child Psychology and Psychiatry*, **33**, 977–985.

Stolarvoa, M., Keil, A. and Moratti, S. (2006) Modulation of the C1 visual event-related component by conditioned stimuli: evidence for sensory plasticity in early affective perception. *Cerebral Cortex*, **16**, 876–887.

Thorell, L.B., Lindqvist, S., Nutley, S.B. *et al.* (2009) Training and transfer of executive functions in preschool children. *Developmental Science*, **12**, 106–113.

Tiffany, S.T. (1990) A cognitive model of drug urges and drug-use behaviour: role of automatic and non-automatic processes. *Psychological Review*, **97**, 147–168.

Warren, S.L., Emde, R.N. and Sroufe, L.A. (2000) Internal representations: predicting anxiety from children's play narratives. *Journal of the American Academy of Child and Adolescent Psychiatry*, **39**, 100–107.

Weems, C. (2008) Developmental trajectories of childhood anxiety: identifying continuity and change in anxious emotion. *Developmental Review*, **28**, 488–502.

Weiss, D.D. and Last, C.G. (2001) Developmental variations in the prevalence and manifestation of anxiety disorders, in *The Developmental Psychopathology of Anxiety* (eds M. Vasey and M.R. Dadds), Oxford University Press, Oxford, pp. 27–44.

Wellman, H.M. (1990) *The Child's Theory of Mind*, MIT Press, Cambridge, MA.

Williams, J.M.G., Watts, F.N., MacLeod, C. and Mathews, A. (2007) *Cognitive Psychology and Emotional Disorders*, John Wiley & Sons, Chichester.

Wolfe, J.M. (1994) Guided search 2.0 – a revised model of visual-search. *Psychonomic Bulletin and Review*, **1**, 202–238.

Yerkes, R.M. and Dodson, J.D., (1908) The relation of strength of stimulus to rapidity of habit-formation. *Journal of Comparative Neurology and Psychology*, **18**, 459–482.

Theoretical and Research Issues

2

Anxiety-Related Reasoning Biases in Children and Adolescents

Peter Muris

muris@fsw.eur.nl

Introduction

Kathy is 10 years old and suffering from a social anxiety disorder. She is very shy when meeting new people or is extremely anxious when she has to do something while others are watching her. For example, last week Kathy had to give an oral report in front of the class. Days before she was continuously thinking about what might go wrong: she predicted that she would forget what she wanted to tell, and most certainly she knew that the class would laugh about her. Her report indeed turned out as a disaster. Kathy was visibly nervous, and although she started rather well with her story, all of sudden she bursted out in crying and ran out of the class. Later she told her mother: 'It was horrible! I was blushing, my hands were trembling, and my heart was pounding. Standing in front of the class, I immediately knew that this was going to be a complete failure! One of the boys was smiling at me all the time: I must have said really stupid things!'

Reasoning refers to the cognitive process that is concerned with deducing conclusions, generating judgements and testing hypotheses in a logical and coherent way. Obviously, this is an important aspect of human functioning as it helps the individual to understand the internal and external world. In anxiety syndromes, reasoning may be erroneous and biased in such a way that it primarily reflects the dominant concerns of these psychological problems (Harvey *et al.*, 2004). For example, in the case of Kathy, it is clear that she already had a strong belief that negative things were going to happen in a future social situation. Further, during the situation itself, she seemed to perceive her physical symptoms as signs of impending danger and interpret ambiguous cues like the smile of her classmate in a negative way. Obviously, Kathy's reasoning habits are not helpful; in fact, they

Information Processing Biases and Anxiety: A Developmental Perspective Edited by Julie A. Hadwin and Andy P. Field
© 2010 John Wiley & Sons, Ltd.

elicit and maintain considerable distress, thereby significantly disturbing her daily functioning.

The current chapter first provides an overview of various types of anxiety-related reasoning biases. Experimental tasks and questionnaires that have been used to assess these cognitive biases in children and adolescents will be described and studies that have employed these assessment methods will be reviewed. The chapter closes with a discussion of the developmental aspects of reasoning biases, their origins as well as their presumed role in the etiology of childhood anxiety problems. Various directions for future research on this anxiety-related phenomenon in youths are described.

Interpretation Bias

Many stimuli and situations that children encounter in daily life are actually ambiguous. A toddler who encounters a snake in the garden, a child who is going to school for the first time or an adolescent who feels dizzy when getting up in the morning – all these scenes could be benign but might also indicate impending danger. How children and adolescents perceive and interpret these situations is important for how they eventually deal with them. Anxious individuals show a tendency to interpret ambiguity in a threatening way, a phenomenon that has been named as *interpretation bias*. It is easy to see how this type of reasoning bias promotes anxiety and instigates children to employ avoidant coping strategies.

Assessment

Previous research studies have employed a variety of assessment methods to measure interpretation bias in youths. Most of these studies have relied on an ambiguous vignette paradigm. This paradigm makes use of short descriptions of everyday situations that may occur in children's daily life and simply asks children to indicate how these situations will proceed. Responses can be provided in either an open or a closed response format. In the open response format, children are simply asked 'What do you think is happening?' Responses to this question are usually coded by trained raters who judge whether the child has interpreted the scenario in a threatening or a non-threatening way. In the closed format, possible threatening and non-threatening interpretations for a scenario are described, and the child has to select the interpretation that, according to him/her, is most applicable (Table 2.1). An important advantage of the ambiguous vignette paradigm is that it is suitable for measuring interpretation bias in youths of various ages. By adapting the content of the vignettes, even children as young as 4 years can be assessed by means of this paradigm. A disadvantage is that this method heavily relies on self-report, which raises questions concerning the potential role of demand bias.

To reduce the influence of demand, experimental paradigms have also been used to examine children's interpretation of ambiguity. For example, Eysenck, MacLeod and Mathews (1987) used a method relying on homophones, which are words

Table 2.1. An example of an ambiguous vignette task that can be employed to measure anxiety-related interpretation bias in children and adolescents

---

Physical threat vignette

On the way to school you feel funny in the tummy.

Open response:

What do you think is happening?

Closed response:

Which of the following explanations is most likely?

(a) You ate some bad food and are going to be really sick at school.[a]
(b) You did not have enough breakfast and you need to eat something.
(c) There is something wrong with your tummy and you might need a big operation.[a]
(d) It is okay and it will go away soon.

Social threat vignette

You see a group of children from another class playing a great game. As you walk over and want to join them, you notice that they are laughing.

Open response:

What do you think is happening?

Closed response:

Which of the following explanations is most likely?

(a) They are telling secrets about you.[a]
(b) They will soon ask you to join in.
(c) One of them is likely to rush up and push you away.[a]
(d) One of them is likely to notice you and smile.

---

[a]Threat interpretation.
Based on Barrett *et al.* (1996).

that sound the same but have different meanings. When studying anxiety-related interpretation bias by means of this method, one needs homophones that have a threatening and a neutral meaning (Table 2.2). Further, one has to make sure that children indeed know both meanings of the word, and the frequency of the two meanings of the homograph in the language should be comparable. There are several ways for assessing children's interpretation of homophones. For example, upon hearing the word, one can show the child two pictures, one representing the threatening meaning and the other representing the neutral meaning, and then ask him or her to point to the picture that (best) represents the meaning of the word. Another possibility is that the experimenter asks the child to construe a sentence with the word, or to make a drawing of the event to which the word refers. To obscure the intention of the task, it is recommended to present the homophones in a list along with some neutral and unambiguously threatening filler items.

It can be argued that a paradigm like the homophone task is still potentially prone to demand and response bias effects. That is, it is possible that anxious children are aware of both meanings simultaneously and then selectively choose to report the threatening meaning. To circumvent these problems, experimental researchers

Table 2.2. Examples of homophones that have been used to index anxiety-related interpretation bias in youths

Homophone	Threat – neutral interpretation
Bark	Dog – tree
Bat	Animal – ballgame
Blind	Man – window
Die/dye	Death – colour
Hanging	Gallow – clothes
Mummy	Egyptian – mother
Sink	Ship – kitchen
Stamp	Foot – postage
Whipping	Rope – cream
Tank	Army – fish

Source: Hadwin *et al.* (1997).

have developed even more sophisticated paradigms to measure anxiety-related interpretation biases. For instance, in the context of social anxiety, one could employ an emotional expression task, which requires children to interpret the meaning of faces with varying levels of different emotions (e.g. happiness, anger). By means of computer manipulations (i.e. morphing), it is possible to present gradually changing facial expressions, which provides the opportunity to assess participants' interpretations online by means of reaction times. The few studies conducted with children have not employed this paradigm in a very consistent way (Creswell *et al.*, 2008; Richards *et al.*, 2007) and so further research is needed to establish whether this paradigm provides a valid index of children's interpretation bias.

Another example is the text comprehension task (MacLeod and Cohen, 1993), which requires participants to read sentences that are presented on a computer screen. After reading a sentence the participant presses a button to indicate that he or she is ready to read the next line of text. In this way, the time is measured that is needed to read and understand various sentences. The basic idea is that sentences that are consistent with the expected interpretation will be read faster than sentences which are not consistent. For example, an anxious person will more easily interpret the sentence 'It was early when the building was lit' in a threatening way, which means that he or she would read the following sentence 'The flames could be seen from a distance' faster than he or she would read the sentence 'The lights could be seen from a distance' (example taken from Harvey *et al.*, 2004). So far, the text comprehension task has been exclusively employed to investigate interpretation bias in adults and hence it remains unclear how adaptable this paradigm is to be used in children, given issues with reading comprehension.

Empirical evidence

In one of the first studies examining anxiety-related interpretation bias in children, Bell-Dolan (1995) presented 9- to 11-year-olds who were high or low on trait anxiety, with a series of videotaped peer-interaction vignettes displaying peer behaviour that was either hostile, non-hostile or ambiguous. Results showed that the high-anxious children were equally accurate in identifying hostile intent in peer interactions as their low-anxious counterparts. However, high-anxious children more frequently interpreted the non-hostile and ambiguous vignettes in a threatening way. In further research by Barrett *et al.* (1996), children with anxiety disorder, children with oppositional-defiant disorder and normal controls (all aged between 7 and 14 years) were exposed to vignettes of ambiguous situations and asked about what was happening in each situation. Following this, children were given two possible neutral outcomes and two possible threatening outcomes and were asked to indicate which outcome was most likely to occur. Results showed that both anxious and oppositional children more frequently perceived ambiguous situations as threatening than did normal controls, with anxious children more often choosing avoidant outcomes and oppositional children more frequently choosing aggressive outcomes (see also Bögels and Zigterman, 2000; Chorpita, Albano and Barlow, 1996).

Hadwin *et al.* (1997) adopted a homophone paradigm to assess anxiety-related interpretation bias in 7- to 9-year-olds. Children completed a standardized measure of anxiety and were then confronted with a series of auditorily presented words, which also included a set of ambiguous homophones. For each word, two pictures were shown from which children had to select the one that best indicated the meaning of the word. Results showed that anxiety levels were positively associated with the tendency to interpret the homophones as threatening. Thus, the higher the children's anxiety level, the more frequently they selected pictures that reflected the threatening meaning of the homophones. A comparable experiment was conducted by Taghavi *et al.* (2000) who presented 9- to 16-year-old children and adolescents with homophones that were printed on cards. For each homophone, participants were asked to construct a sentence which included the ambiguous word. The results of this study indicated that anxious children and adolescents produced significantly more sentences that were consistent with a threatening homophone interpretation than did the control children.

These and other findings (Dineen and Hadwin, 2004; Suarez and Bell-Dolan, 2001; Waters *et al.*, 2008a) warrant the conclusion that a negative interpretation bias is present in anxious youths. However, there is some debate whether this cognitive bias is specific to anxiety pathology. A recent study by Reid, Salmon and Lovibond (2006) examined to what extent information processing biases were specifically associated with symptoms of anxiety, depression and aggression in non-clinical youths aged 8–14 years. As for the negative interpretation of ambiguous situations, no evidence was found indicating that this bias was specifically linked to anxiety. In other words, interpretation bias was found to be related to a broad range of symptoms in youths, suggesting that it reflects a pervasive bias which is relevant for various types of psychopathology. Meanwhile, it should be noted that when studying the content of the negative interpretations in more detail, some evidence for the specificity of this bias has been obtained. More precisely, research by Dalgleish *et al.* (1997) and Dineen and Hadwin (2004) has demonstrated that when children have to interpret ambiguous social scenarios, anxiety is linked to negative interpretations about others, whereas depression is more associated with negative interpretations about the self. These findings fit with the idea that anxiety in children is characterized by negative evaluations of the (threatening) external world, while depression is typified by negative evaluations of the self. Further, Bögels, Snieder and Kindt (2003) have shown that even within the anxiety disorders, there is some support for the content specificity of children's interpretations. In this study, children who scored high on social phobia and separation anxiety disorder predominantly displayed interpretation bias in response to vignettes describing situations that were relevant to their type of fear (i.e. respectively social and separation situations). Taken together, these data indicate that interpretation biases mimic the type of (anxiety) pathology that a child is suffering from, which is nicely in keeping with the premises of cognitive theory (Beck, Emery and Greenberg, 1985). Nevertheless, it is also clear that more research on the specificity of interpretation biases is urgently needed.

Reduced Evidence for Danger (RED) Bias

Daleiden and Vasey (1997) have postulated another cognitive bias that may occur in anxious children. Briefly, these authors hypothesized that in anxious children 'even very minor threat cues may readily trigger subsequent processing and consequently anxious responding. In essence, they may be acutely vigilant for signals of potential threat but, once they have encoded such a signal, they may quickly move through the interpretation stage and conclude that the situation is dangerous even though a search for further information would show it is not. For example, upon seeing a dog, dog-phobic children may quickly jump to the conclusion that they are in danger and, because they have ceased encoding further information, they may fail to notice that the dog is on a leash or that the dog is behaving in a friendly manner' (pp. 411–412). In other words, anxious children only require very little information before deciding that a situation is dangerous, a phenomenon that is known as *reduced evidence for danger (RED) bias*. This type of bias is similar to some of the cognitive errors that were described by Beck (1976) in the more clinical literature. In particular, distortions such as 'arbitrary inference', which involves the drawing of unjust conclusions in the absence of evidence, and 'selective abstraction', which pertains to focusing on a detail while ignoring other important features of a situation, come very close to RED bias. Note also that information processing models of anxiety view a lower threshold of threat perception and interpretation as one of the hallmark features of anxiety vulnerability (e.g. Mogg and Bradley, 1998).

Assessment

RED bias is typically assessed in interview studies in which children are exposed to ambiguous vignettes. Children are told that some of these vignettes are scary (i.e. stories with a bad end), whereas other vignettes are not (i.e. stories with a happy end). Children are instructed to find out as quickly as possible whether

Table 2.3. Examples of vignettes that were used in studies examining reduced evidence for danger (RED) bias in children

Ambiguous vignette

1. Next week is your birthday and you want to organize a birthday party.
2. Mother has told you that you may invite all of your classmates.
3. The teacher allows you to speak to your class so that you can invite everyone.
4. Standing in front of the class, you hear some of your classmates laughing.
5. When you sit down again, everyone suddenly begins to laugh about you.

Non-threatening vignette

1. Next week is your birthday and you want to organize a birthday party.
2. You have made a list of children you want to invite.
3. The children who are invited have told you that they will certainly come.
4. During the break at school, you see some of the invited children.
5. They come to you and say that they are looking forward to your party.

After each sentence, the child is asked 'What do you think? Is this going to be a scary or a non-scary story?' In this way, a *threshold of threat perception* score is obtained which can be defined as the moment at which a child begins to perceive the story as scary. The lower the threshold score, the less information a child needs to perceive threat and the stronger his/her RED bias.
Source: Muris *et al.* (2000b).

the pertinent vignette will be scary or not scary. For this purpose, each vignette is presented sentence by sentence and after each sentence the child is asked whether he or she thinks that the vignette will be scary or not scary (Table 2.3). In this way, one can determine how much information a child needs before deciding that the vignette is going to be threatening.

Empirical evidence

A first test of RED bias was provided by Muris, Merckelbach and Damsma (2000) who exposed 8- to 13-year-old non-clinical children, high and low on social anxiety, to vignettes of social situations which were presented to them in a stepwise manner. The results demonstrated that children with high levels of social anxiety displayed lower thresholds for threat perception (i.e. needed to hear fewer sentences before deciding that a story was going to be threatening) as compared to children with low levels of social anxiety, which is of course a finding that supports the presence of a RED bias (see also Lu, Daleiden and Lu, 2007; Muris *et al.*, 2000a, 2003b). A further investigation by Muris *et al.* (2000b) demonstrated that RED bias in anxious children represents a persistent phenomenon. In this study, 76 normal primary school children aged 8–13 years were once more confronted with vignettes describing social situations. Half of the vignettes were ambiguous and thus contained information that could be interpreted as threatening, whereas the other half of the vignettes were non-threatening; that is, these scenarios clearly had a positive content and contained no obvious trace of threat. Results again indicated that high levels of social anxiety were accompanied by an early detection of threat; but most importantly, this result was not only documented in children's responses to ambiguous vignettes but also in their responses to the non-threatening scenarios. On the basis of these findings, Muris *et al.* (2000b, p. 134) concluded that 'Anxious children seem to have a motto that can be summarized as "Danger is lurking everywhere" which manifests itself in threat perception abnormalities that even occur in relatively non-threatening situations' (see also Muris *et al.*, 2003a).

Altogether, there is sufficient evidence for the presence of RED bias in anxious youths. RED bias can best be viewed as a variant of interpretation bias. The vignettes that are used to demonstrate both biases are just presented in a different way. In the case of interpretation bias children are exposed to the complete vignette, whereas in the case of RED bias children receive the information in a piecemeal fashion, which provides the opportunity to study how easily anxious youths perceive threat in ambiguous and even rather neutral situations. While interpretation bias and RED bias are concerned with the processing of threat-related information about the external world, there are also reasoning biases which pertain to the processing of internal information, such as anxiety-related bodily sensations. Anxious children display a tendency to use this internal information for evaluating the threat in their environment, a phenomenon that is labelled as 'emotional reasoning', which will be the topic of the next section.

Emotional Reasoning

Physical sensations such as palpitations, sweating and trembling are part and parcel of the anxiety response (Lang, 1968) and there is evidence that such sensations also occur in anxious youths (see Fonseca and Perrin, 2001). Arntz, Rauner and Van den Hout (1995) demonstrated that adult patients with anxiety disorders tend to employ these physical anxiety symptoms as a parameter for evaluating the dangerousness of a situation. This phenomenon has been described as emotional reasoning by Beck Emery and Greenberg (1985) who also observed this heuristic in their patients. In their words, 'Many anxious patients use their feelings to validate their thoughts and thus start a vicious circle: "I'll be anxious when I ask for the date so there must be something to fear"' (p. 198). In other words, anxious subjects strongly believe in the proposition 'If I feel anxious, there must be danger'. Obviously, when danger is inferred from physical anxiety responses rather than from objective threat, false alarms are not recognized and anxiety will tend to persist.

Assessment

Although questionnaires can be used to measure whether children interpret physical sensations in a threatening way (Mattis and Ollendick, 1997; Schneider *et al.*, 2002; Unnewehr *et al.*, 1996; see for example Table 2.4), a vignette paradigm is typically employed for assessing emotional reasoning in youths. In this paradigm, children are confronted with a series of scenarios in which objective danger versus

Table 2.4. Example of a questionnaire item for measuring children's anxious interpretations of physical symptoms

Lena is lying on her bed. Suddenly she notices that her heart is pounding and she is dizzy and short of breath. What has happened?

A. Lena is afraid. She thinks that she is seriously sick and needs a doctor (anxious).
B. Lena has just arrived from school. She has run the whole way home and she is tired (neutral).
C. Lena is very excited. It's her birthday and her classmates will be coming to her birthday party right away (positive).

Children have to choose one of the three options, which then receive the following scores: anxious $= +1$, neutral $= 0$ and positive $= -1$.
Source: Schneider *et al*. (2002).

Table 2.5. Examples of scripts for assessing emotional reasoning in youths (aged 8 years and above)

Objective danger/anxiety response	You are invited for a birthday party by one of the children in your class. Because you thought that the party was a costume ball, you are dressed up as a clown. When you enter the party, you see that nobody wears a costume. You start to sweat . . .
Objective danger/no anxiety response	You are invited for a birthday party by one of the children in your class. Because you thought that the party was a costume ball, you are dressed up as a clown. When you enter the party, you see that nobody wears a costume.
Objective safety/anxiety response	You are invited for a birthday party by one of the children in your class. Because you thought that the party was a costume ball, you are dressed up as a clown. When you enter the party, you see that everybody wears a costume that is just as lovely as yours is. You start to sweat . . .
Objective safety/no anxiety response	You are invited for a birthday party by one of the children in your class. Because you thought that the party was a costume ball, you are dressed up as a clown. When you enter the party, you see that everybody wears a costume that is just as lovely as yours is.

Scripts are rated on a 10-point scale anchored with 1 = *not at all scary* and 10 = *very scary*.
Source: Muris, Merckelbach and Van Spauwen (2003).

objective safety and the presence versus absence of anxiety-response information are systematically manipulated. That is, for each scenario, four scripts are written: (i) a scenario with objective danger information and anxiety-response information; (ii) a scenario with objective danger information, but no anxiety response; (iii) a scenario with objective safety information and an anxiety response; and (iv) a scenario with objective safety information and no anxiety response (Table 2.5). After each scenario, children are asked to give a danger rating, that is, they are

Picture

Vignette (without anxiety-related symptom)

Sam walks with his/her friends to the playground.

Vignette (with anxiety-related symptom)

Sam walks with his/her friends to the playground.

While walking, he notices that his/her heart is beating fast.

Question

How scary is this situation?

Rating scale

1 = Not scary   2 = Somewhat scary   3 = Very scary

Figure 2.1 Example of a picture/vignettes that can be employed to assess emotional reasoning in younger children (from age 4). *Source*: Muris *et al.* (2007b).

instructed to rate how scary they evaluate that situation if this would actually happen to them. For younger children, a simplified version of this paradigm has been developed that relies on black-and-white pictures to present each scenario twice, one time with an anxiety-related physical symptom (i.e. 'heart beating fast', 'feeling dizzy', 'tickles in the belly'), the other time without such symptom (Figure 2.1). Note that the face of the main character in the picture has been removed in order to initially avoid priming of the anxiety emotion (see Muris *et al.*, 2004).

Empirical evidence

Muris, Merckelbach and Van Spauwen (2003) asked a sample of 8- to 12-year-old primary school children first to complete questionnaires for measuring trait anxiety and anxiety sensitivity and then to rate the danger levels of scripts in which objective safety or danger and the absence or presence of anxiety-response information were systematically varied. Evidence was obtained for a general emotional reasoning effect. That is, children's danger ratings were not only a function of objective danger information but also, in the case of objective safety scripts, determined by anxiety-response information. Most importantly, high levels of trait anxiety and anxiety sensitivity were accompanied by a greater tendency to use anxiety-response information as a heuristic for evaluating the dangerousness of objective safety scripts. Further studies have replicated these findings and even showed that early manifestations of emotional reasoning seem to be present in children as young as 4 years (Morren, Muris and Kindt, 2004; Muris et al., 2007b; Muris, Vermeer and Horselenberg, 2008).

So far, results have indicated that emotional reasoning occurs in non-clinical youths. Note that this finding is at odds with the results of Arntz Rauner and Van den Hout (1995) who showed that, in adult populations, this reasoning bias was only present in patients with anxiety disorders. The typical participants in their study only based their danger ratings on objective danger information and not on anxiety-response information. Developmental issues may be relevant here. That is, it may well be the case that anxiety-response information sensitizes all children to potential danger and that this phenomenon gradually dissipates as children grow older (note that a similar hypothesis has been formulated for the developmental pattern of attentional bias, e.g. Kindt and Van den Hout, 2001). The basic idea is that only in some children, emotional reasoning may persist as part of a general vulnerability to develop anxiety problems. Clearly, this developmental account warrants further investigation. In addition, it seems important to study whether this bias operates in clinically referred youths with anxiety disorders.

Covariation Bias

Previous sections have described various types of reasoning biases that were all concerned with the interpretation of (internal and external) ambiguous stimuli. A distinct type of bias refers to the reasoning process of covariation detection, which refers to the ability to discover that two stimuli tend to co-occur in a regular and consistent way. This capability is important because it helps people to understand and predict the world, for example, by learning what stimuli indicate upcoming reward and punishment. The 'covariation bias' occurs when people observe an illusory correlation between two stimuli that in fact are correlated to a lesser extent or not related at all (Harvey et al., 2004). In the case of anxiety problems, this bias is concerned with the tendency to overestimate the association between anxiety-relevant stimuli and negative outcomes (Mineka and Tomarken, 1989; Tomarken, Mineka and Cook, 1989). In adults, the following experimental procedure is used to demonstrate covariation bias. Anxious and non-anxious participants are shown a series of slides consisting of anxiety-relevant (e.g. spiders) and neutral (e.g. flowers) pictures. Slide offset is followed by one of three outcomes, namely, an aversive shock (i.e. negative outcome), a tone or nothing. Fear-relevant and neutral pictures are equally often followed by each of the outcomes. After the series of slides, participants are asked to estimate the contingencies between slides and outcomes (e.g. 'Given that you saw a spider picture, on what percentage of those trials was the spider followed by a shock?'). Under these experimental conditions, anxious participants systematically overestimate the contingency between anxiety-relevant stimuli and negative outcomes (e.g. De Jong, Merckelbach and Arntz, 1995; Pauli, Montoya and Martz, 1996).

Assessment

Researchers have encountered problems to demonstrate covariation bias in anxious children (Muris *et al.*, 2005). This is primarily due to the fact that covariation bias experiments typically employ electric shock as aversive outcome to be paired with anxiety-relevant and neutral stimuli, which is of course not considered as an ethical and pro-child procedure. One way to tackle this problem is to employ a thought experiment in which children are asked to *imagine* that they participate in an experiment during which they view a series of pictures showing anxiety-relevant and neutral stimuli that are occasionally followed by a negative outcome (i.e. a mild electric shock): 'Imagine that you participate in a scientific experiment. In the laboratory where you will be tested, the experimenter asks you to sit in a comfortable chair. When seated, the experimenter will attach a small apparatus to your leg. With this apparatus, the experimenter can give you an electric shock. No worries, this shock does not really hurt, but will give you an unpleasant, prickling sensation. Now the experiment can begin: on the table in front of you, there is a pile containing three types of pictures: spiders, guns and flowers. The pictures in the pile are not properly ordered, but in total there are 24 pictures of spiders, 24 pictures of guns and 24 pictures of flowers. You have to turn the pictures one-by-one. On the back of each picture, you will see a smiling or a sad face. When you turn a picture and you see a smiling face, nothing will happen. However, when you turn a card and you see a crying face, you will receive an unpleasant electric shock via the apparatus on your leg. You will receive this shock immediately after you have turned the picture. In this way, you have to turn all 72 pictures'. After this instruction, children are asked to provide estimates of the expected contingencies between the three picture types and the negative outcome in order to assess covariation bias.

The advantage of the employment of such a thought experiment is obvious: one can mimic an original covariation bias experiment without problematic ethical considerations. Another possibility is to develop an experiment in which children are confronted with anxiety-relevant and neutral stimuli that are actually followed by positive and (mildly) negative consequences. Such an approach was adopted by Muris *et al.* (2007a) who developed a computer game to assess spider-fear-related covariation bias in youths. In their experiment, participants received the following instruction: 'You are going to play a computer game. The game is exciting because you can really win pieces of candy! When the game starts, the computer will show you pictures of spiders, guns and flowers. After each picture, the computer will immediately generate a smiley. A happy smiley means that you win three pieces of candy, a sad smiley means that you lose three pieces of candy, whereas when the smiley looks neutral nothing will happen. After each picture and smiley, you have to press the space bar to proceed with the game and to continue with the next picture. At the end of the game, the computer will tell me how many pieces of candy you have won, and I will give you your profits!' A total of 72 pictures were shown in a random order: 24 pictures of spiders, 24 pictures of guns and 24 pictures of flowers, with each picture type being equally often followed by a happy, a sad and a neutral smiley. Figure 2.2 shows some examples of the stimuli that were employed during this experiment as well as the smileys that indicated the consequence of each stimulus.

Empirical evidence

The aforementioned study by Muris *et al.* (2007a) yielded evidence for the existence of an anxiety-related covariation bias in youths aged 8–16 years. The thought

Figure 2.2 Stimuli and smileys that were used during a computerized task to measure covariation bias in youths. *Source*: Muris *et al.* (2007b).

experiment, during which youths had to assess contingencies between pictures of spiders, guns and flowers and electric shock, revealed that children and adolescents provided higher estimates of shocks for pictures of spiders and weapons than flowers, which seems to reflect a general tendency to relate a negative outcome to more negatively valenced stimuli. Most importantly, the data indicated that there was a clear and specific link between youths' level of spider fear and shock estimates for pictures of spiders. That is, higher levels of spider fear were associated with higher estimates of shock following spider pictures, which provides support for the presence of an *a priori* anxiety-related covariation bias. The results of the computer game experiment in which children and adolescents were led to believe that they actually won or lost candy in relation to various picture types again showed that youths displayed an inclination to link a negative outcome to more negatively valenced pictures (i.e. they believed that they more frequently lost candy following pictures of spiders and guns). Furthermore, the results provided support for an *a posteriori* covariation bias in spider fearful youths. More precisely, higher levels of spider fear were accompanied by a tendency to more frequently estimate a negative outcome (i.e. losing candy) following pictures of spiders.

A recent investigation by Field and Lawson (2008) employed a somewhat different approach to examine covariation detection abilities in young people. In that study, 7- to 9-year-old children received negative, positive or no information about unknown animals and then engaged in a causal learning task which measured covariation bias. More precisely, children viewed a series of slides of animals and, following each slide, they had to predict whether there would be a good outcome (i.e. a smiling face) or a bad outcome (i.e. a scared face). Results showed that while children normally underestimated the occurrence of bad outcomes in relation to the unknown animals (i.e. positivity effect), participants in the negative information condition more often predicted bad outcomes so that they provided more accurate estimates of the contingency that they had experienced. Although these findings do not yield straightforward support for the presence of a covariation bias (which is typically characterized by an *over*estimation of bad outcomes in relation to a negative stimulus), this study at least demonstrates that children more easily relate a negatively valenced stimulus to a bad outcome. In the meantime, it is possible that with the inclusion of children as young as 7 years, the covariation detection did not clearly emerge because some of the participants may have lacked the cognitive maturation for displaying this type of reasoning ability.

Altogether, while the results of the studies by Muris *et al.* (2007a) and Field and Lawson (2008) indicate that covariation bias seems to occur in anxious youths, it should be acknowledged that another investigation yielded rather disappointing results (Muris *et al.*, 2005). Thus, it is clear that more research is necessary to demonstrate that this type of reasoning bias indeed operates in children and adolescents with anxiety problems. A similar remark should be made regarding the reasoning bias that will be discussed in the next section, namely probability bias.

Probability Bias

Anxious children and adolescents tend to worry about what may happen in upcoming future events (e.g. Weems, Silverman and La Greca, 2000). In a similar vein, it has been hypothesized that anxious youths may display a probability bias, which implies that they have an inclination to estimate that future negative events are far more likely to occur, in particular to themselves (Butler and Mathews, 1987). Obviously, such a bias may have an impact on the investment of effort and behavioural choices with regard to prospective situations (Harvey *et al.*, 2004). For example, the anxious child who has to present in front of the class and who is certain that he will fail anyway, will likely put less energy in his preparation as he hopes that it is still possible to avoid the dreaded situation.

Assessment

Probability bias in youths can be measured by means of the Subjective Probability Questionnaire (Dalgleish *et al.*, 1997), which simply asks children to estimate the likelihood that a given negative event will happen in the future. For control purposes, the questionnaire not only includes negative events that may happen to the participant himself (i.e. self-referent events) but also negative events that may happen to a generic other child (i.e. other-referent events; see Table 2.6). Of course, it is expected that anxious children provide increased probability estimates of future negative events, in particular for those events that may happen to themselves.

Table 2.6. Examples of items taken from the Subjective Probability Questionnaire, which has been used to measure probability bias in youths

Self-referent events	
Physical threat	How likely is it that you are going to be involved in a road accident during the next 6 months?
Social threat	How likely is it that you are going to be bullied at school during the next couple of months?
Other-referent events	
Physical threat	How likely is it that Josh is going to be involved in a road accident during the next 6 months?
Social threat	How likely is it that Judith is going to be bullied at school during the next couple of months?

Items were given on a 10-point scale with 1 = *This is definitely **not** going to happen* and 10 = *This is definitely going to happen*.
Source: Dalgleish *et al.* (1997).

Empirical evidence

The evidence on probability bias in anxious youths is mixed. On the one hand, studies in non-clinical children and adolescents have provided support for the presence of this type of reasoning bias in youths. For example, Canterbury *et al.* (2004) asked 9- to 18-year-old children who were recruited from regular schools to complete a standardized anxiety scale and the above-described Subjective Probability Questionnaire. Results showed that high-anxious youths estimated negative events as more likely to occur than low-anxious youths. This probability bias effect was present for events referring to themselves as well as for events referring to other children. A further study by Muris and Van der Heiden (2006) employed a similar procedure to assess anxiety-related probability bias in non-clinical children aged between 10 and 13 years. Again, high-anxious children displayed significantly higher probability estimates of future negative events as compared to low-anxious children, but this time the difference only reached statistical significance for the self-referent negative events. On the other hand, research in clinically referred anxious youths has generally yielded negative results. For example, Dalgleish *et al.* (1997) examined the occurrence of probability bias in 9- to 18-year-old children and adolescents with anxiety disorders, depression or no psychiatric disorder. Results demonstrated that neither anxious nor depressed youths estimated negative events to occur more frequently than did non-clinical youths. Furthermore, whereas depressed youths judged negative events as equally likely to occur to themselves and others, anxious youths judged such events as more likely to occur to others. This so-called 'other-referent bias' has been observed in various samples of children and adolescents with anxiety disorders (Dalgleish *et al.*, 2000, 2003; Dineen and Hadwin, 2004).

One has to conclude that the evidence for an anxiety-related probability bias in children and adolescents is not very convincing. Dalgleish *et al.* (1997, 2000) have suggested that this type of bias may occasionally be overshadowed by inhibitory processes and this may be particularly true in youths displaying high anxiety levels. Briefly, such processes may reflect children and adolescents' immature but purposeful strategy to minimize the chance that negative events will actually happen to themselves (i.e. 'strategic inhibition' hypothesis). Otherwise, it is also possible that the relatively low probability estimates for self-referent negative future events in high-anxious youths are simply a result of the fact that they actually avoid a large number of the physically or socially threatening events that are described in the Subjective Probability Questionnaire (i.e. 'avoidance' hypothesis). Future research should test these two possibilities and further explore the role of probability bias in anxious children and adolescents.

Discussion

This chapter demonstrates how various types of reasoning biases can be assessed in children and adolescents and summarizes the empirical evidence on these cognitive phenomena in anxious youths. It can be concluded that there are strong indications that reasoning in youths with anxiety problems is erroneous and biased in several ways. That is, anxious children and adolescents tend to interpret ambiguity in a threatening way (i.e. interpretation bias), require less information before perceiving threat (i.e. RED bias), view physical symptoms as a forecast of impending danger (i.e. emotional reasoning) and more easily associate anxiety-related stimuli with negative outcomes (i.e. covariation bias) and there is also tentative evidence that they may judge threatening events as more likely to occur in the future (i.e. probability bias). This general conclusion can be qualified in a number of ways.

First of all, some of these biases have been demonstrated in high-anxious non-clinical youths as well as clinically referred children and adolescents with anxiety disorders, but it should be noted that a number of these reasoning errors have only been investigated in non-clinical populations (i.e. RED bias, emotional reasoning and covariation bias). While it is generally assumed that normal and abnormal anxiety are part of one and the same continuum (Muris, 2007), suggesting that pathogenic processes are highly similar for non-clinical and clinically referred anxious youths, the mixed results from studies on probability bias illustrate that it is certainly important to examine the generalization of reasoning biases across various populations. Second, from the developmental psychology literature, it is well known that reasoning abilities gradually increase during childhood as a result of cognitive development (e.g. Berk, 2004). This implies that reasoning biases require a minimum level of cognitive maturation before they consistently emerge in (anxious) youths (Alfano, Beidel and Turner, 2002) and hence there should be clear differences in the manifestation of these cognitive distortions across various age groups. Empirical evidence for these ideas, however, is sparse. One exception is the study by Muris *et al.* (2007b) who demonstrated that children's performance on conservation tasks and a theory-of-mind test were significant predictors of anxious interpretations of physical symptoms and emotional reasoning scores, suggesting that these phenomena are influenced by cognitive development. In another study, Muris *et al.* (2007a) showed that a spider-fear-related covariation bias was more clearly present among adolescents (aged 12 and above) than among children (aged 8–11), which is in keeping with the notion that more advanced cognitive skills (e.g. abstract reasoning) are necessary for this type of cognitive distortion. This tentative evidence suggests that at least some of the reasoning biases described in this chapter only become clearly prominent once children have reached a certain level of cognitive maturity, but obviously more research on the developmental patterns of reasoning biases is certainly needed. Third, most of the studies on reasoning biases in youths have been assessed by means of a vignette paradigm. As mentioned earlier, although vignettes represent an appropriate way for measuring these cognitive distortions in youths of various ages, it is also true that this method is susceptible to demand effects. Thus, where possible, future studies should try to employ other, more experimental paradigms to measure reasoning biases in children and adolescents (see Harvey *et al.*, 2004).

Origins of reasoning biases

This chapter has provided an overview of the evidence indicating that various types of reasoning biases occur in anxious children and adolescents. While it is clear that more research is required to further demonstrate these distortions in high-anxious non-clinical and clinical youths of varying ages, one of the key questions also remains as to how these distortions develop. As to the origins of reasoning biases, it is generally assumed that inherited personality characteristics such as neuroticism play an important role (Muris and Field, 2008; Vasey and MacLeod, 2001; see also Chapter 9). However, there is also evidence indicating that environmental influences are involved (see Chapter 12). For example, in the study by Barrett *et al.* (1996), anxious, oppositional-defiant and non-clinical children (aged 7–14 years) and their parents were presented with ambiguous vignettes and asked to provide plans of action for these hypothetical situations. Solutions were categorized in two broad classes of avoidant and aggressive solutions. As predicted, children with anxiety disorders and their parents most frequently chose avoidant solutions, whereas children with oppositional-defiant disorder and their parents clearly preferred aggressive solutions. Interestingly, after a family discussion during which children and parents first deliberated about the possible solutions for the scenarios, it was observed that anxious children's avoidant action plans significantly increased. In a subsequent observational investigation by this research group in which the specific sequences of communications exchanged between parents and children were examined, Dadds *et al.* (1996) revealed that parents of anxious children indeed show the tendency to encourage the fearful avoidant behaviour of their offspring. These and other studies suggest that reasoning biases are passed on from parents to their children (Creswell, Schniering and Rapee, 2005; Creswell, O'Connor and Brewin, 2006; review by Hadwin, Garner and Perez-Olivas, 2006).

Reasoning biases and the pathogenesis of anxiety

While it is generally assumed that information processing abnormalities (such as reasoning biases) play a role in the maintenance and even exacerbation of anxiety problems in youths (Vasey and MacLeod, 2001), almost all the research on this topic has been cross-sectional in nature and so no conclusions can be drawn on the cause–effect relation between reasoning biases and anxiety. Future studies could adopt various approaches to examine this causality issue in more detail. A first approach would be prospective research in which the extent to which reasoning biases are predictive of the development of anxiety symptoms over time is investigated. There are a number of studies that have adopted this approach in adult populations (e.g. Pury, 2002), but so far research of this type in youths is sparse and has yielded quite mixed results. For instance, in a study by Muris, Jacques and Mayer (2004), 9- to 13-year-old children completed a self-report measure of anxiety symptoms and were then interviewed individually using an ambiguous vignette paradigm to assess various threat perception biases (i.e. interpretation bias and RED bias). The assessment was repeated some 4 weeks later so that it became possible to study prospective relationships for threat perception biases and anxiety symptoms. The results indicated that, on both occasions, anxiety disorder symptoms were significantly associated with threat perception biases. Furthermore, no evidence was obtained for a prospective link between these biases and anxiety disorder symptoms, which made Muris *et al.* (2004) conclude that these biases are 'epiphenomena of high levels of anxiety symptoms that make children more sensitive to potentially threatening information' (p. 261). Different findings were obtained by Warren, Emde and Sroufe (2000) who employed a vignette-play approach to measure expectancy (interpretation) biases in young non-clinical children. Results indicated that negative expectations were predictive of children's anxiety disorder symptoms at age 5, as rated by the mothers at a 1-year follow-up. These findings suggest that when studied over longer time periods, reasoning biases may act as an antecedent of childhood anxiety problems. Obviously, more research of this type may shed light on the precise role of various types of reasoning biases in the development of anxiety symptoms in youths.

A second possibility would be to employ an intervention approach for examining the role of reasoning biases in childhood anxiety problems (see Chapter 13). If these biases are indeed involved in the maintenance and/or exacerbations of anxiety symptoms among youths, it seems logical to assume that an undermining of such cognitive distortions results in marked reductions of anxiety. Cognitive techniques may be particularly useful for changing the erroneous interpretations and judgements of anxious youths. More precisely, these children can be taught to recognize their reasoning errors and consciously try to combat them by using more adaptive self-talk (e.g. Barrett, 2001; Ollendick and King, 1998). There is already some evidence indicating that reasoning biases can be effectively reduced by means of cognitive-behaviour therapy (Bögels and Siqueland, 2006) and that residual biases at post-treatment are associated with higher anxiety symptomatology (Waters *et al.*, 2008b), but so far a formal test which indicates that change in cognitive bias mediates reductions in children's anxiety symptoms after treatment has not been carried out (Weersing and Weisz, 2002). Of course, the finding that reasoning biases act as a mediator of change during cognitive-behaviour therapy would underline the role of this variable in the pathogenesis of childhood anxiety.

The third approach is experimental in nature and is based on recent work by Mathews and Mackintosh (2000), who developed a training procedure for manipulating anxiety-related interpretation bias in adults. Recently, Muris *et al.* (2008) adapted the procedure to make it suitable for young people. The resulting 'space odyssey' paradigm is essentially a computer game of an imaginary journey to an unknown planet. During the first part of the game, children get acquainted with the unknown living conditions on the new planet: they are presented with brief scenarios describing unknown stimuli and situations. For each scenario, children have to choose between a negative (i.e. mildly threatening) and a positive outcome. Children continuously receive feedback on the correctness of their choices. In half the children, the choice of negative outcomes is reinforced (i.e. negative training group), whereas in the other half the choice of positive outcomes is reinforced (i.e. positive training group). The second part of the game actually is an interpretation bias task: children are asked to imagine that they still live on the new planet and are confronted with ambiguous scenarios describing everyday situations that could also occur on Earth (e.g. going to school, encountering unfamiliar people). The main task of the children is to rate the level of threat associated with each of these situations.

The results showed that the training stage was successful: children in the negative training condition quickly learned to choose negative outcomes for the unknown scenes, whereas children in the positive training condition rapidly learned to select positive outcomes. Most importantly, children's subsequent threat perception scores were affected by this manipulation. That is, children in the negative training condition displayed higher threat perception scores than children in the positive training condition. Moreover, an additional analysis indicated that this pattern of results was particularly pronounced for children who already exhibited high levels of anxiety symptoms. The latter finding is interesting because it suggests that more vulnerable (i.e. already more anxious) children were especially affected by the experimental manipulation. All in all, the initial results with this interpretation bias training paradigm are promising and obviously more supportive for a causal role of reasoning biases in mediating anxiety vulnerability than the prospective and treatment designs described above (which merely demonstrate a correlational association between biases and anxiety). However, much more work needs to be done. In particular, it should be investigated whether the experimental induction of interpretation bias (and maybe other reasoning biases) also promotes children's anxiety levels.

Taken together, during the past two decades, researchers have begun to study reasoning biases in anxious youths and this research has yielded sufficient evidence to assume that anxiety problems in children and adolescents are accompanied by this type of cognitive distortions. Meanwhile, several issues need further empirical exploration. To begin with, it should be examined whether various types of reasoning biases are related to one another and to what extent each of them accounts for unique variance in children and adolescents' vulnerability to anxiety problems. In addition, the origins of these biases as well as their causal role in aetiology and maintenance of pathological anxiety in youths need to be further established.

References

Alfano, C.A., Beidel, D.C. and Turner, S.M. (2002) Cognition in childhood anxiety: conceptual, methodological, and developmental issues. *Clinical Psychology Review*, **22**, 1209–1238.

Arntz, A., Rauner, M. and Van den Hout, M. (1995) "If I feel anxious, there must be danger": ex-consequentia reasoning in inferring danger in anxiety disorders. *Behaviour Research and Therapy*, **33**, 917–925.

Barrett, P.M. (2001) Current issues in the treatment of childhood anxiety, in *The Developmental Psychopathology of Anxiety* (eds M.W. Vasey and M.R. Dadds), Oxford University Press, New York, pp. 304–324.

Barrett, P.M., Rapee, R.M., Dadds, M.R. and Ryan, S.M. (1996) Family enhancement of cognitive style in anxious and aggressive children. *Journal of Abnormal Child Psychology*, **24**, 187–203.

Beck, A.T. (1976) *Cognitive Therapy and the Emotional Disorders*, International Universities Press, New York.

Beck, A.T., Emery, G. and Greenberg, R.L. (1985) *Anxiety Disorders and Phobias: A Cognitive Perspective*, Basic Books, New York.

Bell-Dolan, D.J. (1995) Social cue interpretation of anxious children. *Journal of Clinical Child Psychology*, **24**, 1–10.

Berk, L. (2004) *Child Development*, Allyn and Bacon, Boston.

Bögels, S.M. and Siqueland, L. (2006) Family cognitive behavioral therapy for children and adolescents with clinical anxiety disorders. *Journal of the American Academy of Child and Adolescent Psychiatry*, **45**, 134–141.

Bögels, S.M., Snieder, N. and Kindt, M. (2003) Specificity of dysfunctional thinking in children with symptoms of social anxiety, separation anxiety, and generalised anxiety. *Behaviour Change*, **20**, 160–169.

Bögels, S.M. and Zigterman, D. (2000) Dysfunctional cognitions in children with social phobia, separation anxiety disorder, and generalized anxiety disorder. *Journal of Abnormal Child Psychology*, **28**, 205–211.

Butler, G. and Mathews, A. (1987) Anticipatory anxiety and risk perception. *Cognitive Therapy and Research*, **11**, 551–565.

Canterbury, R., Golden, A.M., Taghavi, R. *et al.* (2004) Anxiety and judgements about emotional events in children and adolescents. *Personality and Individual Differences*, **36**, 695–704.

Chorpita, B.F., Albano, A.M. and Barlow, D.H. (1996) Cognitive processing in children: relationship to anxiety and family influences. *Journal of Clinical Child Psychology*, **25**, 170–176.

Creswell, C., O'Connor, T.G. and Brewin, C.R. (2006) A longitudinal investigation of maternal and child 'anxious cognitions'. *Cognitive Therapy and Research*, **30**, 135–147.

Creswell, C., Schiering, C.A. and Rapee, R.M. (2005) Threat interpretation in anxious children and their mothers: comparison with nonclinical children and the effects of treatment. *Behaviour Research and Therapy*, **43**, 1375–1381.

Creswell, C., Woolgar, M., Cooper, P. *et al.* (2008) Processing of faces and emotional expressions in infants at risk of social phobia. *Cognition and Emotion*, **22**, 437–458.

Dadds, M.R., Barrett, P.M., Rapee, R.M. and Ryan, S. (1996) Family process and child anxiety and aggression: an observational analysis. *Journal of Abnormal Child Psychology*, **24**, 715–734.

Daleiden, E.L. and Vasey, M.W. (1997) An information-processing perspective on childhood anxiety. *Clinical Psychology Review*, **17**, 407–429.

Dalgleish, T., Moradi, A., Taghavi, R. *et al.* (2000) Judgments about emotional events in children and adolescents with post-traumatic stress disorder and controls. *Journal of Child Psychology and Psychiatry*, **41**, 981–988.

Dalgleish, T., Taghavi, R., Neshat-Doost *et al.* (2003) Patterns of processing bias for emotional information across clinical disorders: a comparison of attention, memory, and prospective cognition in children and adolescents with depression, generalized anxiety, and posttraumatic stress disorder. *Journal of Clinical Child and Adolescent Psychology*, **32**, 10–21.

Dalgleish, T., Taghavi, R., Neshat-Doost *et al.* (1997) Information processing in clinically depressed and anxious children and adolescents. *Journal of Child Psychology and Psychiatry*, **38**, 535–541.

De Jong, P.J., Merckelbach, H. and Arntz, A. (1995) Covariation bias in phobic women: the relationship between a priori expectancy, on-line expectancy, automatic responding, and a posteriori contingency judgment. *Journal of Abnormal Psychology*, **104**, 55–62.

Dineen, K.A. and Hadwin, J.A. (2004) Anxious and depressive symptoms and children's judgements of their own and others' interpretation of ambiguous social scenarios. *Journal of Anxiety Disorders*, **18**, 499–513.

Eysenck, M.W., MacLeod, C. and Mathews, A. (1987) Cognitive functioning and anxiety. *Psychological Research*, **49**, 189–195.

Field, A.P. and Lawson, J. (2008) The verbal information pathway to fear and subsequent causal learning in children. *Cognition and Emotion*, **22**, 459–479.

Fonseca, A.C. and Perrin, S. (2001) Clinical phenomenology, classification, and assessment of anxiety disorders in children and adolescents, in *Anxiety Disorders in Children and Adolescents. Research, Assessment, and Intervention* (eds W.K. Silverman and P. Treffers), Cambridge University Press, New York, pp. 126–158.

Hadwin, J., Frost, S., French, C.C. and Richards, A. (1997) Cognitive processing and trait anxiety in typically developing children: evidence for interpretation bias. *Journal of Abnormal Psychology*, **106**, 486–490.

Hadwin, J., Garner, M. and Perez-Olivas, G. (2006) The development of information processing biases in childhood anxiety: a review and exploration of its origins in parenting. *Clinical Psychology Review*, **26**, 876–894.

Harvey, A., Watkins, E., Mansell, W. and Shafran, R. (2004) *Cognitive Behavioural Processes Across Psychological Disorders. A Transdiagnostic Approach to Research and Treatment*, Oxford University Press, Oxford.

Kindt, M. and Van den Hout, M.A. (2001) Selective attention and anxiety: a perspective on developmental issues and the causal status. *Journal of Psychopathology and Behavioral Assessment*, **23**, 193–202.

Lang, P.J. (1968) Fear reduction and fear behaviour: problems in treating a construct, in *Research in psychotherapy, volume III.* (ed. J.M. Schlien), American Psychiatric Association, Washington, DC.

Lu, W., Daleiden, E. and Lu, S.E. (2007) Threat perception bias and anxiety among Chinese school children and adolescents. *Journal of Clinical Child and Adolescent Psychology*, **36**, 568–580.

MacLeod, C. and Cohen, I. (1993) Anxiety and the interpretation of ambiguity: a text comprehension study. *Journal of Abnormal Psychology*, **102**, 238–247.

Mathews, A. and Mackintosh, B. (2000) Induced emotional interpretation bias and anxiety. *Journal of Abnormal Psychology*, **109**, 602–615.

Mattis, S.G. and Ollendick, T.H. (1997) Children's cognitive responses to the somatic symptoms of panic. *Journal of Abnormal Child Psychology*, **25**, 47–57.

Mineka, S. and Tomarken, A.J. (1989) The role of cognitive biases in the origins and maintenance of fear and anxiety disorders, in *Aversion, Avoidance, and Anxiety: Perspectives on Aversively Motivated Behavior* (eds T. Archer and L.G. Nilsson), Lawrence Erlbaum, Hillsdale, NJ, pp. 195–221.

Mogg, K. and Bradley, B.P. (1998) A cognitive-motivational analysis of anxiety. *Behaviour Research and Therapy*, **36**, 809–848.

Morren, M., Muris, P. and Kindt, M. (2004) Emotional reasoning and parent-based reasoning in normal children. *Child Psychiatry and Human Development*, **35**, 3–20.

Muris, P. (2007) *Normal and Abnormal Fear and Anxiety in Children and Adolescents*, Elsevier, Oxford.

Muris, P., De Jong, P.J., Meesters, C. *et al.* (2005) An experimental study of spider-related covariation bias in 8- to 13-year-old children. *Child Psychiatry and Human Development*, **35**, 185–201.

Muris, P. and Field, A. (2008) Distorted cognition and pathological anxiety in children and adolescents. *Cognition and Emotion*, **22**, 395–421.

Muris, P., Hoeve, I., Meesters, C. and Mayer, B. (2004) Children's conception and interpretation of anxiety-related physical symptoms. *Journal of Behavior Therapy and Experimental Psychiatry*, **35**, 233–244.

Muris, P., Huijding, J., Mayer, B. *et al.* (2007a) Spider fear and covariation bias in children and adolescents. *Behaviour Research and Therapy*, **45**, 2604–2615.

Muris, P., Mayer, B., Vermeulen, L. and Hiemstra, H. (2007b) Theory-of-mind, cognitive development, and children's interpretation of anxiety-related physical symptoms. *Behaviour Research and Therapy*, **45**, 2121–2132.

Muris, P., Huijding, J., Mayer, B. and Hameetman, M. (2008) A space odyssey: experimental manipulation of interpretation bias in children. *Child Psychiatry and Human Development*, **39**, 469–480.

Muris, P., Jacques, P. and Mayer, B. (2004) The stability of threat perception abnormalities and anxiety disorder symptoms in non-clinical children. *Child Psychiatry and Human Development*, **34**, 251–265.

Muris, P., Kindt, M., Bögels, S. *et al.* (2000a) Anxiety and threat perception abnormalities in normal children. *Journal of Psychopathology and Behavioral Assessment*, **22**, 183–199.

Muris, P., Luermans, J., Merckelbach, H. and Mayer, B. (2000b) "Danger is lurking everywhere". The relationship between anxiety and threat perception abnormalities in normal children. *Journal of Behavior Therapy and Experimental Psychiatry*, **31**, 123–136.

Muris, P., Merckelbach, H. and Damsma, E. (2000) Threat perception bias in nonreferred socially anxious children. *Journal of Clinical Child Psychology*, **29**, 348–359.

Muris, P., Merckelbach, H., Schepers, S. and Meesters, C. (2003a) Anxiety, threat perception abnormalities, and emotional reasoning in non-clinical children. *Journal of Clinical Child and Adolescent Psychology*, **32**, 453–459.

Muris, P., Rapee, R., Meesters, C. *et al.* (2003b) Threat perception abnormalities in children: the role of anxiety disorders symptoms, chronic anxiety, and state anxiety. *Journal of Anxiety Disorders*, **17**, 271–287.

Muris, P., Merckelbach, H. and Van Spauwen, I. (2003) The emotional reasoning heuristic in children. *Behaviour Research and Therapy*, **41**, 261–272.

Muris, P. and Van der Heiden, S. (2006) Anxiety, depression, and judgments about the probability of future negative and positive events in children. *Journal of Anxiety Disorders*, **20**, 252–261.

Muris, P., Vermeer, E. and Horselenberg, R. (2008) Cognitive development and the interpretation of anxiety-related physical symptoms in 4- to 12-year-old non-clinical children. *Journal of Behavior Therapy and Experimental Psychiatry*, **39**, 73–86.

Ollendick, T.H. and King, N.J. (1998) Empirically supported treatments for children with phobic and anxiety disorders: current status. *Journal of Clinical Child Psychology*, **27**, 156–167.

Pauli, P., Montoya, P. and Martz, G.E. (1996) Covariation bias in panic-prone individuals. *Journal of Abnormal Psychology*, **105**, 658–662.

Pury, C.L.S. (2002) Information-processing predictors of emotional response to stress. *Cognition and Emotion*, **16**, 667–683.

Reid, S.C., Salmon, K. and Lovibond, P.F. (2006) Cognitive biases in childhood anxiety, depression and aggression: are they pervasive or specific? *Cognitive Therapy and Research*, **30**, 531–549.

Richards, A., French, C.C., Nash, G. *et al.* (2007) A comparison of selective attention and facial processing biases in typically developing children who are high and low in self-reported trait anxiety. *Development and Psychopathology*, **19**, 481–495.

Schneider, S., Unnewehr, S., Florin, I. and Margraf, J. (2002) Priming panic interpretations in children of patients with panic disorder. *Journal of Anxiety Disorders*, **16**, 605–624.

Suarez, L. and Bell-Dolan, D. (2001) The relationship between child worry to cognitive biases: threat interpretation and likelihood of event occurrence. *Behavior Therapy*, **32**, 425–442.

Taghavi, M.R., Moradi, A.R., Neshat-Doost, H.T. *et al.* (2000) Interpretation of ambiguous emotional information in clinically anxious children and adolescents. *Cognition and Emotion*, **14**, 809–822.

Tomarken, A.J., Mineka, S. and Cook, M. (1989) Fear-relevant selective associations and covariation bias. *Journal of Abnormal Psychology*, **98**, 381–394.

Unnewehr, S., Schneider, S., Margraf, J. *et al.* (1996) Exposure to internal and external stimuli: reactions in children of parents with panic disorder or animal phobia. *Journal of Anxiety Disorders*, **10**, 489–508.

Vasey, M.W. and MacLeod, C. (2001) Information processing factors in childhood anxiety: a review and developmental perspective, in *The Developmental Psychopathology of Anxiety* (eds M.W. Vasey and M. Dadds), Oxford University Press, Oxford, pp. 253–277.

Warren, S.L., Emde, R.N. and Sroufe, L.A. (2000) Internal representations predicting anxiety from children's play narratives. *Journal of the American Academy of Child and Adolescent Psychiatry*, **39**, 100–107.

Waters, A.M., Craske, M.G., Bergman, L. and Treanor, M. (2008a) Threat interpretation bias as a vulnerability factor in childhood anxiety disorders. *Behaviour Research and Therapy*, **46**, 39–47.

Waters, A.M., Wharton, T.A., Zimmer-Gembeck, M.J. and Craske, M.G. (2008b) Threat-based cognitive biases in anxious children: comparison with non-anxious children before and after cognitive behavioural treatment. *Behaviour Research and Therapy*, **46**, 358–374.

Weems, C.F., Silverman, W.K. and La Greca, A.M. (2000) What do youth referred for anxiety problems worry about? Worry and its relationship to anxiety and anxiety disorders in children and adolescents. *Journal of Abnormal Child Psychology*, **28**, 63–72.

Weersing, V.R. and Weisz, J.R. (2002) Mechanisms of action in youth psychotherapy. *Journal of Child Psychology and Psychiatry*, **43**, 3–29.

3

The Emotional Stroop Task in Anxious Children

*Zoë C. Nightingale, Andy P. Field
and Merel Kindt*
andyf@sussex.ac.uk

The original paradigm of Stroop (1935) has played a valuable theoretical role in the study of selective information processing and has been an important tool for understanding the processing of intrusive stimuli (MacLeod, 1991). The traditional Stroop task involves presenting participants the names of colours (green, purple, red, brown and blue) printed in different (conflicting) coloured inks. (For example, the word 'blue' is not printed in blue ink, but is printed an equal number of times in green, purple, red and brown ink.) Consequently, word and colour stimuli are presented simultaneously: each word represents the name of one colour, but is printed in the ink of another colour. The control condition consists of a set of coloured non-words. Participants are instructed to name the colour of ink in which the word (or non-word in the control condition) is printed as fast as possible. In a typical set of results, participants are reliably slower to name the colour of the ink when it is presented in a conflicting coloured ink than to name the same colours printed depicting non-words (see MacLeod, 1991; Stroop, 1935). This phenomenon is known as the *Stroop effect* and has been interpreted in terms of response competition: as a result of automatized semantic processing of the colour word, colour naming of the word is prioritized such that it conflicts with the task to name the colour of the ink (see MacLeod, 1991). This chapter discusses a variant of this task known as the *emotional Stroop task*, which has been used as an information processing approach to assess selective information processing of emotional stimuli. This chapter will present an overview of studies that have used the emotional Stroop task to explore cognitive processing in children and adolescents who experience elevated anxiety.

Information Processing Biases and Anxiety: A Developmental Perspective Edited by Julie A. Hadwin and Andy P. Field
© 2010 John Wiley & Sons, Ltd.

The Emotional Stroop Task

The emotional Stroop task involves examining the response latency to name the colours of emotionally aversive words (e.g. 'cancer') relative to emotionally neutral words (e.g. 'plate'). In some experiments, pictures have been used instead of words and in these cases the participant might be required to name the colour of a schematic face, displaying either a neutral or an angry expression (Williams, Mathews and MacLeod, 1996). An important prediction from the task is that participants who are more attentive to threat in their environment, such as those who experience elevated or clinical levels of anxiety, should show a greater latency to colour name an emotionally aversive stimulus relative to an emotionally neutral stimulus, compared to non-anxious individuals (MacLeod, 1991). In many studies an 'interference score' is calculated, which is the time taken to name the colour of threat stimuli minus the time taken to name the colour of control stimuli. As such, a positive interference score indicates that the threat stimuli interfered with the participant's ability to name the colour compared to control stimuli.

Both the traditional and the emotional Stroop tests require the suppression of responses to distracting word information, while maintaining attention on the colour of the word (Compton et al., 2003). In addition, they both elicit comparable behavioural effects (an increased latency to name the colour of words). It is argued, however, that these tests utilize distinct mechanisms of interference (McKenna and Sharma, 2004). The classic Stroop produces a conflict between an incongruent colour and word (the word red in font colour blue), whereas the emotional Stroop concerns only emotional and neutral words; colour does not affect latency because it does not conflict with word meaning.

Although studies using the emotional Stroop task all measure the speed to name colours of negative words or pictures, these stimuli can be presented in two different ways. First, the stimuli can be presented individually using either a tachistoscope or a computer monitor. We will call this the *single-trial format* because each stimulus appears alone as a single trial. An alternative format is the *card format* in which columns of words or pictures are presented on a single card. Unlike the single-trial format, in the card format many trials are presented simultaneously. The choice of format has important implications because processing biases shown using the card format can reflect mood effects (see Richards et al., 1992) and measurement error (see the discussion in Kindt, Brosschot and Everaerd, 1997). As such, the card format might not be an appropriate measure of processing bias. This view should be remembered as we review the various studies.

What does the emotional Stroop task measure?

The emotional Stroop, unlike the traditional Stroop, does not involve an effect of conflict between a word meaning and a colour of ink, but is proposed to be a function of the emotional significance of the semantic content of the word to an individual where this significance leads to increased attention to this word and therefore interferes with the task of colour naming. As such it measures a processing bias[1] towards threat.

Processing bias towards threat has also been demonstrated through the use of other paradigms. For example, another commonly used task is the dot-probe task (see Chapters 4 and 8). Here, a threatening and a neutral cue (e.g. a word or face) are presented simultaneously on a screen; subsequently these cues disappear and a probe appears in the location of either the previous threatening or the neutral cue. High anxious individuals relative to non-anxious controls are faster to react to probes appearing in the location of threatening rather than neutral cues, suggesting that their attention is oriented towards threatening cues, thus facilitating response when the probe appears in that location (e.g. Field, 2006; Heim-Dreger et al., 2006; Lipp and Derakshan, 2005). In visual dot-probe tasks, the emotional cue and the succeeding probe are physically and temporally separated and, therefore, the distribution of attention relates to the visuospatial field. In the emotional Stroop task, however, this is not the case: the emotional cue and the probe (i.e. the colour of the word or picture) are spatially and temporally integrated because the word or picture and colour appear at the same time and in the same physical location. Therefore, attention is distributed cognitively but not physically (i.e. in the visuospatial field). Therefore, the Stroop task and the visual dot-probe task differ in that the visual dot-probe task measures relative attention whereas the Stroop task is a measure of emotional interference (van Strien and Valstar, 2004).

The emotional Stroop task has been frequently employed to explore processing bias in anxious adults (see Logan and Goetsch, 1993; Williams, Mathews and MacLeod, 1996, for reviews). Research carried out since the 1980s has shown that the colour naming of emotionally negative words is typically slower in individuals who are anxious (relative to the colour naming of neutral words of equivalent frequency) and this difference is not found in non-anxious control groups. This phenomenon is proposed to reflect automatic processing of the semantics of the threatening words in anxious individuals, which causes interference with the main task of colour naming (e.g. Watts et al., 1986). The disruption caused by selective attention to emotionally relevant stimuli in anxiety has led some researchers to argue that the emotional adaptation of the Stroop task could be utilized as a measure of psychopathology (Williams et al., 1996). For example, if a person demonstrates a processing bias for spider-related material, it could imply that they have a spider phobia.

Williams, Mathews and MacLeod (1996) wrote an exceptional review of research using the emotional Stroop task and discussed the causes and mechanisms underlying the Stroop effect. On the basis of this review, they suggested that in adult research, both state (anxiety at a particular moment in time such as in a stressful situation) and trait (general feelings of anxiety an individual experiences) components of anxiety affect the degree of interference observed in the emotional Stroop task.

---

[1] Some people describe the emotional Stroop task as measuring attentional bias. However, the task cannot differentiate between the selective processes occurring early after a cue is presented (and in the wider context these early-onset processes are commonly referred to as *attentional bias*) and processing biases occurring later after stimulus onset. To acknowledge this fact we will use the term *processing bias* rather than 'attentional bias' to describe what the emotional Stroop measures.

Individual differences in state and trait anxiety, as assessed by tools such as The State-Trait Anxiety Inventory (Spielberger *et al.*, 1983), appear to interact to create interference effects. Specifically, although individuals high on trait anxiety show more interference for all threatening words, the presence of experimentally induced state anxiety is necessary for the disruption to be observed. Moreover, Williams, Mathews and MacLeod suggest that this interaction is more likely to occur if the current stressor has had time to develop (e.g. worrying about an impending examination), relative to if the current emotional disturbance is only short-lived (e.g. failing an experimental task).

When considering what the emotional Stroop paradigm measures, it is important to rule out the possibility that the observed interference effects are due to artefacts of the experimental procedure. Williams, Mathews and MacLeod (1996) identified three possible alternative explanations of the observed interference effects in adults. First, colour-naming interference could be due to priming effects of a word from a particular category on the subsequent presentation of a word from the same category. However, Williams, Mathews and MacLeod concluded that the available evidence suggests that this interpretation is not the case because several studies showing significant interference effects had used categorized neutral stimuli, which controlled for inter-category priming effects (e.g. Dalgleish, 1995). Second, because nearly all studies use a repeated presentation collection of emotional and neutral stimuli, the resulting interference effects could be due to the repetition of a small collection of emotional words. Williams, Mathews and MacLeod ruled out this explanation by arguing that this repetition is unlikely to influence the Stroop effect because neutral and emotional stimuli are typically presented an equal number of times. One further criticism of the Stroop paradigm is that participants might be consciously attending to the emotional words, undermining the idea of interference being a function of an automatic information processing bias to threat in anxiety. However, studies using subliminal Stroop tasks (e.g. Bradley *et al.*, 1995; Mogg *et al.*, 1993; Mogg, Kentish and Bradley, 1993) have shown that biases can be found using presentation times that do not allow participants time to construct strategies based on conscious awareness of the material. This finding suggests that emotional Stroop interference is not dependent on conscious strategies (Williams, Mathews and MacLeod, 1996). However, research has also shown that attributes of automatic processing, such as being capacity free, unconscious and involuntary, do not all apply to selective processing of threat associated with anxiety. Experimental and clinical findings suggest that processing biases are automatic in the sense of being involuntary (and sometimes unconscious), but not in the sense of being capacity free (McNally, 1995).

Apart from artefacts that might explain the interference effects measured by the emotional Stroop task, there are design issues that often obscure the inferences that can be made from the task. For example, the subjective (and sometimes actual) frequency of the threat stimuli used in the task is not always controlled. The subjective frequency is difficult to control because it will differ across patient groups and normal controls. For example, the subjective frequency with which a spider phobic experiences words such as 'web' or images of spiders is probably greater than for people experiencing social anxiety or controls. This lack of control over subjective prior experience with stimuli in the emotional Stroop task is problematic because performance on this task is not attributable to lexical frequency but to personal relevance (Riemann and McNally, 1995). A related suggestion is that the emotional Stroop effect reflects participant expertise rather than emotional interference. For example, Cohen, Dunbar and McClelland's (1990) connectionist model suggests that variation in colour-conflict Stroop interference could reflect variation in the amount of expertise that an individual has had with the emotional stimuli, the colour of which participants have to name (MacLeod and Dunbar, 1988). Here it is suggested that individuals characterized with elevated anxiety have a tendency to ruminate on negatively laden emotional stimuli and so will have had more practice in using and thinking about these particular concepts compared with non-anxious individuals. This process of rumination may lead to the development of some expertise in processing information associated with personal concern in anxious individuals (Segal et al., 1995). However, emotional Stroop effects have been shown to decrease in anxious individuals after treatment (e.g. Lavy and van den Hout, 1993; Lavy, van den Hout and Arntz, 1993; Watts et al., 1986). Given that treatment does not reduce the amount of expertise with emotional concepts, it can be argued that interference observed in the emotional Stroop task is attributable to the emotional valence of the stimuli and not to cognitive expertise. Furthermore, these findings indicate that the emotional Stroop can be used as an index of whether individuals have recovered from their emotional disturbance.

If we accept, bearing in mind the aforementioned caveats, that the emotional Stroop task is a measure of an automatic information processing bias, then we can move on to try to explain the underlying mechanism that drives this bias. Several cognitive models have been proposed to elucidate the mechanisms underlying the emotional Stroop effect in anxious adults (Williams, Mathews and MacLeod, 1996). The earliest explanatory models were Beck's schema theory (Beck, Emery and Greenberg, 1985) and Bower's (1981) network theory in which potentially threatening stimuli are thought to capture excessive attentional resources because of the activation of specific cognitive structures signifying personal danger (Mogg, Mathews and Weinman, 1989). Other models have proposed that the negative emotional content of the experimental stimuli trigger self-focusing processes that expend attentional resources that interfere with the main task of colour naming (Dawkins and Furnham, 1989) or require greater cognitive effort to override the perception of such stimuli (Holmes, 1974; Ruiter and Brosschot, 1994). However, these older models have been superseded by Mathews and MacLeod's (1994) prioritization model. In this model, anxiety functions to shift attention into a state of hyper-vigilance, resulting in the individual scrutinizing his or her environment for any potentially threatening stimulus, especially those environments that in past experience have been linked to threat. They suggest that in this hyper-vigilant state the cognitive system prioritizes the processing of threat stimuli, but not the deliberate rehearsal of the stimuli for explicit encoding into memory (see Williams, Mathews and MacLeod, 1996). This hyper-vigilance model has a lot of support (see Mathews and MacLeod, 2005, for a review); however, there is some evidence that in some individuals anxiety serves to create avoidance rather than vigilance (e.g. Hock and Krohne, 2004). Nevertheless, some researchers have argued that if the emotional Stroop effect consistently correlates with the presentation of an anxiety disorder, then it is useful (diagnostically or as a research tool) regardless of the underlying mechanism (Benoit et al., 2007).

The Emotional Stroop Task in Children

Methodological and theoretical considerations

A strong aspect of the emotional Stroop task is that it is an experimental paradigm; it is a performance-based task and is therefore less sensitive to reporter bias. For example, Dubner and Motta (1999) concluded that the emotional Stroop shows potential as a research and diagnostic instrument in work with traumatized youths who are reluctant or incapable of revealing the presence of abuse. However, experimental measures of processing bias may suffer from methodological problems, especially when involving young children.

Throughout this section there are two general issues to consider that relate to both methodology and theory. The first is whether processing biases are specific or general. So, for example, do children with panic disorder show a general processing bias for all threat stimuli or for only stimuli related to panic (a specific bias)? The studies we review generally fall into categories of those looking at general anxiety and a processing bias for general threat, and those looking at processing biases for disorder-specific stimuli. The second issue is the downward application of adult models. Cognitively speaking, a 17-year-old is an adult, whereas a 6- or 12-year-old is not. The literature contains studies that have recruited youths with wide-ranging ages. The downward compatibility of adult models of anxiety (such as the hyper-vigilance model described earlier) might be influenced by aspects of cognitive development. So, although adult models of emotional Stroop effects should apply to older adolescents because cognitively they differ little from adults, these models might not extend back to the pre-teenage years in which the child is still developing his or her cognitive abilities. Cognitive development could affect both performance aspects of the task (e.g. younger children might find the task more confusing and get bored more easily, which will affect their reaction times) and also the underlying process (younger children have yet to develop a bias to threat). In Chapter 11 it is argued that the underlying associations that drive attentional biases should be acquired relatively early in life; therefore, age might not affect the underlying mechanism that drives the bias but could affect the expression or measurement of that mechanism. Studies have varied in whether they use word or picture stimuli and this manipulation might affect the strength of interference effects from the emotional Stroop task. Pictures may be the more appropriate stimuli for children because they do not depend upon linguistic skills, are more concrete, ecologically valid and closer to the original source of threat than more abstract word stimuli. As such, we might expect effects from picture-based Stroop tasks to be stronger than those from word-based versions.

The developmental trajectory of processing biases is discussed elsewhere in this book (e.g. Chapter 11), but theories differ in whether they assume a central role for development. The *integral bias hypothesis* proposes that cognitive processes are an innate constituent of emotion (Martin, Horder and Jones, 1992; Martin and Jones, 1995). Specific emotions have evolved to bring about certain cognitive objectives. The integral bias hypothesis predicts that cognitive biases are present in childhood and remain fairly stable from childhood to adulthood (Martin, Horder and Jones, 1992; Rapee, 2000). According to this hypothesis, processing biases seen in adults should transfer downwards to children. As such, age and cognitive development should not affect interference effects and if they do, then it reflects measurement error (such as younger children finding the Stroop task more difficult to perform).

An alternative is to assume that anxiety-related processing biases do not emerge fully formed in a child and that their ongoing cognitive and emotional development and past experience will affect how they interpret information in their environment. Jones (1984, 1987) proposed that the cognitive effects of emotion are not, in general, innate consequences of that emotion but instead they are learned via previous experiences in which certain patterns of emotional and cognitive processing have been associated. As we said earlier, although the underlying associations might be formed early in life, the emotional biases driven by these associations will be influenced by the child's developing cognitive sophistication to think about these associations between certain events and particular emotional states, and also their ever-developing experience with different events as predictors of emotion. This *inferred bias hypothesis* would predict that processing biases should become greater with age.

A variant of this hypothesis assumes that development acts in a different way for anxious and non-anxious children. In essence, the anxiety status of the child sets them off on a different developmental trajectory. The idea is that a processing bias for threatening stimuli is a normal characteristic of young children but this bias decreases with age in non-anxious children and increases with age in the anxious children. This *inhibition hypothesis* suggests that from middle to late childhood normally developing children learn to inhibit automatic processing of potential threat, whereas anxious children do not develop this ability. In other words, anxious children maintain processing biases which are a normal characteristic of young childhood (Kindt, Bierman and Brosschot, 1997; Kindt and van den Hout, 2001). Kindt and van den Hout (2001) suggest that anxiety experienced during childhood creates a failure to inhibit selective attention to threat, which, in turn, increases susceptibility to developing an anxiety disorder in adulthood. This hypothesis is also consistent with Lonigan's temperament model (see Chapter 10), which argues that effortful control mediates the relationship between threat-related processing bias and the beginning of an anxiety disorder (Lonigan *et al.*, 2004). For example, young children (aged 8) may lack adequate effortful control to suppress attentional reactions to threat-related stimuli or information that is relevant to their developmental stage because some stimuli are not threatening for all developmental stages.

Evidence for anxiety-related emotional Stroop effects in children

Having considered what the task measures and some of the methodological and theoretical issues, we will now review the studies that have found threat-related interference effects in the context of childhood anxiety (Table 3.1). We will divide the research into studies from non-clinical and clinical populations because effects might be expected to be stronger in clinical populations. In non-clinical populations, research has looked at both general anxiety by splitting samples into high and low trait anxious children and also children with specific anxiety concerns by defining groups according to those concerns. For example, Martin, Horder and Jones (1992) used the card format of the emotional Stroop task on a group of spider-fearful and non-fearful children (6–13 years old). This study found that spider-fearful children showed greater latencies to colour name spider-related words (e.g. 'creepy' and 'hairy'), but not neutral words (e.g. 'table' and 'cars'). Non-spider-fearful children did not show this difference. Martin and Jones (1995) replicated this finding in a sample of children from three different age groups (4–5 years, 6–7 years and 8–9 years) using a pictorial adaptation of the emotional Stroop paradigm. Here, children were asked to name the ink colour of pictures (instead of words), where these were related to spiders, houses (control stimuli) or teddy bears (filler stimuli). This adaptation was important because it extended the investigation of processing bias to younger groups of children who may not have the necessary reading age to complete word-based tasks. Martin and Jones found that the magnitude of processing bias was consistent across development and was therefore not a function of age.

Another study that looked at interference effects for a specific anxiety focused on social concerns in late childhood (Martin and Cole, 2000). Here 8- to 12-year-olds were asked to colour name words related to acceptance (e.g. 'popular') and rejection (e.g. 'hated') in children who were rated by peers as popular or unpopular. Care was taken to ensure that the task was appropriate for use with children of this age group. For example, children were given the opportunity to practice the task until they clearly understood the procedure. In addition, subsequent to the Stroop task, the computer program repeated the presentation of the stimulus words and phrases but without colour variation (i.e. all words were in black letters on a white background). Children read the words aloud and word-reading reaction times were recorded. The experimenter coded whether or not the child was able to read the word fluently. Words that could not be read fluently by the child were excluded from the analysis. Martin and Cole found that children rated as unpopular showed significantly greater colour-naming interference towards words with a negative social content than were their more popular peers.

In terms of general anxiety, Richards et al. (2007) have utilized the emotional Stroop task in combination with a facial processing task in a group of children aged 10–11 years. This age was deemed suitable for children to cope with the task demands. The reading level of all children was assessed by a teacher and all children were found to be average or above in relation to their chronological age. One useful aspect of this study is the use of different methodologies which can tell us something about the convergent validity of the emotional Stroop task

Table 3.1. Details of experiments finding significant anxiety-related emotional Stroop effects in children

Authors	Format	Sample characteristics	Presentation stimulus (word/picture/face)	Other measures/ control variables	Block/trials	Age/adjustments for use with children
Dubner and Motta (1999)	Card	Clinical: PTSD (sexually abused)	Sexual abuse words (i.e. *sex, privates*), neutral (i.e. *pen, planet*), OCD-like stimuli (i.e. *germs, urine*) and positive stimuli (i.e. *happy, fun*). To assess the base rate for colour naming non-meaningful stimuli; also presented children with a control card of coloured zeroes	To ensure that the children were familiar with the colour names used on the MSP, they first named the colours of five vertical lines on a card Participants who were unable to read all of a sample of the Stroop words ($n = 3$) were excluded from the analysis	B1: Three practice cards, which consisted of coloured pictures and two cards of coloured words not related to the task stimuli B2: 200 test trials – words were printed on four sheets of white paper in a variety of colours (i.e. red, yellow, green, blue and black). Each sheet contained 50 words in capital letters	8–19 None
Hadwin *et al.* (2009)	Single trial (computer)	Non-clinical: Trait anxiety social concern	Angry, happy and neutral face stimuli made up the schematic faces, with each face being made up of a pair of eyes, eyebrows and a mouth (see Hadwin *et al.*, 2003). The facial features from each emotion face were rearranged to make control stimuli with scrambled facial features	None	B1: 72 randomly presented trials	6–12 Used non-integrated face stimuli. Children responded using coloured buttons on a key board

(*continued overleaf*)

Table 3.1. (*Continued*)

Authors	Format	Sample characteristics	Presentation stimulus (word/picture/face)	Other measures/ control variables	Block/trials	Age/adjustments for use with children
Martin, Horder and Jones (1992)	Card	Non-clinical: Spider anxious	Non-words: wpa, doat, ksuiv and mijcat. Colour words: red, blue, green and yellow (the sequence was subject to the constraint that a colour word was never written in ink of the same name). Control words: fly, colours, spots, wings, ladybird. Spider words: web, crawl, hairy, body, legs. Practice words: tail, purr, cute, paws, fluffy.	None	B1: 185 test trials	6–13 None
Martin and Cole (2000)	Single trial (computer)	Non-clinical: Popular vs. unpopular	(i) Negative social words such as 'lonely' and 'hated'; (ii) positive social words such as 'popular' and 'accepted'; (iii) negative control words such as 'broken' and 'smelly' and (iv) positive control words such as 'sweet' and 'easy'	Word-reading test. Pilot test: Children attempted to read each word aloud and quickly into a microphone attached to the timing device. Eliminated words if (i) the word or phrase was not easily pronounced by all children; (ii) the average reading time for the word was greater than 1000 ms (i.e. 1 s)	B1: Three practice trials that were repeated until the child clearly understood the task. B2: 48 test stimulus words and brief phrases	8–12 None

Study	Task type	Group	Stimuli	Additional tests	Trial details	Age	Notes
Martin and Jones (1995)	Card	Non-clinical: Spider anxious	Pictures of spiders, houses or teddy bears	None	B1: 20 practice trials B2: 120 test trials	4–9	Used pictures instead of words
Moradi et al. (1999b)	Single trial (computer)	Clinical: PTSD	Happy (e.g. pleased), categorized neutral (e.g. sheep), depression-related (e.g. helpless), general threat-related (e.g. terrified) and trauma-related (e.g. injured)	Vocabulary and reading tests administered	B1:120 test trials (Sixty words presented twice). These consisted of 12 words from each of the five word categories	9–17	None
Moradi et al. (1999a)	Single trial (computer)	Clinical: PTSD	Happy (e.g. pleased), categorized neutral (e.g. sheep), depression-related (e.g. helpless), general threat-related (e.g. terrified) and trauma-related (e.g. injured)	Vocabulary and reading tests administered	B1:120 test trials (60 words presented twice). These consisted of 12 words from each of the five word categories	9–17	None
Richards, Richards and McGeeney (2000)	Card	Non-clinical: Trait anxiety	Threat-related words and neutral words	None	B1: Practice trials (no description) B2: The authors state that there are 96 threat-related test trials and 96 non-threat-related test trials. However, based on their description it would appear that there are 64 trials of each	16–18	None
Richards et al. (2007)	Card	Non-clinical: Trait anxiety	Anxiety-related, positive and neutral words	Reading level assessed	B1: 96 practice trials (eight neutral words presented 12 times) B2: 288 test trials	10–11	None
Taghavi et al. (2003)	Single trial (computer)	Clinical: GAD	Depression-related, trauma-related, threat-related, happy and neutral words	The British Picture Vocabulary Scale and word-reading test administered	B1: 60 trials (12 words from each category)	$M = 13.47$ (GAD), 14.50 (control)	None

(see later). The emotional Stroop task looked at children's processing bias to threat words and a second task investigated facial processing biases using morphed angry-neutral and happy-neutral expressions that varied in emotional intensity. The results produced the predicted emotional Stroop interference effect, with high trait anxious children demonstrating greater colour-naming interference for anxiety-related words than low trait anxious children. Both state and trait anxiety were found to play a role in this bias: Stroop interference was significantly correlated with both trait ($r = .40$, $p = .004$) and state anxiety ($r = .42$, $p = .002$). Williams, Mathews and MacLeod's (1996) model suggests that emotional Stroop effects in high trait anxious people should be exacerbated by high state anxiety, but this interaction between state and trait anxiety was not tested. The face processing task indicated that high trait anxious children were less able than the low trait anxious children at discriminating happy from angry facial expressions in cases where the happy expressions contained low levels of emotional intensity. The authors argued that both methodologies revealed differences between anxious and non-anxious children in the processing of emotional information and provided support for the suggestion that these two divergent tasks make use of general cognitive processes. Richards *et al.* proposed that the inability to inhibit threat cues (i.e. in the Stroop task) may be related to the inability to discriminate emotional expressions when the emotional intensity is weak.

A similar study was recently done but using picture rather than word stimuli in the Stroop task. Hadwin *et al.*, (2009) examined the effects of self-report trait anxiety, social concern and age on colour matching Stroop interference for angry (relative to neutral) schematic faces in children aged 6–12 years. The results demonstrated that increased social concern was associated with decreased ability to inhibit attention to angry faces (relative to neutral), $r = .24$, and that this relationship was not moderated by age. The failure to inhibit attention to angry faces was argued to be specific to increased social concerns. The authors argue that the developmental course of information processing biases in childhood anxiety can be best understood by matching specific anxieties (such as social concerns) with appropriate experimental stimuli (e.g. facial expressions). However, this conclusion is not as clear-cut as it might seem. First, trait anxiety correlated very highly with social concerns ($r = .83$), implying that they might measure essentially the same thing. Also, although the correlation between processing bias and trait anxiety was not significant, $r = .19$, it was similar in size to that of social concerns.

Processing biases for general anxiety stimuli have also been explored in adolescents. Richards, Richards and McGeeney (2000) used a card-based emotional Stroop paradigm consisting of eight threat-related words and eight matched neutral words in a sample of 16- to 18-year-olds who were classified as either high or low trait anxious adolescents. The results revealed that high trait anxious adolescents displayed comparable colour-naming interference effects to those obtained in the adult literature. Interestingly, their results showed a linear relationship between trait anxiety and the degree of colour-naming interference; specifically, they found that as anxiety increases, the amount of interference produced by the threat-related stimuli compared with the neutral stimuli also increased.

We now turn to studies that have used clinical samples. Taghavi *et al.* (2003) looked at processing bias using the emotional Stroop task in a sample of 19 child and adolescent patients with generalized anxiety disorder (GAD) aged 13 and 14 years. They found that adolescents with a diagnosis of GAD demonstrated significantly greater colour-naming latencies when asked to colour name emotionally aversive words (depression-related and trauma-related) compared with positive and neutral words relative to controls. The effect size for this negative word Stroop bias across groups was tending towards large (Cohen's $d = .75$). This result is consistent with the findings in studies with GAD in adults (Mathews and MacLeod, 1985) and supports the idea that the cognitive features of GAD are comparable across adult, adolescent and child populations (Taghavi *et al.*, 2003). The same research team found interference effects in the predicted direction in children and adolescents with post-traumatic stress disorder (PTSD) aged between 9 and 17 years (Moradi *et al.*, 1999b). In this study, vocabulary and reading tests subsequent to completing the emotional Stroop task were used to ensure that the words presented were not too difficult for this sample of youths. Moradi *et al.* found that youths suffering from PTSD were selectively slower to colour name trauma-related words (e.g. 'injured' and 'emergency') relative to non-emotional words (e.g. 'sheep' and 'duck') compared to non-clinical controls. Additionally, correlational analyses suggested that this effect was not dependent on age and was consistent across the age range of 9–17 years. These findings were replicated in a group of 9- to 17-year-olds with PTSD (Moradi *et al.*, 1999a) and are similar to processing bias effects found in adults with PTSD (Thrasher, Dalgleish and Yule, 1994).

Dubner and Motta (1999) used the modified Stroop procedure (MSP) to assess processing bias and intrusive cognitions of foster care children who had developed PTSD after being either physically or sexually abused. The sample included 40 preadolescents (8–12 years of age), 72 early adolescents (13–15 years of age) and 38 late adolescents (16–19 years of age). Their results showed that children who had been sexually abused demonstrated significantly longer colour-naming latencies of sexual-abuse-related words (e.g. 'naughty' and 'sex') than non-abused children. In addition, sexually abused children with PTSD showed significantly more interference in responding to the Stroop card containing sexual-abuse-related words than those without PTSD. Finally, sexually abused children diagnosed with PTSD were slower to identify the colour of words on the sexual abuse card than words on the obsessive-compulsive disorder (OCD), neutral and positive stimulus cards.

In summary, although the literature is small, several studies have replicated the basic emotional Stroop interference effect in child and adolescent samples: anxious children and adolescents are slower to name the colours of threat-related stimuli. Although some of these studies have used samples close in age to adults, others have used young children. In addition, when studies have specifically explored developmental effects between age and processing bias, none have been found (Martin and Jones, 1995; Moradi *et al.*, 1999b). These studies, therefore, support the integral bias theory (described earlier), which suggests that processing biases are an integral part of emotion that are unaffected by cognitive development. However, it is worth remembering that even the youngest children in the aforementioned research were aged 4 and quite a lot of development has gone on by this age. It is also important to bear in mind that many of the studies just described have used the card format (Table 3.1) and as we argued earlier this format probably does not rule out explanations other than the detection of a processing bias.

Evidence against anxiety-related emotional Stroop effects in children

Despite the apparent similarities between processing biases shown by the emotional Stroop task in anxious adults and children that we have described in the previous section, there have been many reported failures to replicate the anxiety-linked Stroop effect in children (Table 3.2). In some studies, non-anxious and anxious children have demonstrated a similar interference effect for threat stimuli. This set of findings raises questions about the causal role of processing bias towards threat in the onset of anxiety in childhood and adolescence (Kindt, Brosschot and Everaerd, 1997). Again, we will begin by looking at evidence from non-clinical samples and then move on to clinical samples.

Kindt, Brosschot and Everaerd (1997) tested children aged 8 to 9 years classified as non-clinically high and low anxious. A computerized single-trial emotional Stroop task was used in two situations: a neutral situation and a medically stressful situation (i.e. a vaccination session). All children passed tests for reading ability and colour blindness. Based on the hyper-vigilance model, the stressful situation should increase state anxiety and would, therefore, produce selective colour-naming interference for threat words relative to non-threat words in high but not low trait anxious children. This interference was expected to be most marked for concern-related words (i.e. the words associated with physical harm in a vaccination situation). However, contrary to these predictions both high and low trait anxious children demonstrated cognitive interference specific to information related to physical harm, irrespective of the presence of the vaccination stressor. Moreover, in the neutral situation (where the vaccination stressor was absent) both high and low trait anxious girls – but not boys – showed a processing bias for generally threatening information. Similar results were obtained in a subsequent experiment using a computerized single-trial emotional Stroop task (Kindt, Bierman and Brosschot, 1997). Kindt, Bierman and Brosschot compared the computerized and card formats of the emotional Stroop task for spider-fearful and non-fearful children aged 8–12 years and found a bias for spider words in both spider-fearful and control children, regardless of the format used. They also found that in low spider-fearful children spider Stroop interference decreased with age, while in high fearful children, spider Stroop interference increased with age. One explanation is that the fear memory networks are not fully developed such as in anxious adults resulting in less bias, but because the absence of a differential effect was not due to a lack of bias in the anxious group but to the presence of a bias in the control group, a more probable explanation is that the emotional stimuli used were significant not only for the anxious group but also for the non-anxious group.

Table 3.2. Details of experiments finding non-significant anxiety-related emotional Stroop effects in children

Authors	Format	Sample characteristics	Presentation stimulus (word/picture/face)	Other measures/ control variables	Block/trials	Age range/ adjustments for use with children
Benoit et al. (2007)	Single trial (computer)	Clinical: GAD Social phobia Separation anxiety Panic OCD PTSD Anxiety not otherwise specified	A photograph of either an adult or a child displaying one of four expressions: anger, disgust, happiness or neutral. For each expression in the adult group, there were two male and two female models	None	B1: 20 practice trials naming the colours of filters covering pictures of chairs. B2: 64 test trials involving adult faces, 48 trials involving child faces. A total of 112 trials. The 112 presentations occurred in eight blocks, each block consisting of one model/expression combination (i.e. adult happy, child disgust, etc.)	7–17 Used pictures of faces
Dalgleish et al. (2003)	Single trial (computer)	Clinical: GAD PTSD	Positive, categorized neutral, depression-related, threat-related and trauma-related	Vocabulary and reading tests administered	B1: 18 practice trials using uncategorized neutral words. B2: 120 test trials	7–18 None
Freeman and Beck (2000)	Single trial (computer)	Clinical: PTSD (sexually abused)	Abuse-related threat words (e.g. force and suck), developmentally relevant words (e.g. shame and abandoned), general threat words (e.g. cancer and knife), positive words (e.g. happy and smile) and neutral words (e.g. table and window)	Reading difficulty was no higher than fifth-grade level Intelligence and achievement measures	B1: 20 practice trials using number words continued until at least 80% of the colours were named correctly. B2: 150 test trials	11–13 None

(continued overleaf)

Table 3.2. (*Continued*)

Authors	Format	Sample characteristics	Presentation stimulus (word/picture/face)	Other measures/control variables	Block/trials	Age range/adjustments for use with children
Heim-Dreger et al. (2006)	Card	Non-clinical: Trait anxiety	Drawings of faces showing either friendly or threatening expressions	Colour blindness	B1: One card (20 faces with ambiguous expressions) B2: 80 trials (two cards each of threat and friendly expressions with 20 facial expressions on each card)	7–10 Used drawings of facial expressions
Kindt and Brosschot (1999)	Single trial (computer)	Non-clinical: Spider anxious	Six categories of stimuli based on the following three types: (i) pictures (spider pictures versus neutral pictures, i.e. chairs), (ii) non-integrated words, non-integrated spider words (e.g. spider, web) and six neutral words (e.g. chair, table) vs. non-integrated neutral words) and (iii) integrated words (integrated spider words versus integrated neutral words)	Children were selected who had sufficient reading abilities as was verified by asking the teacher	B1: 20 practice stimuli B2: 96 test trials (48 words; integrated and non-integrated and 48 pictures; integrated and non-integrated)	8–12 Used non-integrated words and pictures (words and pictures were superimposed onto coloured circles to simplify the task)
Kindt, Bierman and Brosschot (1997)	Card and Single trial (computer)	Non-clinical: Spider anxious	Standard colour word: Stroop used *incongruent colour words* (red, blue, yellow and green) and *non-words* (loav, tmelw, ernif, muga). The word sets in the spider Stroop were:	Tests were administered to assure whether the subjects had sufficient general reading abilities	B1: 20 practice stimuli consisting of neutral words. B2: Both Stroop formats consisted of 80 test trials. The stimuli were presented in four blocks, each block	8–12 None

The Emotional Stroop Task in Anxious Children

The Emotional Stroop Task in Anxious Children   63

Study	Task	Group	Stimuli	Additional measures	Trials	Age	Notes
			spider words (spider, web, hairy, legs and crawl) and control words (sparrow, nest, feather, flying and bird)	and whether anyone suffered from colour blindness	consisting of one of the four word sets	8–12	None
Kindt, Bögels and Morren (2003)	Single trial (computer)	Clinical: Separation Anxiety Social phobia GAD Controls	Six word categories: separation-threat (e.g. lost, desolate) vs. neutral (e.g. bathroom, chair-leg), social-threat (e.g. boring, deride) vs. neutral (pine-tree, grass), and general threat (e.g. illness, damage) vs. neutral (noise, guitars)	Colour blindness test	B1: 'some' practice trials B2: 120 word test trials	7–18	None
Kindt, Brosschot and Everaerd (1997)	Single trial (computer)	Non-clinical: Trait anxiety	Standard Stroop. Emotional Stroop: concern-related threat; concern-related non-threat; concern-unrelated threat and concern-unrelated non-threat	Reading ability tested Colour blindness tested	B1: 18 practice words B2: 96 test stimuli presented in trials of six blocks, each block consisting of one of the six word categories	8–9	None
Kindt et al. (2000)	Single trial (computer)	Non-clinical: Spider anxious	Words (spider words and neutral words) and pictures (spider pictures and neutral pictures)	None	B1 12 practice trials B2: 48 picture test trials and 48 word test trials	8–11	The words and pictures were superimposed on coloured circles (i.e. non-integrated) Included linguistic training and also a manipulation check of the training

(continued overleaf)

Table 3.2. (*Continued*)

Authors	Format	Sample characteristics	Presentation stimulus (word/picture/face)	Other measures/ control variables	Block/trials	Age range/ adjustments for use with children
Morren et al. (2003)	Single trial (computer)	Non-clinical: Spider anxious	Spider words (e.g. spider and web), control words (e.g. stool and table). Presented as integrated and non-integrated stimuli Integrated stimuli comprised coloured letters on a black background. Non-integrated words were printed in black letters and superimposed on a coloured circle	Colour blindness tested	B1: Three practice trials B2:72 test trials B3: Short break + three practice trials B4: 72 test trials	7–11 Used non-integrated stimuli (which is supposedly easier to process) as well as integrated stimuli
Schneider et al. (2008)	Card	Non-clinical: Parent diagnosed with panic disorder or animal phobia	Panic-relevant words, spider-phobia-relevant words, and neutral words (the list can be requested from the authors)	Excluded children younger than 8 years of age. Selected age-appropriate words	B1: Practice run with a card containing neutral words. B2: 96 test trials	8–15 None.
Schwartz, Snidman and Kagan (1996)	Single trial (computer)	Non-clinical: Behaviourally inhibited vs. uninhibited	Threatening words (e.g. shy, lonely) positive words (e.g. smile, neutral words (e.g. dash, museum)	All words were at a sixth-grade reading level or below. Subjects were screened for reading ability by presenting the 12 most difficult words on index cards and asking the subject to read each word	B1: 54 test trials	12–13 None

In a similar study, Kindt and Brosschot (1999) tested spider-fearful and non-fearful girls aged between 8 and 12 years. Unlike their previous studies, Kindt and Brosschot used pictorial stimuli as well as word stimuli in the Stroop task and presented stimuli in both an integrated and a non-integrated form. In the traditional emotional Stroop paradigm, words and colours are integrated (they are presented simultaneously), which differs from, for example, dot-probe tasks in which stimuli and probes appear consecutively (non-integrated). By using a non-integrated form of the stimuli, Stroop, Kindt and Brosschot could determine whether previous failures to find interference effects in high and low anxious children was because of the integrated nature of the Stroop task. Consistent with their previous studies, Kindt and Brosschot found that the integrated spider words caused interference in both the spider-fearful girls and controls. Non-integrated words (but not pictures) produced some interference in spider-fearful girls, but not in control children. However, this effect was not significant and might have been due to the performance of the older children in the sample. Kindt *et al.* (2000) replicated this study in two experiments. In their first experiment, a group of spider-fearful and non-fearful girls aged between 8 and 11 years were falsely informed that they might have to complete a behavioural approach task, in which they would be faced with a real-life spider. This manipulation was intended to activate threat cognitions. Remember that in the hyper-vigilance model trait anxiety is predicted to cause interference only when state anxiety is high because state anxiety will activate the person's threat detection system. By getting girls to anticipate threat their threat schema should become activated, resulting in a processing bias. Children completed non-integrated forms of the word and picture spider Stroop task. The results showed no significant interference effect for spider-threat words or pictures. However, consistent with Kindt, Bierman and Brosschot (1997), the interference effect became greater with age in the spider-fearful girls and decreased with age in the non-spider-fearing girls. This study did reveal that in 8-year-olds, the presence of spider pictures facilitated colour naming in the spider-fearful group. This finding was followed up in a second experiment using a larger sample and only the word version of the spider Stroop task. Half of the children also completed the behavioural approach task subsequent to the Stroop task as an ecologically valid test of fear and avoidance differences between the spider-fearful and non-fearful children. All children demonstrated interference when colour naming the non-integrated spider words and the expectation of approach to a real spider did not significantly affect the processing bias. The authors suggested that at age 8 a bias to threat words is typical of all children; however, another explanation is that normal fears are focused on animals at this age (Field and Davey, 2001). We mentioned earlier that processing biases are present for personally relevant information; it is possible that there are sensitive periods in which specific stimuli evoke a processing bias. The onset of animal phobia peaks at around 7–9 years; therefore, processing biases for animal-related stimuli might be present in all children during this sensitive time, whereas, for instance, socially relevant stimuli might evoke a general processing bias later on in life.

These studies by Kindt *et al* gave rise to the aforementioned inhibition hypothesis, in which a processing bias is seen as a normal part of development that increases with age in anxious children but slowly withers in non-anxious children. However, one large-scale study seems to contradict this model. Morren *et al.* (2003) used a large sample of high ($N = 170$) and low spider-fearful children ($N = 215$) aged 7–11 years in an emotional Stroop task using both integrated and non-integrated stimuli. Contrary to the inhibition hypothesis, results did not show that all children had a processing bias for spider words; a reverse pattern was found in that children were *faster* to respond to spider-related words relative to control words. In addition, the hypothesis that anxiety group would interact with age in producing interference effects was not support. The authors suggest that the reverse bias that they observed is a consequence of avoidance: children may have avoided aversive processing of spider stimuli by responding speedily. This study supports the integral hypothesis in that age did not mediate interference effects; however, the interference observed was in the opposite direction. One interesting consideration is that this experiment contained significantly more trials (144) than previous studies and for the first block of trials a general bias appeared for the integrated spider stimuli, whereas avoidance appeared only on the second block of trials.

Similarly, Heim-Dreger *et al.* (2006) found evidence in two experiments for *avoidance* of drawings of faces depicting either friendly or threatening expressions in a card format emotional Stroop task. The stimuli in this study were similar to those used by Hadwin *et al.* (2009), but unlike this study, Heim-Dreger found inconsistent evidence of a processing bias: the interference effect was significantly different from zero only in Experiment 2. In both experiments trait anxiety did not significantly predict interference effects, $rs = .16$ and $.14$, and the sizes of these effects are very consistent with those of Hadwin *et al.* (see earlier). Most important in the current context, Heim-Dreger *et al.* found that trait anxiety was better predicted by the absolute values of interference scores (i.e. when you ignore whether the effect shows vigilance or avoidance), which is partly consistent with Morren *et al.*'s (2003) findings.

It could be argued that the inconsistent results that we have reviewed reflect the use of non-clinical samples (in which interference effects might be expected to be weak). However, there is evidence from 'at-risk' children and clinically diagnosed children that suggest that the emotional Stroop does not always consistently produce evidence of a processing bias. Schneider *et al.* (2008) used an 'at-risk' group of children aged 8–15 years who had one parent diagnosed with either panic disorder or animal phobia. Their Stroop task included panic-relevant, animal-phobia-relevant and neutral words that were considered to be age appropriate. Children whose parent was diagnosed with panic disorder showed similar interference scores for panic-related words as children whose parent was diagnosed with animal phobia and children of healthy controls. Schneider *et al.* concluded that their sample included children who were 'at risk', but who had never experienced a panic attack; therefore, they would not necessarily interpret the panic words as threatening. However, we do not know if their explanation is plausible because they did not perform a pretest measuring child threat ratings of the words used in the emotional Stroop. It is also possible that although the words were selected for their age appropriateness, the absence of reading and vocabulary tests in this study raises the possibility that children were simply unable to read (which is unlikely) or understand the words used. The explanation may be that reading of difficult words is less automatized and consequently less word meaning interference would be expected.

Another study using 'at-risk' children focused on the temperaments of the children. Schwartz, Snidman and Kagan (1996) used a computerized single-trial emotional Stroop task with adolescents (12- to 13-years old) who had been previously classified as either behaviourally inhibited or uninhibited when they were 2 years old. Based on temperament theories (see Chapter 10), adolescents who were inhibited at 2 years of age should exhibit greater threat-related interference compared with those who were uninhibited. This prediction was not supported and the results showed that colour-naming latencies were greater for threat and positive words relative to neutral words, but there were no significant differences between the two temperament groups. The authors did not measure concurrent anxiety, but these results seem to support Kindt *et al.*'s data showing a general processing bias for affective stimuli in all children. However, contrary to adult models, this bias was not affected by risk for anxiety.

Data from 'at-risk' populations may be limited because perhaps anxiety has to fully express itself before a processing bias is found. However, this possibility is unlikely because some studies using non-clinical samples do show processing biases using the emotional Stroop task (see the previous section). In addition, some studies using clinical samples have failed to replicate the expected processing biases to threat stimuli.

Freeman and Beck (2000) employed the emotional Stroop paradigm to examine cognitive interference for trauma-related stimuli in sexually abused adolescent girls (aged between 11 and 13 years old) with PTSD. Controlling for verbal IQ and reading achievement, their results indicated that sexually abused adolescent girls with PTSD showed more overall colour-naming interference for all word types presented (developmentally relevant general threat and abuse-related threat, positive and neutral) than non-clinical controls. In addition, interference of colour naming of abuse-related words was found in both abused and non-abused adolescents. The authors did, however, note that the abuse-related threat words (e.g. 'penis') might have caused interference for all adolescents, even controls, simply because all girls would have had less exposure to such taboo words. An alternative explanation is that non-abused adolescents showed cognitive interference for abuse-related words because they were at an age at which their sexuality was emotionally significant. This explanation fits well with Williams, Mathews and MacLeod's (1996) observation that 'relatedness to current concern is necessary to explain Stroop interference in non-clinical participants' (p. 19). Similarly, Dalgleish *et al.* (2003) failed to find a significant Stroop effect in children with GAD and PTSD for threat-related or depression words, but when using the dot-probe task found that GAD patients showed vigilance for threat words, and PTSD patients demonstrated an avoidance for depression words.

Kindt, Bögels and Morren (2003) used the emotional Stroop task to examine processing bias in clinically anxious children and adolescents aged between 7 and 18 years who were diagnosed as experiencing separation anxiety disorder (SAD), social phobia (SP) and/or GAD compared with normal controls. The aim of this study was to investigate whether clinically anxious children present a processing bias towards threat stimuli and also whether this bias was domain specific. To test for domain specificity, words tailored to each anxiety disorder were included: example words included 'lost' (SAD), 'bathroom' (neutral), 'silly' (SP), 'illness' (GAD). They found no significant evidence for either an anxiety-related processing bias towards threat or a domain-specificity effect. Their study contained a large age range (7–18 years), and although theoretically you would expect to find a processing bias in all children, the inclusion of younger children weakened the effect because of performance aspects of the task (see earlier): children of 7 years may have been unable to read or understand some of the words used. Unfortunately though, this hypothesis could not be tested by comparing age groups because the sample size was too small (especially within disorders).

Most recently, Benoit *et al.* (2007) did a picture adaptation of the emotional Stroop task in which children (7–12 years) and adolescents (13– 17 years) with a range of clinically diagnosed anxiety disorders named the colours of filters covering images of both adults and children depicting either a neutral expression or an emotional expression of anger, disgust or happiness (see also Hadwin *et al.*, 2009; Heim-Dreger *et al.*, 2006). They reported that the clinically anxious children, relative to controls, were slower to colour name in general. This finding suggests that social cues create greater interference in individuals with anxiety disorders. However, contrary to what was predicted, anxiety-disordered individuals were no slower than non-clinical controls at colour-naming filters covering threatening facial expressions (i.e. anger and disgust) relative to filters covering faces portraying happy or neutral expressions. This failure to find an interference effect towards threatening facial expressions could reflect the heterogeneity of the sample because the majority of participants had co-morbid diagnoses, and a range of anxiety disorders were included. However, in adults the extent of processing bias is comparable across anxiety disorders, and co-morbidity appears not to be a statistical moderator of processing bias effects (Bar-Haim *et al.*, 2007).

What conclusions can we draw about emotional Stroop effects in child populations?

In summary, findings from the Stroop task have shown a mixed set of results. In non-clinical and vulnerable samples at least there appears to be evidence that all children possess a processing bias for threat material. There are four studies that show some evidence for processing biases in clinical samples, but there are four studies that do not. Bar-Haim *et al.* (2007) conducted a meta-analysis on information processing biases in anxiety across many different paradigms. Their analysis, therefore, included data from the emotional Stroop task in both child and adult samples. Bar-Haim *et al.*'s meta-analysis revealed a significant effect of threat-related bias in anxious adults based on 81 studies ($d = .48$) and in anxious children, based on 11 studies ($d = .50$). The two groups were not significantly different from each other. Only two studies with children used picture stimuli, thus precluding a comparison between adults and children on this variable. For word stimuli, the bias was significant both for anxious adults ($k = 79$, $d = .43$) and for anxious children ($k = 9$, $d = .68$), with children showing a significantly larger effect size than adults ($Q = 3.78$, $p <.05$).

At face value then, this meta-analysis would suggest that interference effects found by the Stroop task in child samples are statistically equivalent (or stronger using word stimuli) to adults. However, studies were included as 'child' samples if the participants were 18 years or under and as we discussed earlier 18-year-old individuals are more or less adults and will have cognitions and cognitive abilities that are very different from those of a young child of 6 years (see Chapter 11). Many of the studies that have looked for Stroop effects have used very heterogeneous age groups (often by necessity when using clinical samples) and so it is impossible to know whether the apparent similarity between adult and child effect sizes in the Bar-Haim meta-analysis are being driven by the older children within the child studies. As such, although the comparisons between adult and child effects in the Bar-Haim *et al.* meta-analysis are the best we can do at present, they are not particularly useful in addressing the issue of the developmental trajectory of processing bias using the emotional Stroop. Bar-Haim *et al.* acknowledge this limitation by pointing out that there were not enough studies with children to allow a more sensitive breakdown of the data by age group.

There is also conflicting evidence about the validity of the emotional Stroop task from studies that have used different methodologies to measure anxiety-related processing biases. When performances on different tasks that measure processing biases do correlate weakly then it suggests one or more of the following: that the tasks measure distinct mechanisms, that one or both mechanisms lack validity or that one or both tasks lack validity. For example, Richards *et al.* (2007) used the emotional Stroop task in combination with a facial processing task (see above) and found that the interference index from the Stroop task correlated significantly with the number of 'anger' responses that children gave to less intense happy faces on the face processing task, $r = .38$. This finding suggests that the emotional Stroop task has convergent validity. However, Kindt, Bierman and Brosschot (1997) compared the card format of the Stroop task for spider words with the single-trial format and found a very low correspondence, $r = .13$. The card format seemed to produce stronger interference effects than the single-trial format. Furthermore, studies have found almost no correlation, $r = .003$ (Dalgleish *et al.*, 2003) and $r = -.04$ (Heim-Dreger *et al.*, 2006) between interference effects as indexed by the emotional Stroop task and the dot-probe task, suggesting that either the two measures are tap different cognitive processes or at least one of the measures is unreliable or invalid. Given that they did not find a significant interference effect using the emotional Stroop task, the strong implication is that it is the task that lacks validity. These are not the only studies to show generally poor correlations between different measures of cognitive biases in anxious youth. For example, processing biases using the dot-probe task correlate poorly when words and pictures are used, $r = -.13$; both formats of this task correlate poorly with memory bias, $rs = .14$ (word dot probe) and .06 (picture dot probe), and measures of cognitive errors, $rs = -.04$ (word dot probe) and .21 (picture dot probe); measures of cognitive errors and memory bias correlate poorly too, $r = .06$ (Watts and Weems, 2006). As such, there is generally a lack of convergent validity in tasks that might be expected to tap similar underlying processing mechanisms in anxious children.

Future research using the emotional Stroop task in anxious children

To explore whether there is a developmental course of processing bias as indexed by the emotional Stroop task as predicted by the inhibition and implied bias hypotheses, researchers will need to use large samples to allow a systematic analysis of trends across ages. Longitudinal designs would also allow researchers to assess causal relations between processing biases and the development of anxiety in childhood. Such research brings with it a unique set of problems because of the difficulty of constructing stimulus materials that are appropriate for both young children and adolescents. It is possible, for example, that the inconsistency in the research findings reflects the inadequacy of the emotional Stroop paradigm in child samples. For example, although there have been some studies that have made adjustments to the traditional version of the emotional Stroop task for use with children, for example, by using pictures rather than words, these adaptations do not systematically explain the success or failure of the task to demonstrate anxiety-related processing bias to threat (see Tables 3.1 and 3.2).

The use of an inhibitory task in children can also reflect cognitive development. For example, children of 3.5–4.5 years of age can find the day–night Stroop-like task challenging (Gerstadt, Hong and Diamond, 1994). When age and task performance is tracked over time, as age increases the task difficulty declines and by the age of 6–7 years, children find the task very easy (Diamond, Kirkham and Amso, 2002). These findings suggest that there is a sensitive phase of attentional control development at roughly 4 years of age tapped by this task. Future studies of processing bias in anxious children would benefit from establishing recognized norms on the emotional Stroop task (Bar-Haim *et al.*, 2007). There are also new inhibitory tasks that have been developed other than the Stroop that might prove useful in exploring processing biases to threat in children. For example, an emotional Go/No Go task has been developed (e.g. Hare *et al.*, 2005), which has been used in anxious children (Ladouceur *et al.*, 2006; Waters and Valvoi, 2009). In this task, participants respond to a particular emotional face on some trials (Go trials) and avoid responding to any other face on other trials (No Go trials). The participants' ability to suppress a behavioural response is indexed by the proportion of presses that they accidentally make on 'No Go' trials. In addition, when No Go trials are sparsely distributed within Go trials (e.g. 30% of trials are 'No Go'), response times tend to be slower on Go trials, reflecting the effect of self-regulatory processes, such as attentional control. However, like the Stroop task, effects from this task are less than clear-cut. For example, Waters and Valvoi (2009) showed that anxious girls were slower to respond to neutral face Go trials than when angry versus happy face No Go trials were present, whereas non-anxious girls were faster to respond. However, in boys there was no corresponding effect of anxiety. Also, anxiety status did not influence the general finding from adults that it is difficult to inhibit responding to happy versus angry faces. Finally, hyper-vigilance as predicted in adult models of anxiety would be shown by effects when emotional faces are the Go trials. However, this effect was not significant. As such, although other inhibition-based tasks might seem like a useful way to complement the research from the emotional Stroop task, it will probably be a long time before a clear picture emerges about the development of processing biases in anxious children.

Acknowledgements

Economic and Social Research Council grant number RES-062-23-0406 awarded to Andy Field and Sam Cartwright-Hatton enabled us to write this chapter.

References

Bar-Haim, Y., Lamy, D., Pergamin, L. *et al.* (2007) Threat-related attentional bias in anxious and nonanxious individuals: a meta-analytic study. *Psychological Bulletin*, **133** (1), 1–24.

Beck, A.T., Emery, G. and Greenberg, R.L. (1985) *Anxiety Disorders and Phobias: A Cognitive Perspective*. Basic Books, New York.

Benoit, K.E., McNally, R.J., Rapee, R.M. *et al.* (2007) Processing of emotional faces in children and adolescents with anxiety disorders. *Behaviour Change*, **24** (4), 183–194.

Bower, G.H. (1981) Mood and memory. *American Psychologist*, **36**, 129–148.

Bradley, B.P., Mogg, K., Millar, N. and White, J. (1995) Selective processing of negative information–effects of clinical anxiety, concurrent depression, and awareness. *Journal of Abnormal Psychology*, **104** (3), 532–536.

Cohen, J.D., Dunbar, K. and McClelland, J.L. (1990) On the control of automatic processes: a parallel distributed processing account of the Stroop effect. *Psychological Review*, **97**, 332–361.

Compton, R.J., Banich, M.T., Mohanty, A. *et al.* (2003) Paying attention to emotion: an fMRI investigation of cognitive and emotional Stroop tasks. *Cognitive, Affective, and Behavioral Neuroscience*, **3**, 81–96.

Dalgleish, T., (1995) Performance on the emotional Stroop task in groups of anxious, expert and control participants: a comparison of computer and card presentation formats. *Cognition and Emotion*, **9**, 341–362.

Dalgleish, T., Taghavi, R., Neshat-Doost, H. *et al.* (2003) Patterns of processing bias for emotional information across clinical disorders: a comparison of attention, memory, and prospective cognition in children and adolescents with depression, generalized anxiety, and posttraumatic stress disorder. *Journal of Clinical Child and Adolescent Psychology*, **32** (1), 10–21.

Dawkins, K. and Furnham, A. (1989) The color naming of emotional words. *British Journal of Psychology*, **80**, 383–389.

Diamond, A., Kirkham, N. and Amso, D. (2002) Conditions under which young children can hold two rules in mind and inhibit a prepotent response. *Developmental Psychology*, **38**, 352–362.

Dubner, A.E. and Motta, R.W. (1999) Sexually and physically abused foster care children and posttraumatic stress disorder. *Journal of Consulting and Clinical Psychology*, **67** (3), 367–373.

Field, A.P. (2006) Watch out for the beast: fear information and attentional bias in children. *Journal of Clinical Child and Adolescent Psychology*, **35** (3), 431–439.

Field, A.P. and Davey, G.C.L. (2001) Conditioning models of childhood anxiety, in *Anxiety Disorders in Children and Adolescents: Research, Assessment and Intervention* (eds W.K. Silverman and P.A. Treffers), Cambridge University Press, Cambridge, pp. 187–211.

Freeman, J.B. and Beck, J.G. (2000) Cognitive interference for trauma cues in sexually abused adolescent girls with posttraumatic stress disorder. *Journal of Clinical Child Psychology*, **29**, 245–256.

Gerstadt, C., Hong, Y. and Diamond, A. (1994) The relationship between cognition and action: performance of 31/2–7 year old children on a Stroop-like day-night test. *Cognition*, **53**, 129–153.

Hadwin, J.A., Donnelly, N., Richards, A. *et al.* (2009) Childhood anxiety and attention to emotion faces in a modified Stroop task. *British Journal of Developmental Psychology*, **27**, 487–494.

Hare, T.A., Tottenham, N., Davidson, M.C. *et al.* (2005) Contributions of amygdala and striatal activity in emotion regulation. *Biological Psychiatry*, **57** (6), 624–632.

Heim-Dreger, U., Kohlmann, C.W., Eschenbeck, H. and Burkhardt, U. (2006) Attentional biases for threatening faces in children: vigilant and avoidant processes. *Emotion*, **6** (2), 320–325.

Hock, M. and Krohne, H.W. (2004) Coping with threat and memory for ambiguous information: testing the repressive discontinuity hypothesis. *Emotion*, **4** (1), 65–86.

Holmes, D.S. (1974) Investigations of repression: differential recall of material experimentally or naturally associated with ego threat. *Psychological Bulletin*, **81**, 632–653.

Jones, G.V. (1984) Fragment and schema models of recall. *Memory and Cognition*, **12**, 250–263.

Jones, G.V. (1987) Independence and exclusivity among psychological processes: implications for the structure of recall. *Psychological Review*, **94**, 229–235.

Kindt, M., Bierman, D. and Brosschot, J.F. (1997) Cognitive bias in spider fear and control children: assessment of emotional interference by a card format and a single-trial format of the Stroop task. *Journal of Experimental Child Psychology*, **66** (2), 163–179.

Kindt, M., Bogels, S. and Morren, M. (2003) Processing bias in children with separation anxiety disorder, social phobia and generalised anxiety disorder. *Behaviour Change*, **20**, 143–150.

Kindt, M. and Brosschot, J.F. (1999) Cognitive bias in spider-phobic children: comparison of a pictorial and a linguistic spider Stroop. *Journal of Psychopathology and Behavioral Assessment*, **21**, 207–220.

Kindt, M., Brosschot, J.F. and Everaerd, W. (1997) Cognitive processing bias of children in a real life stress situation and a neutral situation. *Journal of Experimental Child Psychology*, **64** (1), 79–97.

Kindt, M. and van den Hout, M. (2001) Selective attention and anxiety: a perspective on developmental issues and the causal status. *Journal of Psychopathology and Behavioral Assessment*, **23** (3), 193–202.

Kindt, M., van den Hout, M., de Jong, P. and Hoekzema, B. (2000) Cognitive bias for pictorial and linguistic threat cues in children. *Journal of Psychopathology and Behavioral Assessment*, **22** (2), 201–219.

Ladouceur, C.D., Dahl, R.E., Williamson, D.E. *et al.* (2006) Processing emotional facial expressions influences performance on a Go/NoGo task in pediatric anxiety and depression. *Journal of Child Psychology and Psychiatry*, **47** (11), 1107–1115.

Lavy, E. and van den Hout, M. (1993) Selective attention evidenced by pictorial and linguistic Stroop tasks. *Behavior Therapy*, **24**, 645–657.

Lavy, E., van den Hout, M. and Arntz, A. (1993) Attentional bias and spider phobia: conceptual and clinical issues. *Behaviour Research and Therapy*, **31**, 17–24.

Lipp, O.V. and Derakshan, N. (2005) Attentional bias to pictures of fear-relevant animals in a dot probe task. *Emotion*, **5** (3), 365–369.

Logan, A.C. and Goetsch, V.L. (1993) Attention to external threat cues in anxiety states. *Clinical Psychology Review*, **13**, 541–559.

Lonigan, C.J., Vasey, M.W., Phillips, B.M. and Hazen, R.A. (2004) Temperament, anxiety, and the processing of threat-relevant stimuli. *Journal of Clinical Child and Adolescent Psychology*, **33** (1), 8–20.

MacLeod, C.M. (1991) Half a century of research on the Stroop effect: an integrative review. *Psychological Bulletin*, **109**, 163–203.

MacLeod, C.M. and Dunbar, K. (1988) Training and Stroop-like interference: evidence for a continuum of automaticity. *Journal of Experimental Psychology: Learning, Memory, and Cognition*, **10**, 304–315.

Martin, J.M. and Cole, D.A. (2000) Using the personal Stroop to detect children's awareness of social rejection by peers. *Cognition and Emotion*, **14** (2), 241–260.

Martin, M., Horder, P. and Jones, G.V. (1992) Integral bias in naming of phobia-related words. *Cognition and Emotion*, **6**, 479–486.

Martin, M. and Jones, G.V. (1995) Integral bias in the cognitive processing of emotionally linked pictures. *British Journal of Psychology*, **86**, 419–435.

Mathews, A. and MacLeod, C. (1985) Selective processing of threat cues in anxiety-states. *Behaviour Research and Therapy*, **23** (5), 563–569.

Mathews, A. and Macleod, C. (1994) Cognitive approaches to emotion and emotional disorders. *Annual Review of Psychology*, **45**, 25–50.

Mathews, A. and MacLeod, C. (2005) Cognitive vulnerability to emotional disorders. *Annual Review of Clinical Psychology*, **1**, 167–195.

McKenna, F.P. and Sharma, D. (2004) Reversing the emotional Stroop effect reveals that it is not what it seems: the role of fast and slow components. *Journal of Experimental Psychology: Learning, Memory and Cognition*, **30**, 382–392.

McNally, R.J. (1995) Automaticity and the anxiety disorders. *Behaviour Research and Therapy*, **33** (7), 747–754.

Mogg, K., Bradley, B.P., Williams, R. and Mathews, A. (1993) Subliminal processing of emotional information in anxiety and depression. *Journal of Abnormal Psychology*, **102** (2), 304–311.

Mogg, K., Kentish, J. and Bradley, B.P. (1993) Effects of anxiety and awareness on color-identification latencies for emotional words. *Behaviour Research and Therapy*, **31** (6), 559–567.

Mogg, K., Mathews, A. and Weinman, J. (1989) Selective processing of threat cues in anxiety states: a replication. *Behaviour Research and Therapy*, **27** (4), 317–323.

Moradi, A.R., Neshat-Doost, H., Taghavi, R. *et al.* (1999a) Performance of children of adults with PTSD on the Stroop color-naming task. *Journal of Traumatic Stress*, **12**, 663–672.

Moradi, A.R., Taghavi, M.R., Neshat-Doost, H.T. *et al.* (1999b) Performance of children and adolescents with PTSD on the Stroop colour-naming task. *Psychological Medicine*, **29**, 415–419.

Morren, M., Kindt, M., van den Hout, M. and van Kasteren, H. (2003) Anxiety and the processing of threat in children: further examination of the cognitive inhibition hypothesis. *Behaviour Change*, **20** (3), 131–142.

Rapee, R.M. (2000) Group treatment of children with anxiety disorders: outcome and predictors of treatment response. *Australian Journal of Psychology*, **52**, 125–129.

Richards, A., French, C.C., Johnson, W. *et al.* (1992) Effects of mood manipulation and anxiety on performance of an emotional Stroop task. *British Journal of Psychology*, **83**, 479–491.

Richards, A., French, C.C., Nash, G. *et al.* (2007) A comparison of selective attention and facial processing biases in typically developing children who are high and low in self-reported trait anxiety. *Development and Psychopathology*, **19**, 481–495.

Richards, A., Richards, L.C. and McGeeney, A. (2000) Anxiety-related Stroop interference in adolescents. *Journal of General Psychology*, **127**, 327–333.

Riemann, B.C. and McNally, R.J. (1995) Cognitive processing of personally relevant information. *Cognition and Emotion*, **9** (4), 325–340.

Ruiter, C. and Brosschot, J.F. (1994) The emotional Stroop effect in anxiety: attentional bias or cognitive avoidance? *Behaviour Research and Therapy*, **32** (3), 315–319.

Schneider, S., Unnewehr, S., In-Albon, T. and Margraf, J. (2008) Attention bias in children of patients with panic disorder. *Psychopathology*, **41** (3), 179–186.

Schwartz, C.E., Snidman, N. and Kagan, J. (1996) Early temperamental predictors to Stroop interference to threatening information at adolescence. *Journal of Anxiety Disorders*, **10**, 89–96.

Segal, Z.V., Truchon, C., Horowitz, L.M. *et al.* (1995) A priming methodology for studying self-representation in major depressive disorder. *Journal of Abnormal Psychology*, **104**, 205–213.

Spielberger, C.D., Gorsuch, R.L., Lushene, P.R. *et al.* (1983) *Manual for the State-Trait Anxiety Inventory (Form Y)*, Consulting Psychologists Press, Inc, Palo Alto.

Stroop, J.R. (1935) Studies of interference in serial verbal reactions. *Journal of Experimental Psychology*, **18**, 643–662.

Taghavi, M.R., Dalgleish, T., Moradi, A.R. *et al.* (2003) Selective processing of negative emotional information in children and adolescents with generalized anxiety disorder. *British Journal of Clinical Psychology*, **42**, 221–230.

Thrasher, S.M., Dalgleish, T. and Yule, W. (1994) Information processing in PTSD. *Behavioural Research and Therapy*, **32**, 247–254.

van Strien, J.W. and Valstar, L.H. (2004) The lateralized emotional Stroop task: left visual-field interference in women. *Emotion*, **4**, 403–409.

Waters, A.M. and Valvoi, J.S. (2009) Attentional bias for emotional faces in paediatric anxiety disorders: an investigation using the emotional go/no go task. *Journal of Behavior Therapy and Experimental Psychiatry*, **40**, 306–316.

Watts, F.N., Mckenna, F.P., Sharrock, R. and Trezise, L. (1986) Color naming of phobia-related words. *British Journal of Psychology*, **77**, 97–108.

Watts, S.E. and Weems, C.F. (2006) Associations among selective attention, memory bias, cognitive errors and symptoms of anxiety in youth. *Journal of Abnormal Child Psychology*, **34** (6), 841–852.

Williams, J.M.G., Mathews, A. and MacLeod, C. (1996) The emotional Stroop task and psychopathology. *Psychological Bulletin*, **120** (1), 3–24.

4

Selective Attention to Threat in Childhood Anxiety: Evidence from Visual Probe Paradigms

Matthew Garner

m.j.garner@soton.ac.uk

The efficiency of the attention system mediates individual differences in intelligence and emotional processing (Posner and Fan, 2004). An attentional system that preferentially filters and selects negative, threatening, anxiogenic information is more likely to potentiate perceptions of threat and danger; activate a range of dysfunctional thoughts, feelings and beliefs about the present and future; and, ultimately, increase an individual's vulnerability to anxiety. Furthermore, the frequent capturing of attention by threat-related stimuli is likely to frustrate ongoing goal-directed behaviour (Eysenck, 1992).

In recent years, there has been considerable research into attentional processes thought to characterize anxiety. Much of this has focused on developing a range of experimental paradigms that clarify biases in specific components/aspects of attention, that is, preferential selection of certain stimuli (over others) due to combinations of low-level perceptual, semantic, motivational or higher level (task relevant) attributes that render some stimuli more salient than others. This chapter discusses recent conceptual advances in our understanding of attention and its component processes, with specific reference to the application of visual probe tasks (and variants) to examine biases in selective attention in anxious children and adolescents.

Attentional Bias in Anxiety: Predictions from Cognitive Models

Cognitive (information processing) models of anxiety emphasize the role of attention in the aetiology and maintenance of anxiety, but differ with respect

Information Processing Biases and Anxiety: A Developmental Perspective Edited by Julie A. Hadwin and Andy P. Field
© 2010 John Wiley & Sons, Ltd.

to the cognitive components and attentional mechanisms they consider most important (see Beck, 1976; Bower, 1981; Williams *et al.*, 1988, 1997; Eysenck, 1992; Mathews, 1990; Mogg and Bradley, 1998; Mathews and Mackintosh, 1998; Eysenck *et al.*, 2007). While models differ in the extent to which they consider individual differences in anxiety reflect the direction of attentional bias for threat (i.e. increasingly towards in high trait anxious versus away in low trait-anxious individuals as state anxiety increases – Williams *et al.*, 1997) or the initial evaluation and subsequent allocation of early attentional resources to threat (Mogg and Bradley, 1998) common across models is the prediction that pre-attentive (including appraisal) and attentional biases that promote evaluation and selection of threat increase vulnerability for anxiety. Thus, while an adaptive attentional system should ensure that all individuals (irrespective of anxiety level) direct attention towards stimuli evaluated as being high in threat value, high anxious individuals are more likely to evaluate and, therefore, direct attentional resources towards mild and moderately threatening stimuli, compared with less anxious individuals.

Recent models further propose a vigilance-avoidance pattern of attentional bias in which anxious individuals' increased detection of mild threats in the environment is associated with subsequent avoidance strategies that serve to reduce subjective discomfort (e.g. averting attention from threat; escape – Mogg and Bradley, 1998). Thus, these individuals might be characterized by unstable attention deployment, with a tendency to shift attention repeatedly towards and away from threat, which may, in turn, potentiate sensitization and interfere with habituation, thereby maintaining anxiety (Mogg and Bradley, 1998). This prediction is consistent with those from Attentional Control Theory (ACT; Eysenck *et al.*, 2007) in which bottom-up (stimulus driven) mechanisms drive resource allocation in the absence of appropriate top-down (goal directed) regulation, with attentional bias to threat, particularly pronounced in anxious individuals with poor attention control (Derryberry and Reed, 2002). Similarly, integrative neuro-cognitive models propose that a common amygdala–prefrontal circuitry underlies increased activation of threat-related representations and a failure to use controlled processing to regulate attention and promote alternate non-threat-related representations as vulnerability factors for anxiety (see Bishop, 2007).

Developmental models of anxiety suggest that the regulation of a default attentional bias for threat-related stimuli develops with age in children at low risk for anxiety, but less so in those at risk for anxiety (Kindt and Van den Hout, 2001; Kindt, Bierman and Brosschot, 1997). More recently, cognitive bias in children has been suggested to emerge via a verbal learning pathway in which valenced information about novel stimuli modifies explicit and implicit attitudes and cognitive processes such as selective attention (Field and Lawson, 2003; Field, 2006).

While an emerging literature continues to examine the role of biases in attention in the development of anxiety in childhood and adolescence, to date, the majority of empirical studies have been in adult samples using a range of experimental paradigms, including modified emotional Stroop, visual search and visual probe paradigms (for reviews of the former see Chapters 3 and 5).

Indices of Initial Orienting to Threat: The Visual Probe Task (Dot Probe)

The rationale underlying visual probe tasks is that individuals are faster to respond to probe stimuli presented in an attended (rather than unattended) region of the visual display. In a typical version of the task, stimulus pairs (e.g. threat-neutral words or negative–neutral pictures/faces) are briefly presented on the screen (e.g. for 500 milliseconds). In the pictorial version two pictures are presented together, one on each side of the screen (e.g. angry face and neutral face), and one of the pictures is replaced by a probe stimulus (e.g. dot or arrow). Participants are instructed to respond as quickly and accurately as possible to the probe, classifying its location (left vs. right; above vs. below fixation), type (e.g. : vs. .. ; ↑ vs. ↓) or onset depending on the task version (Figure 4.1).

Reaction times (RTs) to probes are then used to calculate the extent to which participants are quicker to respond to probes that appear in the location of the critical stimulus (e.g. threat word/picture), compared to probes that appear in the location previously occupied by the control stimulus (e.g. neutral word/picture).

An index of attentional bias for each stimulus pair-type (e.g. angry relative to neutral face) can be calculated to express the degree to which RTs are reduced for

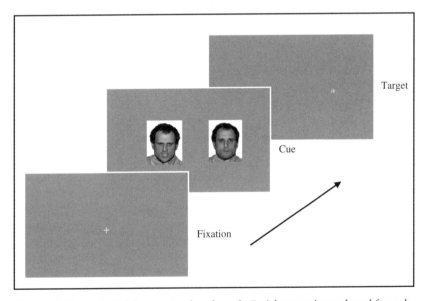

Figure 4.1 Example trial from a visual probe task. Facial expressions selected from the NimStim Set of Facial Expressions (http://www.macbrain.org/resources.htm).[1] (Facial expressions reprinted with permission from Dr. Nim Tottenham.)

[1] Development of the MacBrain Face Stimulus Set was supported by the MacArthur Foundation Research Network; please contact Nim Tottenham (tott0006@tc.umn.edu) for further information.

probes appearing in the location of critical stimuli, compared to control stimuli (cf. Bradley *et al.*, 1998; MacLeod and Mathews, 1988):

$$\frac{(PL|TR - PL|TL) + (PR|TL - PR|TR)}{2}$$

where PL|TR corresponds to RTs to probes appearing on the left following the presentation of the threat stimulus to the right. Thus, attentional bias scores will be 0 in the absence of a bias in selective attention, positive in the presence of an attentional bias towards critical (e.g. threat) stimuli and negative in the presence of an attentional bias away from critical stimuli.[2]

Evidence in Adult Samples

Research in adult samples (both those with anxiety symptoms that meet criteria for clinical diagnosis and those with elevated but subclinical levels of trait anxiety) has reliably shown that anxious individuals are faster to respond to probes that replace threat rather than neutral stimuli considered to reflect vigilance for threat (e.g. Broadbent and Broadbent, 1988; MacLeod, Mathews and Tata, 1986; Mogg, Bradley and Williams, 1995). Evidence of selective attention towards concern-relevant lexical and pictorial threat cues has been observed in a variety of adult anxious populations (see recent reviews by Bar-Haim *et al.* 2007; Frewen *et al.*, 2008), including specific phobia (Lavy, Van den Hout and Arntz, 1993), panic disorder (McNally, Reimann and Kim, 1990), generalized anxiety disorder (GAD) (MacLeod, Mathews and Tata, 1986; Bradley *et al.*, 1999) and social phobia (Mogg, Phillipott and Bradley, 2004). In addition, evidence of an early (often

---

[2]Before entering RT condition means into the above formula raw RTs from incorrect trials are removed and the remaining RTs screened for outliers in an effort to identify those responses that are likely to reflect a mechanism other than that under inspection, for example, uncharacteristically slow responses that might reflect momentary distraction from the task, adjustment of fingers on response device. Outliers are typically identified using statistical methods (e.g. box plots to identify appropriate absolute cut-offs or, winsorizing/removing data according to individual or sample, means and standard deviations).

Visual probe studies typically require participants to classify probes as quickly and accurately as possible with indices of spatial attention calculated from participants' manual RTs to correctly classify probes. However, some studies have used error rates to infer attention allocation to target stimuli by contrasting accuracy on trials where the probe replaces the critical picture against trials where the probe replaces the control picture (e.g. Murphy *et al.*, 2006). While error rates might have some face validity, they do not provide an unambiguous measure of attention in the absence of manual RT data and are often liable to floor effects. As such, researchers wishing to use visual probe paradigms are encouraged to inspect both RT and error data in an effort to identify those participants who might have employed strategies that contaminate RT attentional bias scores, for example, speed–accuracy trade-offs. In doing so, researchers should hope to observe homogenous distributions of error rates across between and within-subject factors. This is particularly necessary when using RT paradigms with children who might be more variable in their performance, effort and adherence to task instructions.

suggested preconscious/automatic) processing bias for threatening information in both clinical and non-clinical anxiety has been inferred from demonstrations of vigilance for masked threat stimuli (presented outside awareness) in visual probe paradigms (Mathews and MacLeod, 1986; Bradley, Mogg and Lee, 1997; Mogg and Bradley, 2002), consistent with findings from visual search paradigms (Byrne and Eysenck, 1995; Gilboa-Schechtman, Foa and Amir, 1999; see Chapter 5).

Evidence in Child and Adolescent Samples

Promising evidence in anxious adult populations continues to encourage researchers to use visual probe paradigms with child and adolescent groups. Table 4.1 details methods and findings from visual probe studies in children, particularly those examining interactions between anxiety and stimulus emotion.

Consistent with developments in the adult literature, the first demonstrations of attentional bias to threat in child and adolescent anxiety used word stimuli. Enhanced vigilance to physical and social threat words (relative to neutral words) has been observed in clinically anxious children (Vasey *et al.*, 1995; Taghavi *et al.*, 1999; Dalgleish *et al.*, 2001; Dalgleish *et al.*, 2003) and those with high levels of test anxiety (Vasey, Elhag and Daleiden, 1996) and to emotional words in children with high levels of anxiety sensitivity (Hunt, Keogh and French, 2007). While studies differ with respect to whether attentional bias to threat in anxiety is inferred from between-group or within-group differences, findings in general concur irrespective of whether children are explicitly asked to read the top word out loud (e.g. Dalgleish *et al.*, 2001), quietly to themselves (HuntHunt, Keogh and French, 2007) or neither (Taghavi *et al.*, 1999). Similarly, vigilance for threat words has been demonstrated in studies that have presented stimuli for relatively long periods (e.g. +1000 milliseconds; e.g. Taghavi *et al.*, 1999) or short (masked) periods (e.g. Helzer, Connor-Smith and Reed, 2009) and in those studies that have attempted to tailor stimulus onset asynchrony (SOA) to childrens' pre-test reading performance (Schippell *et al.*, 2003).

Visual probe studies in children have more recently examined selective attention to pictoral stimuli including emotional images from standardized affective picture sets [e.g. International Affective Picture Set (IAPS), Lang, Bradley and Cuthbert, 1999] and emotional facial expressions (e.g. Ekman and Friesen, 1976; Tottenham *et al.*, 2009). Clinically anxious children have shown increased vigilance to negative pictures (Waters, Lipp and Spence, 2004; Waters *et al.*, 2008a) with some evidence that this negative bias can extend to emotional images more generally (Waters, Lipp and Spence, 2004, Experiment 2).

Evidence of attentional bias to emotional faces is currently mixed. Vigilance for angry facial expressions has been observed in clinically anxious children (Roy *et al.*, 2008), children with current bipolar disorder and a lifetime history of anxiety (but not those without a history of anxiety, Brotman *et al.*, 2007) and non-selected children with increased trait anxiety (Telzer *et al.*, 2008), with some evidence in children with GAD that vigilance extends to both negative and positive facial expressions (Waters *et al.*, 2008a). In contrast, greater avoidance of angry faces has been

Table 4.1. Findings from visual probe studies in anxious children

Study	Paradigm	Participants	Stimuli	SOA	Vigilance (positive bias score)	Avoidance (negative bias score)	Additional findings
Emotional words							
Vasey et al., 1995	Probe detection	Anxiety diagnosis (n = 12) NAC (n = 12)	Threat–neutral word pairs	1250 (read top word)	Threat bias: anxiety > NAC (no bias)		
Vasey, Elhag and Daleiden, 1996	Probe detection	High test anxious (n = 20), aged 11–14 yr Low test anxious (n = 20), aged 11–14 yr	Threat (social and physical) paired with neutral.	1250 (read top word)	High anxious	Low anxious boys	
Schippell et al., 2003	Probe detection	Non-selected (n = 90), aged 11.1–16.5 yr.	Threat (social and physical) paired with neutral	Either 500, 650, 800 or 1250 (based on child's pre-test reading speed)	↑ State anxiety α ↑ social threat bias	↑ Reactive aggression (teacher report) α ↑ social threat avoidance	Social and physical bias scores not related to each other nor interpretation bias score
Ehrenreich et al., 1998 (cited from Ehrenreich and Gross, 2002)	Probe detection	Non-selected, aged 9–12 yr	Threat–neutral word pairs	1250 (read top word)	Females (irrespective of self-report anxiety and depression)	Males (irrespective of self-report anxiety and depression)	

Study	Task	Sample	Stimuli	Presentation			
Dalgleish et al., 2001	Probe detection	PTSD aged 9–17 yr (n = 24) Non-anxious controls aged 9–17 yr (n = 24)	Physical threat Social threat Depression (paired with neutral)	1500 (read top word)	Social threat words:PTSD > NAC	Dep. Words: PTSD > NAC	No group difference on physical threat words
Taghavi et al., 1999	Probe detection	General anxiety (n = 24) Mixed anxiety-depression (n = 18) NAC (n = 24) All aged 9–19 yr	Physical threat Social threat Depression (paired with neutral)	1500	Anxiety group: threat bias > depression words No effects for mixed group or NAC		
Dalgleish et al., 2003	Probe detection	GAD no MDD (n = 24) PTSD no MDD (n = 24) MDD (n = 19) NAC (n = 26) (all aged 7–18)	Threat Depression (paired with neutral)	1500 (read aloud top word)	Threat: GAD + PTSD Null: MDD + NAC	Depression: PTSD Null: MDD + NAC	Performance on word Stroop (no group differences) not correlated with performance on probe detection
Hunt, Keogh and French, 2007	Location classification	High anxiety sensitivity (n = 23) Low anxiety sensitivity (n = 16) High anxiety sensitivity (n = 20) Low anxiety sensitivity (n = 19)	Anxiety Social threat Positive Neutral (paired with neutral) As above	1000 (quietly read word) 14 (+word mask)	Emotional words (high AS groups)	Emotional words (low AS groups)	

(continued overleaf)

Table 4.1. (*Continued*)

Study	Paradigm	Participants	Stimuli	SOA	Vigilance (positive bias score)	Avoidance (negative bias score)	Additional findings
Neshat-Doost et al., 2000.	Probe detection	Clinical depression (n = 19) Controls (n = 26) Aged 9–17 yr	Social threat Physical threat Depression	1500	Null results	Null results	
Helzer, Connor-Smith and Reed, 2009	Location classifica-tion	Non-selected (n = 121), aged 10–13 yr Allocated to low, medium and high social stress (self-report)	Social threat Physical threat (paired with neutral)	1250 or 20 (+mask)	Subliminal social threat (high social stress only)		Fearful temperament predicted biases to supraliminal social threat only for individuals with poor attentional control
Emotional images							
Waters, Lipp and Spence, 2004 (exp 1)	Location classifica-tion	Non-selected children, aged 9–12 yr (n = 105)	Fear-related, pleasant, neutral pictures (IAPS)	1250	Fear bias > pleasant bias particularly in females		Findings mirror those observed in non-selected adult sample (but no effect of adult gender)
		Clinically anxious children (GAD, SA, SP, SpP), aged 9–12 yr (n = 23)	As above	1250	Fear bias > pleasant bias		

Waters, Lipp and Spence, 2004 (exp 2)					Emotion bias in anxious children > bias in random subset of non-selected children. Bias observed in left-visual field
Field (2006)	Type classification	Non-selected (n = 50), aged 7–9 yr. No delay group (n = 23). 24-hr delay (n = 27)	Animal images associated with negative, positive information paired with no information control images.	500	Bias for negative animals both immediately and 24 hrs after receipt of information
Waters et al., 2008b	Location classification	Clinically anxious children (GAD, SA, SP, SpP) aged 8–12 yr (n = 19). Non-anxious matched controls (n = 19)	Fear-related, pleasant, neutral pictures (IAPS)	1250	Threat bias in clinical group both pre- and post-CBT treatment. Threat bias in NAC at time 1 but not time 2. No happy bias observed

(continued overleaf)

Table 4.1. (*Continued*)

Study	Paradigm	Participants	Stimuli	SOA	Vigilance (*positive bias score*)	Avoidance (*negative bias score*)	Additional findings
Legerstee et al., 2009	Probe classification	Clinically anxious children (GAD, SA, SP, SpP) aged 8–16 yr. Pre-CBT treatment (*n* = 131)	IAPS: Severe threat Mild threat Neutral (all paired with neutral)	500	No significant bias (across all)	Mild threat (across all)	Avoidance of severe threat predicted treatment success Treatment responders tended to avoid engaging with severe threat. Nonresponders tended to have difficulty disengaging from severe threat
Kallen et al., 2007	Probe classification	High vs. low test anxious (*n* = 44) aged 10–13 yr.	IAPS: Severe threat Mild threat Neutral (all paired with neutral)	500			General effect of RT slowing on severe threat vs. mild and neutral trials (no interaction with probe location or anxiety)
Emotional faces							
Waters et al., 2008b	Location classification	GAD aged 7–12 yr (*n* = 23) Non-anxious controls (*n* = 25)	Angry–neutral Happy–neutral	500	Angry and happy bias in severely anxious > (null) bias in less severely anxious and controls		Vigilance for anger increased with severity and co-morbid SP (but not SA or SpP)

Study	Method	Sample	Stimuli	SOA (ms)	Low–moderate anxiety	High anxious
Ehrenreich et al., 1998 (cited from Ehrenreich and Gross, 2002)	Location classification	Non-selected children	Threat words Threat faces	500		
Telzer et al., 2008	Location classification	Healthy children and adolescents aged 11–18 yr ($n = 16$)	Angry–neutral Happy–neutral Neutral–neutral	500	↑ Trait anxiety ∝ ↑ angry bias	↑ Trait anxiety ∝ ↑ right DLPFC activation (for angry face contrast)
Roy et al., 2008	Location classification	Clinically anxious children (GAD, SA, SP), aged 7–18 yr ($n = 101$) Non-anxious controls ($n = 51$)	Angry–neutral Happy–neutral Neutral–neutral	500	Anger bias: Clin > NACs Happy: no bias	No correlations between bias scores and severity, specific anxiety diagnoses or co-morbidity
Brotman et al., 2007	Location classification	BD + ANX ($n = 20$) $m = 14.6$ yr BD − ANX ($n = 11$) $m = 14.3$ yr NAC ($n = 14$) $m = 14.0$ yr	Angry–neutral Happy–neutral	500	Anger: BD + ANX > BD − ANX ≡ NAC Happy: no effects	83.9% medicated (no effect of medication type)
Monk et al., 2006	Location classification	GAD ($n = 17$), $m = 13.12$ yr NAC ($n = 12$), $m = 14.3$ yr	Masked face pairs: Angry–neutral Happy–neutral	17 = faces 68 = mask (probe timeout = 1100)	Anger: bias observed in both GAD and NAC No group difference Happy: no effects	Amygdala activity to masked threat: GAD > NAC. Negative connectivity between VLPFC and amygdala: GAD < NAC

(continued overleaf)

Table 4.1. (*Continued*)

Study	Paradigm	Participants	Stimuli	SOA	Vigilance (positive bias score)	Avoidance (negative bias score)	Additional findings
Pine *et al.*, 2005		Maltreated children (*n* = 34) aged 7–13 yr Controls (*n* = 21), aged 7–13 yr	Angry–neutral Happy–neutral	500 (probe timeout = 1100)		Anger: High physical abuse > low physical abuse PTSD > non-PTSD Happy: no effects	
Stirling, Eley and Clark, 2006	Probe classification	Non-selected children (*n* = 79) aged 8–11 yr	Negative (anger, fear, disgust, sad)–neutral Positive–neutral Negative–positive	1000 (diagonal presentation)		↑ Social anxiety α ↑ avoidance of negative (vs. neutral).	
Joorman, Talbot and Gotlib, 2007	Location classification	21 daughters of mothers with history of depression (high risk) 20 daughters of mothers with no Axis I history (all aged 9–14 yr).	Sad–neutral Happy–neutral	1500	Sad faces (high risk) Happy faces (no history)		

Study	Classification	Sample	Stimuli	SOA (ms)	In those trained to attend to threat	No effect in those trained to avoid threat	Findings
Edlar, Ricon and Bar-Haim, (2008)	Type classification	Non-anxious children (n = 26), aged 7–12 yr. Half trained to attend to threat, half to avoid threat.	Angry–neutral	700 (probe timeout = 100)	In those trained to attend to threat	No effect in those trained to avoid threat	Only children trained to attend to threat experienced elevated anxiety in response to stress-induction
Monk et al., 2008	Location classification	GAD (n = 18), m = 12.28 yr NAC (n = 15), m = 13.53 yr	Angry–neutral Happy–neutral Neutral–neutral	500 (probe timeout = 1100)		Anger: GAD > NAC	VLPFC to anger: GAD > NAC. In patients VLPFC activity associated with reduced anxiety

Spatial cueing tasks

Study	Classification	Sample	Stimuli	SOA (ms)			Findings
Pollak and Tolley-Schell (2003)	Location classification	Physically abused children (n = 14) Non-abused controls (n = 14) Aged 8–11 yr.	Angry Happy Neutral 78% valid trials	500 (+200 ISI)			Enhanced engagement for anger (valid trials) and delayed disengagement from anger (invalid trials) in abused group. Group diff. on summary bias score
Bosmans, De Raedt and Braet, 2007	Location classification	Non-selected (n = 40) age 9–13 yr split into high and low secure attachment groups	Own mother and other faces (neutral) presented as single cues	200 1000 (blocked)			Mother vs. others engagement bias and disengagement bias in low secure > high secure

observed in children with post-traumatic stress disorder (PTSD) (vs. controls; Pine *et al.*, 2005; children who have experienced high levels of physical abuse (Pine *et al.*, 2005), non-selected children with high levels of social anxiety (Stirling, Eley and Clark, 2006) and those with a diagnosis of GAD (Monk *et al.*, 2008).

Evidence of attentional bias in non-anxious control groups and unselected samples is mixed, with demonstrations of vigilance to negative images (relative to vigilance also observed for positive images; Waters, Lipp and Spence, 2004, Experiment 1), threat words (Ehrenreich *et al.*, 1998 cf. Ehrenreich and Gross, 2002), pictures of novel animals associated with threat (Field, 2006), angry facial expressions presented outside awareness (Monk *et al.*, 2006) and happy faces in those with no maternal history for any axis I disorder (Joorman, Talbot and Gotlib, 2007). In non-selected child samples, increased state anxiety has been associated with greater attention to social threat, contrary to predictions from cognitive models that assume strong interactions between state and trait anxiety (Williams *et al.*, 1988, 1997) though significant avoidance has been observed in non-selected/control samples to mild threat images (Legerstee *et al.*, 2009) and emotional words (Hunt, Keogh and French, 2007). In other studies, no significant evidence of attentional bias (vigilance or avoidance) has been observed in non-selected or non-anxious control groups (e.g. Waters *et al.*, 2008a).

Equivocal findings are not readily explained by methodological differences between studies. Indeed, evidence of (greater) vigilance for threat in children with anxiety has been demonstrated to word, picture and face stimuli, in clinical groups comprising mixed anxiety subtypes, subclinical groups, in groups with co-morbid psychiatric disorders and those currently receiving medication (e.g. Brotman *et al.*, 2007), and positive results have been observed in visual probe onset, location and type variants (with recent studies preferring location classification designs).[3] While word studies typically display stimuli for over 1 second, vigilance in anxious children

---

[3] While various versions of the visual probe task have been developed to assess attentional biases in anxiety, there is debate about their relative merits in terms of reliability and sensitivity to such biases (see Mogg and Bradley, 1999 for extended discussion). For example, in probe *detection* ('press the button when you have detected the onset of the probe') and *location* classification ('press the left button for a probe appearing on the left of the screen and the right button for a probe appearing on the right of the screen') studies, participants might adopt a biased monitoring strategy that favours one region of the display more than another, and perform the task by determining probe onset via its presence in or absence from the attended region. This strategy is particularly problematic when the time between a manual response and the presentation of the probe in the subsequent trial is fixed (i.e. due to an inter-trial interval of fixed duration) as motor responses will more likely become time-locked as the task progresses. Thus, visual probe studies are encouraged to manipulate the ITI (e.g. randomly between 750 and 1250 milliseconds) and use catch trials (where no probe follows the stimuli).

In contrast, *probe type* classification tasks benefit from requiring participants to attend to both sides of the display, albeit that the relationship between the stimulus and the response is arbitrary and more difficult for participants to learn. Despite this, direct comparisons of location and probe type classification tasks have produced attentional bias scores of comparable effect size (Mogg

to pictorial threat has been observed at various time points following picture onset; for example, under 100 milliseconds (Monk *et al.*, 2006), 500 milliseconds (Roy *et al.*, 2008) and 1250 milliseconds (Waters *et al.*, 2008b).

Most studies match comparison groups on gender and are not powered to systematically examine interactions with child gender. Nevertheless, there is some initial (*a posteriori*) evidence that girls might more likely show vigilance for threat stimuli (Waters, Lipp and Spence, 2004, Experiment 1; Ehrenreich *et al.*, 1998) and boys avoidance (Vasey, Elhag and Daleiden, 1996; Ehrenreich *et al.*, 1998), findings that perhaps suggest one mechanism that may contribute to the greater prevalence of anxiety in females than males.

The studies reviewed above have recruited children and adolescents who range in age from 7 to 19 with most reporting mean ages between 9 and 14 years. Of these, none have directly compared age groups (e.g. young children vs. adolescents), nor reported strong evidence that age moderates or mediates relationships between anxiety and attentional bias to threat. Indeed, to date, empirical evaluations of the cognitive-inhibition hypothesis (Kindt, Bierman and Brosschot, 1997; Kindt and Van den Hout, 2001) using other paradigms (e.g. Stroop) have failed to find evidence that (i) selective attention to threat is evident in young children irrespective of anxiety level and (ii) attentional bias to threat decreases with age in low anxious children but persists in high anxious children (see Hadwin *et al.*, 2009; Morren *et al.*, 2003). It therefore remains for prospective longitudinal studies to clarify the development of biases in selective attention to threat through infancy and adolescence to adulthood. In doing so, visual probe methods will need modification (e.g. concurrent eye tracking) to clarify potentially insensitive RT data from very young children (e.g. pre-school).

In contrast, the verbal pathway to fear (Field and Lawson, 2003) has received some support from initial tests. Field (2006) gave children between 7 and 9 years positive, negative and no information about different novel animals and measured attentional bias to each animal type using a pictoral dot-probe task immediately or 24 hours after description. Regardless of delay, children acquired an attentional bias towards the animal about which they held negative beliefs compared to the control animal, consistent with proposals that verbal fear information may contribute to acquired fear by manipulating cognitive bias.

Taken together, emerging evidence from visual probe tasks in children supports its continued use as a tool to examine biases in selective attention to a range of emotional stimuli. Indeed, very recent findings in children support conclusions from a recent meta-analysis that significant threat-related biases exist in both

---

and Bradley, 1999) although responses were generally slower, more variable and contained more errors in the probe type classification variant. Thus, while it is reassuring that both versions have successfully revealed anxiety-related differences in attentional bias to threat, research with children might prefer the probe location variant (with a variable inter-trial interval) as this does not require the greater trial numbers to counterbalance the additional probe type factor across pair type × critical stimulus location × probe location conditions and thus reduces task length.

anxious children and adults, and do not differ between the two groups (Bar-Haim *et al.*, 2007).

Spatial Cueing Tasks – Evidence of Delayed Disengagement from Threat

While cognitive models and findings reviewed above place particular emphasis on early pre-attentive mechanisms and biases in initial orienting to threat, other models discuss in detail component processes and regulatory mechanisms that can be considered to coordinate attention allocation following initial orienting.

Specifically, studies have questioned whether threat-related stimuli better draw attentive processes towards themselves or whether the initial shift component of attention may be encapsulated and impervious to higher level variables (Stolz, 1996). If so, anxious individuals' preferential processing of threat in visual probe tasks may be better characterized by a difficulty to disengage from threat-related stimuli (see Fox *et al.*, 2001). Fox *et al.* argue that in visual probe tasks where both stimuli are presented within foveal vision, critical stimuli never appear in truly unattended locations (as both locations are task relevant and inattention to foveal stimuli is highly unlikely, Treisman, 1969). Thus, during a typical 500 milliseconds SOA presentation (and particularly when longer SOAs are used, e.g. 1250 milliseconds), both stimuli are likely to receive attentive processing with subsequent RTs to probes likely to reflect an unquantifiable combination of (i) initial orienting to the threat stimulus and (ii) tendency to dwell on the attended threat stimulus.

In order to determine the relative contributions of these two components of attention, researchers have used a modified version of Posner's (1980) spatial cueing paradigm in which a single cue (e.g. threat face/word) appears in one of the two locations and is followed by a target presented at the cued location on a majority of trials (valid-cues) and at the alternative location on a minority of trials (invalid cues, Figure 4.2).

In an initial study in adults, Fox, Russo and Dutton (2002) found that heightened anxiety was associated with increased attentional dwell time on emotional facial stimuli, relative to neutral faces, but was not linked to facilitated shifting towards threat stimuli. Specifically, high and low anxious participants did not show significant variations across the different cue types (angry, happy and neutral) in responding to a target on valid trials. However, the valence of the face did affect RTs on invalid trials with longer RTs to negative and positive (cf. neutral) invalid face cues. Furthermore, follow-up studies that used a cueing task with a longer SOA to examine inhibition of return (IOR - a reluctance to re-allocate attention to a recently attended location) found that threat-related and ambiguous cues diminished the magnitude of the IOR effect, particularly in high anxious individuals (Fox, Russo and Dutton, 2002), consistent with delayed disengagement from threat.

It is unclear whether the absence of individual differences in attentional shift to threat summarized above reflects the encapsulation of the initial shift component of attention or whether other methodological factors/task demands bias the

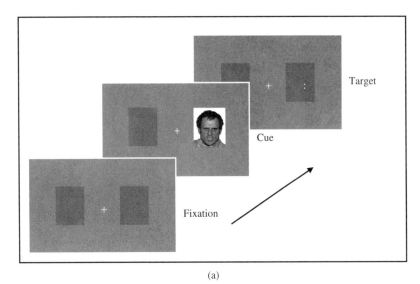

(a)

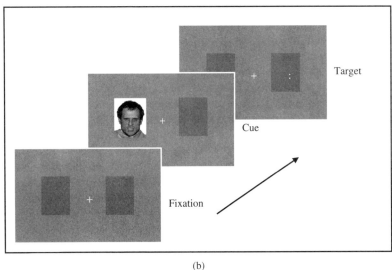

(b)

Figure 4.2 Example trial from spatial cueing task ((a) a valid trial; (b) depicts an invalid trial). (Facial expressions reprinted with permission from Dr. Nim Tottenham.)

aforementioned tasks in favour of observing disengagement rather than shift/engage effects. One factor that seems particularly important is the ratio of valid and invalid trials. For example, studies using a 75 (valid):25 (invalid) ratio have not reported biases in shift, but instead biases in disengagement (Fox *et al.*, 2001; Fox, Russo and Dutton, 2002) suggesting that cueing tasks might be less sensitive to individual differences in exogenous orienting when the endogenous relationship (covariation) between cue and target location (often made explicit to participants) encourages greater orienting to cues than might naturally be expected. Indeed, it is interesting to note that those spatial cueing tasks that have modulated the shift component of attention (as a function of stimulus content or individual differences) have used a 50:50 ratio between cue and target location (e.g. Van Damme *et al.*, 2004; Koster *et al.*, 2007). Therefore, given that participants (particularly young children) may differ in the extent to which they detect the covariation between cue and probe location, researchers might best use 50:50 ratios which are made explicit to participants.

To date, spatial cueing tasks (employing single cues) have not been used to examine attentional bias in child and adolescent anxiety. However, individual differences have been revealed in other populations. For example, in a non-referred sample of 9- to 13-year-olds, Bosmans, De Raedt and Braet (2007) observed faster engagement and delayed disengagement from single cue pictures of their mother (relative to non-mother cues) in children with low secure attachment compared to those with high attachment. In a similar face cueing task Pollak and Tolley-Schell (2003) found that physically abused children demonstrated faster engagement to angry faces (on valid trials) and delayed disengagement for angry faces (on invalid trials) compared to non-abused children (aged 8–11). Taken together, these findings support the use of spatial cueing RT tasks in children to examine individual differences in processing concern-relevant and emotionally/motivationally salient stimuli.

An important conceptual consideration for researchers wishing to use spatial cueing tasks (irrespective of population) relates to the extent to which performance on invalid and valid trials directly maps to disengage and shift/engage components, respectively. Evidence of delayed disengagement from threat in anxiety is typically inferred from significant contrasts between RTs on threat cue trials relative to neutral cue trials (with anxiety status × cue valence interactions evident on invalid rather than valid cue trials). However, on spatial cueing tasks, high trait anxious individuals have also been found to have generally slower RTs following high threatening stimuli (e.g. Experiments 2 and 3 in Yiend and Mathews, 2001). Therefore, differences in RTs between threat cue and neutral cue trials may stem from a slowing effect of threat on RT, as well as effects on allocation of visuospatial attention (Mogg *et al.*, 2008; Yiend and Mathews, 2001). In a recent study, Mogg *et al.* (2008) examined the importance of response slowing when interpreting the effects of cue validity. High and low anxious individuals completed a central cue task, which assessed threat-related response slowing, and a spatial cueing task, which assessed attentional biases for angry, happy and neutral faces. Crucially, results suggested that interpretation of the anxiety-related bias for threat (i.e. bias in disengagement or bias in shift components) depends on whether the effect of response slowing is taken into account (i.e. subtracted from RTs on spatial cueing trials). Given that conventional spatial cueing tasks may reflect both threat-related attentional cueing and response slowing effects, it is important that future studies obtain independent indices of response slowing when seeking to clarify shift and disengagement components of attentional bias within spatial cueing tasks.

Extending the use of visual probe methods in children – implications from studies in adults

Differentiating vigilance and difficulty to disengage using the visual probe task

Within the visual probe task, threat and neutral stimuli are presented simultaneously. While this allows researchers to directly index participant's allocation of attention between two competing stimuli (i.e. selection as a function of the resolution of differences between the two competing stimuli), in its common form, it is not able to isolate whether attentional effects for threat might be due to the faster direction of attention to threat or difficulties in shifting attention away from threat (Fox *et al.*, 2001; Koster *et al.*, 2004) or vigilance for one stimulus versus avoidance of the other. While this later point can be in part mitigated by pairing different categories of critical stimuli (e.g. threat and positive words) with multiple matched sets of control stimuli, the former can be addressed by interspersing conventional threat–neutral trials with neutral–neutral pairings and examining whether individual differences in attentional bias scores are driven by facilitated performance on threat-congruent trials (i.e. when probe appears in threat location) or impaired performance on threat-incongruent trials (when probe appears in non-threat location) relative to neutral–neutral baseline probe RTs (see Koster *et al.*, 2004 for extended discussion). Interestingly, studies in children often do include neutral–neutral filler trials (presumably to reduce the frequency with which critical stimuli appear throughout the task), but do not use data from these trials to clarify shift versus disengage components (but see Legerstee *et al.*, 2009 for a recent use of this method in anxious children).

Mapping the time course of attentional bias to threat using the visual probe task

The vigilance-avoidance hypothesis proposes that anxiety-related attentional biases vary over time (i.e. initial vigilance for high threat cues, followed by avoidance). Several studies have employed the visual probe task to examine attentional processes at comparatively early and late stages of stimulus processing by manipulating the SOA between picture onset and probe onset. For example, Mogg *et al.* (2004) presented pictorial stimuli in a visual probe task for two exposure durations: 500 milliseconds and 1500 milliseconds. Results revealed evidence that high trait anxious participants were more vigilant for high threat scenes at the shorter exposure duration (500 milliseconds) relative to low trait anxious individuals and that participants with high levels of blood injury fear demonstrated significant avoidance of high threat scenes at the longer (1500 milliseconds) exposure duration (see also Bradley *et al.*, 1998). While these findings question whether anxiety and fear reflect two distinct aversive motivational systems, characterized by different patterns of attentional bias, they do support the use of visual probe designs to map the temporal characteristics of attentional bias.

More recently, spatial cueing paradigms have examined the time course of component processes (engagement and disengagement) by manipulating SOA. For example, Koster *et al.* (2006) reported that at short stimulus durations (100 milliseconds) high trait anxious individuals more strongly engaged attention with and showed impaired disengagement from highly aversive threat pictures compared to low anxious controls but showed a stronger tendency to avoid threat at 200 and 500 millisecond presentations. Similarly, in a non-selected sample, facilitated attentional capture by threat has been observed at 100 milliseconds (but not 28 milliseconds) with some evidence of reduced attentional capture by threat (relative to neutral) stimuli emerging at later time points (200 and 500 milliseconds; Koster *et al.*, 2007).

Attentional shifting, engagement and disengagement can be covert (in the absence of eye movements) or overt (characterized by observable shifts in eye gaze/fixations). While probe detection paradigms can provide robust indices of attention allocation at stimulus offset (i.e. probe onset) the measure only provides a snap shot of attention allocation at a selected time point and not a continuous measure of attention throughout stimulus presentation. While careful sampling of attentional bias scores can be used to map participant's attention trajectory, temporal resolution is considerably hampered by the need to keep task length manageable for participants (a bias score for a given SOA is typically generated from a minimum of 16 trial RT data points). As such, recent studies have used visual probe tasks with concurrent eye movement monitoring (infra-red or electro-oculography) to supplement RT indices of attentional bias with convergent measures of overt orienting (see also Chapter 6).

Studies of eye movements during visual probe tasks have demonstrated faster and more frequent initial orienting to threat faces in patients with GAD relative to both normal controls and individuals with depressive disorder (Mogg, Millar and Bradley, 2000; see also Mogg, Garner and Bradley, 2007). In addition, individuals with high trait social anxiety have been found to be faster to initially orient towards and subsequently disengage eye gaze from emotional faces compared to low anxious controls (Garner, Mogg and Bradley, 2006) within a visual probe task. Furthermore, both eye movement indices of initial orienting (e.g. proportion of initial eye movements to threat stimuli) and attentional bias scores derived from manual RTs have been found to reveal similar patterns between groups (Mogg, Garner and Bradley, 2007; but see Mogg, Miller and Bradley, 2000) and correlate positively with one another (Bradley, Mogg, and Millar, 2000).

The temporal resolution of attentional bias to threat will be further informed by electrophysiological evidence from studies that examine event-related brain potentials during visual probe tasks. Using a visual probe task with non-selected adults Holmes *et al.* (2009) have recently revealed that attentional orienting to threatening faces (N2pc component) emerged earlier than orienting to positive faces consistent with models of attention and emotion that posit rapid onset of neural processes involved in the attentional prioritization of threat. Using concurrent electroencephalogram (EEG) recording Pollak and Tolly-Schell (2003) found that abused children demonstrated behavioural evidence of delayed disengagement from angry expressions and a selective increase in P3b on invalid angry trials, reflecting increased resources required to disengage from the previously cued location. These findings converge with more recent event-related potential (ERP) evidence that attention allocation to threat mediates the relationship between physical abuse and child-reported anxiety such that extreme emotional experiences may promote vulnerability for anxiety by influencing the development of attention regulation abilities (Shackman, Shackman and Pollak, 2007).

Concurrent Neuroimaging: Implications for Neuro-Cognitive Models

Neuro-cognitive models of anxiety converge with predictions from cognitive models in proposing a common amygdala–prefrontal circuitry that underlies increased activation of threat-related representations, and a failure to use controlled processing to regulate attention and promote alternate non-threat-related representations as vulnerability factors for anxiety (see Bishop, 2007).

Findings from functional magnetic resonance imaging (fMRI) show amygdala hyperactivity to threat in high state anxious and clinically anxious individuals (e.g. Bishop, Duncan and Lawrence, 2004a; Tillfors et al., 2001; Yoon et al., 2007), with evidence that this specialized subcortical network can prioritize the processing of threat information that is presented outside of attention (Bishop, Duncan and Lawrence, 2004b) and awareness (i.e. subconsciously; Etkin et al., 2004). Potentiation of fear-related defense (e.g. startle) behaviours coordinated by the amygdaloid complex and associated structures has also been demonstrated in anxious children (Waters, Lipp and Spence, 2005), children at greater risk of developing anxiety due to parental anxiety (Grillon, Dierker and Merikangas, 1998) and numerous adult populations (PTSD: Grillon et al., 1998; obsessive-compulsive disorder (OCD): Kumari et al., 2001; panic disorder: Grillon et al., 1994; and individuals with subclinical levels of social anxiety: Cornwell et al., 2006; Garner et al., 2008).

fMRI studies have confirmed the role of prefrontal cortical regions in regulating the subcortical fear system (e.g. Hariri, Bookheimer and Mazziotta, 2000) while dysfunction in prefrontal regulatory structures during behavioural attention tasks has been observed in high state anxious adults (Bishop, Duncan and Lawrence, 2004b) and in children with GAD (Monk et al., 2008; see Chapter 8). Concurrent fMRI during visual probe tasks has shown that children with GAD who demonstrate attentional vigilance for masked angry faces exhibit greater amygdala activation in response to angry expressions compared to non-anxious controls, and reduced connectivity between ventrolateral prefrontal cortex (VLPFC) and amygdala compared to non-anxious controls (Monk et al., 2006). Similarly, children with GAD who avoided angry faces had greater VLPFC activity, with increased activity in VLPFC associated with reduced anxiety (Monk et al., 2008). Taken together, initial findings in children provide some support for neuro-cognitive models that suggest that amygdala hyperactivity and hypo-activity in prefrontal structures underlies attentional bias to threat, with greater recruitment of prefrontal control structures associated with reduced anxiety vulnerability (Bishop, 2007). Indeed, it would be interesting to examine in child samples the extent to which known genetic risk factors (polymorphisms in SERT, COMT) shown to affect anxiety-related behaviours (You *et al.*, 2005), attentional bias (Osinsky *et al.*, 2008; Bishop *et al.*, 2006) and neural mechanisms involved in threat processing (review by Munafo, Brown and Hariri, 2008) interact with environmental risk factors throughout development (e.g. low social support and parenting style, Hadwin, Garner and Perez-Olivaz, 2006) to further promote dysfunction in neural and cognitive mechanisms involved in emotion activation and regulation (e.g. Fox *et al.*, 2005).

Attention Control and Selective Attention to Threat in Anxiety

ACT (Eysenck *et al.*, 2007) predicts that attention dysfunction in anxiety results from bottom-up (stimulus driven) mechanisms prioritizing resource allocation in the absence of appropriate top-down (goal directed) regulation. The importance of (or the lack of) attention control in the (dys)regulation of attentional bias to threat in anxiety is evidenced by findings from visual probe paradigms that high trait anxious individuals with poor attention control (assessed using self-report measures) show a threat bias, whereas those with good control are better able to shift attention from threat locations (Derryberry and Reed, 2002). More recently, Reinholdt-Dunne, Mogg and Bradley (2009) investigated the role of executive attention control (objectively determined using the Attention Network Task; Fan *et al.*, 2002) in modulating cognitive interference (emotional Stroop). Individuals with high anxiety and poor attention control showed greater cognitive interference by emotional faces (including angry faces), compared to neutral faces, whereas participants with high anxiety/high attentional control and low anxious individuals did not.

In children, psychopathological symptom severity (across a range of dimensions including anxiety, depression and hyperactivity) has been associated with reduced attention control (self-report), though broader associations between severity and neuropsychological measures of attention control have yet to be established (Muris *et al.*, 2008a, 2008b). Thus, to the extent that emerging evidence continues to implicate low cognitive regulation in moderating the relationship between anxiety and biases in emotion processing (e.g. selective attention), future studies are encouraged to include subjective and preferably objective measures of attention control in order to clarify predicted interactions between anxiety and selective attention to threat.

The Effects of Psychological Treatment on Biases in Selective Attention

The beneficial effects of psychological therapies on maladaptive biases in selective attention to threat have been demonstrated in several anxiety disorders including spider phobia following exposure treatment (Lavy, Van den Hour and Arntz, 1993); GAD following treatment comprising relaxation, cognitive coping and gradual exposure (Mathews *et al.*, 1995); and social phobia following cognitive behavioural therapy (CBT) (Mattia, Heimberg and Hope, 1993), with some evidence that treatments moderate selective processing of unconscious material (Van den Hout *et al.*, 1997; Mogg *et al.*, 1995).

In children, while CBT has been shown to reduce negative interpretative bias to within normal limits (Waters *et al.*, 2008a), it is yet to produce demonstrable change in clinically anxious children's attentional bias to threat (Waters *et al.*, 2008a). However, an attentional bias away from severe threat (greater avoidance) prior to treatment has been associated with response to CBT (Legerstee *et al.*, 2009).

Attention Training Using Visual Probe Paradigms: Clinical Implications

The extent to which selective attention to threat is an important mechanism in the emergence of anxiety or simply an epiphenomenon observed in those with elevated levels of anxiety remains the subject of continued debate (Kindt and Van den Hout, 2001). Recent studies have directly tested whether training an individual to selectively attend to or avoid threat information moderates emotional vulnerability and anxiety (see review by Mathews and MacLeod, 2002 and Koster, Fox and MacLeod, 2009 for extended discussion). Using a modified visual probe task in which participants were trained to attend to threat rather than neutral word stimuli (by manipulating threat location–probe location contingencies) MacLeod *et al.* (2002) modified emotional reactions to a standardized (anagram) stress task.

While it is not clear whether attentional biases trained using visual probe tasks lead to associated change in related processing biases (e.g. as measured by Stroop – Harris and Menzies, 1998), these findings provide empirical support that attentional bias can causally mediate emotional vulnerability and suggest the possibility that cognitive-experimental procedures designed to modify selective information processing may have potential therapeutic value (MacLeod *et al.*, 2002).

Rather than inducing negative bias, of more obvious clinical interest is recent evidence that modified visual probe paradigms that train attentional bias to positive stimuli (e.g. happy faces) can reduce some elements of self-report social anxiety (Li *et al.*, 2008) and modify eye gaze to negative stimuli (Wadlinger and Isaacowitz, 2008). Reassuringly, the beneficial effects following training sessions in the laboratory seem to also occur in adult patients who self-administer visual probe training paradigms at home (MacLeod *et al.*, 2007).

One might expect that compared to adults, children's developing attentional system might be more amenable to, and therefore benefit more greatly from, attention training. While, unfortunately, to date this seems largely untested, recent findings do show promise. Eldar, Ricon and Bar-Haim (2008) demonstrated in healthy 7- to 12-year-old children that an attentional bias to threat can be induced and lead to increases in self-report anxiety. Unfortunately, attempts to train attention away from threat did not modify attention nor alter self-report mood.

Thus, evidence in adults and emerging evidence in children do suggest that modified visual probe tasks can create changes in selective attention, self-report mood and response to stress. It, therefore, seems necessary to clarify (i) whether potentially protective attentional biases can be induced in children, (ii) whether biases in selective attention promote change in other aspects of information processing, (iii) which factors persist changes in cognition and emotion that result from attention training and (iv) whether attention training paradigms can be easily incorporated into psychological treatments for child and adolescent anxiety and improve efficacy.

Summary

Visual probe tasks continue to show promise as a tool with which to clarify biases in selective attention to threat in child and adolescent anxiety. Research to date has revealed considerable evidence of greater vigilance to lexical and pictorial threat (e.g. affective images and emotional facial expressions) in anxious children, with evidence of avoidance more likely in children who have experienced extreme levels of threat (physical abuse) and/or are tested in potentially anxiogenic environments [i.e. within magnetic resonance imaging (MRI) scanner]. While evidence in anxious children is broadly consistent with findings in adult samples and appears consistent with predictions from cognitive models of threat processing in anxiety, future studies need to clarify the development, component processes and time course of attentional bias in child and adolescent populations. To this end, studies in children should be mindful of developments in the adult literature, particularly regarding the psychonomics of visual probe indices of selective attention.

Mechanisms that underlie the development and regulation of attentional bias to threat throughout childhood remain unclear, and longitudinal studies are necessary to test predictions from original developmental models and extend promising initial evidence that supports verbal learning pathways to cognitive bias. In doing so, interactions between environmental and genetic risk factors that modulate neural and cognitive mechanisms that underlie bias in selective attention should be explored.

The clinical utility of attention retraining techniques for child and adolescent anxiety has yet to be realized; however, evidence from visual probe training paradigms in adult anxiety and initial findings in children identify attentional bias as a mechanism through which anxiety may emerge and resolve.

Convergent evidence from concurrent eye tracking and event-related potentials will help clarify the time course of attention allocation to threat in children, particularly younger children for whom manual RT data alone may prove insensitive to individual differences, while continued integration of visual probe paradigms with functional imaging (e.g. fMRI) techniques will further delineate the neural structures and functional connectivity involved in the activation and control of selective attention to threat. This data should inform recent connectionist network models of attentional bias within visual probe tasks (e.g. Frewen *et al.*, 2008) with a view to providing biologically plausible dynamic models of selective attention to threat and its development.

References

Bar-Haim, Y., Lamy, D., Pergamin, L. *et al.* (2007) Threat-related attentional bias in anxious and nonanxious individuals: a meta-analytic study. *Psychological Bulletin*, **133** (1), 1–24.

Beck, A.T. (1976) *Cognitive Therapy and the Emotional Disorders*, International Universities Press, New York.

Bishop, S.J., Duncan, J. and Lawrence, A.D. (2004a) State anxiety modulation of the amygdala response to unattended threat-related stimuli. *Journal of Neuroscience*, **24** (46), 10364–10368.

Bishop, S.J., Duncan, J. and Lawrence, A.D. (2004b) Prefrontal cortical function and anxiety: controlling attention to threat-related stimuli. *Nature Neuroscience*, **7** (2), 184–188.

Bishop, S.J. (2007) Neurocognitive mechanisms of anxiety: an integrative account. *Trends in Cognitive Sciences*, **11** (7), 307–316.

Bishop, S.J., Cohen, J.D., Fossella, J. *et al.* (2006) COMT genotype influences prefrontal response to emotional distraction. *Cognitive Affective and Behavioral Neuroscience*, **6** (1), 62–70.

Bosmans, G., De Raedt, R. and Braet, C. (2007) The invisible bonds: does the secure base script of attachment influence children's attention toward their mother? *Journal of Clinical Child and Adolescent Psychology*, **36** (4), 557–567.

Bower, G.H. (1981) Mood and memory. *American Psychologist*, **36**, 129–148.

Bradley, B.P., Mogg, K., Falla, S.J. and Hamilton, L.R. (1998) Attentional bias for threatening facial expressions in anxiety: manipulation of stimulus duration. *Cognition and Emotion*, **12** (6), 737–753.

Bradley, B.P., Mogg, K., White, J. *et al.* (1999) Attentional bias for emotional faces in generalized anxiety disorder. *British Journal of Clinical Psychology*, **38**, 267–278.

Bradley, B.P., Mogg, K. and Lee, S.C. (1997) Attentional biases for negative information in induced and naturally occurring dysphoria. *Behaviour Research and Therapy*, **35** (10), 911–927.

Bradley, B.P., Mogg, K. and Millar, N.H. (2000) Covert and overt orienting of attention to emotional faces in anxiety. *Cognition and Emotion*, **14** (6), 789–808.

Broadbent, D. and Broadbent, M. (1988) Anxiety and attentional bias: state and trait. *Cognition and Emotion*, **2**, 165–183.

Brotman, M.A., Rich, B.A., Schmajuk, M. *et al.* (2007) Attention bias to threat faces in children with bipolar disorder and comorbid lifetime anxiety disorders. *Biological Psychiatry*, **61** (6), 819–821.

Byrne, A. and Eysenck, M.W. (1995) Trait anxiety, anxious mood, and threat detection. *Cognition and Emotion*, **9** (6), 549–562.

Cornwell, B.R., Johnson, L., Berardi, L. and Grillon, C. (2006) Anticipation of public speaking in virtual reality reveals a relationship between trait social anxiety and startle reactivity. *Biological Psychiatry*, **59** (7), 664–666.

Dalgleish, T., Moradi, A.R., Taghavi, M.R. *et al.* (2001) An experimental investigation of hypervigilance for threat in children and adolescents with post-traumatic stress disorder. *Psychological Medicine*, **31** (3), 541–547.

Dalgleish, T., Taghavi, R., Neshat-Doost, H. *et al.* (2003) Patterns of processing bias for emotional information across clinical disorders: a comparison of attention, memory, and prospective cognition in children and adolescents with depression, generalized anxiety, and posttraumatic stress disorder. *Journal of Clinical Child and Adolescent Psychology*, **32** (1), 10–21.

Derryberry, D. and Reed, M.A. (2002) Anxiety-related attentional biases and their regulation by attentional control. *Journal of Abnormal Psychology*, **111** (2), 225–236.

Ehrenreich, J. T., Coyne, L. W., O'Neill, P. and Gross, A. M. (1998) Attentional bias to threat cues in childhood anxiety: a preliminary investigation of lexical and facial cues. *Poster session presented at the annual convention of the Association for the Advancement of Behavior Therapy*, Washington, DC.

Ehrenreich, J.T. and Gross, A.M. (2002) Biased attentional behavior in childhood anxiety – a review of theory and current empirical investigation. *Clinical Psychology Review*, **22** (7), 991–1008.

Ekman, P. and Friesen, W.V. (1976) *Pictures of Facial Affect*, Consulting Psychologists Press, Palo Alto, CA.

Eldar, S., Ricon, T. and Bar-Haim, Y. (2008) Plasticity in attention: implications for stress response in children. *Behaviour Research and Therapy*, **46** (4), 450–461.

Etkin, A., Klemenhagen, K.C., Dudman, J.T. *et al.* (2004) Individual differences in trait anxiety predict the response of the basolateral amygdala to unconsciously processed fearful faces. *Neuron*, **44** (6), 1043–1055.

Eysenck, M.W. (1992) *Anxiety and Cognition: A Cognitive Perspective*, Erlbaum, Hove, England.

Eysenck, M.W., Derakshan, N., Santos, R. and Calvo, M.G. (2007) Anxiety and cognitive performance: attentional control theory. *Emotion*, **7** (2), 336–353.

Fan, J., McCandliss, B.D., Sommer, T. *et al.* (2002) Testing the efficiency and independence of attentional networks. *Journal of Cognitive Neuroscience*, **14** (3), 340–347.

Field, A.P. (2006) Watch out for the beast: fear information and attentional bias in children. *Journal of Clinical Child and Adolescent Psychology*, **35** (3), 431–439.

Field, A.P. and Lawson, J. (2003) Fear information and the development of fears during childhood: effects on implicit fear responses and behavioural avoidance. *Behaviour Research and Therapy*, **41** (11), 1277–1293.

Fox, E., Russo, R., Bowles, R. and Dutton, K. (2001) Do threatening stimuli draw or hold visual attention in subclinical anxiety? *Journal of Experimental Psychology-General*, **130** (4), 681–700.

Fox, N.A., Nichols, K.E., Henderson, H.A. *et al.* (2005) Evidence for a gene-environment interaction in predicting behavioral inhibition in middle childhood. *Psychological Science*, **16** (12), 921–926.

Fox, E., Russo, R. and Dutton, K. (2002) Attentional bias for threat: evidence for delayed disengagement from emotional faces. *Cognition and Emotion*, **16** (3), 355–379.

Frewen, P.A., Dozois, D.J.A., Joanisse, M.F. and Neufeld, R.W.J. (2008) Selective attention to threat versus reward: meta-analysis and neural-network modeling of the dot-probe task. *Clinical Psychology Review*, **28** (2), 307–337.

Garner, M., Clarke, G., Graystone, H. and Baldwin, D.S. (2008) Potentiated startle to emotional expressions in social anxiety. *Journal of Psychopharmacology*, **22**, A38.

Garner, M., Mogg, K. and Bradley, B.P. (2006) Orienting and maintenance of gaze to facial expressions in social anxiety. *Journal of Abnormal Psychology*, **115** (4), 760–770.

Gilboa-Schechtman, E., Foa, E.B. and Amir, N. (1999) Attentional biases for facial expressions in social phobia: the face-in-the-crowd paradigm. *Cognition and Emotion*, **13** (3), 305–318.

Grillon, C., Ameli, R., Goddard, A. *et al.* (1994) Base-line and fear-potentiated startle in panic disorder patients. *Biological Psychiatry*, **35** (7), 431–439.

Grillon, C., Dierker, L. and Merikangas, K.R. (1998) Fear-potentiated startle in adolescent offspring of parents with anxiety disorders. *Biological Psychiatry*, **44** (10), 990–997.

Grillon, C., Morgan, C.A., Davis, M. and Southwick, S.M. (1998) Effects of experimental context and explicit threat cues on acoustic startle in Vietnam veterans with posttraumatic stress disorder. *Biological Psychiatry*, **44** (10), 1027–1036.

Hadwin, J. A., Donnelly, N. *et al.* (2009) Childhood anxiety and attention to emotion faces in a modified Stroop task. *British Journal of Developmental Psychology*, **27**, 487–494.

Hadwin, J.A., Garner, M. and Perez-Olivaz, G. (2006) The development of information processing biases in childhood anxiety: a review and exploration of its origins in parenting. *Clinical Psychology Review*, **26** (7), 876–894.

Hariri, A.R., Bookheimer, S.Y. and Mazziotta, J.C. (2000) Modulating emotional responses: effects of a neocortical network on the limbic system. *Neuroreport*, **11** (1), 43–48.

Harris, L.M. and Menzies, R.G. (1998) Changing attentional bias: can it effect self-reported anxiety? *Anxiety Stress and Coping*, **11** (2), 167–179.

Helzer, E.G., Connor-Smith, J.K. and Reed, M.A. (2009) Traits, states, and attentional gates: temperament and threat relevance as predictors of attentional bias to social threat. *Anxiety Stress and Coping*, **22** (1), 57–76.

Holmes, A., Bradley, B.P., Kragh Nielsen, M. and Mogg, K. (2009) Attentional selectivity for emotional faces: evidence from human electrophysiology. *Psychophysiology*, **46** (1), 62–68.

Hunt, C., Keogh, E. and French, C.C. (2007) Anxiety sensitivity, conscious awareness and selective attentional biases in children. *Behaviour Research and Therapy*,
45 (3), 497–509.

Joormann, J., Talbot, L. and Gotlib, I.H. (2007) Biased processing of emotional
information in girls at risk for depression. *Journal of Abnormal Psychology*,
116 (1), 135–143.

Kallen, V. L., Ferdinand, R. F. *et al.* (2007) Early attention processes and anxiety in
children. *Perceptual and Motor Skills*, **104** (1), 221–235.

Kindt, M., Bierman, D. and Brosschot, J.F. (1997) Cognitive bias in spider fear and
control children: assessment of emotional interference by a card format and a
single-trial format of the Stroop task. *Journal of Experimental Child Psychology*,
66 (2), 163–179.

Kindt, M. and Van den Hout, M. (2001) Selective attention and anxiety: a perspective on developmental issues and the causal status. *Journal of Psychopathology
and Behavioral Assessment*, **23** (3), 193–202.

Koster, E.H.W., Crombez, G., Verschuere, B. and De Houwer, J. (2004) Selective
attention to threat in the dot probe paradigm: differentiating vigilance and
difficulty to disengage. *Behaviour Research and Therapy*, **42** (10), 1183–1192.

Koster, E.H.W., Crombez, G., Verschuere, B. *et al.* (2006) Components of attentional bias to threat in high trait anxiety: facilitated engagement, impaired
disengagement, and attentional avoidance. *Behaviour Research and Therapy*, **44**
(12), 1757–1771.

Koster, E.H.W., Crombez, G., Verschuere, B. *et al.* (2007) A time-course analysis
of attentional cueing by threatening scenes. *Experimental Psychology*, **54** (2),
161–171.

Koster, E.H.W., Fox, E. and MacLeod, C. (2009) Introduction to the special section
on cognitive bias modification in emotional disorders. *Journal of Abnormal
Psychology*, **118** (1), 1–4.

Kumari, V., Kaviani, H., Raven, P.W. *et al.* (2001) Enhanced startle reactions
to acoustic stimuli in patients with obsessive-compulsive disorder. *American
Journal of Psychiatry*, **158** (1), 134–136.

Lang, P.J., Bradley, M.M. and Cuthbert, B.N. (1999) *International Affective Picture
System (IAPS): Instruction Manual and Affective Ratings (Tech Rep. No A-4)*,
University of Florida, Gainsville, FL.

Lavy, E., Van den Hout, M. and Arntz, A. (1993) Attentional bias and spider phobia
-conceptual and clinical issues. *Behaviour Research and Therapy*, **31** (1), 17–24.

Legerstee, J.S., Tulen, J.H.M., Kallen, V.L. *et al.* (2009) Threat-related selective
attention predicts treatment success in childhood anxiety disorders. *Journal of
the American Academy of Child and Adolescent Psychiatry*, **48** (2), 196–205.

Li, S.W., Tan, J.Q., Qian, M.Y. and Liu, X.H. (2008) Continual training of attentional
bias in social anxiety. *Behaviour Research and Therapy*, **46** (8), 905–912.

MacLeod, C. and Matthews, A. (1988) Anxiety and the allocation of attention
to threat Quarterly. *Journal of Experimental Psychology: Human Experimental
Psychology*, **38**, 659–670.

Macleod, C., Mathews, A. and Tata, P. (1986) Attentional bias in emotional
disorders. *Journal of Abnormal Psychology*, **95** (1), 15–20.

MacLeod, C., Rutherford, E., Campbell, L. *et al.* (2002) Selective attention and emotional vulnerability: assessing the causal basis of their association through the experimental manipulation of attentional bias. *Journal of Abnormal Psychology*, **111** (1), 107–123.

MacLeod, C., Soong, L.Y., Rutherford, E.M. and Campbell, L.W. (2007) Internet-delivered assessment and manipulation of anxiety-linked attentional bias: validation of a free-access attentional probe software package. *Behavior Research Methods*, **39** (3), 533–538.

Mathews, A. (1990) Why worry? The cognitive function of anxiety. *Behaviour Research and Therapy*, **28**, 455–468.

Mathews, A. and Mackintosh, B. (1998) A cognitive model of selective processing in anxiety. *Cognitive Therapy and Research*, **22** (6), 539–560.

Mathews, A. and Macleod, C. (1986) Discrimination of threat cues without awareness in anxiety-states. *Journal of Abnormal Psychology*, **95** (2), 131–138.

Mathews, A. and MacLeod, C. (2002) Induced processing biases have causal effects on anxiety. *Cognition and Emotion*, **16** (3), 331–354.

Mathews, A., Mogg, K., Kentish, J. and Eysenck, M. (1995) Effect of psychological treatment on cognitive bias in generalized anxiety disorder. *Behaviour Research and Therapy*, **33** (3), 293–303.

Mattia, J.I., Heimberg, R.G. and Hope, D.A. (1993) The revised Stroop color-naming task in social phobics. *Behaviour Research and Therapy*, **31** (3), 305–313.

McNally, R.J., Riemann, B.C. and Kim, E. (1990) Selective processing of threat cues in panic disorder. *Behaviour Research and Therapy*, **28** (5), 407–412.

Mogg, K. and Bradley, B.P. (1998) A cognitive-motivational analysis of anxiety. *Behaviour Research and Therapy*, **36** (9), 809–848.

Mogg, K. and Bradley, B.P. (1999) Some methodological issues in assessing attentional biases for threatening faces in anxiety: a replication study using a modified version of the probe detection task. *Behaviour Research and Therapy*, **37** (6), 595–604.

Mogg, K. and Bradley, B.P. (2002) Selective orienting of attention to masked threat faces in social anxiety. *Behaviour Research and Therapy*, **40** (12), 1403–1414.

Mogg, K., Bradley, B.P., Miles, F. and Dixon, R. (2004) Time course of attentional bias for threat scenes: testing the vigilance-avoidance hypothesis. *Cognition and Emotion*, **18** (5), 689–700.

Mogg, K., Bradley, B.P., Millar, N. and White, J. (1995) A follow-up-study of cognitive bias in generalized anxiety disorder. *Behaviour Research and Therapy*, **33** (8), 927–935.

Mogg, K., Bradley, B.P. and Williams, R. (1995) Attentional bias in anxiety and depression – the role of awareness. *British Journal of Clinical Psychology*, **34**, 17–36.

Mogg, K., Garner, M. and Bradley, B.P. (2007) Anxiety and orienting of gaze to angry and fearful faces. *Biological Psychology*, **76**, 163–169.

Mogg, K., Holmes, A., Garner, M. and Bradley, B.P. (2008) Effects of threat cues on attentional shifting, disengagement and response slowing in anxious individuals. *Behaviour Research and Therapy*, **46** (5), 656–667.

Mogg, K., Millar, N. and Bradley, B.P. (2000) Biases in eye movements to threatening facial expressions in generalized anxiety disorder and depressive disorder. *Journal of Abnormal Psychology*, **109** (4), 695–704.

Mogg, K., Philippot, P. and Bradley, B.P. (2004) Selective attention to angry faces in clinical social phobia. *Journal of Abnormal Psychology*, **113** (1), 160–165.

Monk, C.S., Nelson, E.E., McClure, E.B. *et al.* (2006) Ventrolateral prefrontal cortex activation and attentional bias in response to angry faces in adolescents with generalized anxiety disorder. *American Journal of Psychiatry*, **163** (6), 1091–1097.

Monk, C.S., Telzer, E.H., Mogg, K. *et al.* (2008) Amygdala and ventrolateral prefrontal cortex activation to masked angry faces in children and adolescents with generalized anxiety disorder. *Archives of General Psychiatry*, **65** (5), 568–576.

Morren, M., Kindt, M., van den Hout, M. and van Kasteren, H. (2003) Anxiety and the processing of threat in children: further examination of the cognitive inhibition hypothesis. *Behaviour Change*, **20** (3), 131–142.

Munafo, M.R., Brown, S.M. and Hariri, A.R. (2008) Serotonin transporter (5-HTTLPR) genotype and amygdala activation: a meta-analysis. *Biological Psychiatry*, **63** (9), 852–857.

Muris, P., Mayer, B., van Lint, C. and Hofman, S. (2008a) Attentional control and psychopathological symptoms in children. *Personality and Individual Differences*, **44** (7), 1495–1505.

Muris, P., van der Pennen, E., Sigmond, R. and Mayer, B. (2008b) Symptoms of anxiety, depression, and aggression in non-clinical children: relationships with self-report and performance-based measures of attention and effortful control. *Child Psychiatry and Human Development*, **39** (4), 455–467.

Murphy, S.E., Longhitano, C., Ayres, R.E. *et al.* (2006) Tryptophan supplementation induces a positive bias in the processing of emotional material in healthy female volunteers. *Psychopharmacology*, **187** (1), 121–130.

Neshat-Doost, H. T., Moradi, A. R. *et al.* (2000) Lack of attentional bias for emotional information in clinically depressed children and adolescents on the dot probe task. *Journal of Child Psychology and Psychiatry*, **41** (3), 363–368.

Osinsky, R., Reuter, M., Kupper, Y. *et al.* (2008) Variation in the serotonin transporter gene modulates selective attention to threat. *Emotion*, **8** (4), 584–588.

Pine, D.S., Mogg, K., Bradley, B.P. *et al.* (2005) Attention bias to threat in maltreated children: Implications for vulnerability to stress-related psychopathology. *American Journal of Psychiatry*, **162** (2), 291–296.

Pollak, S.D. and Tolley-Schell, S.A. (2003) Selective attention to facial emotion in physically abused children. *Journal of Abnormal Psychology*, **112** (3), 323–338.

Posner, M.I. (1980) Orienting of attention. *Quarterly Journal of Experimental Psychology*, **41A**, 19–45.

Posner, M.I. and Fan, J. (2004) Attention as an organ system, in *Topics in Integrative Neuroscience: From Cells to Cognition* (eds J.R. Pomerantz and M.C. Crair), Cambridge University Press, Cambridge, UK.

Reinholdt-Dunne, M.L., Mogg, K. and Bradley, B.P. (2009) Effects of anxiety and attention control on processing pictorial and linguistic emotional information. *Behaviour Research and Therapy*, **47** (5), 410–417.

Roy, A.K., Vasa, R.A., Bruck, M. *et al.* (2008) Attention bias toward threat in pediatric anxiety disorders. *Journal of the American Academy of Child and Adolescent Psychiatry*, **47** (10), 1189–1196.

Schippell, P.L., Vasey, M.W., Cravens-Brown, L.M. and Bretveld, R.A. (2003) Suppressed attention to rejection, ridicule, and failure cues: a unique correlate of reactive but not proactive aggression in youth. *Journal of Clinical Child and Adolescent Psychology*, **32** (1), 40–55.

Shackman, J.E., Shackman, A.J. and Pollak, S.D. (2007) Physical abuse amplifies attention to threat and increases anxiety in children. *Emotion*, **7**, 838–852.

Stirling, L.J., Eley, T.C. and Clark, D.M. (2006) Preliminary evidence for an association between social anxiety symptoms and avoidance of negative faces in school-age children. *Journal of Clinical Child and Adolescent Psychology*, **35** (3), 431–439.

Stolz, J.A. (1996) Exogenous orienting does not reflect an encapsulated set of processes. *Journal of Experimental Psychology-Human Perception and Performance*, **22** (1), 187–201.

Taghavi, M.R., Neshat-Doost, H.T., Moradi, A.R. *et al.* (1999) Biases in visual attention in children and adolescents with clinical anxiety and mixed anxiety-depression. *Journal of Abnormal Child Psychology*, **27** (3), 215–223.

Telzer, E.H., Mogg, K., Bradley, B.P. *et al.* (2008) Relationship between trait anxiety, prefrontal cortex, and attention bias to angry faces in children and adolescents. *Biological Psychology*, **79** (2), 216–222.

Tillfors, M., Furmark, T., Marteinsdottir, I. *et al.* (2001) Cerebral blood flow in subjects with social phobia during stressful speaking tasks: a PET study. *American Journal of Psychiatry*, **158** (8), 1220–1226.

Tottenham, N., Tanaka, J. W., Leon, A.C. *et al.* (2009). The NimStim set of facial expressions: judgments from untrained research participants. *Psychiatry Research*, **168** (3), 242–249.

Treisman, A.M. (1969) Strategies and models of selective attention. *Psychological Review*, **76**, 282–299.

Van Damme, S., Lorenz, J., Eccleston, C. *et al.* (2004) Fear-conditioned cues of impending pain facilitate attentional engagement. *Neurophysiologie Clinique-Clinical Neurophysiology*, **34** (1), 33–39.

Van den Hout, M., Tenney, N., Huygens, K. and DeJong, P. (1997) Preconscious processing bias in specific phobia. *Behaviour Research and Therapy*, **35** (1), 29–34.

Vasey, M.W., Daleiden, E.L., Williams, L.L. and Brown, L.M. (1995) Biased attention in childhood anxiety disorders – a preliminary study. *Journal of Abnormal Child Psychology*, **23** (2), 267–279.

Vasey, M.W., ElHag, N. and Daleiden, E.L. (1996) Anxiety and the processing of emotionally threatening stimuli: distinctive patterns of selective attention among high- and low-test-anxious children. *Child Development*, **67** (3), 1173–1185.

Wadlinger, H.A. and Isaacowitz, D.M. (2008) Looking happy: the experimental manipulation of a positive visual attention bias. *Emotion*, **8** (1), 121–126.

Waters, A.M., Lipp, O.V. and Spence, S.H. (2004) Attentional bias toward fear-related stimuli: an investigation with nonselected children and adults and children with anxiety disorders. *Journal of Experimental Child Psychology*, **89** (4), 320–337.

Waters, A.M., Lipp, O.V. and Spence, S.H. (2005) The effects of affective picture stimuli on blink modulation in adults and children. *Biological Psychology*, **68** (3), 257–281.

Waters, A.M., Mogg, K., Bradley, B.P. and Pine, D.S. (2008a) Attentional bias for emotional faces in children with generalized anxiety disorder. *Journal of the American Academy of Child and Adolescent Psychiatry*, **47** (4), 435–442.

Waters, A.M., Wharton, T.A., Zimmer-Gembeck, M.J. and Craske, M.G. (2008b) Threat-based cognitive biases in anxious children: comparison with non-anxious children before and after cognitive behavioural treatment. *Behaviour Research and Therapy*, **46** (3), 358–374.

Williams, J.M.G., Watts, F.N., MacLeod, C. and Mathews, A. (1988) *Cognitive Psychology and Emotional Disorders*, 1st edn, John Wiley & Sons, Chichester.

Williams, J.M.G., Watts, F.N., MacLeod, C. and Mathews, A. (1997) *Cognitive Psychology and Emotional Disorders*, 2nd edn,. John Wiley & Sons, Chichester.

Yiend, J. and Mathews, A. (2001) Anxiety and attention to threatening pictures. *Quarterly Journal of Experimental Psychology Section A-Human Experimental Psychology*, **54** (3), 665–681.

Yoon, K.L., Fitzgerald, D.A., Angstadt, M. *et al.* (2007) Amygdala reactivity to emotional faces at high and low intensity in generalized social phobia: a 4-Tesla functional MRI study. *Psychiatry Research-Neuroimaging*, **154** (1), 93–98.

You, J.S., Hu, S.Y., Chen, B.L. and Zhang, H.G. (2005) Serotonin transporter and tryptophan hydroxylase gene polymorphisms in Chinese patients with generalized anxiety disorder. *Psychiatric Genetics*, **15** (1), 7–11.

5

The Use of Visual Search Paradigms to Understand Attentional Biases in Childhood Anxiety

Nick Donnelly, Julie A. Hadwin,
Tamaryn Menneer and Helen J. Richards
nd5@soton.ac.uk

Introduction

The notion that affective (i.e. threatening) stimuli capture attention automatically is a feature of influential models of attention and anxiety (review by Bar-Haim *et al.*, 2007). Within the adult literature two distinct issues have been considered. First, researchers have asked whether there are objects and/or events that evolution has determined to be sufficiently threatening that detection has been automated. Such automation is defined as occurring in parallel and without capacity limitation, thus representing a qualitative difference in processing compared with the serial and limited capacity processing otherwise used. At the population level, this issue has been explored by examining whether threatening or negative faces are detected differently from non-threatening faces (e.g. Fox *et al.*, 2000), and whether spiders and snakes are detected in a different way from other animals and objects (e.g. Lipp and Waters, 2007). These threat objects are chosen for experimentation on the basis that they are found to be aversive in the general population. The second issue that has been explored is whether, through experience and conditioning, some objects or events have acquired significance for individuals with elevated anxiety, such that their level of anxiety influences target detection (e.g. Byrne and Eysenck, 1995; Gilboa-Schechtman, Foa and Amir, 1999).

In this review, we focus on how the visual search paradigm has been used to explore threat detection. Our interest is in visual search and threat detection in

Information Processing Biases and Anxiety: A Developmental Perspective Edited by Julie A. Hadwin and Andy P. Field
© 2010 John Wiley & Sons, Ltd.

childhood anxiety; however, there is little research that addresses this issue directly. Nevertheless, considering the literature on threat detection in adults, both within the population generally and for those individuals with heightened levels of anxiety, has allowed us to consider a framework that may be useful to understand the roles of development and anxiety in visual search for threat.

The Experimental Study of Visual Search in Anxiety and Development

The fundamental design of visual search studies requires searching for targets set amongst distractors. The response time (RT) and accuracy (% correct) of present and absent responses is measured. RT is typically used to compute a measure of search efficiency. Calculating the slope of change in RT as a function of the number of items in the display (set size) generates a search slope, where shallower slopes indicate more efficient search.

If participants know target identity in advance, then search is guided by a mental representation or template of the target, and is said to be 'top-down', for example, when participants are required to search for a specific category of emotional face set amongst neutral faces (e.g. Horstmann, 2007). If participants have to detect the odd-one-out from sets of distractors (participants are asked to find, for example, any emotional face amongst neutral faces), then search is said to be 'bottom-up' (e.g. Lundqvist and Öhman, 2005).

In most real-world search tasks, detection results from the conjoined activity of neural systems responsible for goal-driven (top-down) and salience-driven (bottom-up) search (Yantis, 1998). The goal- and salience-driven systems are synonymous with the anterior attentional system and posterior attentional systems, respectively (Posner and Petersen, 1990). Highlighting the significance of goals and salience for anxiety research, these same attentional systems form an important part of Attentional Control Theory (ACT; Eysenck *et al.*, 2007). ACT is a recent theoretical framework developed to understand attention in anxiety. Anxious individuals are proposed to spread their attention widely to enable them to monitor or attend to potential threat in their environment. This broadening of attention is suggested to reflect bottom-up (or stimulus driven) cognitive processing that operates at the cost of top-down (or goal directed) processing. Placing the visual search literature within this theoretical framework would suggest that heightened anxiety leads to poor attentional guidance in visual search and to the increased influence of bottom-up salience relative to top-down goals. Therefore, a key issue to explore in the context of ACT is the proposed increased influence of distractor salience for high relative to low anxious individuals. In this chapter, we will see evidence of this effect when individuals with heightened anxiety are searching for neutral targets amongst threatening distractors.

In terms of the developmental psychology of visual search there have been multiple studies showing that fundamental visual-search processes operate in infancy, although they become more efficient with age (Gerhardstein and

Rovee-Collier, 2002; Trick and Enns, 1998). One study, for example, explored developmental trends of top-down versus bottom-up search (Donnelly *et al.*, 2007). Donnelly *et al.* (2007) tested children in middle to late childhood on a range of bottom-up odd-one-out and top-down conjunction search tasks. With respect to the top-down tasks, they found that search slopes were inversely related to age, even after factoring out baseline differences in RT (defined as the intercept).[1] One interpretation of this finding is that search is guided more effectively with increasing age. With respect to bottom-up searches, the data showed that young children (6- to 7-year-olds) could not search for differences across three feature dimensions simultaneously (colour, orientation, size) without a cost, relative to search for differences in only one feature dimension. In addition, 6- to 7-year-olds responded to colour targets more quickly than orientation targets – a difference that was not found in any other age group. The evidence points to a limitation in young children's ability to monitor across multiple possible target dimensions effectively. In Donnelly *et al.*'s experiment, this limitation was resolved by focussing on the colour dimension (see also Pick and Frankel, 1973). In summary, there is evidence that the basic mechanisms of visual search are functional in infancy, but that visual guidance and the capacity to search simultaneously across multiple dimensions develops with age.

When considering the effect of anxiety and development on visual search for threat the effects are likely to be complex. Before considering any moderating effects of anxiety in search, the evidence of development in bottom-up and top-down search systems indicates a changing baseline to visual search across development.

Underlying Framework for Understanding Visual Search

Within research on visual search, three core questions have provided a framework for interpreting bottom-up and top-down search. First, is search parallel or serial? Second, does visual search operate with limited or unlimited capacity? Third, is visual search self-terminating or exhaustive? When considering these questions

---

[1] Although mathematically independent, there is a concern in developmental studies that the slopes might be inversely related to age simply because of differences in baseline RTs (as measured by intercept). In the same way that standard deviation tends to scale with overall RT, it is possible that RT/per item slopes might also be similarly affected by baseline differences in RT. One approach to this issue is to use intercept values as a covariate in the analysis of slopes (see Burack *et al.*, 2000 for a related argument when trying to establish baseline RTs) to ensure that any differences in slope magnitude are not a by-product of an uninteresting difference in simple reaction times, an effect known to be subject to developmental differences. By covarying out baseline differences across age groups, we can be sure that it is the development of the search process itself that is being tested rather than some effect of search efficiency being scaled with baseline differences in reaction time. In the study by Burack *et al.* (2000), where slope values were used as a covariate when analysing from the smallest set size condition only, no significant relationship was found between RT/per item slope and RT to the smallest set size. In contrast, when Donnelly *et al.* (2007) covaried intercept values in an analysis of RT/per item absent and present slopes, the covariate was significant for absent trials. These data suggest that some attempt to covary developmental differences in RT is appropriate to clarify effects of visual search alone.

in the context of the neural and psychological changes through maturation and learning in development and how these interact with psychopathology, the resolution of these questions is complex. Moreover, we believe that these questions cannot be answered using data from visual search experiments alone. For this reason, we make some comment on the processing architecture that is likely to underpin performance on all visual search tasks.

Despite the popularity of asking the three questions outlined above, there are a number of reasons why characterizing the processing architecture underlying visual search as parallel or serial, of limited or unlimited capacity, or self-terminating or exhaustive is problematic. Wolfe (1998) reviewed multiple visual search studies containing data from over 1 million trials and showed that slope gradients varied continuously in a unimodal distribution and could not be classified into slope distributions reflecting either parallel or serial search. In addition, experimental data show that target-absent decisions do not result from exhaustive searches, but rather from a complex judgement influenced by factors usually associated with signal detection theory, as well as both the perceived similarity of distractors to targets and the time since an error was made (Chun and Wolfe, 1996). Furthermore, making the decision that targets are present must be influenced by the rate of information accumulation and the target threshold to be reached (e.g. Ratcliff and McKoon, 1978). Therefore, decisions about target presence are based on factors that vary on a continuum, rather than comprising the discrete categories present in the three core questions.

Given the importance of these issues, we conclude that choosing between mutually exclusive processing architectures (i.e. parallel vs. serial, limited vs. unlimited, self-terminating vs. exhaustive) will always be problematic. Of course, we are not the first to point this out. In a series of papers, Townsend (1971, 2001) has shown that several parallel processing models can account for data that would, by these problematic classifications, have been taken as evidence for serial processing, namely, slope gradients of significant magnitude and target-absent slopes being greater than target-present slopes. A critical aspect to showing how data produced by parallel systems can take on many forms relates to the notion that decision thresholds, information processing rates towards thresholds for activating mental templates and decision criteria are dynamic. These considerations mean that data apparently indicative of serial and self-terminating processing (steep slopes, with absent slopes twice as steep as present slopes) could be generated by a parallel system with higher thresholds to make decisions about absent trials, or by a slower processing rate due to the absence of signal from the target.

In the context of the present discussion, we suggest that effects of maturation and learning on visual search should be understood as quantitative effects of parameter changes, rather than qualitative changes in processing or discrete shifts in architecture. Such parameters include the information processing rate and the threshold at which enough information has been acquired to signify a match with the known target for a decision about its presence to be made. Processing speed, for example, will tend to increase with age. Furthermore, given that threshold setting and decision criteria are probably reflective of goals set by the frontal attention system, the development of this system will also impact on the efficiency of visual search. Likewise, psychopathological states can also be understood as influencing these same parameters, through basic learning processes (see Chapter 11) or genetic influences (see Chapter 9).

One consequence of understanding the impact of changing parameters, thresholds and decision criteria on data from visual search experiments is that contrasting data patterns, which might be thought to require different processing architectures, in fact, do not. We should not, therefore, seek evidence for automated threat detection in a parallel unlimited capacity system to be contrasted with search for non-threat items using a serial and limited capacity system. Rather, we should seek to understand how quantitative changes to various measures influence visual search. Indeed, it is our view that Occam's razor demands acceptance of the fact that simple parameter changes are capable of generating the different patterns observed in visual search tasks: we will not, therefore, interpret any study as revealing data that demand acceptance of one processing architecture over another (e.g. Öhman, Flykt and Esteves, 2001; Öhman, Lundqvist and Esteves, 2001; Frischen, Eastwood and Smilek, 2008). Rather, development and psychopathology will be interpreted as potentially leading to changes in processing rate and decision thresholds.

There are manifestations of this same debate regarding processing architectures in discussions within psychological theories of visual search as to whether selection is early (e.g. Treisman and Gelade, 1980; Wolfe, Cave and Franzel, 1989) or late (e.g. Duncan and Humphreys, 1989) and those accounts which are not based on a view of a split between pre-attentive and attentive vision (e.g. Di Lollo et al., 2001). Early and late selection accounts share a view of the architecture of early vision: that basic features (e.g. colours, basic form features, movement) are represented in extrastriate cortex and form the basic building blocks of vision, but differ in the level of processing that is applied in parallel prior to selection. More recent theories of visual search have focussed on considering search efficiency as a trade-off between scale and resolution (e.g. Di Lollo et al., 2001; Nakayama and Joseph, 1998). These accounts are less wedded to a fixed architecture for early vision. For example, central to Di Lollo et al.'s (2001) account is the notion that perceptual input is handled by a set of dynamically configurable input filters, where these are set according to high-level goals (probably determined by prefrontal cortex). Under this account, selection is implemented via input filters for central and peripheral visual processing areas. The dynamic nature of input filters enables them to respond reasonably efficiently to the presence of complex feature conjunctions, so long as they are relevant to current goals and form part of the current task set.

In relation to the current chapter, dynamically configural input filters may change with maturation and learning, as well as with psychopathology. In this case, the moderating factors (i.e. learning and conditioning) that lead to changes in information processing are likely to be the same as those underpinning development and psychopathology. In this spirit, we seek evidence that (i) threat objects are detected faster than non-threat objects in the general population, (ii) raised anxiety levels further speeds the detection of threat and (iii) there is a developmental time course to threat detection that is influenced by anxiety.

Animals

There are multiple papers which suggest that search for phylogenetically threat-relevant items (e.g. snakes and spiders) is efficient whereas search for non-threat items (e.g. mushrooms or flowers) is not, for both adults and children (e.g. Öhman, Flykt and Esteves, 2001; LoBue and DeLoache, 2008; Waters, Lipp and Spence, 2008). It is a seductive argument that evolutionary threats, by their very nature, are detected efficiently. Reviewing the visual search literature this claim, however, does not stand up to close examination. Recent evidence suggests that the search advantage typically associated with phylogenetically threat-relevant stimuli can also be found with other object categories. For example, a threat advantage has been reported for objects only recently defined as threatening (e.g. guns and knives; Brosch and Sharma, 2005; Blanchette, 2006; Fox, Griggs and Mouchlianitis, 2007), as well as for non-threatening objects such as animals and fruits (e.g. Tipples et al., 2002).

These inconsistencies across studies led Cave and Batty (2006) to argue that findings across different categories of stimuli can be explained by the detection of simple features. In order to control for feature effects in visual search Batty, Cave and Pauli (2005) used an implicit association task (IAT; see Chapter 7) to explore search for threat-associated abstract stimuli and found no evidence for automatic attentional biases for these stimuli. A second factor that may contribute to any apparent differences in search efficiency is difference in category consistency. Lipp (2006) suggested that flower and mushroom categories are more heterogeneous than spider and snake categories and it is likely that there are differences in search efficiency resulting from category heterogeneity (e.g. Smith et al., 2005; Quinlan and Binney, 2008). If so, then the greater homogeneity in the threat-relevant categories will aid target detection relative to non-threat categories.

In conclusion, although some experiments indicate efficient detection of phylogenetically threatening animal targets, there are alternative accounts of these experiments. We conclude that the current evidence does not support the view that phylogenetically threatening animals are detected efficiently in the general population by virtue of their threat-related properties.

Faces

Experiments purporting to show qualitative difference in search for angry faces relative to other emotional faces (Hansen and Hansen, 1988; Öhman, Lundqvist and Esteves, 2001) have been the subject of detailed critique (Horstmann, 2007), successful replications (e.g. Schubo et al., 2006) and failures to replicate (Purcell, Stewart and Skov, 1996; Purcell and Stewart, 2002). The evidence for threat faces being processed in a qualitatively different fashion from non-threat faces is not robust. While we can accept that differences in the detection of angry and happy faces have been reported across several studies, these differences disappear when seemingly minor changes are made to the experimental paradigm (e.g. when face outlines are removed; Schubo et al., 2006). In other studies, differences between threat and non-threat faces remain even when faces are restructured to create non-face controls (Purcell and Stewart, 2002) or when faces are inverted and so do not convey emotion (e.g. Eastwood, Smilek and Merikle, 2001). These two facts support the view that findings interpreted as showing qualitative difference in the search for angry relative to other emotional faces are likely to result from simple feature differences (see Purcell and Stewart, 2002).

A growing body of work has found more efficient search for angry versus happy faces (e.g. Hahn and Gronlund, 2007, Experiment 2). These studies are also open to the same kind of critique as offered above for qualitative differences in search for angry versus other emotional faces. For example, differences in RTs between emotional expressions are maintained when faces are inverted (Calvo and Nummenmaa, 2008). Often, an effect added to provide further weight to the special status of angry faces is the search asymmetry (Treisman and Gormican, 1988) between detecting angry faces embedded in happy face distractors and happy face targets embedded in angry face distractors (e.g. Hahn and Gronlund, 2007; Horstmann, 2007). Of course, it remains possible that it is feature differences between angry and other emotional faces that account for this effect. However, a factor contributing to the occurrence of these search asymmetries is the fact that angry faces also hold attention and so acts to slow down search for other emotional faces when used as distractors (e.g. Fox et al., 2001).

Resolving the question of whether specific facial expressions are captured or held by attention has also been addressed using eye movement methodology but the results have been equivocal. Work from our own laboratory by Richards, Benson and Hadwin (Unpublished) has found that initial saccades to detect angry target faces (presented in angry inverted distractors) were more accurate compared with initial saccades to neutral target faces, especially when search was more difficult (i.e. with set sizes of one target and either three or seven distractor faces, compared with a set size of two with one face and one distractor). Other eye movement studies have also found that negative target faces are fixated more rapidly compared with positive target faces (Reynolds et al., 2009). However, other studies have failed to find any effect of facial expression (Hunt et al., 2007) using eye movement paradigms or have found that happy, surprised and disgusted target faces are fixated more rapidly compared with angry, fearful and sad target faces (Calvo, Nummenmaa and Avero, 2008). For example, Hunt et al. (2007, Experiment 1) asked participants to orient attention to faces that changed from a neutral to a task-relevant emotional expression (angry or happy). At the same time as the target change happened, there was also a task-irrelevant change in one of the distractor faces from neutral to an emotional expression that was to be ignored. The experiment was performed with upright and inverted stimuli. Hunt et al. found no evidence that angry target faces attracted attention more than happy faces. Nor did they find evidence that task-irrelevant angry faces distracted attention more than task-irrelevant happy faces. Their results suggest that anger has no special status in terms of attracting attention.

In conclusion, studies in the general population have found some evidence for angry faces leading to more efficient visual search compared with happy faces. This finding has also been replicated in children (see Hadwin et al., 2003; Waters and Lipp, 2008b). However, the effects are relatively modest and are certainly not sufficient to argue that anger is detected in a qualitatively different manner to happiness. Indeed, when considering the power of visual search studies to provide evidence in support of various processing architectures, we argued that it is impossible, in principle, for visual search experiments to provide this evidence, even if it were true. There is some evidence that there is increased efficiency of detection of angry faces relative to happy faces when set in the context of other emotional faces: an effect that might result from difficulties disengaging attention from angry face distractors. However, there is no reliable evidence of generalized efficient searching to other categories of evolutionarily important threat objects.

Visual Search for Threat Faces and Objects in Adults and Children with Anxiety

We have argued that search efficiency is subject to the influence of change in information processing speed, the threshold for matching targets to mental templates and decision criteria for rejecting target-absent displays. Each of these parameters could be subject to influence from anxiety. In other words, effects of threat that may be difficult to show in group studies within the general population might be made more transparent in the context of those individuals more sensitive to threat. In the next section, we review findings from studies of threat detection with anxious individuals.

Animals

Adult anxiety

Empirical work suggests that individual differences in spider and snake fear influence search for feared threat-relevant target stimuli (Öhman, Flykt and Esteves, 2001; Flykt and Caldara, 2006; Soares, Esteves and Flykt, 2008). Öhman, Flykt and Esteves (2001) identified participants who scored high in self-reported spider or snake fear and compared performance with non-fearful participants. Responses to threat targets (spiders and snakes) were compared to non-threat targets, in displays comprising threat targets set amongst non-threat distractors and vice versa. Öhman *et al.* reported that all participants were faster to detect threat-relevant targets compared with threat-irrelevant targets. In addition, participants with specific fears were faster to detect the feared threat-relevant target compared with the non-feared threat-relevant target (e.g. the detection of spider (vs. snakes) targets in spider fearful participants), whilst non-fearful participants displayed comparable reaction times for spider and snake targets. They concluded that the threat advantage was enhanced in fearful participants, suggesting that specific fears are associated with enhanced attentional engagement with feared threatening stimuli in the environment.

An additional finding of Öhman, Flykt and Esteves (2001) was that participants with specific fears were less accurate than control participants when detecting threat-irrelevant targets and concluded that the feared distractors interfered with target detection. This latter result is consistent with the proposal that fearful individuals have difficulties disengaging from feared stimuli. However, this finding has been explored in more detail by others (e.g. Miltner *et al.*, 2004; Lipp and Waters, 2007). Following Öhman, Flykt and Esteves (2001), Lipp and Waters (2007; Experiment 2) identified a spider fearful and snake fearful group. They asked participants to indicate the presence or absence of a cat target amongst horse, fish or bird distractors. On some trials, displays also contained a single threat-relevant (snake or spider) distractor. Participants were slower to detect targets in the presence of a non-feared threat-relevant distractor (compared with no distractor), and a feared threat-relevant distractor caused additional slowing in detection (compared with a non-feared threat-relevant distractor). Lipp and Waters (2007) concluded that the adverse effect of individual threat-relevant distractors was selectively enhanced in fearful participants, although whether this effect was caused by individual distractors capturing or holding attention remains unclear. This finding has recently been replicated among children aged 9–13 years using the same methodology (see Waters and Lipp, 2008a).

In relation to attentional engagement, Miltner *et al.* (2004) used a visual search task to ask individuals with and without spider phobia to search for spider or mushroom target stimuli displayed amongst flowers. In order to explore whether feared distractors would slow down search times for targets, a spider or mushroom distractor replaced one flower distractor in some displays. The results showed that spider phobics were slower to find target mushrooms in the presence of an individual spider distractor both compared with non-phobic controls and compared with all other types of search. Furthermore, spider phobia was associated with eye movements to individual spider distractors before fixating the target, with these participants making these eye movements to spider and mushroom distractors on 30.2% and 10.8% of the trials respectively. Corresponding figures in the non-phobic control participants were 12.2% to individual spider distractors and 14.1% to individual mushroom distractors. These data indicate that distraction by feared objects was specific to the phobic group and was not characteristic of the sample as a whole.

The relationship between anxiety and attentional disengagement has been investigated using visual search in a number of studies (e.g. Gerdes, Alpers and Pauli, 2008; Rinck *et al.*, 2003, 2005; Rinck and Becker, 2005; Pineles *et al.*, 2007). Typically, individual differences in attentional disengagement were investigated by comparing the time taken to detect targets amongst different types of distractors: feared threat-relevant, positive or neutral. In general, these studies have found that anxious (compared with non-anxious) individuals are slower to detect a target when the display contains feared threat-relevant distractors. For example, Rinck *et al.* (2005) found that spider fearful individuals were slower to indicate the presence of a target amongst spider distractors compared with non-fearful individuals. Rinck *et al.* also explored participants' eye movements during visual search. They reported that spider fearful individuals fixated on the spider distractors for significantly longer than controls. In contrast, there was no significant difference between the groups in reaction times or gaze duration for butterfly or beetle distractors. Slower disengagement from feared threat-relevant distractors has been replicated in adults with post-traumatic stress disorder (Pineles *et al.*, 2007), generalized anxiety disorder (Rinck *et al.*, 2003), social phobia and depression (Rinck and Becker, 2005; Baños, Quero and Botella, 2008) in visual search tasks using disorder-relevant word stimuli.

Faces

Adult anxiety

As for threat object search, findings from studies with schematic and photographic faces have generally reported an enhanced threat advantage in anxious individuals relative to controls (e.g. Byrne and Eysenck, 1995; Eastwood *et al.*, 2005; Juth *et al.*, 2005, Experiment 5; Gilboa-Schectman, Foa and Amir, 1999). In addition, studies have also found specificity of these effects between anxiety disorders. Eastwood *et al.* (2005), for example, found that the search slope for negative target faces was significantly shallower than the search slope for positive target faces in individuals with social phobia or panic disorder. There was no difference between the search slopes for negative and positive faces in a non-clinical control group or individuals with obsessive–compulsive disorder.

Further research has suggested that individuals with social anxiety are slower (Gilboa-Schectman, Foa and Amir, 1999) and less accurate (Juth *et al.*, 2005) in detecting happy faces. Similarly, Suslow *et al.* (2004) found that individuals with comorbid anxiety were slower to detect positive faces compared with control participants.

As with visual search for threat objects, we should also consider whether anxiety influences attentional engagement and/or disengagement from threat faces. With respect to attentional engagement, work from our own laboratory (Richards, Benson and Hadwin Unpublished) has used eye movement methodology to explore search for photographs of angry, happy and neutral faces (amongst inverted face distractors) in adults with elevated social anxiety. Our findings extended previous work demonstrating attentional capture to threat faces in individuals with elevated anxiety to show that the initial orienting response (i.e. the first eye movement) to angry faces was more accurate compared with happy faces in individuals with higher levels of social anxiety. This effect was moderated by attentional control, with the threat advantage emerging most clearly in individuals with high social anxiety and low attentional control. This work indicates that both increased anxiety and attentional control should be explored when investigating attentional processes to threat.

Considering disengagement from distractors, Byrne and Eysenck (1995) found evidence of inter- and intra-group differences in anxiety: high trait anxious (relative to low trait anxious) participants were slower to detect a happy target among angry distractors and, furthermore, they were slower to detect a happy target among angry distractors compared with neutral distractors. This intra-group difference was not found for low trait anxious participants. This finding suggests that there is delayed disengagement from angry faces in anxious individuals (Byrne and Eysenck, 1995).

Childhood anxiety

Few studies have used the visual search paradigm to explore attentional biases to threat in childhood anxiety. Work within our own laboratory has found that increased trait anxiety in children aged 7–10 years of age was associated with flatter slopes to decide when angry schematic (Experiment 1) or cartoon-like faces (Experiment 2) were absent (Hadwin *et al.*, 2003). In addition, it highlighted that this pattern of results was not associated with elevated depressed affect in this group of children. There was no evidence of any relationship between anxiety and target detection for threat faces.

A further study did, however, highlight evidence for increased efficiency for the detection of threat faces in anxious children. Perez-Olivas, Stevenson and Hadwin (2008) used the visual search paradigm to explore links between parenting, childhood anxiety and search times for angry versus happy or neutral schematic faces. The study found no direct links between over-involved parenting and elevated separation anxiety in children. However, it did reveal a partially mediated pathway linking parental over-involvement to increased efficiency to detect angry versus happy or neutral schematic faces in children, which was associated with increased separation anxiety. This mediated model emerged across development and was most evident in children aged 10 years and above (see Kindt and van den Hout, 2001, described in Chapter 3, for a developmental argument related to the emergence of attentional biases). The results are consistent with theoretical models that aim to understand links between parenting, information processing and psychopathology in childhood (e.g. Hudson and Rapee, 2004). Specifically, they indicate that attentional biases for threat partially mediate a more distal relationship between parenting factors and anxiety in adolescence.

Further research with children has found that those with low anxiety were faster to search for angry (compared with sad and happy) among neutral distractors (Waters and Lipp, 2008b). Those with high anxiety were faster to find angry and sad target faces compared with happy faces among neutral distractors. This study indicates a more general influence of anxiety in search with children that extends to a broader category of negative emotions, where this result warrants further research.

Summary and Discussion

The research literature suggests that several conclusions can be supported in relation to adults with and without anxiety. Research using visual search paradigms does not generally support the proposition that visual search has been automated for objects determined as threat objects through evolution. Second, there is evidence of a moderating influence of anxiety on visual search for threat objects, such that individuals with high versus low anxiety respond differently to the presentation of threat objects. Several papers support the proposition that elevated anxiety is typically associated with enhanced detection of and slower disengagement from threat targets. Finally, high levels of anxiety are associated with speeded termination times on target-absent trials where the distractors are neutral.

These conclusions can be understood within the explanatory framework outlined above. Learning history in anxious individuals seems to adjust target template thresholds (see Field, Crompton and Rohani, 2009), information processing speed and decision criteria so that we detect and hold on to objects likely to be threatening. One future goal for research should be the pursuit of neurobiological or neurophysiological data gathered in response to presentations of threat objects/faces. This research could explore how variations in, for example, the amplitude or latency or event-related potential (ERP) markers associated with object categorization of threat and non-threat items might also correlate with performance on visual search tasks for these same items. A recent study used functional magnetic resonance imaging (fMRI) to measure amygdala reactivity in relation to detecting positive and negative faces amongst neutral faces. It used right amygdala reactivity to photographs of emotional fearful faces as an index of 'neurobiologically defined threat sensitivity' (Ohrmann et al., 2007, p. 57) and looked at links between this index and search times for positive and negative faces. They reported that amygdala reactivity to threat was associated with faster reaction times both to find negative faces and to terminate search in the absence of a target face, suggesting that fundamental aspects of neurobiology and neurophysiology may be influencing visual search behaviour.

With respect to development, some of our conclusions based on a review of the adult literature have been supported with studies of anxiety in children. However, the lack of evidence in relation to any specific conclusion has more to do with the absence of studies and not the likelihood that conclusions will hold in children as they do in adults. Assuming the same explanatory framework is adopted and the appropriate statistical controls are employed for studying visual search across different ages, then our default position would be that all other conclusions would hold for children as they do for adults. It is possible that these effects may emerge across childhood (see Perez-Olivas et al., 2008), but further research is required to explore attentional processes across anxiety within a developmental framework.

This review has demonstrated the utility of the visual search methodology for exploring threat detection. Across our review of the work using this paradigm, the use of visual search has been reasonably standard. However, other work in experimental psychology has utilized visual search in novel ways, where these studies are likely to be relevant to future work on anxiety and development. Examples include, for example, searching for two or more targets and searching for targets that appear at very low frequency. There is curiously little research on multiple-target search (e.g. Kaplan and Carvellas, 1965; Schneider and Shiffrin, 1977; Dzmura, 1991) with and without threat items. An exception to this general rule are the studies of Menneer et al. (2009) who explored simultaneous visual search for two categories of threat item (guns/knives and bombs) with only one target appearing on each trial. The task was designed to simulate the visual search of X-ray baggage screeners. This study demonstrated that simultaneous search for two types of threat led to significant costs in accuracy, relative to single-target visual search baselines. The so-called dual-target cost was resistant to change over many thousands of trials, and was reliable when targets differed from each other such that the mental representation guiding search was so coarse that to incorporate both targets it also included distractor items similar to both targets.

Comparable dual-target studies can be designed in domains that are of more immediate relevance to anxiety researchers. For example, searching for emotional faces set amongst neutral faces can easily be characterized as searching for happy or sad, angry or worried faces set amongst neutral faces. In fact, Öhman, Lundqvist and Esteves (2001) conducted exactly this study, except that no condition was run in which participants searched only for a single type of target and so the cost of searching for multiple targets relative to searching for a single target remains unknown. Within the context of this task, we predict that anxiety may preserve detection for threat-related targets at single-target levels in dual-target search, but no preservation of performance would be found with non-threat targets in dual-target search.

The dual-target search paradigm could also be used to investigate biases in anxiety by manipulating the frequency at which threat or non-threat targets appear across trials. In single-target search, manipulation of target frequency produces the prevalence effect, in which targets that appear infrequently tend to be missed on those few trials when they are present (Wolfe et al., 2007). With regard to the prevalence effect in visual search, in which infrequent targets are often missed, a key question for anxiety researchers is whether threat mitigates this effect. In addition, the effect of different relative target prevalence in dual-target search provides a window into the salience of threatening items for high versus low anxiety participants. While control participants would perform well on the high prevalence target and poorly on the low prevalence target, high anxiety participants might be predicted to show preference for the threatening target over the neutral target and achieve better performance on threat targets compared with controls, thus strengthening or attenuating the effect of relative target prevalence. Further work can explore whether this better performance is linked to developmental effects of anxiety in children.

One question we have sought to address is whether anxiety correlates with estimates for the occurrence of low frequency threat targets. Exploratory studies (Menneer and Donnelly, 2009) have used face stimuli that displayed negative, potentially threatening emotions (fearful and angry) and positive emotions (happy). Participants searched for the presence of an emotional face amongst distractor faces with neutral expressions. The relative frequencies of the three emotions (fearful, angry and happy) were manipulated between participants, such that one emotion was presented on 50% of target-present trials, while the other two were presented on 25% of target-present trials. After completing the task, participants judged the percentage frequencies of the three emotions throughout the search task, with the requirement of summing the frequencies to 100%. For half of the participants, this judgement was made immediately, and for the other half, it was made following a 10-minute filler task (sudoku). For each emotion, the ratio of the recalled frequency to the actual frequency was calculated as a measure of overestimation of the frequency of occurrence. Correlations revealed that when participants experienced a delay between the task and recall, those with high trait anxiety levels (as measured by Profile of Moods trait questionnaire, McNair, Lorr and Droppleman, 1981) underestimated the frequency of positive emotions compared with those with low anxiety levels. Given that estimates summed to 100%, high anxiety participants were therefore overestimating the frequency of negative emotions.

In conclusion, anxiety has been found to influence visual search for threat in the ways we have outlined above. Effects of anxiety on search are reasonably easy to explain using simple concepts that relate learning to processing rate, template thresholds and decision criteria. The visual search paradigm has a lot to offer to explore links between anxiety and visual search (e.g. in relation to dual-target search and target prevalence). In addition, the paradigm is ideal for exploring selective attention and attentional disengagement in development, since the paradigms used with adult samples do not need to be adapted for use with children.

Acknowledgements

An Economic and Social Research Council studentship number PTA-031-2006-00179 awarded to Helen Richards and funding from the School of Psychology, University of Southampton awarded to Tammy Menneer supported the writing of this chapter.

References

Bañnos, R.M., Quero, S. and Botella, C. (2008) Detection and distraction effects for threatening information in social phobia and change after treatment. *Depression and Anxiety*, **25**, 55–63.

Bar-Haim, Y., Lamy, D., Pergamin, L. *et al.* (2007) Threat-related attentional bias in anxious and nonanxious individuals: a meta-analytic study. *Psychological Bulletin*, **133**, 1–24.

Batty, M.J., Cave, K.R. and Pauli, P. (2005) Abstract stimuli associated with threat through conditioning cannot be detected preattentively. *Emotion*, **5**, 418–430.

Blanchette, I. (2006) Snakes, spiders, guns, and syringes: how specific are evolutionary constraints on the detection of threatening stimuli? *Quarterly Journal of Experimental Psychology*, **59**, 1484–1504.

Brosch, T. and Sharma, D. (2005) The role of fear-relevant stimuli in visual search: a comparison of phylogenetic and ontogenetic stimuli. *Emotion*, **5**, 360–364.

Burack, J.A., Enns, J.T., Iarocci, G. and Randolph, B. (2000) Age differences in visual search for compound patterns: long- versus short-range grouping. *Developmental Psychology*, **36**, 731–740.

Byrne, A. and Eysenck, M.W. (1995) Trait anxiety, anxious mood and threat detection. *Cognition and Emotion*, **9**, 549–562.

Calvo, M.G. and Nummenmaa, L. (2008) Detection of emotional faces: salient physical features guide effective visual search. *Journal of Experimental Psychology-General*, **137**, 471–494.

Calvo, M.G., Nummenmaa, L. and Avero, P. (2008) Visual search of emotional faces: eye-movement assessment of component processes. *Experimental Psychology*, **55**, 359–370.

Cave, K.R. and Batty, M.J. (2006) From searching for features to searching for threat: drawing the boundary between preattentive and attentive vision. *Visual Cognition*, **14**, 629–646.

Chun, M.M. and Wolfe, J.M. (1996) Just say no: how are visual searches terminated when there is no target present? *Cognitive Psychology*, **30**, 39–78.

Di Lollo, V., Kawahara, J., Zuvic, S.M. and Visser, T.A. (2001) The preattentive emperor has no clothes: a dynamic redressing. *Journal of Experimental Psychology: General*, **130**, 479–492.

Donnelly, N., Cave, K., Greenway, R. *et al.* (2007) Visual search in children and adults: top-down and bottom-up mechanisms. *Quarterly Journal of Experimental Psychology*, **60**, 120–136.

Duncan, J. and Humphreys, G.W. (1989) Visual-search and stimulus similarity. *Psychological Review*, **96**, 433–458.

Dzmura, M. (1991) Color in visual-search. *Vision Research*, **31**, 951–966.

Eastwood, J.D., Smilek, D. and Merikle, P.M. (2001) Differential attentional guidance by unattended faces expressing positive and negative emotion. *Perception and Psychophysics*, **63**, 1004–1013.

Eastwood, J.D., Smilek, D., Oakman, J.M. *et al.* (2005) Individuals with social phobia are biased to become aware of negative faces. *Visual Cognition*, **12**, 159–179.

Eysenck, M.W., Derakshan, N., Santos, R. and Calvo, M.G. (2007) Anxiety and cognitive performance: attentional control theory. *Emotion*, **7**, 336–353.

Field, A.P., Crompton, K. and Rohani, S. (2009) Finding the beast: visual search for novel animals after verbal threat information in children. Manuscript in preparation.

Flykt, A. and Caldara, R. (2006) Tracking fear in snake and spider fearful participants during visual search: a multi-response domain study. *Cognition and Emotion*, **20**, 1075–1091.

Fox, E., Griggs, L. and Mouchlianitis, E. (2007) The detection of fear-relevant stimuli: are guns noticed as quickly as snakes? *Emotion*, **7**, 691–696.

Fox, E., Lester, V., Russo, R. *et al.* (2000) Facial expressions of emotion: are angry faces detected more efficiently? *Cognition and Emotion*, **14**, 61–92.

Fox, E., Russo, R., Bowles, R. and Dutton, K. (2001) Do threatening stimuli draw or hold visual attention in subclinical anxiety? *Journal of Experimental Psychology: General*, **130**, 681–700.

Frischen, A., Eastwood, J.D. and Smilek, D. (2008) Visual search for faces with emotional expressions. *Psychological Bulletin*, **134**, 662–676.

Gerdes, A.B.M., Alpers, G.W. and Pauli, P. (2008) When spiders appear suddenly: spider-phobic patients are distracted by task-irrelevant spiders. *Behaviour Research and Therapy*, **46**, 174–187.

Gerhardstein, P. and Rovee-Collier, C. (2002) The development of visual search in infants and very young children. *Journal of Experimental Child Psychology*, **81**, 194–215.

Gilboa-Schechtman, E., Foa, E.B. and Amir, N. (1999) Attentional biases for facial expressions in social phobia: the face-in-the-crowd paradigm. *Cognition and Emotion*, **13**, 305–318.

Hadwin, J.A., Donnelly, N., French, C.C. *et al.* (2003) The influence of children's self-report trait anxiety and depression on visual search for emotional faces. *Journal of Child Psychology and Psychiatry and Allied Disciplines*, **44**, 432–444.

Hahn, S. and Gronlund, S.D. (2007) Top-down guidance in visual search for facial expressions. *Psychonomic Bulletin and Review*, **14**, 159–165.

Hansen, C.H. and Hansen, R.D. (1988) Finding the face in the crowd: an anger superiority effect. *Journal of Personality and Social Psychology*, **54**, 917–924.

Horstmann, G. (2007) Preattentive face processing: what do visual search experiments with schematic faces tell us? *Visual Cognition*, **15**, 799–833.

Hudson, J.L. and Rapee, R.M. (2004) From anxious temperament to disorder: an etiological model of generalized anxiety disorder, in *Generalized Anxiety Disorder: Advances in Research and Practice* (eds R.G. Heimberg, C.L. Turk and D.S. Mennin), Guildford Press, New York, pp. 51–74.

Hunt, A.R., Cooper, R.M., Hungr, C. and Kingstone, A. (2007) The effect of emotional faces on eye movements and attention. *Visual Cognition*, **15**, 513–531.

Juth, P., Lundqvist, D., Karlsson, A. and Öhman, A. (2005) Looking for foes and friends: perceptual and emotional factors when finding a face in the crowd. *Emotion*, **5**, 379–395.

Kaplan, I.T. and Carvellas, T. (1965) Scanning for multiple targets. *Perceptual and Motor Skills*, **21**, 239–243.

Kindt, M. and van den Hout, M. (2001) Selective attention and anxiety: a perspective on developmental issues and the causal status. *Journal of Psychopathology and Behavioral Assessment*, **23**, 193–202.

Lipp, O.V. (2006) Of snakes and flowers: does preferential detection of pictures of fear-relevant animals in visual search reflect on fear-relevance? *Emotion*, **6**, 296–308.

Lipp, O.V. and Waters, A.M. (2007) When danger lurks in the background: attentional capture by animal fear-relevant distractors is specific and selectively enhanced by animal fear. *Emotion*, **7**, 192–200.

LoBue, V. and DeLoache, J.S. (2008) Detecting the snake in the grass: attention to fear-relevant stimuli by adults and young children. *Psychological Science*, **19**, 284–289.

Lundqvist, D. and Öhman, A. (2005) Emotion regulates attention: the relation between facial configurations, facial emotion, and visual attention. *Visual Cognition*, **12**, 51–84.

McNair, D.M., Lorr, M. and Droppleman, L.F. (1981) *Manual for the Profile of Mood States*. Educational and Industrial Testing Service, San Diego, CA.

Menneer, T., Cave, K. and Donnelly, N. (2009). The cost of searching for multiple targets: effects of practice and target similarity. *Journal of Experimental Psychology: Applied* **15**, 125–139.

Menneer, T. and Donnelly, N. (2009) Effects of anxiety on perceived frequency of negative emotions. Manuscript in preparation.

Miltner, W.H.R., Krieschel, S., Hecht, H. *et al.* (2004) Eye movements and behavioral responses to threatening and nonthreatening stimuli during visual search in phobic and nonphobic subjects. *Emotion*, **4**, 323–339.

Nakayama, K. and Joseph, J.S. (1998) Attention, pattern recognition, and pop-out visual search, in *The Attentive Brain* (eds R. Parasuraman and R. Parasuraman), The MIT Press, Cambridge, MA, pp. 279–298.

Öhman, A., Flykt, A. and Esteves, F. (2001) Emotion drives attention: detecting the snake in the grass. *Journal of Experimental Psychology: General*, **130**, 466–478.

Öhman, A., Lundqvist, D. and Esteves, F. (2001) The face in the crowd revisited: a threat advantage with schematic stimuli. *Journal of Personality and Social Psychology*, **80**, 381–396.

Ohrmann, P., Rauch, A.V., Bauer, J. *et al.* (2007) Threat sensitivity as assessed by automatic amygdala response to fearful faces predicts speed of visual search for facial expression. *Experimental Brain Research*, **183**, 51–59.

Perez-Olivas, G., Stevenson, J. and Hadwin, J.A. (2008) Do anxiety-related attentional biases mediate the link between maternal over involvement and separation anxiety in children? *Cognition and Emotion*, **22**, 509–521.

Pick, A.D. and Frankel, G.W. (1973) A study of strategies of visual attention in children. *Developmental Psychology*, **9**, 348–357.

Pineles, S.L., Shipherd, J.C., Welch, L.P. and Yovel, I. (2007) The role of attentional biases in PTSD: is it interference or facilitation? *Behaviour Research and Therapy*, **45**, 1903–1913.

Posner, M.I. and Petersen, S.E. (1990) The attention system of the human brain. *Annual Review of Neuroscience*, **13**, 25–42.

Purcell, D.G. and Stewart, A.L. (2002) The face in the crowd: yet another confound. Poster, presented at the 43rd Annual Meeting of the Psychonomic Society, Kansas City.

Purcell, D.G., Stewart, A.L. and Skov, R.B. (1996) It takes a confounded face to pop out of a crowd. *Perception*, **25**, 1091–1108.

Quinlan, P. and Binney, J. (2008) Category search efficiency is, in part, determined by mental grouping. Presented at the 25th Anniversary Annual British Psychological Society Cognitive Section Conference, Southampton, UK.

Ratcliff, R. and Mckoon, G. (1978) Priming in item recognition: evidence for propositional structure of sentences. *Journal of Verbal Learning and Verbal Behavior*, **17**, 403–417.

Reynolds, M.G., Eastwood, J.D., Partanen, M. *et al.* (2009). Monitoring eye movements while searching for affective faces. *Visual Cognition*, **17**, 318–333.

Richards, H.J., Benson, V. and Hadwin, J.A. The effects of social anxiety and attentional control on eye movements in visual search for emotional faces. (Unpublished).

Rinck, M. and Becker, E.S. (2005) A comparison of attentional biases and memory biases in women with social phobia and major depression. *Journal of Abnormal Psychology*, **114**, 62–74.

Rinck, M., Becker, E.S., Kellermann, J. and Roth, W.T. (2003) Selective attention in anxiety: distraction and enhancement in visual search. *Depression and Anxiety*, **18**, 18–28.

Rinck, M., Reinecke, A., Ellwart, T. *et al.* (2005) Speeded detection and increased distraction in fear of spiders: Evidence from eye movements. *Journal of Abnormal Psychology*, **114**, 235–248.

Schneider, W. and Shiffrin, R.M. (1977) Controlled and automatic human information-processing I. Detection, search, and attention. *Psychological Review*, **84**, 1–66.

Schubo, A., Gendolla, G.H.E., Meinecke, C. and Abele, A.E. (2006) Detecting emotional faces and features in a visual search paradigm: are faces special? *Emotion*, **6**, 246–256.

Shiffrin, R.M. and Schneider, W. (1977) Controlled and automatic human information-processing II. Perceptual learning, automatic attending, and a general theory. *Psychological Review*, **84**, 127–190.

Smith, J.D., Redford, J.S., Washburn, D.A. and Taglialatela, L.A. (2005) Specific-token effects in screening tasks: possible implications for aviation security. *Journal of Experimental Psychology: Learning, Memory and Cognition*, **31**, 1171–1185.

Soares, S.C., Esteves, F. and Flykt, A. (2008) Fear, but not fear-relevance, modulates reaction times in visual search with animal distractors. *Journal of Anxiety Disorders*, **23**, 136–144.

Suslow, T., Dannlowski, U., Lalee-Mentzel, J. *et al.* (2004) Spatial processing of facial emotion in patients with unipolar depression: a longitudinal study. *Journal of Affective Disorders*, **83**, 59–63.

Tipples, J., Young, A.W., Quinlan, P. *et al.* (2002) Searching for threat. *Quarterly Journal of Experimental Psychology Section A: Human Experimental Psychology*, **55**, 1007–1026.

Townsend, J.T. (1971) A note on the identifiability of parallel and serial processes. *Perception and Psychophysics*, **10**, 161–163.

Townsend, J.T. (2001) A clarification of self-terminating versus exhaustive variances in serial and parallel models. *Perception and Psychophysics*, **63**, 1101–1106.

Treisman, A.M. and Gelade, G. (1980) Feature-integration theory of attention. *Cognitive Psychology*, **12**, 97–136.

Treisman, A. and Gormican, S. (1988) Feature analysis in early vision: evidence from search asymmetries. *Psychological Review*, **95**, 15–48.

Trick, L.M. and Enns, J.T. (1998) Lifespan changes in attention: the visual search task. *Cognitive Development*, **13**, 369–386.

Waters, A.M. and Lipp, O.V. (2008a) The influence of animal fear on attentional capture by fear-relevant animal stimuli in children. *Behaviour Research and Therapy*, **46**, 114–121.

Waters, A.M. and Lipp, O.V. (2008b) Visual search for emotional faces in children. *Cognition and Emotion*, **22**, 1306–1326.

Waters, A.M., Lipp, O. and Spence, S.H. (2008) Visual search for animal fear-relevant stimuli in children. *Australian Journal of Psychology*, **60**, 112–125.

Wolfe, J.M. (1998) What can 1 million trials tell us about visual search? *Psychological Science*, **9**, 33–39.

Wolfe, J.M., Cave, K.R. and Franzel, S.L. (1989) Guided search: an alternative to the feature integration model for visual-search. *Journal of Experimental Psychology-Human Perception and Performance*, **15**, 419–433.

Wolfe, J.M., Horowitz, T.S., Van Wert, M.J. *et al.* (2007) Low target prevalence is a stubborn source of errors in visual search tasks. *Journal of Experimental Psychology: General*, **136**, 623–638.

Yantis, S. (1998) The attentive brain. *Nature*, **395**, 857–858.

6

Using Eye Tracking Methodology in Children with Anxiety Disorders

Tina In-Albon and Silvia Schneider
tina.in-albon@unibas.ch

The first studies of eye movements, conducted using direct observations, go back as far as the 1800s. Thereafter, the process of reading was observed and found not to involve a smooth sweeping of the eyes along the text, but to consist of a series of short stops (fixations) and quick movements (saccades). The scientific methodology has since advanced considerably. From corneal reflection for objective eye measurements in 1901, contact lenses were used to improve accuracy in the 1950s. This invasive measurement relied on physical contact to the eyeball and, although it provided a sensitive measurement, it required wearing contact lenses and was sometimes painful. Non-invasive (also called remote) eye trackers rely on the measurement of visible features of the eye, for example, the pupil or a corneal reflection of closely positioned, directed light source. Video-based corneal reflection eye trackers (head or table mounted) are currently the most practical devices. Similarly, the areas of applications for eye tracking studies have also increased and are diverse. Application areas are usability studies, advertising testing and psychological research, including research on infants, reading, clinical research on schizophrenia and patients with frontal brain damages.

The current chapter provides an overview of the eye tracking methods. It highlights technical issues to be considered when using this task in child samples, and reviews the use of eye tracking in individuals with anxiety disorders, as well as current research of attentional biases in childhood anxiety with reference to eye tracking. Suggestions for future research are also made. Because eye tracking studies in children and adolescents are still very rare, the chapter also includes results of studies with adult populations.

Information Processing Biases and Anxiety: A Developmental Perspective Edited by Julie A. Hadwin and Andy P. Field
© 2010 John Wiley & Sons, Ltd.

Eye Tracker in Anxiety Research: What is the Idea?

The eye tracker is a device for measuring eye positions, eye movements and pupil dilation and assesses either the point of gaze ('where we are looking') or the motion of an eye relative to the head.

The general rationale for relying on these visual behaviours is based on the idea that the area one looks at is closely tied to what one sees. Although the direction of gaze is not perfectly correlated with the uptake of visual information, there is a strong presumption that the direction of gaze can provide important information about visual stimuli (Aslin and McMurray, 2004). Therefore, it can be assumed that by tracking someone's eye movements, we can follow the path of visual attention deployed by the observer (Just and Carpenter, 1976). This process may give us some insight into what the observer found interesting and what drew and held his or her attention, and it may provide some clues to how a person perceived the viewed stimuli over a period of time. Pupillary response is a physiological correlate of cognitive activity in that the pupil dilates as the subject gazes at a point which stimulates cognition.

The Association of Anxiety and Attention

One of the most important functions of anxiety is to facilitate the early detection of threat in potentially dangerous environments, enabling the individual to react quickly.

The information processing approach assumes that there is a competition within the processing system between various streams of information, due to capacity or resource limitations. This competition leads to a selection of information, commonly referred to as *selective attention*. In a cognitive system with limited resources, information that potentially has immediate and important consequences for the organism will be given priority selectively processed (Dalgleish, 2003). Therefore, attentional processes are assumed to be particularly essential in the aetiology and maintenance of anxiety disorders. The role of cognition and attention in anxiety has been well elaborated in many papers (e.g. Eysenck, 1992, 1997; Mogg and Bradley, 1998; Williams *et al.*, 1988).

Cognitive-motivational theories (Mogg and Bradley, 1998) propose that hyper-vigilance and avoidance co-occur in a temporally ordered manner. Anxious individuals initially direct their attention towards threat, but may then avoid detailed processing of such stimuli in an attempt to reduce their anxious mood state. According to this vigilance-avoidance model, anxious individuals vigilantly monitor the environment for threatening stimuli and detect threatening stimuli more quickly compared with non-anxious individuals. Hyper-vigilance may also have a protective purpose, as it allows early activation of defences (Öhman, Flykt and Lundqvist, 2000). The detection of threat leads to increased anxiety, which causes anxious individuals to avoid the source of the threat in an attempt to reduce anxiety. This pattern of avoidance is believed to maintain anxiety, as it prevents anxious individuals from evaluating ambiguous stimuli as non-threatening or habituating to threatening stimuli. The eye tracking method is an effective methodology for testing this model. Using an eye tracking method, it would be expected that the first fixation of anxious individuals would be on the threatening stimuli and that these individuals would show shorter gaze time and fixation counts on these stimuli.

Methods of Assessing the Attention Bias and Their Limitations

To understand the relative merits of eye tracking studies in individuals with anxiety disorders, it is useful to briefly reiterate the limitations of other paradigms for investigating selective attention. The aim of this section is to elucidate how these limitations can be addressed using eye movement methodology. The vast majority of research investigating the relation between anxiety and selective attention utilized one of two methods: the emotional Stroop task (see Chapter 3) and the dot-probe paradigm (see Chapter 4).

Emotional Stroop task

As reviewed in Chapter 3, Stroop studies with clinical and non-clinical anxious children have so far provided inconsistent results: while several studies could show a threat-related attentional bias, other studies failed to detect this bias. However, the Stroop task has been criticized on several grounds.

Increased emotion instead of increased attention

Typically, the Stroop tasks demonstrate increased reaction time (RT) to colour name threatening or fear-related words or pictures in anxious compared with non-anxious children (see Chapter 3). Previous researchers have questioned whether this observed lag in colour-naming times is due to increased attention to threat cues or increased emotionality in response to the presentation of threat words (MacLeod, Mathews and Tata, 1986). Anxious individuals might attend to both threat-related and neutral words in a similar manner, but a negative emotional reaction caused by threat-related words may impair their ability to react as quickly to threat-related words. This response bias would most likely only exist in anxious individuals and would thus create differential responses on the emotional Stroop task (Puliafico and Kendall, 2006). Some studies have, however, found results that are inconsistent with this emotionality hypothesis (e.g. McNally *et al.*, 1992, 1994). McNally *et al.* (1992), for example, found that although patients with panic disorder rated positive words as more emotional than catastrophe words, they took longer to colour name catastrophe words than positive words. The authors concluded that anxious patients selectively process positive information, but that emotionality does not completely account for the interference effect.

Definition of attention

Further questions have been raised as to whether the Stroop task assesses selective attention (e.g. Williams, Mathews and MacLeod, 1996), since the interference in this task may still be the result of processes that are related to the response rather than to the input stage of information processing (Mineka, Rafaeli and Yovel, 2003). In their discussion of the different definitions of attention, Kindt and van den Hout (2001), for example, argued that the Stroop task measures relatively late selection processes, which are based on a semantic analysis of a word or picture. Some researchers suggest that only relatively early selection processes should be regarded as part of the attentional processes. Consistent with the delayed disengagement model (Fox *et al.*, 2001), Fox (2004) proposed that the emotional Stroop effect may be an index for the delay in *disengaging* from the threat content of words, rather than a measure of the movement of attention towards the source of threat. In support of this proposition, a recent meta-analysis by Phaf and Kan (2007) concluded that the emotional Stroop effect seems to rely more on a slow disengagement process than on a fast, automatic bias. Similarly, Mogg and Bradley (2004) also questioned the common interpretation of the Stroop effect as indicator of vigilance for fear-relevant information. Further, researchers have suggested that the effects may not necessarily reflect an attentional bias for threat, but may instead reflect an attempt to avoid processing the aversive information (De Ruiter and Brosschot, 1994; Hermans, Vansteenwegen and Eelen, 1999; Tolin *et al.*, 1999).

Dot-probe paradigm

As outlined in Chapter 4, the dot-probe paradigm requires the participant to indicate the location or identity of a probe by a key press following stimulus presentation. The dot-probe paradigm has also been criticized on several grounds. There is evidence, for example, which suggests that the intention to act (e.g. press a key) operates on pre-existing motor representations of possible responses (Tucker and Ellis, 1998). In other words, it is possible that an anxious individual's pre-existing motor response to threat is avoidance, whereas the dot-probe task requires the *opposite* response of approach (in the form of the motor response of pressing a key). As such, inferring attentional processes from data from the dot-probe task is confounded by instructing anxious individuals to give a motor response (approach) that may be contrary to their reflexive motor response (avoidance). In the dot-probe paradigm, the advantage in performance on trials in which the target probe appears at the location of the threat-related stimulus might result either from faster engagement with the threat stimulus or from a difficulty to disengage from it (Bar-Haim *et al.*, 2007).

Emotional Stroop Task and Dot-Probe Paradigm: Reliability and Validity

Strauss *et al.* (2005) investigated test–retest reliability of the emotional Stroop task in undergraduate students. When investigating latencies, test–retest reliability was found to be high; however, when using difference scores, reliability was very low. In a study by Eide *et al.* (2002) with adults, high test–retest reliability was found for RTs derived from the individual emotion conditions, but low test–retest reliability for the interference indices. Kindt, Bierman and Brosschot (1996) compared the card format and the single-trial format of the standard colour word Stroop task and the emotional Stroop task. There is no convergent validity between the two formats for either the standard Stroop effect or the emotional Stroop effect. Test–retest reliability of the emotional Stroop effects was very low. Concluding from these studies, the emotional Stroop task appears to be only suitable to determine group differences between anxious and non-anxious subjects and is not suitable for assessing individual interference as a stable characteristic. Furthermore, cognitive paradigms should investigate their psychometric data.

Research on the psychometric properties of the dot-probe paradigm is rare. Schmukle (2005) examined the reliability of the dot-probe task in university students using words and pictures as stimulus material. Estimates of both internal consistency and test–retest reliability over a 1-week period lead Schmukle to the conclusion that the dot-probe paradigm is an unreliable measure of attentional allocation in non-clinical samples.

Dalgleish *et al.* (2003) examined the relationship between the indexes of threat-related bias on the modified Stroop and dot-probe tasks. These two tasks, both suggested to measure attention using emotional words, showed a near-zero correlation, suggesting that they are unlikely to be assessing identical underlying cognitive processes. Similarly, in the study of Heim-Dreger *et al.* (2006) using the same pictorial stimuli the performance on the Stroop task and the dot-probe task also showed no correlation. Summarizing these results, it must be concluded that psychometric properties of these two tasks are not well established and that further research is needed.

Another limiting factor for both the Stroop and dot-probe tasks is that they often use words as stimuli, and it is unclear whether anxious participants are simply more familiar with and/or more frequently use threatening words compared with their less anxious peers (Bradley *et al.*, 1997). In support of this argument, Dalgleish (1995) showed comparable colour-naming interference effects in a Stroop task for threat words in anxious adults and bird words in ornithologists. This finding suggests that what the task may assess is an attentional bias for personally significant stimuli. If it is difficult to be confident that words convey a generally clear threat message accurately, then attentional bias findings based on verbal stimuli and resulting conclusions about information processing abilities must be questioned or supported with nonverbal forms of stimuli (Bradley *et al.*, 1997; Lundh and Öst, 1996).

The major limitation of these two paradigms is that they measure only a snapshot of attention, which depends on the presentation time of the stimulus pair. No information is provided about either the pattern or the course of attention deployment before or after the moment of measurement.

In this section, we have overviewed some of the main problems of the Stroop and dot-probe paradigms. Many of these limitations can be overcome using eye tracking, and it has, therefore, become a popular methodology for studying attentional processes. Against this backdrop of problems inherent in the Stroop and dot-probe task, we now look at the relative benefits of eye tracking.

The Relative Benefits of Eye Tracking

One way in which eye movement studies can address one of the aforementioned problems is that they are not influenced by motor responses because participants are not instructed to engage in any activity that may contradict their eye movements to the presented stimuli. Furthermore, the most important advantage compared to the other paradigms is its continuous measure of gaze, whereas the other paradigms assessed only a snapshot of attention. Assessing the course of attention also resolves the problem of the definition of attention. Bögels and Mansell (2004), for example, argued that the use of an eye tracking apparatus might be the most direct method to assess selective attention. It records the exact position of eye gaze as a continuous measure without requiring the participant to provide an explicit response. Furthermore, Caseras et al. (2007) suggested that eye movement recording possess good ecological validity, as people typically look at the stimuli that they attend to. In addition, as will be reported further below, there are several studies confirming that eye tracking has good reliability and test–retest reliability. Stimuli used in eye movement studies are predominantly pictures, which have the advantage over words that they can be used in children with no or limited reading abilities.

Unlike using RTs as indices of attention, eye movements enable researchers to test predictions linked to different theoretical models because they provide measures of biases in initial orienting, as indexed by the direction and latency of the first shift in gaze, as well as in the maintenance of attention, as reflected by the duration of gaze. Eye movement data provide an index of overt orienting, which is often assumed to follow closely to and be directed by shifts in covert attention (Kowler et al., 1995). Although the precise relationship between overt and covert attention is controversial, recent research suggests that the eye movement system plays an important role in covert attention and that common mechanisms underlie both overt and covert orienting (Smith, Rorden and Jackson, 2004).

Types of Eye Trackers

Several types of eye trackers are available: electro-oculography (EOG) and video-based eye trackers. The EOG relies on measurement of the skin's electric potential differences with electrodes placed around the eye. This method is still used today, but to a much lesser extent than a few years ago. The EOG is based on the fact that the eye has a standing electrical potential, with the cornea being positive relative to the retina. However, this potential is not constant and variations cause the EOG to be somewhat unreliable for measuring slow eye movements and fixations.

At present, the most widely used designs are video-based eye trackers, which are relatively non-invasive and fairly accurate. Video-based corneal reflection trackers work by capturing video images of the eye (illuminated by an infra-red light source), processing the video frames and outputting the eye's x- and y-coordinates relative to the screen being viewed. Video-based eye trackers can be either table mounted or head mounted. The head-mounted system involves a binocular eye tracker fitted inside the system. It provides the advantage of mobility and can be used outside of the lab. However, the observer has to wear a helmet or relatively big 'glasses', which can result in an unnatural test situation. The table-mounted eye tracker, also called remote systems, has a camera focus on one or both eyes and records their movement as the viewer looks at some kind of stimulus.

Tobii Eye Tracker System

As an example of a table-mounted eye tracker system, the Tobii 1750 (Tobii Technology AB, Sweden) eye tracker will be described. Although the following descriptions are based on Tobii, procedures should apply to most remote eye tracking systems. The Tobii is a table-mounted eye tracker with cameras and infra-red light emitting diode (LED) optics embedded beneath a liquid-crystal display (LCD) flat panel (Figure 6.1). Data are collected simultaneously for both eyes for each gaze data item. There are several advantages to this: binocular tracking

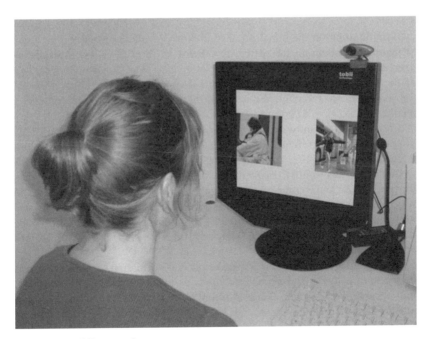

Figure 6.1 Tobii eye tracker.

can yield higher accuracy, less drift and better robustness than tracking only one eye.

The Tobii 1750 eye tracker samples the position of the user's eyes around every 20 milliseconds (i.e. 50 Hz) and at an accuracy of about 0.5° (bias error). The latest model of the Tobii eye tracker (Tobii T120) provides recordings every 10 milliseconds (120 MHz). It is characterized by the unobtrusive addition of the eye tracking hardware to the display frame. This design aspect helps promote more natural user behaviour in that it does not place unnatural restrictions on participants such as the need to use helmets or head/chest rests.

Tobii eye tracking metrics

- Fixation count (number of fixations on each area of interest (AOI)[a] per recording)
- Gaze time (total time each AOI was viewed during each recording)
- Average gaze time (average time of fixation per AOI and recording)
- Time to first fixation (time it took a participant to look at an AOI for the first time)
- Fixation order (order in which each AOI was fixated)

[a]AOI: an area of the stimuli that is of interest to the researchers.

Gaze duration on the initially fixated picture provides a relatively pure index of maintained attention for testing hypotheses. In most cases, the immediately proceeding stimulus is a neutral central fixation cue. Thus, the emotional content of the preceding fixated stimulus is controlled, whereas this control is absent for subsequent fixations on the items of the presented stimuli, for example, a picture pair.

ClearView is the software provided by Tobii and is used with the Tobii 1750 to examine the eye movements by means of a *post hoc* analysis of visual fixations within two target pictures. The eye tracking data are then examined in regard to the fixations recorded within these pictures (areas of interest, AOI). The fixation data for these AOIs can be compared in a number of ways, including (i) the order in which each AOI was first fixated on, (ii) the number of fixations recorded in each AOI and (iii) the cumulative dwell time of fixations recorded in each AOI. These data provide a means to determine which picture is generally looked at first, how often and for how long.

The advantages of the Tobii eye tracker for use in children are the customized calibration for low-attention subjects, the large tolerance towards head motion, thus removing all need for chinrests and other restraints, and the easy set up of highly attention-grabbing stimuli.

Components of Eye Movements

Eye movements are typically divided into saccades, fast movements of the eye, and fixations, the periods between saccades when the eye pauses in a certain position and visual information is encoded. The resulting series of fixations and saccades is called a *scan path*.

Saccades are rapid eye movements used in repositioning the fovea to a new location in the visual environment in order to allow for high acuity vision. Saccadic movements are both voluntary and reflexive. They range in duration from 10 to 100 milliseconds (Duchowski, 2007).

Fixations are eye movements that stabilize the retina over a stationary object of interest. 90% of viewing time is devoted to fixations and their duration ranges from 150 to 600 milliseconds (Irwin, 1992).

Implications for Eye Movement Analysis

The primary requirement of eye movement analysis is the identification of fixations and saccades. It is assumed that these movements provide evidence of voluntary and overt visual attention. However, this assumption does not preclude plausible involuntary movement, or the covert non-use of these eye movements. Furthermore, properties of the stimuli such as colour, contrast and movement cause involuntary eye movements. Fixations naturally correspond to the desire to maintain one's gaze on an object of interest. Saccades are considered manifestations of the desire to voluntarily change the focus of attention (Duchowski, 2007).

Eye Tracker: Reliability

In a recent review, Karatekin (2007) summarized eye tracking studies of typical and atypical development and psychometric characteristics of eye tracking studies in children. Reliability of eye tracking measures was examined in several studies. Internal consistency of anti-saccade errors on a 20-trial task with a large sample of healthy children was found to be 0.81 for 11-year-olds and 0.82 for 17-year-olds (Malone and Iacono, 2002). In the anti-saccade task, the subject has to wilfully terminate a 'reflexive' saccade to a suddenly appearing visual stimulus (i.e. actively engage response inhibition) and then generate a voluntary saccade – the anti-saccade – in the opposite direction to the mirror location of the original visual target.

Test–retest reliability over 3–6 weeks with a sample of 22 children with attention-deficit hyperactivity disorder (ADHD) was .79 for anti-saccade errors and .62 for predictive saccades (O'Driscoll *et al.*, 2005).

In the largest developmental study of reliability of saccadic measures in children, internal consistency and split-half reliability of pro- and anti-saccades were assessed in 327 healthy 9- to 88-year-olds (Klein and Fischer, 2005). With age partialed out, instrumental reliabilities were high for pro- and anti-saccade RTs (.91–.96 for odd–even reliability, .81–.90 for split-half reliability) and anti-saccade errors (.95 for odd–even, .83 for split-half). Test–retest reliability over 19 months was assessed for 6- to 18-year-olds, showing moderate reliability for pro- and anti-saccade RTs (.65–.66), but low reliability for anti-saccade errors (.43; possibly due to individual differences in the rate of maturation of the neural substrates of anti-saccades). Klein and Fischer (2005) noted that the instrumental (within-session) and test–retest reliability estimates were not affected by age.

The use of eye movement methodologies has been found to show good internal consistency and test–retest reliability. Furthermore, eye tracking has the advantage of assessing a continuous measure of gaze, which is very important in investigating attention at an early information processing stage. Studies on the reliability of emotional stimuli, as well as the validity of eye movements are, however, missing in the developmental literature.

Eye Movement Studies in Adults with Anxiety Disorders

The vigilance-avoidance model proposes that attention is directed to stimuli that are relevant to the concerns of the specific anxiety disorders (specificity hypothesis). The following section will describe eye movement studies conducted with adults with anxiety disorders. Most of the studies in this research area were investigated with adults who experience spider phobia.

In an early study, Hermans, Vansteenwegen and Eelen (1999) tested high and low spider-anxious participants with a series of slides depicting spiders and flowers, while their eye movements were recorded continuously for 3 seconds. During the first 500 milliseconds, there was no difference between the groups, as both groups focused more on the spider pictures. From 500 to 3000 milliseconds, there was a significant and increasing difference between the groups, in that high spider-anxious individuals started to increasingly look away from the spiders. From 2000 to 3000 milliseconds, the high spider-anxious individuals looked significantly more often at the flowers. The control group showed a more stable viewing pattern and looked at the spider pictures more than 50% of the time throughout the stimulus presentation. This study provides partial support for the hyper-vigilance-avoidance model, where high spider-anxious individuals demonstrated the avoidance component, but not the hyper-vigilance in comparison to low spider-anxious individuals. Similarly, Tolin et al. (1999) found that individuals with spider phobia showed reduced viewing time on a picture of a spider, suggesting an attentional bias away from the spider.

Further work has found increased scanning in adults with spider phobia. Lange et al. (2004), for example, investigated the viewing behaviour of spider-anxious individuals compared to controls and found that spider-anxious individuals make more shifts in gaze when presented with threat stimuli, suggesting that they scan their environment as part of their safety behaviour.

A study by Rinck and Becker (2006) provides further evidence for the attention-avoidance sequence in spider-fearful individuals. Compared with non-anxious control participants, these individuals spent more time looking at the spider picture for the first 500 milliseconds. This attentional bias towards the spider was quickly followed by avoidance of the spider pictures. From 1501 to 3000 milliseconds, spider fearfuls (compared with controls) spent less time looking at the spider pictures. These results support the vigilance-avoidance model. Comparably, Pflugshaupt *et al.* (2005) found further support for this model. They used another paradigm by administering a visual task with spider phobics and controls, requiring participants to search for spiders in everyday scenes. The results indicated that spider phobics detected spiders faster, fixated closer to spiders during the initial search phase and subsequently fixated further from spiders compared to controls.

Miltner *et al.* (2004) presented fear-relevant (spider) or neutral targets (mushroom) in visual matrices of neutral objects (flowers) to spider-phobic and non-phobic subjects. All subjects responded faster to the neutral target than to the fear-relevant target. However, phobics were slower to respond when a neutral target was presented with a spider distractor than non-phobics. The authors concluded that the attentional bias to visual threat primarily occurs when subjects are confronted with different stimuli of different emotional valence, which compete for selective attention, processing priority and behavioural adaptation. Because control subjects showed faster manual response and faster saccades, the authors assume that the processing system of control subjects may change when the amount of fear-relevant stimuli exceeds a critical value. In other words, non-fearful subjects might show the same kind of priority processing of threat as fearful individuals. Miltner *et al.* (2004) did not, however, assess the course of attention with eye movement data.

The results of eye movement studies conducted with facial stimuli are comparable to those with spider stimuli. Similar to the study by Lange *et al.* (2004), Horley *et al.* (2004) found increased scanning in adults with social phobia when viewing angry faces. Rohner (2002), who assessed the eye movements with EOG, found (similar to Hermans, Vansteenwegen and Eelen, 1999), support for a late threat avoidance of angry faces in high trait anxious individuals, but no vigilance compared to low trait anxious individuals on angry faces compared to happy faces. Both Rohner (2002) and Hermans, Vansteenwegen and Eelen (1999) expected, but were unable to demonstrate, the vigilance effect. Hermans, Vansteenwegen and Eelen (1999) suggested that the lack of vigilance was a function of the high spider-anxious group being selected on the basis of questionnaires, where these individuals were not necessarily seeking treatment.

Mogg, Millar and Bradley (2000) investigated attentional bias to emotional face stimuli in generalized anxiety disorder (GAD), depressive disorder and normal controls. There were four face types: threatening, sad, happy and neutral. Their results indicated that adults with GAD were more likely to first look towards threat faces, rather than neutral faces, compared to normal controls and those with depression disorder. The results provide evidence of a bias in initial orienting to threat in GAD supporting cognitive models of anxiety (e.g. Eysenck, 1992). Garner, Mogg and Bradley (2006) monitored eye movements in high and low social anxious individuals while viewing pictures of faces. High social anxious individuals were relatively quick to look at emotional faces rather than neutral faces, but viewed emotional faces for a shorter time compared to low social anxious individuals, which is consistent with the vigilant-avoidant hypothesis.

In summary, eye movement studies with feared objects (e.g. spiders) and facial stimuli lend some support for the vigilance-avoidance hypothesis. However, there are also studies with these stimuli, which could show only partial support for the vigilance-avoidance model.

The disparate findings may be explained with the following explanations. The applied duration of stimulus exposure was possibly not long enough to allow for elaborative processing that prompts avoidance behaviour. Results of eye tracking studies indicate that the time frame should be long enough for the avoidance pattern to become evident, which needs at least 1700 milliseconds of stimulus exposure to occur (Pflugshaupt et al., 2005). Another explanation for the discrepancy between study results, as suggested by Rinck and Becker (2006), is that frequent but short gaze durations for threat compared to less frequent but longer threat gaze durations cancel each other out in an epoch-related analysis.

Eye Tracking Studies in Anxious Children and Adolescents

Regarding the typical development of saccades in children, Karatekin (2007) stated that findings consistently show that the basic dynamics of pro-saccades and the subcortical regions mediating them do not change substantially after age 4. Furthermore, pro-saccades and anti-saccades have different developmental trajectories.

The following section describes eye tracking studies in anxious children and adolescents. So far, there are only two published eye tracking studies with anxious children. Two studies were published after the deadline of this book (Gamble & Rapee, 2009; In-Albon, Kossowsky & Schneider, 2009). The first study investigated cognitive control and error processing under contingencies (Jazbec et al., 2005). They used a new monetary reward anti-saccade task. The task measured rapid reflexive and voluntary eye movements in three contingency contexts: monetary gain (reward condition), monetary loss (punishment condition), and no incentive (neutral condition). The task consisted of three phases: (i) the initial phase, which informed the subject with cues about the type of trial (pro-saccade or anti-saccade, reward, punishment or neutral); (ii) the target or saccade phase; and (iii) the feedback phase. To succeed on a trail, subjects had to fixate the correct location until receiving feedback (monetary gain or loss). The task included a total of 144 trials and task length was around 12 minutes. The authors anticipated that anxiety would affect performance on punishment trials more strongly than on reward trials due to the negative bias found in anxiety disorders (Dalgleish et al., 2003). The sample consisted of 28 healthy, 11 anxious and 12 depressed adolescents. Performance parameters used included accuracy, saccade latency and saccade peak velocity.

The results demonstrated that attention-related processes engaged during errant execution of a saccade are sensitive to experimentally manipulated reward contingencies. The hypotheses were partly supported. Accuracy improved under reinforcement conditions (reward or punishment) and did not differ between the groups. Cognitive control, indexed by saccade latency and peak velocity of errant anti-saccades, was facilitated by contingencies in healthy subjects. Latency of incorrect anti-saccades for the anxious group was increased in the punishment trials. Therefore, the punishment condition was the most affected condition (longest latencies) in anxious adolescents. This result suggests that negative contingencies were more disruptive than positive contingencies. The authors interpreted this finding as being consistent with the negative attention bias in anxious children. They proposed that the presence of contingencies, positive or negative, creates an interference effect. The authors noted that the possibility of reward or punishment might induce a state in which attentional resources are partly diverted away from cognitive control processes towards emotion-based processes. This attention alteration would result in a reduction of the attentional resources allocated to inhibiting a pro-saccade.

The second study by Fulcher, Mathews and Hammerl (2007) conducted three experiments to investigate the relationship between evaluative learning and attentional preference in children with varying degrees of anxiety. One of these experiments tested the prediction that anxious children and/or children with anxious parents would show a bias in evaluative learning using an eye tracker system. Another goal was to determine whether vulnerable children show an attentional bias not only to unpleasant images, but also to images imbued with valence. Two pictures were presented on the left and the right of the monitor consisting of either one smiling or one frowning face. The participant's task was to press a key if the target image appeared on the left side of the monitor. First eye fixations, mean fixations on the trail type and RTs to respond to the target were recorded. Fourty-four children of 7–8 years of age participated in this study. All participants tended to fixate on the frowning faces earlier than the smiling faces. A preference for emotional faces could not be predicted by anxiety symptoms. Children scoring high on the panic/separation subscale of the MASC (multidimensional anxiety scale for children, March et al., 1997) had longer fixation times on frowning faces than did low panic/separation anxious (PSA) children. Results indicated differences between children high and low on panic/separation symptoms in learning and attention. The authors concluded that their results provide support for a learning mechanism in the development of attentional bias. Fulcher, Mathews and Hammerl, (2007) describe a cognitive style in which children with elevated panic/separation anxiety learn quickly about emotional information. Second, they selectively attend to new stimuli associated with a threat and they are then slow to disengage from threatening material.

In our own recently conducted study (In-Albon, Kossowsky and Schneider, 2009), we aimed to investigate whether eye movements are a useful tool in assessing the attentional bias in children with separation anxiety disorder (SAD) in comparison to normal controls. The majority of studies within the developmental literature have explored cognitive biases in children with anxiety disorders as a general phenomenon. There is a lack of studies in children that explore whether specific anxiety disorders are associated with specific attentional biases. In this study, pictures were used as stimuli material. Colour photographs representing disorder-specific threat stimuli for SAD were developed and empirically validated with school children, indicating that the pictures trigger emotional response, and show evidence for content specificity of separation (see In-Albon *et al.*, 2008). Separation situation pictures represent arrival and departure situations between a mother and a child. Girls and boys had separate sets of gender-specific pictures. Each slide contained two pictures, both matched for complexity and brightness, depicting contrasts (arrival/departure) in these two situations. Children underwent nine trials, each consisting of the viewing of 33 slides.

Eye tracking was measured using the Tobii 1750 eye tracker (Tobii Technology AB). After calibration, participants were presented with the pictures for 4 seconds. Prior to each picture, a central fixation cross was shown. The instruction given to the child was, 'Your task will be to look at the pictures on the screen until it disappears, move your eyes, but not your head'. A pair of pictures was then presented on the left and the right side of the screen. Pictures were presented for 4 seconds, which were divided into eight intervals of 500 milliseconds each.

The primary focus of this research was to explore whether children with SAD would show a vigilant-avoidance pattern when viewing disorder-specific pictures. Following the vigilant-avoidance model, we proposed that the first fixation of children with SAD would be on threatening (separation/departure related) pictures followed by a shorter gaze time and fewer fixation counts. The preliminary results indicated that at the beginning of the slide presentation there was no difference between children with SAD and normal controls (first fixation). After 1000 milliseconds children with SAD looked significantly more at the departure pictures. The pattern then reversed and after 2000 milliseconds children with SAD started to avoid looking at the departure picture. Therefore, partial support was found for the vigilance-avoidance hypothesis. Specifically, the study did not find hyper-vigilant behaviour (time to first fixation). However, a late vigilance behaviour to threat and as expected an avoidance behaviour was shown, which is in line with results of eye movement studies with adults.

In summary, these three studies using eye tracking technology with anxious children provide preliminary support for this method as a mechanism for exploring attentional processes in anxiety. Jazbec *et al.* (2005) demonstrated that attention-related processes engaged during errant execution of a saccade are sensitive to experimentally manipulated reward contingencies. Results from the study by Fulcher, Mathews and Hammerl (2007) indicate differences between children high and low on panic/separation symptoms in learning and attention. The results of our own study (In-Albon *et al.*, 2009) indicated a different course of attention allocation between children with SAD and non-anxious controls, which is in line with the vigilance-avoidance model.

The research questions of these studies were very different, therefore they are difficult to compare and due to the small number of studies, clear conclusions cannot be made. Certainly, more studies are needed in this area.

Limitations of Eye Tracking

As mentioned above, the major advantage of the eye tracking method over other methods assessing attention is its continuous measure of gaze; there are also some limitations of this approach that have to be mentioned. A problem with eye tracking research is that humans can voluntarily dissociate attention from the foveal direction of gaze. An eye tracker can only track the overt movements of the eyes. It cannot, however, track the covert movement of visual attention. Thus, in all eye tracking work, an implicit but important assumption is usually accepted: 'we assume that attention is linked to foveal gaze direction, but we acknowledge that it may not always be so' (Duchowski, 2007, p. 12). Performance on eye tracking tasks is a function not only of task difficulty but also of contextual factors, including task parameters and state variables, such as anxiety and fatigue (Karatekin, 2007).

Another limitation of eye tracking highlighted is the extent to which inferences can be drawn from the oculomotor system about other motor systems (Connoly et al., 2005). There is evidence that these two systems may not have a parallel organization. For example, pointing away and looking away from visual targets recruit overlapping but separable regions and may be accomplished through somewhat different mechanisms. Therefore, generalizations across systems have to be made with caution. In other words, eye movements in the laboratory may not necessarily portray eye movements in the real world.

Another important issue is that no standard paradigm for assessing eye movements during scene or face perception exists. Some progress has been made to establish the psychometric properties in eye movement studies. However, the psychometric properties of eye tracking methodology should be further investigated with different paradigms and stimuli. A further limitation of the current attentional bias literature is the lack of multi-method validation of attentional bias measures (Puliafico and Kendall, 2006; Vasey, Dalgleish and Silverman, 2003).

Issues Relevant in Eye Tracking Studies with Children

There are several issues that have to be considered when doing eye tracking studies with children compared to studies with adults. Issues such as calibration and showing a fixation cross between stimuli presentation are important in adult, as well as child studies. However, some differences have to be considered. The calibration process in child studies should not take too long because children can get tired more quickly, leading to attention decreases. For a child adequate example of a calibration procedure, Evans and Saint-Aubin (2005) used tiny faces of a cartoon character and encouraged the children to look closely to examine its features. The role of the fixation cross is that the previous and the following targets should not interact. In studies with children, the fixation cross can be presented, for example, as a smile or another icon, which will be displayed in the middle of the screen. The following issues are specific to eye tracking studies in children.

The number of trials and the task length of eye tracking studies with children have to be reduced compared to studies with adults. Task length varies considerably in the reviewed studies. An inadequate number of trails reduce the reliability of the measure. However, estimating the effect of task length on performance is not easy, since shorter tasks reduce the likelihood of tiredness in children, while longer tasks may also assess participant's ability to improve their performance with practice. Thus, Karatekin (2007) suggested that the effect of task length might differ depending on the nature of the task, as well as the age and clinical status of the participants (e.g. increase of error rates in ADHD children, Klein, Raschke and Brandenbusch, 2003). Furthermore, she noted that in studies including younger children or clinical populations of children, tasks tend to be shorter. From our own experience, a task length of 30 minutes is manageable with children with anxiety disorders. However, it is important to control for order effects if studies involve multiple conditions.

Future Research

Future research using eye tracker methodology looks very promising. This method is valuable, especially for use with children, because it is easy to administer and pictures can be used as stimuli. This chapter has highlighted that eye tracking studies in children and adolescents with anxiety disorders are rare. It has yet to be investigated whether the use of pictures as stimuli will be effective in assessing attentional biases in anxiety and whether children demonstrate a disorder-specific bias comparable to that found in adults with anxiety disorders. In addition, longitudinal studies with children at risk for anxiety disorders (e.g. behaviourally inhibited children, children of parents with anxiety disorder) could be utilized to investigate whether biases represent a causal risk factor or is a consequence of anxiety. In addition to the study of attentional biases as risk factors in anxiety, further research could utilize these methodologies to examine children pre- and post-treatment of their anxiety disorder.

Concerning attentional mechanisms, Garner, Mogg and Bradley (2006) noted that attentional mechanisms such as distinctions between covert versus overt orienting and between initial orienting and maintained attention have to be considered in more detail. One means of exploring these issues is through monitoring eye movements. The distinction between orienting and maintained attention also suggests that opposing biases may operate in different aspects of attentional responses (e.g. relatively more rapid orienting to, but reduced maintenance of attention on emotional faces in socially anxious individuals under stress).

This chapter presented an overview of eye tracking methods and discussed the association of anxiety and attention. Limitations of paradigms (emotional Stroop task and dot-probe paradigm) used to assess the attentional bias were reported. Compared to RTs as indices of attention as assessed by Stroop task and dot-probe paradigm, the assessment of eye movements is beneficial to investigate attention. The major benefit of eye movement methods is that they provide researchers with the possibility of assessing a continuous measure of gaze, which allows an exploration of the attentional bias consisting of vigilance and avoidance. Because there are currently only very few eye tracking studies in anxious children, results of studies with anxious adult population with reference to eye tracking were presented. In sum, results of eye movement studies suggest that there is at least partial support for the vigilance-avoidance model of different anxiety disorders. Practical issues relevant in eye tracking studies in children relate to the number of trials and the task length; because of shorter attention span in children the number of trials should be less and task length should be shorter than in adult studies. These issues, as well as the distinction between covert and overt orienting have to be investigated in future studies.

Acknowledgements

We would like to thank Thomas Roderer and Javier Bargas-Avila for their helpful comments and suggestions during the preparation of this chapter.

References

Aslin, R.N. and McMurray, B. (2004) Automated corneal-reflection eye tracking in infancy: methodological developments and applications to cognition. *Infancy*, **6** (2), 155–163.

Bar-Haim, Y., Lamy, D., Pergamin, L. *et al.* (2007) Threat-related attentional bias in anxious and nonanxious individuals: a meta-analytic study. *Psychological Bulletin*, **133** (1), 1–24.

Bögels, S. and Mansell, W. (2004) Attention processes in the maintenance and treatment of social phobia: hypervigilance, avoidance and self-focused attention. *Clinical Psychology Review*, **24**, 827–856.

Bradley, B.P., Mogg, K., Millar, N. *et al.* (1997) Attentional biases for emotional faces. *Cognition and Emotion*, **11**, 25–42.

Caseras, X., Garner, M., Bradley, B.P. and Mogg, K. (2007) Biases in visual orienting to negative and positive scenes in dysphoria: an eye movement study. *Journal of Abnormal Psychology*, **116** (3), 491–497.

Connoly, J.D., Goodale, M.A., Goltz, H.C. and Munoz, D.P. (2005) fMRI activation in the human frontal eye field is correlated with saccadic reaction time. *Journal of Neurophysiology*, **94**, 605–611.

Dalgleish, T. (1995) Performance on the emotional Stroop task in groups of anxious, experts and control subjects: a comparison of computer and card presentation formats. *Cognition and Emotion*, **9**, 341–362.

Dalgleish, T. (2003) Information processing approaches to emotion, in *Handbook of Affective Science* (eds R.J. Davidson, K.R. Scherer and H.H. Goldsmith), Oxford University Press, Oxford, pp. 661–673.

Dalgleish, T., Taghavi, R., Neshat-Doost, H. *et al.* (2003) Patterns of processing bias for emotional information across clinical disorders: a comparison of attention, memory and prospective cognition in children and adolescents with depression, generalized anxiety and posttraumatic stress disorder. *Journal of Clinical Child and Adolescent Psychology*, **32** (1), 10–21.

De Ruiter, C. and Brosschot, J.F. (1994) The emotional Stroop interference effect in anxiety: attentional bias or cognitive avoidance? *Behavior Research and Therapy*, **32**, 315–319.

Duchowski, A.T. (2007) *Eye Tracking Methodology Theory and Practice*, 2nd edn, Springer, London.

Eide, P., Kemp, A., Silberstein, R.B. *et al.* (2002) Test–retest reliability of the emotional Stroop task: examining the paradox of measurement change. *The Journal of Psychology*, **136** (5), 514–520.

Eysenck, M.W. (1992) *Anxiety: The Cognitive Perspective*, Erlbaum, Hove.

Eysenck, M.W. (1997) *Anxiety: The Cognition: A Unified Theory*, Erlbaum, Hove.

Evans, M.A. and Saint-Aubin, J. (2005) What children are looking at during shared storybook reading: evidence from eye movement monitoring. *Psychological Science*, **16**, 913–920.

Fox, E. (2004) Maintenance or capture of attention in anxiety-related biases? in *Cognition, Emotion, and Psychopathology: Theoretical, Empirical, and Clinical Approaches* (ed. J. Yiend), Cambridge University Press, Cambridge, pp. 86–105.

Fox, E., Russo, R., Bowles, R. and Dutton, K. (2001) Do threatening stimuli draw or hold visual attention in subclinical anxiety? *Journal of Experimental Psychology*, **130**, 681–700.

Fulcher, E.P., Mathews, A. and Hammerl, M. (2007) Rapid acquisition of emotional information and attentional bias in anxious children. *Journal of Behavioral Therapy and Experimental Psychiatry*. **39** (3), 321–339

Gamble, A.L. and Rapee, R.M. (2009) The time-course of attentional bias in anxious children and adolescents. *Journal of Anxiety Disorders*, **23** (7), 841–847.

Garner, M., Mogg, K. and Bradley, B.P. (2006) Orienting and maintenance of gaze to facial expressions in social anxiety. *Journal of Abnormal Psychology*, **115** (4), 760–770.

Heim-Dreger, U., Kohlmann, C.-W., Eschenbeck, H. and Burkhardt, U. (2006) Attentional biases for threatening faces in children: vigilant and avoidant processes. *Emotion*, **6** (2), 320–325.

Hermans, D., Vansteenwegen, D. and Eelen, P. (1999) Eye movement registration as a continuous index of attention deployment: data from a group of spider anxious students. *Cognition and Emotion*, **13** (4), 419–434.

Horley, K., Williams, L.M., Gonsalvez, C. and Gordon, E. (2004) Face to face: visual scanpath evidence for abnormal processing of facial expressions in social phobia. *Psychiatry Research*, **127**, 43–53.

In-Albon, T., Klein, A., Rinck, M., *et al.* (2008) Development and evaluation of a new paradigm for the assessment of anxiety disorder-specific interpretation bias using picture stimuli. *Cognition and Emotion*, **22**, 422–436.

In-Albon, T., Kossowsky, J. and Schneider, S. (2009) Vigilance and avoidance in children with separation anxiety disorder using an eye movement paradigm. *Journal of Abnormal Child Psychology*., DOI.

Irwin, D.E. (1992) Visual memory within and across fixations, in *Eye Movements and Visual Cognition: Scene Perception and Reading* (ed. K. Rayner), Springer-Verlag, New York, pp. 146–165.

Jazbec, S., McClure, E., Hardin, M. *et al.* (2005) Cognitive control under contingencies in anxious and depressed adolescents: an antisaccade task. *Biological Psychiatry*, **58**, 632–639.

Just, M.A. and Carpenter, P.A. (1976) Eye fixations and cognitive processes. *Cognitive Psychology*, **8** (4), 441–480.

Karatekin, C. (2007) Eye tracking studies of normative and atypical development. *Developmental Review*, **27**, 283–348.

Kindt, M. and van den Hout, M. (2001) Selective attention and anxiety: a perspective on developmental issues and the causal status. *Journal of Psychopathology and Behavioural Assessment*, **23**, 193–202.

Kindt, M., Bierman, D. and Brosschot, J.F. (1996) Stroop versus Stroop: comparison of a card format and a single-trial format of the standard color-word Stroop task and the emotional Stroop task. *Personality and Individual Differences*, **21** (5), 653–661.

Klein, C. and Fischer, B. (2005) Instrumental and test–retest reliability of saccadic measures. *Biological Psychology*, **68**, 201–213.

Klein, Ch., Raschke, A. and Brandenbusch, A. (2003) Development of pro- and antisaccades in children with attention-deficit hyperactivity disorder (ADHD) and healthy controls. *Psychophysiology*, **40**, 17–28.

Kowler, E., Anderson, E., Dosher, B. and Blaser, E. (1995) The role of attention in the programming of saccades. *Vision Research*, **35**, 1897–1916.

Lange, W.G.T., Tierney, K.J., Reinhardt-Rutland, A.H. and Vivekananda-Schmidt, P. (2004) Viewing behaviour of spider phobics and non-phobics in the presence of threat and safety stimuli. *British Journal of Clinical Psychology*, **43**, 235–243.

Lundh, L.G. and Öst, L.G. (1996) Recognition bias for critical faces in social phobics. *Behaviour Research and Therapy*, **34** (10), 787–794.

MacLeod, C., Mathews, A. and Tata, P. (1986) Attentional bias in emotional disorders. *Journal of Abnormal Psychology*, **95**, 15–20.

Malone, S.M. and Iacono, W.G. (2002) Error rate on the antisaccade task: heritability and developmental change in performance among preadolescent and late-adolescent female twin youth. *Psychophysiology*, **39**, 664–673.

March, J.S., Parker, J.D.A., Sullivan, K. *et al.* (1997) The multidimensional anxiety scale for children (MASC): factor structure, reliability, and validity. *Journal of the American Academy of Child and Adolescent Psychiatry*, **63**, 554–565.

McNally, R.J., Amir, N., Louro, C.E. *et al.* (1994) Cognitive processing of idiographic emotional information in panic disorder. *Behaviour Research and Therapy*, **32** (1), 119–122.

McNally, R.J., Riemann, B.C., Louro, C.E. *et al.* (1992) Cognitive processing of emotional information in panic disorder. *Behaviour Research and Therapy*, **30** (2), 143–149.

Miltner, W.H.R., Krieschel, S., Hecht, H. *et al.* (2004) Eye movements and behavioural responses to threatening and nonthreatening stimuli during visual search in phobic and nonphobic subjects. *Emotion*, **4** (4), 323–339.

Mineka, S., Rafaeli, E. and Yovel, I. (2003) Cognitive biases in emotional disorders: social-cognitive and information processing perspectives, in *Handbook of Affective Science* (eds R. Davidson, H. Goldsmith and K. Scherer), Oxford University Press, New York.

Mogg, K. and Bradley, B.P. (1998) A cognitive-motivational analysis of anxiety. *Behaviour Research and Therapy*, **36**, 809–848.

Mogg, K. and Bradley, B.P. (2004) A cognitive-motivational perspective on the processing of threat information and anxiety, in *Cognition, Emotion, and Psychopathology: Theoretical, Empirical, and Clinical Approaches* (ed. J. Yiend), Cambridge University Press, Cambridge, pp. 68–85.

Mogg, K., Millar, N. and Bradley, B.P. (2000) Biases in eye movements to threatening facial expressions in generalized anxiety disorder and depressive disorder. *Journal of Abnormal Psychology*, **109** (4), 695–704.

O'Driscoll, G.A., Dépatie, L., Holahan, A.V. *et al.* (2005) Executive functions and methylphenidate response in subtypes of attention-deficit/hyperactivity disorder. *Biological Psychiatry*, **57**, 1452–1460.

Öhman, A., Flykt, A. and Lundqvist, D. (2000) Unconscious emotion: evolutionary perspectives, psychophysiological data, and neuropsychological mechanisms, in *Cognitive Neuroscience of Emotion* (eds R.D. Lane and L. Nadel), Oxford University Press, New York, pp. 296–327.

Pflugshaupt, T., Mosimann, U.P., von Wartburg, R. *et al.* (2005) Hypervigilance-avoidance pattern in spider phobia. *Anxiety Disorders*, **19**, 105–116.

Phaf, R.H. and Kan, K. (2007) The automaticity of emotional Stroop: a meta-analysis. *Journal of Behavior Therapy and Experimental Psychiatry*, **38**, 184–199.

Puliafico, A.C. and Kendall, P.C. (2006) Threat-related attentional bias in anxious youth: a review. *Clinical Child and Family Psychology Review*, **9**, 162–180.

Rinck, M. and Becker, E.S. (2006) Spider fearfuls attend to threat, then quickly avoid it: evidence from eye movements. *Journal of Abnormal Psychology*, **115** (2), 231–238.

Rohner, J.-C. (2002) The time-course of visual threat processing: high trait anxious individuals eventually avert their gaze from angry faces. *Cognition and Emotion*, **16** (6), 837–844.

Schmukle, S.C. (2005) Unreliability of the dot-probe task. *European Journal of Personality*, **19**, 595–605.

Smith, D.T., Rorden, C. and Jackson, S.R. (2004) Exogenous orienting of attention depends upon the ability to execute eye movements. *Current Biology*, **14**, 792–795.

Strauss, G.P., Allen, D.N., Jorgensen, M.L. and Cramer, S.L. (2005) Test–retest reliability of standard and emotional Stroop tasks: an investigation of color-word and picture-word version. *Assessment*, **12** (3), 330–337.

Tobii Technology AB. http://www.tobii.com. 2005

Tolin, D.F., Lohr, J.M., Lee, T.C. and Sawchuk, C.N. (1999) Visual avoidance in specific phobia. *Behaviour Research and Therapy*, **37**, 63–70.

Tucker, M. and Ellis, R. (1998) On the relations between seen objects and components of potential action. *Journal of Experimental Psychology: Human Perception and Performance*, **24** (3), 830–846.

Vasey, M.W., Dalgleish, T. and Silverman, W.K. (2003) Research on information-processing factors in child and adolescent psychopathology: a critical commentary. *Journal of Clinical Child and Adolescent Psychology*, **32**, 81–93.

Williams, J.M.G., Mathews, A. and MacLeod, C. (1996) The emotional Stroop task and psychopathology. *Psychological Bulletin*, **120**, 3–24.

Williams, J.M.G., Watts, F.N., MacLeod, C. and Mathews, A. (1988) *Cognitive Psychology and Emotional Disorders*, Wiley, Chichester, UK.

7

The Assessment of Fear-Related Automatic Associations in Children and Adolescents

Jorg Huijding, Reinout W. Wiers and Andy P. Field
Huijding@fsw.eur.nl

Introduction

Cognitive models of adult, adolescent and childhood anxiety disorders assume that dysfunctional cognitive structures in memory are at the core of these emotional problems (e.g. Beck, Emery and Greenberg, 1985; Kendall and Ronan, 1990). With the increasing popularity of such models, research on information processing in psychopathology has been thriving in the adult literature (reviews by Harvey *et al.*, 2004; Williams *et al.*, 1997), and is becoming more widely researched in the child and adolescent literature (see Muris, 2007, for a recent overview). The hypothesized cognitive structures (schemata) can be thought of as maladaptive lenses that distort the way the world is perceived (i.e. disorder congruent) and are assumed to automatically influence all stages of information processing (e.g. Daleiden and Vasey, 1997). Researchers trying to empirically test the validity of these types of cognitive models have focused on information processing biases (e.g. Vasey, Dalgleish and Silverman, 2003; Muris, 2007).

Although such biases are functionally related to the hypothesized schemata, they provide rather indirect information concerning the content and structure of these schemata. Recently, however, a new class of measurement instruments has been developed that promises to offer more direct information on these aspects of schemata: various indirect measures of automatic associations. Some authors view these measures as indices of schema or memory biases (e.g. Teachman, 2005).

The indirect measures discussed in this chapter are all varieties of reaction time (RT) paradigms developed in social cognition research. It should be noted, however, that there are also other indirect measures of memory associations not involving RTs that have been successfully used in adolescents (e.g. Ames *et al.*, 2007; Thush *et al.*, 2007; Stacy, 1997). In these tests, derived from the basic memory literature, adolescents react to homographs that may or may not be related to the behaviour of interest. For example, heavy drinkers' first associations to a word like 'draft' will more often be alcohol-related than the associations of light drinkers and abstainers. However, these studies were in the domain of substance use and misuse and are, therefore, not discussed in detail here.

This chapter discusses why indirect (RT-based) measures of automatic associations may be informative in the context of child and adolescent anxiety disorders and provides an overview of studies that have used such measures in that context. Although research in adults with indirect measures is popular and rapidly expanding (e.g. Wittenbrink and Schwarz, 2007; Petty, Fazio and Briñol, 2008), this field of research is also relatively new and few studies have been carried out with child and adolescent samples. As a consequence, all of the indirect measures were initially developed for adult samples. Therefore, we frequently rely on the adult literature as the starting point of our discussions. We start with explaining why researchers are interested in assessing automatic associations in the context of anxiety. After providing a brief summary of findings in adult anxiety, we describe the indirect measures of automatic associations that have been applied to child and adolescent anxiety, followed by an overview of the studies that have been conducted so far. Given the dearth of research with these measures in children and adolescents we also review studies outside anxiety. Special attention is paid to the extent to which researchers have modified the tasks to make them more suitable for children and adolescents.

First, however, it is important to clarify some of the terminology used in this chapter.

What Are We Talking about?

In the quickly growing literature concerning indirect measures of automatic associations, such measures are often referred to as *implicit measures*. This term has, however, raised some confusion. While some scholars have argued that the term refers to a certain measurement procedure (e.g. Fazio and Olson, 2003), others have used the term to refer to what is presumably being measured, that is, automatically activated associations (e.g. Wilson, Lindsey and Schooler, 2000; Cunningham, Preacher and Banaji, 2001). Addressing this confusion, De Houwer (2006) proposed that the terms *direct* and *indirect* should be reserved to refer to measurement procedures, while the term *implicit* should be used for denoting the type of cognitions that are being assessed with indirect measures. In the present chapter, we mostly refrain from using the term implicit altogether. The reason is that the term implicit is often used to imply that the individual is *not conscious* of the cognitions or associations that are being measured, while this awareness is rarely measured. In addition, for most indirect measures it seems doubtful whether the individual is truly unaware of what is being assessed (e.g. Fazio and Olson, 2003). Therefore, we use the term automatic rather than implicit. The term *automatic* is traditionally used to refer to a wide range of characteristics (unintentional, goal-independent, unconscious and efficient), but several authors have argued that it is important to look at these characteristics separately, and define in what way a certain process is assumed to be automatic (e.g. Moors and De Houwer, 2006). In the present context, we use the term *automatic association* to refer to the unintentional activation of knowledge upon presentation of specific cues.

Why Assess Automatic Associations?

Individuals with an anxiety disorder, by definition, perceive relatively innocuous disorder-related stimuli as being excessively threatening or dangerous (e.g. American Psychiatric Association, 2000). Contemporary cognitive models assume that such dysfunctional associations are at the core of the problem in anxiety disorders (e.g. Beck and Clark, 1997). For example, individuals with panic disorder associate bodily sensations of arousal or anxiety (e.g. palpitations, trembling, sweating) with catastrophic consequences like having a heart attack (e.g. Clark, 1986), and individuals with spider phobia associate spiders with danger and physical harm (e.g. Arntz et al., 1993).

The existence of such associations has traditionally been examined using self-report measures by simply asking about the feared catastrophe (e.g. Arntz et al., 1993; Muris, 2002). An important feature of self-reports is, however, that individuals will report only what they are willing and able to report (e.g. Nisbett and Wilson, 1977). This limitation is potentially problematic because pertinent associations are not necessarily available for conscious introspection. In addition, an individual may discard certain spontaneously emerging associations as unimportant or irrelevant when asked to verbalize idiosyncratic fear-related associations, or may simply not want to disclose certain information. As a result, self-reports may be biased towards the social norm and certain information may remain unreported (e.g. Bijttebier, Vasey and Braet, 2003). For this reason, researchers, during the last decade, have started to complement self-report measures with *indirect* measures of associations. These instruments are called indirect because respondents are not directly asked to provide the information of interest. Instead, the desired information is inferred from task performance. The attractive feature of such tasks is that they require neither verbalization nor (conscious) introspection (e.g. Fazio and Olson, 2003; Bijtebier, Vasey and Braet, 2003, but see Vasey, Dalgleish and Silverman, 2003 for a discussion of limitations of performance-based measures in child and adolescent psychopathology). Indirect measures may be particularly useful in children, who might be more prone to respond to experimenter demands compared with adults (see Ceci and Bruck, 1993). An additional important feature of such indirect measures is that they are often assumed to assess *automatic* associations.

The emergence of indirect measures of automatic associations and the idea that they can provide important complementary information next to self-reports went hand in hand with the development of so-called dual process models for information processing (e.g. Fazio and Towles-Schwen, 1999; Wilson, Lindsey and Schooler, 2000; Strack and Deutsch, 2004; Gawronski and Bodenhausen, 2006). These models differentiate between fast automatic and slower more deliberate components of information processing and assign to each different functional properties. For instance, the Reflective Impulsive Model developed by Strack and Deutsch (2004) distinguishes an impulsive system, which is based on automatically activated associations between 'knowledge elements', from a reflective system, which uses knowledge elements for logic reasoning. Strack and Deutsch argued that our reactions and behaviours are influenced by both the impulsive and the reflective system, but that the relative influence of each system may vary widely from moment to moment and situation to situation. For example, watching a good horror movie will, in many cases, lead to the automatic activation of fear-related associations in the impulsive system. As a result, the film might give you a good scare or make you feel anxious. You might also want to avoid certain scenes by, for example, looking away from the screen. However, because the reflective system can strategically employ additional information (e.g. 'there is no real danger, it's only a movie'), the fear and accompanying avoidance tendencies can be kept under control.

An individual's strategic control will be more or less successful, depending on the strength of the activated fear associations and the extent to which there is opportunity (e.g. time, processing resources) and motivation to engage in strategically controlling the automatic 'impulses'. You may, for instance, be able to force yourself not to look away during a particularly gruesome scene, but you will inadvertently be very startled when something suddenly appears during an exciting scene with a lot of tension. In addition, there is emerging evidence that individual differences in executive capacity (related to self-control capabilities) moderate the impact of automatic associations on behaviour. For example, alcohol use and cigarette smoking are better predicted by tests of automatic appetitive associations in adolescents with limited executive capacity (assessed with a self-ordered pointing task) than in adolescents with better developed executive capacity (Grenard *et al.*, 2008; Thush *et al.*, 2008). To the extent that these findings also generalize to the domain of anxiety, it seems plausible that executive capacity also moderates the impact of automatic fear-related associations in children and adolescents. This idea is strengthened by research in the context of anxiety-related attentional biases that has found executive capacity (in this context referred to as attentional control) to moderate the impact of automatic versus more strategic attention allocation on task performance. That is, skilled control of voluntary attention may keep rein of the effects of automatic attentional biases, thereby allowing anxious individuals to limit the impact of threatening information (e.g. Derryberry and Reed, 2002).

Given the often uncontrollable and spontaneous character of many fears, the differentiation between the automatic and more controlled processes has been utilized in models of anxiety. Beck and Clark (1997), for instance, argued that the identification of a personally relevant negative stimulus activates a specific threat processing template. This template is assumed to direct automatically activated responses on the basis of the initial threat impression. If there are enough means available (time, motivation and processing resources), then this first stage of fast automatic information processing is followed by slower secondary processing of the threat information. This secondary processing, taking into account the context and coping abilities, offers the opportunity to react with more controlled responses. Following this, automatically initiated fear responses may deviate from more elaborated fear responses. This framework offers an explanation for the observation that adult individuals with specific fears often report knowing that their fear is unreasonable, but nevertheless show strong spontaneous fear responses when confronted with anxiogenic stimuli. This dissociation is mentioned in the *Diagnostic and Statistical Manual for Mental Disorders* (American Psychiatric Association (APA), 2000) as part of the diagnosis of specific phobia. In a similar vein, it may explain the observation that different components of the fear response (verbal, physiological and overt behaviour) are only loosely coupled (Lang, 1985). It is important to note, however, that while in most anxiety disorders impulsive as well as reflective processes can be argued to be involved, it is likely that the relative influence of each system will vary across aspects of the disorder. For instance, the characteristic avoidance reactions in anxiety disorders (APA, 2000) or the negative ruminative thoughts in generalized anxiety (APA, 2000) are likely to be fuelled largely by reflective processes. In contrast, more immediate and spontaneous fear reactions in response to disorder-related stimuli are likely to be primarily determined by automatic processes. In fact, some scientists have argued that a fast preconscious reaction to threat is specific for fear reactions and has evolutionary value (e.g. Mineka and Öhman, 2005).

The importance of distinguishing between automatic and more controlled processes now seems widely recognized and has also been used to understand other aspects of anxiety-related information processing. One example is the attentional control theory of Eysenck *et al.*, which uses this distinction to explain the impact of anxiety on task performance (Eysenck *et al.*, 2007). Attentional control theory proposes that anxiety decreases the influence of the top-down, goal-directed attentional system and increases the influence of the bottom-up, stimulus-driven attentional system. In effect, this impairs the ability to prevent attentional resources being allocated to task-irrelevant stimuli and responses and the ability to shift the allocation of attention to remain focused on task-relevant stimuli. A major difference between the attentional control theory and the dual process models described above is that the former is focused primarily on the influence of anxiety on the allocation of attentional resources, whereas the latter focus on the influence of deliberately versus automatically activated information in memory on subsequent responses. Similarities between these models involve the importance of distinguishing between automatic and more controlled processes, the notion that fear and anxiety-related information is processed with priority and the idea that executive functions of working memory are important in determining the extent to which the (influences of) automatic processing of fear and anxiety-related information can be controlled.

From a dual process perspective on anxiety, the appeal of indirect measures of automatic associations is that they are assumed to capture the automatically activated information in memory, whereas self-reports are assumed to tap into more reflective processes. Recent empirical studies modelling the processes underlying RT tests such as the popular Implicit Association Test (IAT) and the extrinsic affective Simon task (EAST) have confirmed this theoretical distinction (e.g. Conrey *et al.*, 2005; Nosek and Smyth, 2007; Stahl and Degner, 2007). Indirect measure of automatic associations may thus provide important complementary information to self-reports.

A Brief Summary of Findings in Adults

In adults many studies have examined hypotheses that follow from applying the dual process framework to cognitive models of anxiety, using a variety of indirect measures of automatic associations (see Huijding, 2006 for a review). Such studies have found evidence that high fearful individuals are characterized by fear-related automatic associations in a variety of anxiety-related problems, including spider fear (e.g. Teachman, Gregg and Woody, 2001; Huijding and de Jong, 2005a), social anxiety (de Jong *et al.* 2001; de Jong, 2002; Tanner, Stopa and De Houwer, 2006), panic (Schneider and Schulte, 2007; Teachman, Smith-Janik and Saporito, 2007), high anxiety sensitivity (Teachman, 2005) and symptoms of post-traumatic stress (Engelhard *et al.*, 2007). In addition, such associations have been found to have specific predictive power for relatively uncontrollable fear responses in social anxiety (Egloff and Schmuckle, 2002) and fear of spiders (Huijding and de Jong, 2006).

Researchers have also investigated the malleability of fear-related associations over the course of treatment. While dysfunctional associations appear relatively robust to change with single-session exposure (e.g. Huijding and de Jong, 2009), there are data suggesting that with more practice these associations do change (Teachman and Woody, 2003). An important question that remains is the extent to which changes in fear-related automatic associations are necessary for long-term symptom alleviation. Some authors have proposed that residual fear-related automatic associations may not hamper symptom alleviation in the short term, but may be related to relapse (Huijding and de Jong, 2009). Researchers in the field of adult anxiety are now starting to address the question of whether the dysfunctional fear-related associations are a causal factor in the onset of anxiety. This research will require the experimental manipulation of fear-related associations, but as yet there are no published studies that have tried to do this in the context of anxiety. There is a lack of corresponding work in child and adolescent samples. However, given that most anxiety disorders are assumed to have their origins in childhood, it would make sense to address these issues in younger populations. In the next section, we discuss the few studies in this field and describe measures that have been used to this purpose.

How to Assess Automatic Associations?

A number of indirect measures of automatic associations have been developed, but here we will discuss only the measures that have been used with children and adolescents in the domain of anxiety. These tasks are the IAT, the affective priming paradigm (APP), and the EAST.[1]

Affective priming paradigm (APP)

The APP, developed by Fazio et al. (1986), was the first RT paradigm developed to assess automatic associations. In this paradigm, participants are presented with two stimuli in quick succession. The first stimulus is the prime, to which no response is required. After a short period, the prime is replaced by the second stimulus, the target. Participants are asked to evaluate this target stimulus as either positive or negative and as fast as possible. The idea behind the APP is that when the valence of the prime is congruent with the valence of the target (e.g. 'love' – 'happy'), participants will be faster to evaluate the target than when the valence of the prime–target pair is incongruent (i.e. 'love' – 'awful') (e.g. Fazio et al., 1986; Hermans, De Houwer and Eelen, 2001). By comparing whether participants are faster naming the valence of positive or negative targets following a certain prime, the valence of the prime can be inferred.

Application to child and adolescent anxiety

One of the first studies to employ the APP with children was carried out by Field (2006) to test whether preferences towards novel stimuli can be conditioned in children aged 7–9 years. He found that pairing novel cartoon characters [conditioned stimulus (CS)] with either Brussels sprouts [negative unconditioned stimulus (US)] or ice cream (positive US), resulted in US congruent affective reactions to these characters on both a self-report measure (Experiment 1) and the APP (where the CSs were the primes; Experiment 2). In Experiment 2, children were instructed to evaluate target words as being 'nice' (good, happy, joy, love, pretty and smile) or 'nasty' (bad, dead, cry, sick, hate and sad) that were preceded by the cartoon characters. The main purpose for using the APP in this study was to circumvent the potential influence of experimental demand when assessing preferences following a conditioning procedure in which participants may have been aware of the CS–US contingencies. In designing the task, particular care was taken in selecting the labels (e.g. using the labels 'nice' and 'nasty' instead of pleasant and unpleasant) and stimulus materials, ensuring that children within the age range of this sample could easily read the target words and knew their evaluative meaning. Although this study did not look at the acquisition of anxiety as such,

---

[1] Again note that there are memory-based measures that have been successfully applied in other domains, which may be applied in this domain as well (see Ames et al., 2007; Thush et al., 2007).

it does show that the APP can be useful to measure negative emotional responses (disliking) in children.

Field *et al.* have also used the APP in several studies as an indirect measure of fears to novel stimuli induced by either verbal information or vicarious learning. Lawson, Banerjee and Field (2007), for example, gave children threat, positive or no information about three novel social situations (going to a summer camp, appearing on TV and meeting a celebrity) and measured the effect that this information had on their self-reported fear beliefs about these situations. Following Field (2006), they also included an APP, except that the primes were photographs representing the situations associated with positive and threat information.

A similar APP was used by Askew and Field (2007) to measure preferences for novel animals to which responses had been previously conditioned using emotional facial expressions (scared or happy) as USs. The APP again used the CSs as primes (in this case, pictures of the two animal CSs that were previously paired with the scared or happy faces) to nice and nasty target words. Askew and Field also followed up the children at 1 week, 1 month and 3 months. They found significant priming effects post-experiment and at 1 week, and although these effects were non-significant at 1 month, they re-emerged at 3-month follow-up. These findings imply that the affective priming task has poor test–retest reliability, although it is possible that the weakness of the APP effects reflect a weak conditioning effect because self-report measures also weakened over time. Despite the initial success with the APP in demonstrating the utility of using indirect measures to reflect attitude change in children, Askew (2007) reported six further studies in children of the same age in which differential attitudes to novel animals conditioned with vicarious learning did show up in self-reports, but not in an APP task. This failure to replicate the APP findings may suggest two things. First, it is possible that the self-report data reflected experimental demand rather than a true conditioning effect, and the APP results simply highlighted that the conditioning procedure was ineffective. This explanation does not seem very likely, however, as in one experiment a US revaluation manipulation after the conditioning procedure had no effect on self-report. Second, the failure to find differential attitudes on the APP in some, but not all conditioning studies, may indicate that the APP does not reliably pick up vicariously conditioned anxiety cognitions.

Spence *et al.* (2006) used the APP to explore whether anxious and non-anxious children show different emotional priming effects and whether such differences are age dependent (7- to 10-year-olds vs. 11- to 14-year-olds). In their APP, Spence *et al.* used pleasant pictures (e.g. puppies) and threat pictures (e.g. a man with a gun) as primes and pleasant words (e.g. friend) and unpleasant words (e.g. nightmare) as targets that had to be evaluated. Although all children (independent of age and anxiety status) were faster to respond to positive targets following congruent compared with incongruent primes, the 11- to 14-year-olds responded equally fast to positive and negative target following negative primes, whereas the 7- to 10-year-old children showed a reverse priming effect (i.e. faster responses to positive than to negative targets following a negative prime). Referring to findings in adults (Glaser and Banaji, 1999; Maier, Berner and Pekrun, 2003) they suggest that the direction of priming effects (congruency or contrast effects) may depend on activation level of the evaluative representation in memory. Strong activation, resulting from highly salient primes and/or high levels of anxiety, would cause contrast effects. The authors note that 'It is plausible that the threshold at which inhibition rather than facilitation occurs in response to congruent negatively valenced prime–target stimuli is lower for younger children' (Spence *et al.*, 2006, p. 108). In addition, younger children may have evaluated the threat stimuli as more negative, making them more salient. However, these *post hoc* explanations are speculative and more research is warranted. Furthermore, the results showed that there were no differences between the anxious and non-anxious children. The lack of effect of anxiety status may be explained by the fact that the group of anxious children included children with different diagnoses [e.g. generalized anxiety disorder, separation anxiety disorder, social phobia, specific phobia] and no disorder specific stimuli were used. The authors took care with the selection of age-appropriate stimulus materials for the APP, and children's understanding of the task was always verified. Nevertheless, given the rather small sample size (i.e. $N = 50$) in this study, it is difficult to decide what to make of these findings.

In sum, research using the APP as an indirect measure of conditioned preferences produces rather mixed results. In addition, in the one study (i.e. Spence *et al.*, 2006) that explored moderating effects of anxiety in emotional priming no significant differences were found between high and low anxious children. It is unclear, however, whether this null finding should be attributed to insensitivity of that version of the APP, the particular design of the study (e.g. the sample that was used) or to a 'true' lack of difference between the two groups. Taken together, research using the APP with children has produced inconsistent results. To understand whether this task is a useful indirect indicator of learned fears across development or in children with anxiety, further research should aim to explore its potential using larger sample sizes and stimuli that have more relevance to specific anxiety disorders (Table 7.1).

Unresolved issues and the APP

Although there has been a lot of research with the APP in adults samples, both its internal consistency and test–retest reliability are often found to be low (e.g. Bosson, Swann and Pennebaker, 2000; Fazio and Olson, 2003, but see Cunningham, Preacher and Banaji, 2001). In the studies published thus far in child and adolescent anxiety, no reliability data are reported.

Implicit Association Test (IAT)

The IAT, developed by Greenwald, McGhee and Schwarz (1998), is a RT sorting task in which participants are instructed to sort stimuli into four different categories using two response keys. In a typical IAT, two of the categories represent so-called target concepts (e.g. flowers vs. insects), while the other two categories represent the poles of an attribute dimension (e.g. positive vs. negative). The IAT has two critical phases during which each response key is assigned to one of the targets and one of the attribute categories. The two phases differ with respect to the target-attribute

Table 7.1. Details of affective priming tasks used with children

Authors	Primes/targets	Blocks/trials	Timing	Adjustments
Field, 2006	P: 1 positively and 1 negatively conditioned novel cartoon character T: 6 'Nice' and 6 'Nasty' words	B 1: 12 practice trials B 2: 48 test trials	500 ms fixdot 200 ms prime 100 ms blank Target 2000 ms ITI	Stimulus selection age appropriate. Labels: 'Nice' and 'Nasty' rather than 'Pleasant' and 'Unpleasant'
Lawson, Banerjee and Field, 2007	P: photographs of 3 social situations for one of which children had received positive, 1 negative and 1 no information T: 'Nice' and 'Nasty' words (no n's reported)	B 1: 12 practice trials B 2: 72 test trials	See Field, 2006	See Field, 2006
Askew and Field, 2007	P: 3 photographs of each of 3 unknown animals that were paired with either happy, scared or no facial expressions T: 6 'Nice' and 6 'Nasty' words	B 1: 12 practice trials B 2: 72 test trials	See Field, 2006	See Field, 2006
Spence et al., 2006	P: 6 pleasant and 6 unpleasant International Affective Picture Set (IAPS) pictures (child rated) T: 6 pleasant and 6 threat words (child rated)	B 1: 10 practice trials B 2–5: 36 test trials each	200 ms fixdot 13 ms blank 200 ms prime 100 ms blank Target 1000 ms ITI	Stimulus selection age appropriate. To check understanding of target words children read them out loud before start

P, prime; T, target; B, block; Fixdot, fixation dot; ITI, inter-trial interval.

combinations that share the response keys. For example, in the first critical phase participants may be instructed to press the left response key for stimuli from the categories 'flowers' and 'positive' and the right response key for stimuli from the categories 'insects' and 'negative'. Then, in the second critical phase, participants are instructed to press the left response key for stimuli from the categories 'insects' and 'positive' and the right response key for stimuli from the categories 'flowers' and 'negative'. The idea behind the IAT is that participants will find it easier to sort the stimuli during a critical phase (i.e. will work faster and/or more accurately) when the target and attribute category that share a response key are associated in memory (compatible) than when they are not (incompatible). The difference in performance between the compatible and the incompatible phases is referred to as the *IAT effect* and interpreted as the relative strength of automatic associations between the target and attribute categories (Greenwald, McGhee and Schwarz, 1998).

Using the IAT in child and adolescent anxiety

Only four studies have used the IAT in the context of anxiety in child and adolescent samples. Field and Lawson (2003) and Field, Lawson and Banerjee (2008), for example, employed the IAT to circumvent potential influence of experimental demand on self-reported affective ratings. More specifically, they used the IAT as an indirect measure of automatic associations with unknown animals concerning which participants received positive or threat information. The aim of these studies was to test the idea that information might be important in the development of fears (see Rachman, 1977). In their IAT, children sorted pictures of unknown animals (the targets) together with nice and nasty words (the attributes) using two response keys. Results showed that, as expected, children were faster sorting the stimuli when an animal for which they had received positive information shared the response key with 'nice' and the animal for which they received negative information with 'nasty' than when the response assignments were reversed (Field and Lawson, 2003) and that these effects remained up to 6 months later (Field, Lawson and Banerjee, 2008). Immediately post-experiment, the information manipulation had similar effects on self-reported fear beliefs and behavioural avoidance (i.e. more fear and avoidance of 'threat' animals) (Field and Lawson, 2003). No correlations between these measures were reported in the paper; however, the correlation between the IAT effect (incompatible trial RTs – compatible trial RTs) and self-reported fear beliefs (change in fear beliefs for the threat animal – change in fear beliefs for the positive animal) was $r = -.035$, and between the IAT and the behavioural task (approach time for the negative animal – approach times for the positive animal) was, $r = -.013$. As mentioned above, these low correlations are not surprising, given that different measures of anxiety are frequently asynchronous (Lang, 1968; review by Zinbarg, 1998). Perhaps the most interesting finding that emerged from this series of studies was that IAT responses to the information given about the animals (like self-reported fear) persisted up to 6 months despite there being no further information delivered to the children during this period (see Field, Lawson and Banerjee, 2008). This finding implies that the IAT is reliable over time in child samples.

Teachman and Allen (2007) used the IAT in a prospective, 6-year longitudinal study that aimed to evaluate the predictive power of peer interactions (i.e. perceived social acceptance and social behaviours with peers) at the ages 13, 14 and 15 for fear of negative evaluation (FNE) at the age of 17–18. They distinguished between 'implicit' FNE (i.e. automatic associations with rejection) and explicit (i.e. self-reported) FNE. Both methods were used in this study because of the potential influence of self-presentational concerns on self-reported FNE and to address the prediction that follows from dual process models (e.g. Wilson, Lindsey and Schooler, 2000) that both measures provide complementary information. The IAT was used to assess the extent to which adolescents associated the category 'me' (relative to 'not me') with the attributes 'liked' versus 'rejected'.[2] Results showed that perceived social acceptance predicted explicit FNE, whereas observer-rated intensity of social interactions with a close friend concerning a problem (in terms of reassurance-seeking, dependence and making social comparisons) predicted 'implicit' FNE. These are exciting results because they are the first to show that automatic associations and more reflective beliefs are differentially related to spontaneous and more deliberated behaviours in adolescence.

Finally, following the idea that low self-esteem may be a risk factor for the development of social anxiety, Sportel *et al.* (2007) used the IAT to test whether automatic and self-reported evaluations of the self are related to social anxiety in adolescents. In this IAT participants sorted words from the target categories 'me' and 'other' together with social evaluation-related positive (e.g. smart, nice, pleasant) and negative (e.g. stupid, mean, unpleasant) attribute words. In contrast to their expectations, only an explicit measure of self-reported self-esteem was related to a self-report measure of social anxiety. However, if indirect measures of automatic associations and self-report tap different cognitive motivational systems (see above), then the lack of a relation between the self-esteem IAT and the social phobia scale may explain this discrepancy. It will be interesting to see what results this ongoing prospective study will yield in the future.

Applications of the IAT task

A similar self-esteem IAT as used by Sportel *et al.* (2007) was used by Huijding, Bos and Muris (in press) to assess whether automatic positive associations can be bolstered using an evaluative conditioning procedure. Primary school children aged between 9 and 13 years were randomly assigned to either an experimental group that completed the IAT before and after an evaluative conditioning procedure or a control group that completed the IAT before and after a neutral conditioning procedure. Across five experiments no consistent evidence was found that the evaluative conditioning procedure had the desired effect. In addition, no meaningful relations were found between the IAT and self-report measures of self-esteem or another measure of 'implicit' self-esteem (i.e. the name letter preference task, see

---

[2] Note that it is not entirely clear whether the IAT measures *FNE* or the extent to which a person automatically associates him or herself with rejection. In the latter case, the results could be a reflection of *fear* of rejection, but also experienced *actual* rejection.

Nuttin, 1985). Perhaps most important in the present context is that this study reported reliabilities of the IAT in a child sample. Over five experiments Spearman-Brown corrected split-half reliabilities were on average $r = .63$ at the first assessment but lower at subsequent assessments at 1-week and 1-month follow-up (around $r = .44$ for the second and third assessment over 2 experiments). This pattern of data suggests that the internal consistency of this version of the IAT is lower than that reported for adult samples but still higher than reliabilities reported for other latency-based measures in adult samples (e.g. Nosek, Greenwald and Banaji, 2007). Over two experiments, the test–retest correlations in the control group were all small but significant: on average $r = .26$ between the first and second (1-week interval), $r = .25$ between the first and third (5-week interval) and $r = .36$ between the second and third assessments (4-week interval). These test–retest reliabilities are clearly lower than what has been reported for IATs in adults (Nosek, Greenwald and Banaji, 2007), but still higher than those reported for other RT-based indirect assessments like the APP (Bosson, Swann and Pennebaker, 2000). In addition, over three experiments approximately only 4% of the children were excluded because they made more than 25% errors, suggesting that the task is not too difficult for children in this age group. This version of the IAT was adjusted to the child sample, following Field and Lawson (2003). In addition, while all instructions were displayed on screen, they were also always explained verbally by the experimenter.

In the field of social psychology, researchers have also used the IAT in adolescent samples in the context of racial attitudes. Similar to what has been found in adults, Rutland *et al.* (2005) found a preference for white over black faces in a group of 6- to 8-year-old, 10- to 12-year-old, and 14- to 16-year-old children. Baron and Banaji (2006) found a similar preference in 6- and 8-year-old children. In addition, they found that this preference did not differ significantly from that in a group of adults. Dunham, Baron and Banaji (2006) replicated these results in an American (Experiment 1) and a Japanese sample (Experiment 2). Interestingly, whereas in all these studies an automatic preference for white over black faces was evident in all age groups, on self-reports this preference was evident only in the youngest age groups and disappeared with age. The implication that follows from this pattern of results is that early automatic preferences may be enduring, while explicit preferences change over time as more information (e.g. cultural norms, experience) becomes available. Similar findings have been reported in other domains. For example, in substance misuse, negative associations are prevalent in adolescents and adults (see for a review, Wiers *et al.*, 2006) and some authors have argued that these reflect early childhood negative experiences (e.g. dad's smoking in the car, Rudman, Greenwald and McGhee, 2001). Translated to the context of fear and anxiety, this finding raises the possibility that automatic negative associations with certain stimuli that were acquired during childhood may persist, even though they are inconsistent with explicit knowledge acquired later in life. For example, even though an individual who became afraid of dogs after a single aversive event in childhood may learn later in life that dogs are mostly harmless, the negative associations with dogs that were acquired in childhood may persist.

Sinclair, Dunn and Lowery (2005) also found that 10- to 11-year-olds showed an automatic preference for white over black faces on an IAT. In addition, parents were asked to complete a self-report measure of racial attitudes. Results showed that children and parents' implicit and explicit racial attitudes corresponded to the degree that the children identified with their parents. Identification was measured with four items asking whether the children cared about making their parents proud, how often they did what their parents told them, how much they enjoyed spending time with, and how much they wanted to be like the parent who completed the IAT. Interestingly,

[...] among highly identified children, parental prejudice was significantly related to children's implicit prejudice but only marginally related to children's explicit prejudice, while among less identified children, parental prejudice was unrelated to children's implicit prejudice but *negatively* related to children's explicit prejudice. It is possible, then, that children who identify with their parents may adopt the racial attitudes of their parents more on an implicit than an explicit level, whereas children who do not identify with their parents may actually reject their parents attitudes, but only on an explicit level.' (p. 287).

Although no strong claims about the origins of children's preferences can be made on the basis of these correlational data, these results may be of interest to researchers in the field of child and adolescent anxiety because they show that explicitly endorsed views of parents potentially have an influence on their children's automatic preferences.

Researchers using the IAT in the context of racial prejudice have made a number of adjustments to the IAT to make it more suitable for use with children. For instance, with respect to children's reading abilities pilot work of Rutland *et al.* (2005) indicated that 6- to 7- year-old children have difficulty understanding a word-based IAT (in particular a racial prejudice IAT in which the exemplars for the target categories 'black' and 'white' were names like Latishia and Ebony). For this reason, Rutland *et al.* (2005) used pictures of black and white faces as exemplars of the target categories. In addition, simple line drawings of happy and sad cartoon faces were used as exemplars for the attribute categories 'happy' and 'sad'.[3] Baron and Banaji (2006) also used pictorial target stimuli, but made the additional adjustment of using pictures of child instead of adult faces.[4] To circumvent the problem of variability in reading level among children with respect to the attribute stimuli these authors presented the attribute words auditorily (through speakers) instead of visually on the computer screen. For the same reason, children received spoken instructions from the experimenter. One might question

[3] There is a potential drawback of using the categories 'happy' and 'sad' as alternatives for 'pleasant' and 'unpleasant'. A relative dislike of black faces or white faces may be different from associating racial facial features with happiness or sadness. It is conceivable that children perceive black individuals as less happy than white individuals, but not necessarily more negative.

[4] It is not clear how this modification would make the task better suited for children, because it is not evident that children would make stronger or different racial evaluations of children compared to adults.

whether this adapted IAT of Baron and Banaji (2006) is similar to the standard IAT, because it is no longer a purely visual task but requires participants to continually switch between modalities (visual and auditory) to make the correct responses. However, pilot work showed high correlations (>.75) between the child IAT and the standard IAT, suggesting that the adapted IAT does not measure anything different (S. Baron, personal communication, 9 January 2008).

Researchers have also tried to accommodate children's limited motor skills. Baron and Banaji (2006) facilitated easy manual responses by using large buttons instead of keyboard keys as response keys. Following pilot work showing that some children had difficulty using keypad responses, Rutland *et al.* (2005) decided to use mouse movements towards or away from the screen as responses. By incorporating approach-avoidance-like motions in the responses, this task essentially becomes an approach-avoidance task in which the responses have an intrinsic evaluative connotation that is absent in standard IATs using a left and a right response key. It is therefore hard to make a direct comparison between this task and the standard IAT.

Finally, some researchers have tried to adjust the lengths of the IAT to the generally shorter attention span of (young) children compared to adults. For instance, Rutland *et al.* (2005) observed that 6- to 8-year-olds appeared to become bored and fatigued during the standard IAT, and therefore reduced the number of practice trials for this younger group with 12 trials. It is unclear, however, why a reduction of 12 trials was chosen and what kind of difference this reduction made for the younger children.

Thomas, Smith and Ball (2007) recently developed an IAT that integrated the response keys in the screen. Stimuli were presented on a touch screen and participants were instructed to respond by touching a response area on the left or the right side of the screen. Each response area held small logos as a reminder of the response requirements. Using this version of the IAT they replicated the standard flower–insect IAT effects (see Greenwald, McGhee and Schwarz, 1998) in a sample of 3- to 7-year-old children. In addition, they found that these children also showed a preference for images of thin adult female models over images of fat models. Interestingly, they reported that the magnitude in both IATs was independent of age, but that (as may be expected) children in the younger age groups were on average slower to respond than children in the older age groups.

A final adaptation to the IAT was made by Banse *et al.* (2006), who greatly simplified the task. In their so-called Action Interference Task (AIT) children aged 5-, 8- and 11-years were asked to help Santa Claus sort the presents for different children. After a brief training phase participants were presented with a picture of a boy and a girl in the opposite lower corners of the screen and were presented with a series of pictures of toys that they had to drag to the correct picture. Half of these toys were stereotypically for boys (e.g. cars, tools), the other half for girls (e.g. dolls, dolls clothes). During the stereotype-compatible phase the boys' toys had to be dragged to the picture of the boy and the girls' toys to the picture of the girl. During the stereotype-incompatible phase these assignments were reversed. Results showed that although children's overall response latencies decreased with age, children of all age groups were faster during the gender stereotype compatible than during the incompatible phase. However, it should be noted that, unlike the IAT, the response assignments in the AIT can easily be recoded to reduce or eliminate the interference. For instance the task boys' toys → girl/girls' toys → boy can easily be recoded to boys' toys → left and girls' toys → right, excluding any interference that might be caused by assigning a gender-incompatible toy. Although most young children do not appear to use this spatial strategy, results show that in an adult sample the task is no longer sensitive (R. Banse, personal communication, 17 December 2007).

In sum, a number of studies have used the IAT in child and adolescent samples, adjusting the task in a number of ways and to various degrees to accommodate the study of developing populations. In the context of anxiety, the IAT is found to be sensitive to differences in automatic associations with unknown animals for which children just received positive or negative information (Field and Lawson, 2003; Field, Lawson and Banerjee, 2008), but no correlation was found between a self-esteem IAT and self-reported social symptoms of social anxiety (Sportel et al., 2007). This lack of association might be explained by the fact that indirect measures of automatic associations and self-report tap different cognitive motivational systems. In line with such an explanation, further research has found that spontaneous insecure social behaviours best predicted automatic associations between oneself and rejection, whereas self-reported perceived social acceptance best predicted self-reported social anxiety symptoms (see Teachman and Allen, 2007). Outside the area of anxiety research the IAT has mostly been used in child and adolescent samples in the context of racial prejudice. In these studies the IAT reliably detects a preference of white over black faces, similar to what has frequently been found in adults, suggesting that the IAT is a useful tool for assessing implicit preferences in child and adolescent samples. Researchers have varied in the extent to which and in what way they adjusted the IAT for use with children. The fact that converging findings are nevertheless found suggests that IAT effects in children seem relatively robust against procedural variations. At the same time, these findings make it difficult to decide how best to adjust the IAT to child and adolescent samples. However, there does seem to be some consensus that responses should be facilitated, for instance using large response keys, and that reading difficulties should be avoided where possible, for instance, by using pictorial stimuli (Table 7.2).

Unresolved issues and the IAT

The IAT owes its popularity to the fact that it is easily adapted to suit diverse research topics and shows relatively good internal consistency in adult samples (e.g. Bosson, Swann and Pennebaker, 2000, see Nosek, Greenwald and Banaji, 2007 for a review). It is important to note, however, that the single study which reported internal consistencies and test–retest correlations in a sample of children found both reliability indices to be lower than what is usually reported in studies using adult samples. Nevertheless, both indices still indicated better reliability than most other RT-based indirect measures. Furthermore, it is encouraging that some studies have shown that the error rates and the percentage of very fast and slow responses appear not to be very extreme (Huijding, Bos and Muris, in press) and similar to what is reported for adults (Sinclair, Dunn and Lowery, 2005). Consistent with

Table 7.2. Details of Implicit Association Tests used with children

Authors	Targets/attributes	Blocks/trials	Effect measure	Timing/procedure	Adjustments
		Studies in the context of anxiety			
Field and Lawson, 2003 Field Lawson and Banerjee, 2008	T: 6 photographs of 2 out of 3 unknown animals (Quokka, Quoll, Cuscus) for which children had just received positive or negative information A: 8 'Nice' and 8 'Nasty' words	B 1: 24 attrib. prac. B 2: 24 target prac. B 3: 36 comb. prac. B 4: 40 comb. test B 5: 24 rev. target prac. B 6: 36 rev. comb. prac. B 7: 40 rev. comb. test (224 trials)	None calculated. Analysis with untransformed RTs of correct trials in B 4 and B 7. RTs > 2 SD's from the child's mean were excluded	Error feedback: red X	Instructions were adjusted
Teachman and Allen, 2007	T: 3 'Me' and 3 'Not Me' words A: 3 'Rejected' and 3 'Liked' words	B 1: 20 comb. prac. B 2: 36 comb. test B 3: 20 rev. comb. prac. B 4: 36 rev. comb. test (112 trials)	D-measure, Greenwald data reduction (Errors and RTs)	After error first correct response had to be given	None reported
Sportel et al., 2007	T: 5 'Me' and 5 'Other' words. A: 5 'Positive' and 5 'Negative' words	B 1: attrib. prac. B 2: target prac. B 3: comb. prac. B 4: comb. test B 5: rev. target prac. B 6: rev. comb. prac. B 7: rev. comb. test (N trials not reported)	No details reported		Instructions were adjusted

(continued overleaf)

Table 7.2. (*Continued*)

Authors	Targets/attributes	Blocks/trials	Effect measure	Timing/procedure	Adjustments
		Studies outside the context of anxiety			
Huijding, Bos and Muris, in press	T: 5 'Me' and 5 'Other' words A: 5 'Positive' and 5 'Negative' words	B 1: 10 target prac. B 2: 10 attrib. prac. B 3: 20 comb. prac. B 4: 40 comb. test B 5: 30 rev. target prac. B 6: 20 rev. comb. prac. B 7: 40 rev. comb. test (170 trials)	D-measure (D4)	500 ms fixdot, then stimulus After correct resp. immediately next trial. After error red X appeared under the stimulus and correct response had to be given	Based on Field and Lawson, 2003. Instructions were adjusted. (more instructions, slower paced, more repeating)
Sinclair, Dunn and Lowery, 2005	T: 6 photographs of Black and 6 of White faces (50% female each) A: 8 'Good' and 8 'Bad' words	B 1: 20 target prac. B 2: 20 attrib. prac. B 3: 20 comb. prac. B 4: 40 comb. test B 5: 30 rev. target prac. B 6: 20 rev. comb. prac. B 7: 40 rev. comb. test (190 trials)	Website automatic calculation. Probably the old algorithm	Website version for adults was used, no further details reported	No adjustments reported
Rutland et al., 2005	T: **Study 1** Photographs of Black and White faces (sex was matched with sex of participant?)	**6- to 8-year-olds** B 1: 12 attrib. prac. B 2: 12 target prac. B 3: 32 comb. test B 4: 12 rev. target prac.	Old algorithm and median RTs (no differences in results)	Not explicitly reported but probably similar to the Greenwald et al. (1998) procedure	Instead of keypad responses participants had to move the mouse towards or away

Reference	Target (T) and Attribute (A) materials	Blocks	Analysis	ITI	Comments
	T: **Study 2** Photographs of Black and White faces with British or German flag superimposed on it. (N exemplars per category is not reported) A: **Study 1 and 2** line drawings of happy and sad cartoon faces	B 5: 32 rev. comb. test (100 trials) **10- to 16-year-olds** B 1: 16 attrib. prac. B 2: 16 target prac. B 3: 32 comb. test B 4: 16 rev. target prac. B 5: 32 rev. comb. test (112 trials)			from the computer screen. Arrows were attached to the screen as reminders
Baron and Banaji, 2006	T: **Flower–Insect IAT** 4 pictures of insects and 4 of flowers **Race IAT** 4 photographs of black and 4 of white child faces A: **Both IATs** 4 'Good' and 4 'Bad' words	B 1: 20 target prac. B 2: 20 attrib. prac. B 3: 20 comb. prac. B 4: 40 comb. test B 5: 30 rev. target prac. B 6: 20 rev. comb. prac. B 7: 40 rev. comb. test (190 trials)	D-measure, but first calculated separately for target and attribute trials and then averaged	1000 ms ITI, no fixdot	Age-appropriate attribute words, presented verbally Large response keys. In race IAT child instead of adult faces were used
Dunham, Baron and Banaji, 2006	T: **White–Black IAT** 4 photographs of black and 4 of white children, **White–Japanese IAT** 4 photographs of Japanese and 4 of white children A: **both IATs** 4 'Good' and 4 'Bad' words	See Baron and Banaji, 2006	Multilevel modelling of square root transformed raw latencies (excl RTs >6500 ms and > 5 sds from mean of that test and age group	See Baron and Banaji, 2006	See Baron and Banaji, 2006

(continued overleaf)

Table 7.2. (*Continued*)

Authors	Targets/attributes	Blocks/trials	Effect measure	Timing/procedure	Adjustments
Thomas, Smith and Ball, 2007	T: **Flower–Insect IAT** Photographs of flowers and insects **Thin–Fat IAT** images of fat and thin adult female models A: **both IATs** Sad (labelled 'bad') and smiling (labelled 'good') emoticons. (N exemplars not reported)	B 1: 20 attrib. prac. B 2: 10 target prac. B 3: 30 comb. test B 4: 10 rev. target prac. B 5: 30 rev. comb test (100 trials)	Old algorithm on untransformed raw latencies (excluding RTs >7500 ms). >25% errors were excluded	Not reported	Stimuli presented on a touch screen, participants had to press response areas on the screen that contained a label as reminder (small emoticons and small flower/insect or thin/fat logo)

T, target; A, attribute; B, block; Prac., practice; Attrib., attribute; Comb., combined; Rev., reversed; RTs, reaction times; Fixdot, fixation dot; ITI, inter-trial interval.

what has been reported for the APP, overall response times increase as participants get younger (e.g. Rutland *et al.*, 2005).

Despite the popularity of the IAT, the task does have several drawbacks. For example, inherent to its design, the IAT can be used only to assess relative attitudes for bipolar target concepts (e.g. self vs. others, men vs. women). This is not necessarily a problem, but renders the task suboptimal for assessing unipolar concepts that have no obvious meaningful contrast, such as 'spiders' (de Jong *et al.*, 2003). In a similar vein, the relative nature of the attribute dimension (e.g. positive–negative) can be problematic when one expects individuals to have ambivalent or multiple associations with a certain target. To overcome this limitation, researchers have designed the so-called *single-category* IAT (SC-IAT, Karpinski and Steinman, 2006) and the single-attribute IAT (SA-IAT, Penke, Eichstaedt and Asendorpf, 2006). Both IAT types are structurally very similar to the IAT, but use a single target or a single-attribute category, rather than two (bipolar) categories. Thush and Wiers (2007) used an SC-IAT to assess alcohol associations in young adolescents and this measure showed good predictive validity, predicting binge-drinking a year later in 12-year-old boys. This finding suggests that the SC-IAT may be a good measure to use in young samples.

Other concerns focus on the validity of the IAT as a measure of automatic associations. Briefly, it has been argued that the IAT effect (i.e. being relatively fast when a certain target-attribute combination shares the same response requirement) is based on the extent to which the target and attribute categories are similar (see De Houwer, Geldof and De Bruycker, 2005). Ideally, one would want that the similarity in valence is the cause of relatively fast responses in one block and relatively slow responses in the other. However, it has been shown that similarities on other features may cause IAT effects as well, for instance, category salience (Rothermund and Wentura, 2004) or perceptual features (De Houwer, Geldof and De Bruycker, 2005). Related to this, Mierke and Klauer (2003) argued that while in the compatible phase all stimuli can be categorized according to a single dimension, because the categories that share response keys are in some respect 'similar' this categorization effect is not possible during the incompatible phase. During this phase, the target and attribute categories that share response keys are (by definition) dissimilar. As a result, participants will continually have to switch between the task requirements for sorting target stimuli and the requirements for sorting the attribute stimuli.

Mierke and Klauer (2003) showed that there are stable inter-individual differences in task-switch ability and that this ability influences the size of the IAT effect. It is conceivable that task-switch ability may vary more among children than adults and may influence IAT results, especially when comparing children who are in different stages of development. Although analysing the data using the D-measure (Greenwald, Nosek and Banaji, 2003) removes this method-specific variance from the IAT in adults, the D-measure has been criticized for other reasons (e.g. Rothermund, Wentura and De Houwer, 2005) and may be suboptimal in within-subject designs (e.g. Wiers *et al.*, 2005). A final point of which researchers should be aware is the effect of category labels versus individual category exemplars. Some studies suggest that IAT effects are primarily based on category labels (De Houwer, 2001), while other data have shown that the individual exemplars do have an effect (Bluemke and Friese, 2006). Some argue that the category labels provide a context in which individual exemplars are interpreted (Mitchell, Nosek and Banaji, 2003), whereas others argue that the individual exemplars define how the categories are interpreted (Govan and Williams, 2004). Whatever the case, researchers should be aware that both the specific category labels that are chosen and the exemplar stimuli can impact the IAT effects, and care should be taken with the selection of both.

Extrinsic affective Simon task (EAST)

The final indirect measure that has been used in the context of child and adolescent automatic association assessment is the EAST (De Houwer, 2003). In his seminal experiment, De Houwer (2003) asked participants to sort stimulus words that were displayed in white as fast as possible on the basis of their valence using two response keys. All white words were clearly positively or negatively valenced. In a subsequent phase, stimulus words were presented, which were sometimes displayed in green and sometimes in blue. Participants had to sort these words on the basis of their colour, using the same response keys as before. In the critical phase, the presentation of white and coloured words was intermixed, and participants sorted the white words on the basis of their valence and the coloured words on the basis of their colour. The idea behind the EAST is that by pairing each response key consistently with either positive or negative white words, the keys acquire an *extrinsic* positive or a negative valence. As a consequence, during the test phase participants have to respond to the coloured words by pressing either the (extrinsically) positive or the negative key, depending on the print colour. By presenting each word equally often in each colour and considering whether participants find it easier to give a positive or a negative response to a certain stimulus, inferences can be made about the extent to which valence is associated with the word (e.g. De Houwer, 2003). The EAST can easily be adapted to allow for the use of pictorial stimuli as well, for instance, by presenting target pictures in portrait or landscape format (e.g. Huijding and de Jong, 2005a, 2005b).

Using the EAST in child and adolescents anxiety
The only study that used the EAST in the context of child and adolescent anxiety is that of Vervoort *et al.* (2008). Vervoort *et al.* (2008) explored whether evaluative differences between neutral, negative and general anxiety-relevant pictures would emerge on a pictorial version of the EAST in an unselected sample of children (6- to 12-years old), adolescents (13- to 18-years old) and adults (older than 18 years). When using a colour filter over the target pictures as the relevant stimulus feature (i.e. the feature that determined the correct response), no significant differences between the stimuli were found, independent of age group (Experiment 1). One explanation for this null result is that when using a colour filter, the content of the target pictures is too easily ignored. In line with this, negative and anxiety-related pictures were found to be more strongly associated with negative than were neutral pictures. A second experiment used picture format (portrait or landscape) as the

relevant stimulus feature for the target pictures. In this task, general anxiety pictures were associated more strongly with negative than the negative pictures in adults. The EAST scores for the positive stimuli did not differ from zero, but as the positive pictures were also rated as neutral rather than positive on a self-report measure, this finding may be due to the particular stimuli that were used rather than an insensitivity of this version of the EAST. In line with previous studies in adults using this version of the EAST (Huijding and de Jong, 2006, 2009), effects emerged only in the EAST scores based on error percentages. In addition, the EAST scores were not significantly related to state or trait anxiety.

Vervoort *et al.* (2008) made two important adjustments compared to previously used versions of the pictorial EAST. First, in their version of the EAST there were more attribute (i.e. evaluation) trials than target trials during the test phase, making evaluation the primary task (usually there are more target than attribute trials during the test phase.) Second, a sticker of a happy or a sad emoticon (i.e. 'smiley') was placed on each response key to remind participants of the response assignments and strengthen the extrinsic valence of the responses. Internal consistency (inter-item stability, based on item variance) for the different target pictures ranged from .43 to .54. The intraclass correlation (inter-individual stability, based on inter-individual variance) was high at .88, indicating that participants completed the EAST in a consistent manner. Similar to the other RT measures discussed in this chapter, error rate and response times decreased with age. Importantly, however, even in the group of 6- to 12-year-old children the median percentage of errors did not seem to be excessively high (approximately 10%), suggesting that this version of the pictorial EAST is not too difficult for children.

Applications of the EAST

The EAST has also been used in child and adolescent samples in other areas relating to psychopathology. For instance, Craeynest *et al.* (2005), employed the EAST to assess differences in automatic associations with healthy and unhealthy food, and sedentary and intense physical activities between obese and matched control children and adolescents (aged between 9- and 18-years old). In this EAST target stimuli were pre-selected words. Attribute stimuli were provided by the participants themselves and consisted of words for foods and physical activities that the participants really (dis)liked. Results showed that obese children and adolescents associated both healthy and unhealthy food more strongly with positive than with negative, whereas lean controls showed a neutral attitude towards both types of food. With respect to physical activity both groups responded equally fast with the positive and negative response keys irrespective of the type of activity. In this study, the mean percentages of errors ranged between 6% and 12%, suggesting that this verbal EAST was not too difficult for the children. However, it is not entirely clear whether the younger participants made more errors or not.

The EAST has also been employed to assess automatic substance use-related associations in high-risk adolescents. Ames *et al.* (2007) and Thush *et al.* (2007) both found no significant relationship of the EASTs used with marijuana and alcohol use, respectively, in contrast to the IATs and explicit measures used. A likely cause for this null finding was the low reliability of the EAST in both studies. However, there were some meaningful correlations with the IAT (e.g. the IAT assessing marijuana-relaxed associations correlated with the EAST assessing the same associations), indicating that the measure had at least some validity in this adolescent sample.

Unresolved issues with the EAST

The main difficulty with the EAST is that studies that have employed the task in adult samples report low internal consistencies, although the pictorial version of the EAST seems to provide somewhat better results (Huijding and de Jong, 2005a, 2005b). De Houwer and De Bruycker (2007) argued that one reason for the low reliability of the EAST might be that its effects depend on the processing of a task-irrelevant stimulus feature, namely valence. Because there may be a number of factors that influence when and to what extent the valence of the target is actually processed, reliability of these tasks may be relatively easily compromised. This process may be especially problematic in young children with limited reading capabilities. For them the meaning of target words may be easily ignored, yielding little interference and thus weak and potentially unreliable effects. Following this line of reasoning the use of pictorial stimuli may be preferable in young children. Note that this argument can be extended to APP effects as well. That is, while APP effects also crucially depend on processing of the valence of the primes, usually participants are not instructed to do anything with or pay special attention to the primes. The study of Vervoort *et al.* (2008) indeed shows that the internal consistency of the EAST is not very high.

Another problem with the EAST is that it may be rather difficult for children, because they need to keep the response requirements of two tasks active at the same time (i.e. the affective categorization of the attributes and the non-affective categorization of the targets (e.g. on the basis of colour or format)). The studies that have employed the EAST in child and adolescent samples thus far, however, have not reported excessively high error rates, even in young children, suggesting that this requirement may be problematic. One way to make the task easier would be to present labels in the upper corners of the screen (as is the case with the IAT) that remind participants of the task requirement.

Conclusions

The major appeal of using indirect measures of automatic associations in studying anxiety and psychopathology and health-related behaviours more generally is that these measures provide important complementary information in addition to self-reports and other performance-based measures of cognitive biases. Indirect measures are less susceptible to self-presentation biases and introspective limitations. This benefit may be an especially important advantage in research with children, who are more likely to respond to experimenter demands

(Ceci and Bruck, 1993). In addition, indirect measures of automatic associations are assumed to tap into relatively spontaneously activated knowledge in memory, whereas self-reports would tap more reflective knowledge. As such, some authors have argued that indirect measures of automatic associations offer unique insight into the content and structure of the dysfunctional schemata that are at the core of cognitive models (e.g. Teachman, 2005). Although most research using indirect measures of automatic associations in the context of psychopathology and health-related behaviours has focused on adults, a growing number of researchers have also started to include these measures in studying child and adolescent samples.

Overall, it seems that indirect measures of automatic associations can successfully be used in children and adolescents and that these measures can yield interesting additional information besides other measures, like self-reports. Although RTs and error rates increase in young children, the effects still seem to be informative. Until now most of this research has used the IAT as an indirect measure of automatic associations in children and adolescents. Compared to the APP and the EAST, the IAT seems to yield the most reliable effects. On the other hand, the IAT does present some interpretative problems. That is, associative as well as non-associative accounts have been proposed for IAT effect. Following this, IAT effects may, in some cases, be inflated by artifacts of the measurement procedure. Tasks like the EAST may some day provide a good alternative, but as yet there has been too little research using this task in child and adolescent samples to assess the reliability and validity of this task. Based on findings with adults it seems reasonable to expect that problems with the reliability of the EAST will limit its use in research with child and adolescents. Although there are no non-associative explanations for priming effects, priming procedures often yield relatively small effects, and the studies that have used priming in samples of children have thus far yielded mixed results.

From the review of the literature one could conclude that given the current information available the IAT seems to be the measure of choice. The fact remains, however, that there is an absolute need for more research to develop and assess valid and reliable indirect measures of automatic associations in children. In general, the indirect measures of automatic associations discussed in this chapter, like any RT measure, will have higher measurement error than self-report measures. This is probably especially true in child samples, because children tend to have relatively short attention spans and the tasks we have described are relatively long and (from a child's perspective) boring. This makes them less reliable and therefore limits their validity. This is a very serious issue as the reliability of a measure limits the strength of the maximally possible correlations with other measures. Nosek, Greenwald and Banaji (2007, p. 277) noted that when a measure with a reliability of .10 is correlated with a perfectly reliable measure, the maximal meaningful correlation is only .32. If the second measure has a more realistic reliability of, say, .50, the maximal meaningful correlation would be reduced to .22. This illustrates that the unreliability of a measure can lead to a serious underestimation of correlations, and underlines the need to keep on searching for ways to improve the reliability of our experimental measures.

One possible solution could be to use non-RT indirect measures (e.g. memory association measures, Ames *et al.*, 2007; Stacy, 1997; Thush *et al.*, 2007). Another solution could be to use multiple indirect measures and to estimate latent variable estimates of the underlying associations (e.g. Ames *et al.*, 2007; Cunningham, Preacher and Banaji, 2001).

Another issue that researchers should be aware of is that, depending on their age, children may find the task more or less difficult. Although this may not systematically influence the direction of the effects, it could dampen the strength of the effects because of increased error variance. This would call for caution when comparing the strength of effects between age groups. In addition, greater error variance may lead to the apparent absence of group differences or significant correlations between the indirect measure and other (indirect) measures within age groups. In theory, this could result in an apparent absence of effects in a group of young children, with the effects being present in older children. One solution for such undesirable influences of age is to standardize the effects based on individual's standard deviations, as is done, for instance, when calculating the D-measure for the IAT (see Greenwald, Nosek and Banaji, 2003). However, some researchers have argued that applying such an approach may also filter out interesting information (Smulders, Wiers and Roefs, 2004). More specifically, with respect to applying the IAT D-measure on child data, the RT adjustments suggested for the D-measure are based on adult norms (Greenwald, Nosek and Banaji, 2003). Children, in general, have slower RTs, and therefore this particular correction will have relatively less impact on child data.

Despite the fact that indirect measures of automatic associations are not without their limitations and that future research should focus on trying to improve existing methods or develop alternative measures, these measures provide a useful tool for researchers in child and adolescent anxiety to circumvent response biases, focus on spontaneously activated knowledge in memory or both. As yet, there are only a handful of studies that have used this type of measures in the context of child and adolescent anxiety. It should be clear that there are a host of issues that are as yet unexplored. For instance, there are a number of hypotheses that follow from cognitive models that have already been (partially) addressed in adults and that could also be explored in children. These include whether (specific) anxiety-related automatic associations differentiate between children with and without certain anxiety complaints or an anxiety disorder, whether certain automatic associations predict (specific) types of (disorder-related) behaviours, whether certain associations predict future complaints, whether dysfunctional associations change over treatment and whether the extent to which certain associations *do not* change predicts relapse. In addition, there are a number of developmental issues that could be explored – for instance, whether there are normative developmental changes in the strength of certain associations in children of different ages and whether there are certain developmental stages in which certain (dysfunctional) associations are more easily acquired. Furthermore, research could focus on the emergence of certain associations in relation to other processing biases like attentional bias or covariations bias. In short, the use of indirect measures of automatic associations enables researchers to test several hypotheses that could improve our knowledge of the onset and maintenance of anxiety disorders in children and adolescents.

References

American Psychiatric Association (2000) *Diagnostic and Statistical Manual of Mental Disorders*, 4th edn, text revision (DSM-IV-TR), American Psychiatric Association, Washington, DC.

Ames, S.L., Grenard, J.L., Thush, C. *et al.* (2007) Comparison of indirect assessments of association as predictors of marijuana use among at-risk adolescents. *Experimental and Clinical Psychopharmacology*, **15**, 204–218.

Arntz, A., Lavy, E., van den Berg, G. and van Rijsoort, S. (1993) Negative beliefs of spider phobics: a psychometric evaluation of the Spider Phobia Beliefs Questionnaire. *Advances in Behaviour Research and Therapy*, **15**, 257–277.

Askew, C. (2007) Vicarious learning and the development of fear in childhood. Unpublished Doctoral Thesis, University of Sussex, UK.

Askew, C. and Field, A.P. (2007) Vicarious learning and the development of fears in childhood. *Behaviour Research and Therapy*, **45**, 2616–2627.

Banse, R., Hayou-Thomas, E., Rebetez, C. and Gawronski, B. (2006) The action interference task as an indirect measure of stereotypes. 53rd British Psychological Society Social Psychology Section Annual Conference, September 6–8, 2006, Birmingham.

Baron, A.S. and Banaji, M.A. (2006) The development of implicit attitudes: evidence of race evaluations from ages 6 to 10 and adulthood. *Psychological Science*, **17**, 53–58.

Beck, A.T. and Clark, D.A. (1997) An information processing model of anxiety: automatic and strategic processes. *Behaviour Research and Therapy*, **35**, 49–58.

Beck, A.T., Emery, G. and Greenberg, R.L. (1985) *Anxiety Disorders and Phobias: A Cognitive Perspective*, Basic Books, New York.

Bijttebier, P., Vasey, M.W. and Braet, C. (2003) The information-processing paradigm: a valuable framework for clinical child and adolescent psychology. *Journal of Clinical Child and Adolescent Psychology*, **32**, 2–9.

Bluemke, M. and Friese, M. (2006) Do features of stimuli influence IAT effects? *Journal of Experimental Social Psychology*, **42**, 163–176.

Bosson, J.K., Swann W.B. Jr. and Pennebaker, J.W. (2000) Stalking the perfect measure of implicit self-esteem: the blind men and the elephant revisited? *Journal of Personality and Social Psychology*, **79**, 631–643.

Ceci, S.J. and Bruck, M. (1993) Suggestibility of the child witness: a historical review and synthesis. *Psychological Bulletin*, **113**, 403–439.

Clark, D.M. (1986) A cognitive approach to panic. *Behaviour Research and Therapy*, **24**, 461–470.

Conrey, F.R., Sherman, J.W., Gawronski, B. *et al.* (2005) Separating multiple processes in implicit social cognition: the quad model of implicit task performance. *Journal of Personality and Social Psychology*, **89**, 469–487.

Craeynest, M., Crombez, G., De Houwer, J. *et al.* (2005) Explicit and implicit attitudes towards food and physical activity in childhood obesity. *Behaviour Research and Therapy*, **43**, 1111–1120.

Cunningham, W.A., Preacher, K.J. and Banaji, M.R. (2001) Implicit attitude measures: consistency, stability, and convergent validity. *Psychological Science*, **12**, 163–170.

Daleiden, E.L. and Vasey, M.W. (1997) An information-processing perspective on childhood anxiety. *Clinical Psychology Review*, **17**, 407–429.

De Houwer, J. (2001) A structural and process analysis of the implicit association test. *Journal of Experimental Social Psychology*, **37**, 443–451.

De Houwer, J. (2003) The extrinsic affective Simon task. *Experimental Psychology*, **50**, 77–85.

De Houwer, J. (2006) What are implicit measures and why are we using them? in *Handbook of Implicit Cognition and Addiction* (eds R.W. Wiers and A.W. Stacy), SAGE, Thousand Oaks, CA, pp. 11–28.

De Houwer, J. and De Bruycker, E. (2007) The identification-EAST as a valid measure of implicit attitudes toward alcohol-related stimuli. *Journal of Behavior Therapy and Experimental Psychiatry*, **38**, 133–143.

De Houwer, J., Geldof, T. and De Bruycker, E. (2005) The implicit association test as a general measure of similarity. *Canadian Journal of Experimental Psychology*, **59**, 228–239.

Derryberry, D. and Reed, M.A. (2002) Anxiety-related attentional biases and their regulation by attentional control. *Journal of Abnormal Psychology*, **111**, 225–236.

Dunham, Y., Baron, A.S. and Banaji, M.R. (2006) From American city to Japanese village: a cross-cultural investigation of implicit race attitudes. *Child Development*, **77**, 1268–1281.

Egloff, B. and Schmukle, C.S. (2002) Predictive validity of an implicit association test for assessing anxiety. *Journal of Personality and Social Psychology*, **84**, 1441–1455.

Engelhard, I.M., Huijding, J., van den Hout, M. and de Jong, P.J. (2007) Vulnerability associations and symptoms of posttraumatic stress disorder after peacekeeping duties in Iraq. *Behaviour Research and Therapy*, **45**, 2317–2325.

Eysenck, M.W., Derakshan, N., Santos, R. and Calvo, M.G. (2007) Anxiety and cognitive performance: attentional control theory. *Emotion* **7**, 336–353.

Fazio, R.H. and Olson, M.A. (2003) Implicit measures in social cognition research: their meaning and use. *Annual Review of Psychology*, **54**, 297–327.

Fazio, R.H., Sanbonmatsu, D.M., Powell, M.C. and Kardes, F.R. (1986) On the automatic activation of attitudes. *Journal of Personality and Social Psychology*, **50**, 229–238.

Fazio, R.H. and Towles-Schwen, T. (1999) The MODE model of behaviour-attitude processes, in *Dual-Process Theories in Social Psychology* (eds S. Chaiken and Y. Trope), Guilford, New York, pp. 97–116.

Field, A.P. (2006) I don't like it because it eats sprouts: conditioning preferences in children. *Behaviour Research and Therapy*, **44**, 439–455.

Field, A.P. and Lawson, J. (2003) Fear information and the development of fears during childhood: effects on implicit fear responses and behavioural avoidance. *Behaviour Research and Therapy*, **41**, 1277–1293.

Field, A.P., Lawson, J. and Banerjee, R. (2008) The verbal threat information pathway to fear in children: the longitudinal effects on fear cognitions and the immediate effects on avoidance behaviour. *Journal of Abnormal Psychology*, **117**, 214–224.

Gawronski, B. and Bodenhausen, G.V. (2006) Associative and propositional processes in evaluation: an integrative review of implicit and explicit attitude change. *Psychological Bulletin*, **132**, 692–731.

Glaser, J. and Banaji, M.R. (1999) When fair is foul and foul is fair: reverse priming in automatic evaluation. *Journal of Personality and Social Psychology*, **77**, 669–687.

Govan, C.L. and Williams, K.D. (2004) Changing the affective valence of the stimulus items influences the IAT by re-defining the category labels. *Journal of Experimental Social Psychology*, **40**, 357–365.

Greenwald, A.G., McGhee, D.E. and Schwarz, J.L.K. (1998) Measuring individual differences in implicit cognition: the implicit association test. *Journal of Personality and Social Psychology*, **74**, 1464–1480.

Greenwald, A.G., Nosek, B.A. and Banaji, M.R. (2003) Understanding and using the implicit association test: I. An improved scoring algorithm. *Journal of Personality and Social Psychology*, **85**, 197–216.

Grenard, J.L., Ames, S.L., Wiers, R.W. *et al.* (2008) Working memory moderates the predictive effects of drug-related associations. *Psychology of Addictive Behaviors*, **22**, 426–432.

Harvey, A., Watkins, E., Mansell, W. and Shafran, R. (2004) *Cognitive Behavioural Processes Across Psychological Disorders: A Transdiagnostic Approach to Research and Treatment*, Oxford University Press, Oxford.

Hermans, D., De Houwer, J. and Eelen, P. (2001) A time course analysis of the affective priming effect. *Cognition and Emotion*, **15**, 143–165.

Huijding, J. (2006) Implicit attitudes and psychopathology. *The Netherlands Journal of Psychology*, **62**, 60–72.

Huijding, J. and de Jong, P.J. (2005a) A pictorial version of the extrinsic affective Simon task: sensitivity to generally affective phobia-relevant stimuli in high and low spider fearful individuals. *Experimental Psychology*, **52**, 289–295.

Huijding, J. and de Jong, P.J. (2005b) A modified extrinsic affective Simon task (EAST) to assess the affective value of pictorial stimuli: no influence of age or educational level. *Psychologica Belgica*, **45**, 241–255.

Huijding, J. and de Jong, P.J. (2006) Specific predictive power of automatic spider-related affective associations for controllable and uncontrollable fear responses. *Behaviour Research and Therapy*, **44**, 161–176.

Huijding, J. and de Jong, P.J. (2009). Implicit and explicit attitudes toward spiders: sensitivity to treatment and predictive validity for generalization of treatment effects. *Cognitive Therapy and Research*, **33**, 211–220.

Huijding, J., Bos, A.E.R. and Muris, P. (in press) Enhancing implicit self-esteem in children: can a smile make you feel worthwhile? *Netherlands Journal of Psycology*.

de Jong, P.J. (2002) Implicit self-esteem and social anxiety: differential self-favouring effects in high and low anxious individuals. *Behaviour Research and Therapy*, **40**, 501–508.

de Jong, P.J., Pasman, W., Kindt M. and van den Hout, M.A. (2001) A reaction time paradigm to assess (implicit) complaint-specific dysfunctional beliefs. *Behaviour Research and Therapy*, **39**, 101–113.

de Jong, P.J., van den Hout, M.A., Rietbroek, H. and Huijding, J. (2003) Dissociations between implicit and explicit attitudes toward phobic stimuli. *Cognition and Emotion*, **17**, 521–545.

Kendall, P.C. and Ronan, K.R. (1990) Assessment of children's anxieties, fears, and phobias: cognitive–behavioral models and methods, in *Handbook of Psychological and Educational Assessment of Children* (eds C.R. Reynolds and K.W. Kamphaus), Guilford Press, New York, pp. 223–244.

Karpinski, A. and Steinman, R.B. (2006) The single category implicit association test as a measure of implicit social cognition. *Journal of Personality and Social Psychology*, **91**, 16–32.

Lang, P.J. (1968) Fear reduction and fear behavior: problems in treating a construct, in *Research in Psychotherapy*, vol. 3 (ed. J.M. Schlien), American Psychological Association, Washington, DC, pp. 90–103.

Lang, P.J. (1985) The cognitive psychophysiology of emotion: fear and anxiety, in *Anxiety and the Anxiety Disorders* (eds A. Tuma and J.D. Maser), Lawrence Erlbaum Associates, Hillsdale, NJ, England, pp. 131–170.

Lawson, J., Banerjee, R. and Field, A.P. (2007) The effects of verbal information on children's fear beliefs about social situations. *Behaviour Research and Therapy*, **45**, 21–37.

Maier, M.A., Berner, M.P. and Pekrun, R. (2003) Directionality of affective priming: effects of trait anxiety and activation level. *Experimental Psychology*, **50**, 116–123.

Mierke, J. and Klauer, K.C. (2003) Method-specific variance in the implicit association test. *Journal of Personality and Social Psychology*, **85**, 1180–1192.

Mineka, S. and Öhman, A. (2005) Phobias and preparedness: the selective, automatic, and encapsulated nature of fear. *Biological Psychiatry*, **52**, 927–937.

Mitchell, J.P., Nosek, B.A. and Banaji, M.R. (2003) Contextual variations in implicit evaluation. *Journal of Experimental Psychology: General*, **132**, 455–469.

Moors, A. and De Houwer, J. (2006) Automaticity: a theoretical and conceptual analysis. *Psychological Bulletin*, **132**, 297–326.

Muris, P. (2002) An expanded childhood anxiety sensitivity index: its factor structure, reliability, and validity in a non-clinical adolescent sample. *Behaviour Research and Therapy*, **40**, 299–311.

Muris, P. (2007) *Normal and Abnormal Fear and Anxiety in Children and Adolescents*. BRAT Series in Clinical Psychology, Elsevier, Amsterdam.

Nisbett, R.E. and Wilson, T.D. (1977) Telling more than we can know: verbal reports on mental processes. *Psychological Review*, **84**, 231–295.

Nosek, B.A., Greenwald, A.G. and Banaji, M.A. (2007) The implicit association test at age 7: a methodological and conceptual review, in *Social Psychology and the Unconscious: The Automaticity of Higher Mental Processes* (ed. J. Bargh), Psychology Press, New York, pp. 265–292.

Nosek, B.A. and Smyth, F.L. (2007) A multitrait–multimethod validation of the implicit association test: implicit and explicit attitudes are related but distinct constructs. *Experimental Psychology*, **54**, 14–29.

Nuttin, J.M. Jr. (1985) Narcissism beyond Gestalt and awareness: the name letter effect. *European Journal of Social Psychology*, **15**, 353–361.

Penke, L., Eichstaedt, J. and Asendorpf, J. (2006) Single-attribute implicit association tests (SA-IAT) for the assessment of unipolar constructs: the case of sociosexuality. *Experimental Psychology*, **53**, 283–291.

Petty, R.E., Fazio, R.H. and Briñol, P. (eds) (2008) *Attitudes: Insights from the New Implicit Measures*, Psychology Press, New York.

Rachman, S. (1977) The conditioning theory of fear-acquisition: a critical examination. *Behaviour Research and Therapy*, **15**, 375–387.

Rothermund, K. and Wentura, D. (2004) Underlying processes in the implicit association test: dissociating salience from associations. *Journal of Experimental Psychology: General*, **133**, 139–165.

Rothermund, K., Wentura, D. and De Houwer, J. (2005) Validity of the salience asymmetry account of the implicit association test: reply to Greenwald, Nosek, Banaji, and Klauer (2005). *Journal of Experimental Psychology: General*, **134**, 426–430.

Rudman, L.A., Greenwald, A.G. and McGhee, D.E. (2001) Implicit self-concept and evaluative implicit gender stereotypes: self and ingroup share desirable traits. *Personality and Social Psychology Bulletin*, **27**, 1164–1178.

Rutland, A., Cameron, L., Milne, A. and McGeorge, P. (2005) Social norms and self-presentation: children's implicit and explicit intergroup attitudes. *Child Development*, **76**, 451–466.

Schneider, R. and Schulte, D. (2007) Panic patients reveal idiographic associations between anxiety symptoms and catastrophes in a semantic priming task. *Behaviour Research and Therapy*, **45**, 211–223.

Sinclair, S., Dunn, E. and Lowery, B.S. (2005) The relationship between parental racial attitudes and children's implicit prejudice. *Journal of Experimental Social Psychology*, **41**, 283–289.

Smulders, F.T.Y., Wiers, R. and Roefs, A. (2004) Understanding and using the new and original scoring algorithms for the Implicit Association Test (IAT): a comparison of Lab data. Unpublished manuscript, Maastricht University, The Netherlands.

Spence, S.H., Lipp, O.V., Liberman, L. and March, S. (2006) Examination of emotional priming among children and young adolescents: developmental issues and its associations with anxiety. *Australian Journal of Psychology*, **58**, 101–110.

Sportel, E., de Hullu, E., de Jong, P.J., Nauta, M. and Mindera, R. (2007) *Implicit Self-esteem and Social Anxiety in Adolescents: Work in Progress*. Poster presented at the 5th World Congress of Behavioural and Cognitive Therapy, July 11–14, 2007, Barcelona, Spain.

Stacy, A.W. (1997) Memory activation and expectancy as prospective predictors of alcohol and marijuana use. *Journal of Abnormal Psychology*, **106**, 61–73.

Stahl, C. and Degner, J. (2007) Assessing automatic activation of valence: a multinomial model of EAST performance. *Experimental Psychology*, **54**, 99–112.

Strack, F. and Deutsch, R. (2004) Reflective and impulsive determinants of social behaviour. *Personality and Social Psychology Review*, **8**, 220–247.

Tanner, R.J., Stopa, L. and De Houwer, J. (2006) Implicit views of the self in social anxiety. *Behaviour Research and Therapy*, **44**, 1397–1409.

Teachman, B.A. (2005) Information processing and anxiety sensitivity: cognitive vulnerability to panic reflected in interpretation and memory biases. *Cognitive Therapy and Research*, **29**, 479–499.

Teachman, B.A. and Allen, J.P. (2007) Development of social anxiety: social interaction predictors of implicit and explicit fear of negative evaluation. *Journal of Abnormal Child Psychology*, **35**, 63–78.

Teachman, B.A., Gregg, A.P. and Woody, S.R. (2001) Implicit associations for fear-relevant stimuli among individuals with snake and spider fears. *Journal of Abnormal Psychology*, **110**, 226–235.

Teachman, B.A., Smith-Janik, S.B. and Saporito, J. (2007) Information processing biases and panic disorder: relationships among cognitive and symptom measures. *Behaviour Research and Therapy*, **45**, 1791–1811.

Teachman, B.A. and Woody, S.R. (2003) Automatic processing in spider phobia: implicit fear associations over the course of treatment. *Journal of Abnormal Psychology*, **112**, 100–109.

Thomas, S., Smith, R.B. and Ball, P. (2007) Implicit attitudes in very young children: an adaptation of the IAT. *Current Research in Social Psychology*, **13**, 75–85.

Thush, C. and Wiers, R.W. (2007) Explicit and implicit alcohol-related cognitions and the prediction of future drinking in adolescents. *Addictive Behaviors*, **32**, 1367–1383.

Thush, C., Wiers, R.W., Ames, S.L., *et al.* (2007) Apples and oranges? Comparing indirect measures of alcohol-related cognition predicting alcohol use in at-risk adolescents. *Psychology of Addictive Behaviors*, **21**, 587–591.

Thush, C., Wiers, R.W., Ames, S.L. *et al.* (2008) Interactions between implicit and explicit cognition and working memory capacity in the prediction of alcohol use in at-risk adolescents. *Drug and Alcohol Dependence*, **94**, 116–124.

Vasey, M.W., Dalgleish, T. and Silverman, W.K. (2003) Research on information-processing factors in child and adolescent psychopathology: a critical commentary. *Journal of Clinical Child and Adolescent Psychology*, **32**, 81–93.

Vervoort, L., Wolters, H.W., Hogendoorn, S.M. *et al.* (2008) A pictorial version of the extrinsic affective Simon task: sensitivity to normally valenced and anxiety relevant stimuli in children, adolescents and adults. Manuscript submitted for publication.

Wiers, R.W., Houben, K., Smulders, F.T.Y. *et al.* (2006) To drink or not to drink: the role of automatic and controlled cognitive processes in the etiology of alcohol-related problems, in *Handbook of Implicit Cognition and Addiction* (eds R.W. Wiers and A.W. Stacy), SAGE, Thousand Oaks, CA, pp. 339–361.

Wiers, R.W., Van de Luitgaarden, J., Van den Wildenberg, E. and Smulders, F.T.Y. (2005) Challenging implicit and explicit alcohol-related cognitions in young heavy drinkers. *Addiction*, **100**, 806–819.

Williams, J.M.G., Watts, F.N., MacLeod, C. and Mathews, A. (1997) *Cognitive Psychology and Emotional Disorders*, John Wiley & Sons, Chichester.

Wilson, T.D., Lindsey, S. and Schooler, T.Y. (2000) A model of dual attitudes. *Psychological Review*, **107**, 101–126.

Wittenbrink, B. and Schwarz, N. (eds) (2007) *Implicit Measures of Attitudes*, Guilford Press, New York.

Zinbarg, R. (1998) Concordance and synchrony in measures of anxiety and panic reconsidered: a hierarchical model of anxiety and panic. *Behavior Therapy*, **29**, 301–323.

8

Application of Cognitive Neuroscience Techniques to the Study of Anxiety-Related Processing Biases in Children

Koraly Pérez-Edgar and Yair Bar-Haim
kperezed@gmu.edu

Over the past two decades, considerable evidence has accumulated for the notion that threat-related cognitive biases play a significant role in individual differences in anxiety (for reviews, see Bar-Haim *et al.*, 2007; Mogg and Bradley, 1998). Most cognitive models of threat processing in anxiety delineate a sequence of steps describing how information is processed as it progresses through the cognitive system (Beck and Clark, 1997; Beck, Emery and Greenberg, 1985; Mogg and Bradley, 1998; Rapee and Heimberg, 1997; Williams *et al.*, 1988). Theory-driven parsing of these cognitive mechanisms provides a particularly useful framework for organizing predictions when examining the specific brain structures and neural mechanisms that are involved in biased threat processing. The current chapter reviews how available neuroscience techniques, in conjunction with classic cognitive tasks, may be applied to examine both the chronometry and the neural architecture associated with threat biases in anxious individuals. Special consideration will be given to the application of such techniques in paediatric populations and in a developmental context. Finally, we selectively review studies using neuroscience techniques to investigate anxiety as an illustration of the potential this approach has for bettering our understanding of these disorders. In doing so, we will focus on a classic attention paradigm – the dot-probe task. Readers who are interested in more exhaustive reviews of this literature are referred to Pine (2007); Rauch, Shin and Wright (2003) and Ochsner and Gross (2008).

Information Processing Biases and Anxiety: A Developmental Perspective Edited by Julie A. Hadwin and Andy P. Field
© 2010 John Wiley & Sons, Ltd.

Why Image Brain Function When Studying Anxiety-Related Processing Biases in Children?

Functional neuroscience techniques are used in the context of cognitive research in general, and processing biases in anxiety as a particular example, to reveal two major aspects of a documented behavioural effect: (i) the chronometry and time course of specific cognitive computations (e.g. when in time do between-group deviations occur during the processing of a particular class of stimuli?) and (ii) the specific locations in the brain and the related neural architecture that support specific cognitive processes. Neural timing information can be particularly useful in elucidating and validating cognitive models of individual differences in anxiety. The precise localization of the relevant neural architecture can provide important links to analogous animal research. This is particularly important as analyses at the systems, molecular and genetic levels are more advanced in animal models than in studies carried out with human subjects (Pine, 2007; Pine *et al.*, 2009). In each case, neuroscience techniques can advance our understanding of the mechanisms that give rise to more readily observed patterns of behaviour. Both types of contributions will be discussed more thoroughly below, following an introduction to the potential and limitations of the available neuroscience techniques.

Cognitive Neuroscience Techniques – A Practical Overview

An impressive array of functional imaging techniques is available to the interested researcher. These include, among others, intracranial single-cell recordings, positron emission tomography (PET), magnetoencephalography (MEG), near-infrared spectroscopy (NIRS), scalp-recorded event-related potentials (ERPs) and functional magnetic resonance imaging (fMRI). Although all of these methods have been used in human research, the invasive nature of some of these techniques considerably limits their application to human participants, in general, and to children, in particular. For instance, PET relies on the injection of radioactive traces to measure changes in brain activity – thereby limiting its use to medical conditions in which such application is absolutely mandatory. In contrast, non-invasive methods may be used in standard research contexts with a wide range of individuals. Two major non-invasive functional brain imaging techniques have been used in the context of affect-cognition research: Recordings of brain electrical activity (ERPs) and imaging of brain–blood oxygenation levels (fMRI). Additional non-invasive methods of functional brain imaging (e.g. MEG and NIRS) could also be readily applied in this research context. However, as of this writing, relevant research using these techniques have yet to emerge, and thus it will not be reviewed here.

Time and space

Perhaps the most critical concern when applying functional neuroimaging techniques to cognitive brain research is the currently inescapable trade-off between

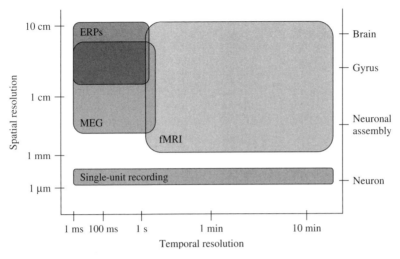

Figure 8.1 Spatial versus temporal resolution trade-off for different functional imaging techniques.

the available resolutions of each technique in the domains of time and space. Inspection of Figure 8.1 clarifies the nature of this trade-off.

Specifically, scalp-recorded ERPs provide excellent temporal resolution (at the millisecond range), but poor spatial resolution. In contrast, fMRI provides high spatial resolution (at the order of millimeters), but poor temporal resolution. These trade-offs dictate the types of research questions that can be tackled with each method, as well as the nuts and bolts of the research designs being applied. These limitations also mean that complex research questions cannot be addressed via a single method. Rather, a multi-method approach is needed if one wishes to create a multidimensional understanding of a complex phenomenon. While there is emerging work attempting to more closely fuse ERP and fMRI data through simultaneous collection protocols (Riera *et al.*, 2005), this work is still in the early stages and has yet to be used in developmental studies.

Next, we provide a brief description of the nature of the brain activity examined via ERPs and fMRI, their specific strengths and weaknesses in the context of research with children, and the limitations of each method in testing theoretical assumptions relevant to processing biases in anxiety. We will then provide an illustration of a cognitive neuroscience approach to the topic of attentional biases in anxiety.

Event-related potentials (ERPs)

While measurements of electrical changes in the brain via ERPs have a long history of use in cognitive research (Kostandov and Azumanov, 1977; Taylor, 1988), these methods have only recently been applied to the study of processing biases in anxiety

(Bar-Haim, Lamy and Glickman, 2005; Ladouceur *et al.*, 2006; Mogg *et al.*, 2008). ERPs are voltage fluctuations that are associated in time either with a physical event in the environment (e.g. appearance of a threat stimulus in the visual field) or with an internal mental event (e.g. covert monitoring of errors in performance). These potentials can be recorded from the scalp and extracted from the ongoing electroencephalogram (EEG) by means of filtering and signal averaging. The typical use of ERPs in the context of threat processing and anxiety research has been in the time domain. That is, the ERP waveform plots as a function of time the change in voltage recorded on the scalp in response to experimental conditions. These waveforms contain components that are very fast-occurring and determined by the physical properties of an eliciting event in the external world (exogenous potentials), as well as components that typically reflect more advanced information processing (endogenous potentials). Since the temporal resolution of these measurements is on the order of milliseconds, ERPs can accurately measure when processing activities take place in the human brain. Specific inferences about anxiety-related modulations in the ERP may be achieved by building on the extensive basic research delineating the cognitive function represented by particular ERP components. For instance, extensive research (Hillyard and Anllo-Vento, 1998; Hillyard, Luck and Mangun, 1994) has detailed a modulation of a specific ERP component, the P1 (a positive-going wave peaking at around 100 milliseconds following stimulus onset), by spatial attention. These studies show that P1 amplitude is typically enhanced by stimuli presented in an attended location relative to unattended ones. Applying this basic knowledge to the study of threat-related attention biases in anxiety, researchers can now generate specific hypotheses about P1 modulations in anxious versus non-anxious individuals during performance on the classic attention tasks being used in the study of processing biases in anxiety. Finally, although the spatial resolution of ERP measurements is limited, both theoretically and technologically, multichannel recordings allow for a rough estimation of the intracranial sources of the electrical activity recorded on the scalp (Ladouceur *et al.*, 2006; Reynolds and Richards, 2005; Santesso *et al.*, 2008).

Functional magnetic resonance imaging (fMRI)

Much like the ERP research, fMRI studies non-invasively track the brain's natural pattern of response to a specific event. The initial uses of magnetic resonance (MR) technology in anxiety research focused on detailing the structure of disease-relevant neural architecture. For example, work has been done detailing across populations the relative size or volume of structures, like the amygdala, that have been found through animal research to play a key role in the fear circuit (De Bellis *et al.*, 2000; Szeszko *et al.*, 1999). From a developmental perspective, MR technology also allows researchers to track the physical maturation of cortical and subcortical regions, which are important to the development of specific psychological functions, such as the link between maturation of the prefrontal cortex (PFC) and the emergence of executive functions (Diamond, Kirkham and Amso, 2002; Munakata, Casey and Diamond, 2004).

Technological advances now allow tracking changes and individual differences in both the structural and functional circuitry of the brain using fMRI. This advance is particularly important since much of our interest lies not just in the maturation of certain brain structures (e.g. variations in volume and shape), but also in whether a brain region works, alone or in concert with other brain regions, to shape behaviour. The combined value of structural and functional imaging research may be illustrated in research on brain–behaviour interactions during adolescence, a period of life in which many brain regions approach adult proportions structurally, but functionally may respond quite differently to provoking stimuli (Nelson *et al.*, 2005; Paus, 2005).

Unlike ERPs, which reflect synchronous electrical activity in fields of neuronal dendrites, fMRI relies on an indirect measurement of neuronal activity to track brain processes via magnetic differences in blood oxygenation. Active areas of the brain are thought to trigger localized increases in levels of oxygenated blood. This is coupled with a decrease in deoxygenated haemoglobin, which is paramagnetic and can therefore act as a natural contrast to the oxygenated blood. As the level of deoxygenated blood decreases in a region, the MR signal will increase, giving rise to blood-oxygenation-level-dependent (BOLD) imaging. The timing of the haemodynamic response cycle from baseline to peak activation and then back to baseline is on the order of seconds, meaning that stimulus presentation in an experimental setting must have longer trials or inter-trial intervals than typically used in behavioural cognitive research and with ERPs.

Finally, it is important to note that fMRI does not provide an absolute quantification of BOLD levels in any one region of the brain. Rather, analyses of fMRI data examine the relative difference in activation levels in a region across conditions (e.g. processing threat cues vs. neutral cues) or across groups (e.g. anxious children vs. healthy children).

Initially, most fMRI studies relied on block designs in which 'runs' of trials from one condition were repeated. Then, the BOLD response over the course of one block (e.g. threat cues) would be compared to BOLD levels from a second block of trials (e.g. appetitive cues). This method led to concerns that block designs could not track changes in neural response over the course of trials, leaving open the possibility of undetected habituation or learning effects. Recent technical and statistical advances have allowed the use of event-related fMRI designs. Mirroring behavioural and ERP studies, event-related designs allow trials from different conditions to be intermingled and presented within the same block of trials or runs. This has decreased the time needed to collect stable data and has allowed for inter-trial intervals on the order of 2–3 seconds. As with the ERP literature, fMRI was initially used to examine simple sensory or cognitive processes. Recent years have seen the emergences of studies examining higher order cognitive and socio-emotional processes in children and adults (Guyer *et al.*, 2008; McClure *et al.*, 2004; Nelson *et al.*, 2003).

Application of ERP and fMRI Techniques in Child Populations

Conducting research with child populations has always required a dose of persever-ance, creativity and humility on the part of researchers. This is particularly so when attempting to apply cognitive neuroscience techniques to the study of children in general – and anxious children in particular. The obstacles typically fall into two categories: (i) age-related cognitive and behavioural limitations on performance, which are evident in any study with children and (ii) the unique demands that cognitive neuroscience techniques place on individual participants. Some of these challenges are shared by both ERP and fMRI techniques, while others are unique to each method.

Neuroscience techniques require a large number of experimental trials

Most of the research on processing biases in anxiety relies on behavioural response time (RT) and accuracy measures. In such studies, researchers are concerned with extracting the pattern of response that is specific to the stimuli or manipulations of interest (signal) from the ambient, and hopefully random, responses that track the other myriad cognitive processes at play in an individual (noise). Both techniques of interest (ERPs and fMRI) examine physiological processes (electrical activity and blood flow in the brain) that are evident and ongoing regardless of the specific demands of the experimental task being studied. As such, researchers work to extract the neural correlates of the effect of interest by manipulating the ratio of signal to noise, allowing the specific effect (e.g. an ERP wave recorded over frontal electrodes or BOLD levels in the amygdala) to stand out in relief.

Researchers studying healthy adult populations often address this challenge by having participants complete a large number of experimental trials. They then mathematically average out the non-systematic response (i.e. the noise). Unfortunately, children often have difficulty tolerating the time and repetition involved in collecting a large number of experimental trials and researchers are often forced to make do with the minimal number of repetitions needed to extract a meaningful signal from the ongoing noise. Many consider 30–50 repetitions per experimental condition as the minimum number of trials needed for meaningful signal extraction, although publications involving child populations routinely set a floor of 15–20 trials per condition. Neuroscientists studying children must therefore work to maximize the data available from their participants. This process can involve breaking down testing into more manageable time units, incorporating rest periods in between testing runs and restricting the study to the most crucial experimental conditions of interest.

Adapting tasks made for adult populations for use with children

Most of the data on processing biases in anxiety has been generated using adaptations of classic cognitive tasks originally developed for adult populations.

With a large number of repetitions, these tasks are often viewed as rather boring by adults and even more so by children. The context and content of testing can be shaped to engage the interest of the child and motivate his or her compliance. For example, a simple stimulus–response task (e.g. press the left button when you see a blue square) can be re-imagined as a hide-and-seek computer game (e.g. press the 'tag' button when you see the picture of a teddy bear).

For example, to measure the development of error-monitoring, researchers have modified the traditional flanker task (Eriksen, 1995), replacing the letters or arrows often used for stimuli with more child-friendly stimuli, such as shapes (e.g. diamonds vs. circles) or animals (left vs. right facing fish) (McDermott, Perez-Edgar and Fox, 2007). Along the same lines, Rothbart and colleagues (Rothbart et al., 2003) have designed inhibitory control tasks in which children have to 'lead' animals to their correct habitats, while varying the spatial compatibility of the animal and its home.

The need to modify tasks goes beyond the need to stimulate the child's motivation to participate. Many times, children cannot meet the linguistic and behavioural demands inherent in testing protocols originally designed for adults. As such, tasks must be streamlined and simplified. For example, Adele Diamond and colleagues (Diamond, Kirkham and Amso, 2002; Gerstadt, Hong and Diamond, 1994) have designed a Day–Night Stroop variant that asks young children to say 'Day' when presented with a picture of the moon and 'Night' when shown a picture of the sun.

Of course, there is always a concern that one may inadvertently change the nature of the task in the attempt to ensure participation. Even when a task seems identical on the surface (e.g. a letter flanker task), inadvertent confounds may still be present. For example, developmental researchers often employ a points and prizes system to motivate children to perform as well and as long as possible. However, the introduction of a new psychological process (potential reward for performance) may alter how the child goes about meeting task demands. One may argue that every task involving performance entails incentives for action; in adult participants these might be driven by internal motives for compliance. However, these motives could be very different from a material reward. Importantly, different types of incentives and different reward intensities may differentially call into action a whole new set of brain regions supporting reward processing, thereby obscuring the response pattern of interest.

In attempting to address this issue, a cognitive neuroscience approach may prove advantageous since it allows the research to supplement behavioural (RT and accuracy) patterns by examining the chronometry (ERP) and neural architecture (fMRI) of performance in both the traditional and new variants of the task. If performance on both tasks yields similar neuronal activation patterns then one can assume that the two tasks tap into a similar process.

This added source of information is particularly important given that similarities in behaviour across tasks, populations or time, may mask differences in underlying mechanisms. For example, Durston et al. (2006) had children engage in a cognitive control task at age 9 and again at age 11. Reaction times and target detection improved over the course of 2 years. There was no improvement in the ability to override a response to non-targets. The results suggest that even though the number of false alarms did not improve, there was a shift within the pattern of cortical activation that paralleled enhanced responding to targets. Activation in areas related to task performance (e.g. the ventral prefrontal regions) increased while non-relevant areas (e.g. the dorsolateral PFC) diminished. This suggests that with development, children streamline the neural regions recruited for behaviour, even though these changes may not be fully evident at the behavioural level.

Brain maturation and task performance

With any experimental paradigm, developmental neuroscientists must be cognizant of the interplay between brain maturation and task performance. There is very little clear normative data on children's performance on standardized cognitive tasks across development. The same holds true for tasks measuring processing biases in anxiety. Without clear age norms, it is difficult to successfully choose a task for experimental use, generate sound hypotheses, and then interpret the subsequent data. For example, it has been carefully documented that children 3.5–4.5 years of age find the Day–Night Stroop variant extremely difficult (Gerstadt, Hong and Diamond, 1994). Diamond, Kirkham and Amso, (2002) further demonstrated that whereas 4-year-olds perform at a chance rate (53% correct) on this task, 4.5-year-olds perform at an almost 80% correct rate, and for 6- to 7-year-olds, the task becomes trivially easy. These findings indicate that around 4 years of age, there is a maturational shift in the development of the attention control functions tapped by this particular task. In this example, researchers would do well to focus on age 4 when examining the maturation of neural processes supporting performance on this task and be aware that there will be little variance in performance with older children. Unfortunately, such age norms are not available for any of the cognitive tasks that have been adopted for use in the study of processing biases in anxiety.

The presence of psychopathology brings an added layer of complexity to the endeavour. For example, one could presume that anxiety differentially affects performance across development, even when holding the level of severity constant. That is, the maturation of regulatory neural mechanisms (e.g. dorsolateral PFC) may better equip older children to cope when exposed to anxiety triggers. From the alternate perspective, the developmental trajectory of anxiety may differentially pressure cognitive mechanisms over time, such that the severity of disorder may ebb and flow, in line with other developmental mechanisms. In particular, the presence and severity of anxiety and other mood disorders has been linked to pubertal development and the corresponding biological and social perturbations (Angold, Costello and Worthman, 1998; Hayward and Sanborn, 2002; Pine, 2007).

ERP research with child populations

As noted above, ERP waves are recorded by placing electrodes on the scalp either through the use of a stretchy lycra cap with embedded electrodes or a net of electrodes connected by thin wires (Figure 8.2). Once the cap or net is in place, researchers must insure that electrodes are properly arranged on the scalp and that

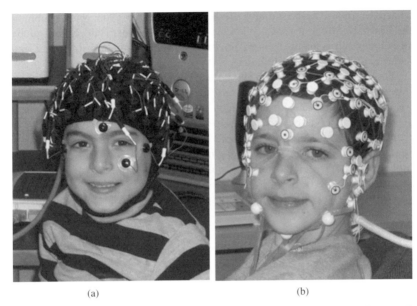

(a)   (b)

Figure 8.2 EEG/ERP recordings involve application of electrodes to the scalp. Stretch lycra cap with embedded electrodes (a), hydro-cell net of electrodes connected by thin wires (b).

impedances are kept as low as possible in order to maximize the quality of the recorded signal.

Although preparation time can vary with the system used (between 15 and 45 minutes for the experienced researcher), the recent push to acquire high-density EEG increases the number of electrodes in use, lengthening the necessary preparation time. This can seem tedious and uncomfortable for all but the most patient child, and runs the risk of negatively impacting their performance on the subsequent tasks. Researchers have attempted to minimize this possibility by placing preparation in the context of a game ('you are an undersea explorer with a diving cap' or 'you are an astronaut with a special space helmet') and allowing the child to watch videos during electrode placement (e.g. Fox, Hane and Perez-Edgar, 2006; Fox *et al.*, 2001a). However, well-trained researchers who are swift and sure in their electrode placement will always be the 'best line of defence'.

Once the task has begun, the child must refrain from speaking or making large head movement, as this will introduce movement artefacts that swamp the relatively weak signal generated by the brain during task performance. Keeping the child compliant often requires repeated prompts by researchers and short, well-paced blocks of trials that the child can tolerate.

One advantage of the ERP technique is that it can be applied across the lifespan from newborn to senescence. It allows researchers to examine the chronometry of processing even when the participant is too young or too impaired to produce an active response to the stimulus. However, care must be taken when examining the ERP waves of very young children and infants. In older children and adults, stimuli typically generate distinct components that are distinguishable across time and space, although the chronometry will vary with maturation.

However, in the very young child, these components are not evident and are instead replaced by broad and less defined deflections in the ERP wave. For example, Richards (Reynolds and Richards, 2005; Richards, 2003) has shown that infants generate a broad Nc (negative component) that is comparable in some ways to the N1 and N2 components seen in older children and adults. The differences in wave morphology suggest that a developmental approach with clear age norms for both the psychophysiological and behavioural response are needed in order to best interpret the data generated by a specific task or paradigm across age groups.

More extensive reviews of the theory and practice of ERP research with children can be found in Fox, Schmidt and Henderson (2000) and Fox, Hane and Pérez-Edgar (2006).

fMRI research with child populations

In many ways, the fMRI environment places even greater demand on the child than EEG/ERP collection. Children must approach a quite large, noisy and unusual machine, place themselves on a long table, and agree to be slowly entered into the 'mouth' of the machine (Figure 8.3).

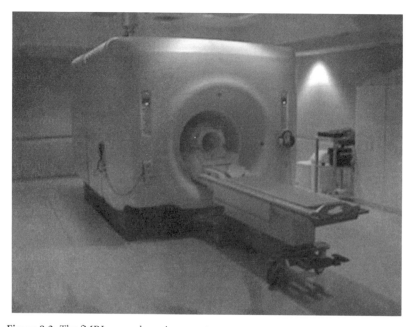

Figure 8.3 The fMRI research environment.

Once testing begins, participants must remain extremely still since head movement of only a few millimeters will swamp the BOLD signal with artefact. Experimental tasks are performed while lying on the back in this constricted environment. Clearly, this is a difficult challenge for children and many adults, and many times proves impossible for an anxious child. As a useful heuristic, many researchers would be reluctant to functionally scan a child younger than 7 years of age as is reflected in the typical age range of the extant published reports. However, some labs are currently attempting to conduct large-scale studies with children as young as 4 years of age, although none have reached the publication stage to date. Studies with slightly older children (ages 5–7) are now beginning to emerge, although many are still in the proof of concept stage (Overy *et al.*, 2005).

Successful fMRI research with young children requires extensive preparation of the child. This often involves having the child acclimate to being alone in the small confines of the magnet. The child can first crawl into a small plastic tube, similar to those found in many playgrounds and backyards. Then, the child may enter a mock scanner, which simulates the sights and sounds of the actual machine. Many laboratories also work to train the child to remain still during the simulation process (Davidson, Thomas and Casey, 2003). For instance, children can be shown a video on a monitor while in the simulator. The monitor is programmed to turn off when it detects movement in the child. Remaining still turns the program back on. In this way, young children can learn the acceptable boundaries of movement while in the fMRI environment. In the actual scanner, padding and side head restraints are also used to further minimize movement.

Recent reviews by Casey, Davidson and Rosen (2002); Davidson, Thomas and Casey (2003), and Paus (2005) provide greater details on the methodological and theoretical considerations of paediatric fMRI research.

A note of encouragement

While developmental neuroscience researchers have to tolerate more noise or ambiguity than ideal, recent work has shown that reliable and replicable findings are possible with young children. The research cited above has already provided a firm and growing foundation for future research. More important than the answers these initial studies have provided are the new questions now being generated. We, as a field, are in the fortunate position of having an even larger 'tool box' at our disposal when attempting to find the answers.

Neural Correlates of Threat-Related Attention Bias in Anxiety

Threat-related attention biases have been extensively studied in anxious versus non-anxious individuals using a variety of attention tasks (e.g. dot probe, emotional Stroop, spatial attention cuing, visual search). Here, we review the literature on

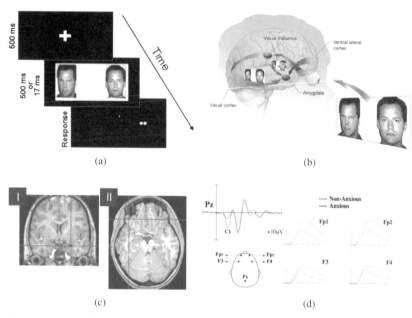

Figure 8.4 Neural correlates of performance on the dot-probe task. (a) Events in a dot-probe trial. (b) Neural pathways of threat processing. (c) Increased amygdala and VLPFC activation during a dot-probe task in GAD versus healthy adolescents. (d) Greater C1 amplitude to faces and lower P3 amplitude to targets in anxious versus non-anxious adults.

the dot-probe task as an example of the ways by which cognitive neuroscience approach can be applied to the study of individual differences in threat processing to enhance our understanding of paediatric anxiety.

In the dot-probe task (Figure 8.4a), two stimuli, one threat-related and one neutral are shown briefly in each trial, and their removal is followed by a small probe in the location just occupied by one of the stimuli. Participants are required to respond as quickly as possible to the probe without compromising accuracy (see Chapter 4 for further details). Response latencies to the probe are thought to provide a 'snap-shot' of the distribution of participants' attention, with faster responses to probes evident for the attended location relative to the unattended location (e.g. Navon and Margalit, 1983). Attention bias towards threat is revealed when participants are faster to respond to probes that replace threat-related rather than neutral stimuli. The opposite pattern would indicate avoidance of threat stimuli. An additional advantage of this paradigm is that manipulating the time interval between presentation of the critical stimuli and presentation of the probe (stimulus onset asynchrony) can assist in revealing the time course of attention allocation.

The processing mechanisms underlying performance on the dot-probe task, as well as other threat-related attention tasks, are shaped by dedicated neural circuits that support threat–attention computations. Research in rodents and non-human primates delineates a distributed neural circuitry that is engaged during threat-orienting behaviour. This network involves a direct neural pathway from the sensory thalamus to the amygdala, and a cortical ventral pathway that also feeds back to the amygdala and other limbic structures (LeDoux, 1995; Morris, Öhman and Dolan, 1998). The direct pathway affords rapid and coarse analysis of threat, whereas the cortical pathway supports a more elaborate analysis that interacts with attention allocation systems and other top-down processes in threat evaluation. A stimulus tagged with high threat value through processing in the fast and crude pathway may trigger a psychophysiological alert state that disrupts ongoing activity and promotes orienting towards threat. However, if detailed analyses determine that the stimulus is benign, cortical top-down processes may override the alert state (LeDoux, 1995). In particular, the PFC has been implicated in threat monitoring by modulating limbic engagement in response to environmental threats (Blair *et al.*, 1999; Hariri *et al.*, 2003; Monk *et al.*, 2003).

These neuro-functional models of threat processing provide a useful framework for the study of individual differences in anxiety. Indeed, recent work has demonstrated perturbations in amygdala–PFC circuitry in humans with anxiety disorders (McClure *et al.*, 2007; Monk *et al.*, 2006). The data suggest that anxious individuals are prone to unsuccessful attempts by the PFC to modulate amygdala hyperactivity (Monk *et al.*, 2006) or are hampered in their ability to recruit the PFC to regulate amygdala hyperactivation (Bishop, Duncan and Lawrence, 2004).

Figure 8.4b describes how performance on the dot-probe task might map onto the neuro-functional model of threat processing described above. Hypersensitivity in the amygdala may play a role in anxiety-related attentional biases manifest in the immediate response to threat. Thus, exposure to threat (e.g. an angry face) in the context of a dot-probe trial could produce excessive amygdala engagement in anxious, compared with non-anxious, participants. In contrast, activity in the PFC may reflect efforts to down-regulate amygdala response to threat (Eysenck *et al.*, 2007). This suggests that perturbed interactions between PFC and the amygdala may be at the core of the attentional biases observed in anxious participants when confronted with threat cues, such as in the dot-probe task.

Of the six fMRI dot-probe studies published to date, three examined the neural correlates of performance in healthy adult samples. Pourtois *et al.* (2006) found increased responses in temporo-parietal areas and occipito-parietal cortex for threat faces relative to happy faces. Monk *et al.* (2004) showed that threat trials engaged the amygdala and ventrolateral PFC (VLPFC) in healthy adults, while also revealing plasticity in the time-related behavioural and neural response to threat trials. Finally, taking an individual differences approach, Amin, Constable and Canli (2004) correlated levels of extraversion and neuroticism with fMRI activation in 11 adults during a dot-probe task. While they found a pattern of activation unique to Extraversion, there were no significant associations with Neuroticism, possibly due to issues of methodology and statistical power.

fMRI studies using the dot-probe task to study anxiety in children have only recently begun to emerge. Monk *et al.* (2006) compared brain activation to angry-neutral face pairs in a dot-probe task in adolescents with generalized anxiety disorder

(GAD) and healthy adolescent controls (ages 8–17 years). The data indicated that healthy children display an attention bias towards the threat faces, while the anxious children directed attention away from the threat faces. While no between-group differences emerged in amygdala activation, adolescents with GAD exhibited increased activation in the right VLPFC while viewing the angry-neutral face pairs, as well as a negative correlation between VLPFC activation and anxiety severity (Figure 8.4c-II). In a second study, also in GAD and healthy adolescents (Monk *et al.*, 2008), a similar dot-probe paradigm was used, now with a masked (17 milliseconds) presentation of the threat cues. In this study, attention bias towards angry faces was observed in both healthy and anxious adolescents with no between-group difference. Unlike Monk *et al.* (2006), the subliminal presentations in this study revealed between-group differences in amygdala activation to angry-neutral face-pair trials, relative to neutral–neutral face-pair trials (Figure 8.4c-I), with GAD patients showing stronger amygdala activation compared to controls. The most recent study (Telzer *et al.*, 2008) found that trait anxiety in healthy children was positively associated with attention bias towards angry faces. Neurophysiologically, trait anxiety was associated with increased right dorsolateral PFC activation reflecting attention bias for angry faces (i.e. angry-incongruent vs. angry-congruent trials).

Taken together, these studies begin to map out the neural circuitry underlying attentional biases to threat during performance on the dot-probe task. Specifically, brief (subconscious) exposure to threat may be preferentially processed by the rapid thalamo-amygdala pathway, triggering hyper-responsivity in the limbic system. In contrast, longer exposure to a threat cue may allow the cortical pathway (centred on the orbital frontal and ventrolateral PFC) to down-regulate the initial limbic response. One could speculate that the extent to which this cortical pathway is effectively engaged may track the severity and/or developmental course of anxiety (Pine *et al.*, 2009). Future studies may build on these results to delineate the developmental course of this neuro-functional link, as well as potential links to individual differences in developmental trajectories leading to anxiety.

There is a general agreement on the relevance of threat-related processing biases to elevated anxiety, and studies identifying the brain structures involved are now emerging. Yet, cognitive accounts of anxiety differ in the roles they assign to biases in attention, interpretation, memory and judgement in its aetiology and maintenance. For instance, according to schema theories (e.g. Beck, 1976; Beck and Clark, 1997; Beck, Emery and Greenberg, 1985; Bower, 1981; Bower, 1987) cognitive processing is guided by schemata that largely determine how information is attended to, interpreted and remembered. In anxious individuals, schemata may be biased towards danger and vulnerability, and thus, threat-related material would be favoured at all stages of processing. This includes early processes such as attention and stimulus encoding, and later processes such as memory and interpretation (see also Bar-Haim *et al.*, 2007 for a compatible account). Other theories (Foa and Kozak, 1986; Fox *et al.*, 2001b; Mogg *et al.*, 1997; Williams *et al.*, 1988) suggest that anxious individuals are prone to biases at more specific stages of information processing (e.g. early attention orienting) but not in others (e.g. disengagement of attention). A closer look at these questions using ERPs can help pinpoint when activation in the PFC engages to regulate the amygdala.

ERP studies have assessed the neural correlates of performance of healthy adults on the dot-probe task. Pourtois *et al.* (2004) used a modified dot-probe task with ERP recordings and found increased C1 amplitude to threat relative to neutral stimuli, which correlated with increased P1 amplitude to target-probe stimuli. The C1 findings (~80 milliseconds following the faces display onset) were interpreted as reflecting increased neural activation during very early processing of threat, most probably indexing the activity of reentrants from the amygdala to the primary visual cortex. This early response to threat may facilitate attention allocation during target processing as reflected in the correlation between the C1 amplitude to the presentation of affective faces and P1 amplitude to the target probes.

Santesso and colleagues (2008), also using the dot-probe task, found increased P1 amplitude towards targets in the same location as angry faces. In this study, no ERP effects were found during the processing of the faces display. Finally, studies from our own laboratory using the dot-probe task indicate that anxious individuals show greater amplitudes in the C1 component to angry-neutral face pairs relative to non-anxious individuals. In addition, anxious individuals show lower P3 amplitudes to the target displays relative to non-anxious individuals (Figure 8.4d). In light of relevant information processing models (McNally, 1998; Vasey, Dalgleish and Silverman, 2003), it may be that threat cues trigger the early deployment of attentional processes. This allocation may subsequently diminish the amount of processing resources deployed for the target that follows.

These results demonstrate that threat faces can act as exogenous cues by increasing sensory processing in extra striate cortex. This response may affect frontal recruitment during the subsequent processing of a target presented in the same location.

As a whole, fMRI and ERP studies illuminate the chronometry and neural architecture of performance of anxious and non-anxious individuals on the dot-probe task, providing detail on the processes giving rise to attentional biases in anxious children. In particular, it appears that anxious individuals are marked by limbic systems that are acutely sensitive to exposure to potential threat cues. This hyper-reactivity is evident in the rapid and persistent allocation of attention to these perceived threats and the relative effectiveness of potential down-regulators to modify this initial response. The coexistence of these two functional patterns may be crucial in distinguishing between children prone to anxious behaviour but are healthy (i.e. they exhibit heightened limbic response but can engage effective cognitive control) and children who meet diagnostic criteria (i.e. limbic hyper-reactivity is coupled with ineffective cognitive control).

Future Directions

Epidemiological data suggest that a developmental perspective is crucial to attempts to treat and prevent anxiety. Anxiety, in the form of either a diagnosable disorder or its developmental precursors, is often evident early in life (Pine, 2007; Pine *et al.*, 1998). Indeed, the vast majority of lifetime cases of social anxiety are evident by age 20, with an initial upwards inflection at age 9 (Beesdo *et al.*, 2007). The early emergence of anxiety places a child at greatly increased risk for anxiety disorders, as well as co-occurring mood disorders, across the lifespan. Our brief review of the literature suggests that a cognitive neuroscience approach may be particularly useful, contributing to many of the central questions concerning the role of processing biases in anxiety (Keller, Hicks and Miller, 2000).

In this review, we have presented a multi-method approach which, by definition, calls on researchers to integrate data from both behaviour and neuroscience. Within the broader neuroscience literature, it is often the case that behavioural differences are relatively ignored or actively discouraged in favour of an approach that focuses exclusively on differences at the neural level. Tasks that do not have a behavioural component (e.g. passive viewing of threat faces) can reveal individual differences in neural activation, but are limited in terms of the inferences that can be made about underlying psychological processes. In some cases, this limitation is unavoidable. Indeed, as we noted above, the neuroscience approach broadens our ability to examine the breadth of development by reflecting processing in populations, such as infants, with limited behavioural repertoires. However, this should not be taken as a sign that behavioural profiles are unimportant or do not provide additional, and partially independent, information concerning the processes of interest.

When applying a behavioural paradigm that requires an active response from the participant, generating a pattern of responses that can be interpreted at the behavioural level (e.g. the dot-probe task), the results may fall within a 2×2 pattern crossing results at the behavioural and neural levels. First, comparable individual differences may be evident at both the behavioural and neural levels. For example, Pérez-Edgar and Fox (2005a) found that shy children under stress had more difficulty (increased errors and slower RTs) in a Posner attention-shifting task than non-shy children. At the neural level, the shy children also showed increased EEG alpha activation and larger peak ERP amplitudes.

Some researchers have argued that such findings complicate our ability to interpret neural differences as a function of group membership versus the alternate explanation that neural differences are simply a reflection of variations in performance. However, as noted throughout this chapter, there are methodological (e.g. task parametrization) and statistical (e.g. separate age, group and performance-based analyses) strategies that can work to tease apart these factors.

The second possibility would have evident differences at the behavioural level, but not in neural mechanisms. This pattern may point to a lack of sensitivity or specificity in the neuroscience method employed. For example, the difficulty in overcoming signal-to-noise ratios in developmental studies may contribute to this dissociation. Alternately, the dissociation may reflect 'real' developmental differences in how children go about performing tasks and how this is reflected in neural processes. In the case of ERP's, for example, individual components are more diffuse (or even absent) in young children. Therefore, group or age differences may not be reflected in the sharp amplitude and latency shifts often evident in older children and adults. The lack of neural differences may, in the end, also indicate that a priori assumptions about the mechanisms underlying behaviour are incorrect or incomplete. This would then allow the field to refine or broaden its understanding of the processes of interest. Indeed, this is a vital process for the advancement of the field.

The third possibility, quite prevalent in the field, finds no behavioural differences across groups, but significant differences at the neural level (e.g. Guyer *et al.*, 2006; Pérez-Edgar *et al.*, 2006). This pattern of results is often prized because neural differences can then be judged without the 'confound' of differences in behaviour. However, in line with the argument above, much of our initial interest in the neuroscience approach lies in its ability to add new insight to the behavioural patterns that characterize and define the group differences of interest. Typically, it is these behavioural differences that motivate our use of neuroscience techniques, not the other way around.

Of course, there are circumstances when this pattern of findings is of great interest. For example, Durston and colleagues (Durston *et al.*, 2002) found that in completing a 'go-no go' task, children must recruit more diffuse neural structures in order to match adult performance. This finding is in line with the general consensus that brain regions that correlate with task performance become more focal or fine-tuned with age, whereas brain regions not correlated with such task performance diminish in activity with age (Amso and Casey, 2006). However, much research has actively worked to eliminate behavioural differences, relying on simple passive viewing or employing extremely constrained and simple tasks – above and beyond the modifications that are normally needed to match the methodological demands of the neuroscience technique. This approach may to some extent limit the generalizability and applicability of the data generated, while also constricting our ability to comment on how neural processes are translated into behaviour.

The fourth potential outcome, of course, is the absence of group differences at both the behavioural and neural levels. Given current publication practices, these data are unlikely to survive the peer-review process. As such, any insights into preserved or resilient processes when comparing disordered or healthy groups are likely to be limited.

When applied to the specific questions surrounding paediatric anxiety, cognitive neuroscience techniques can help determine when and how processing in anxious children diverges from healthy controls. These techniques may also allow us to note differences in processing even in the absence of marked behavioural differences in any given task. By the same token, cognitive neuroscience techniques can point to neural perturbations that may be evident even before classic behavioural or cognitive symptoms of anxiety emerge. For example, children who fit the temperamental profile of behavioural inhibition are at increased risk for anxiety and much of this link may be bound to shared characteristics that are evident through neuroscience techniques, such as an over-reactive amygdala response to threat, regardless of current diagnostic status (Pérez-Edgar and Fox, 2005b).

These insights may be crucial to improving our ability to identify early risk for anxiety. It may also help specify the multiple pathways that can lead to anxiety, distinguishing perhaps between biological (e.g. temperament) and socially mediated (e.g. child rearing environment) mechanisms that can give rise to psychopathology. In this way, coupling data from neuroscience with more traditional measures of cognition and behaviour allows researchers to create multidimensional profiles of children. These profiles, in turn, may eventually aid researchers and clinicians in monitoring populations that are non-verbal (e.g. young children) or otherwise cognitively compromised (e.g. children with pervasive developmental disorders), target for intervention children at high risk and choose and evaluate treatment outcomes. In treatment studies, for example, this approach would help characterize the level of treatment effect. That is, do interventions shape only observed behaviour or do they also modify underlying neural functioning? This approach may help in understanding questions of aetiology, disease maintenance, and individual differences in levels of remittance and relapse.

Summary

The literature reviewed in the current chapter examines the potential link between attention and paediatric anxiety through the lens of cognitive neuroscience. The available research suggests that anxiety disorders likely represent the end result of complex interactions among multiple risk factors that, over the course of development, operate at increasing levels of complexity (Fox, Hane and Pine, 2007; McClure and Pine, 2006). In order to manage this complexity and maximize the clarity of our argument, we have chosen a single task, the dot probe, to illustrate the issues facing cognitive neuroscientists today. However, even here, the complexities involved are still quite evident. The emerging literature is only now beginning to integrate new data on the timing (via ERP) and neural structures (via fMRI) of processing into our understanding of phenotypic displays of affect and behaviour. This multi-method approach is beginning to yield dividends, shaping our understanding of causal mechanisms, discernible risk factors for later disorder, and the processes by which interventions shape subsequent functioning. It is our belief that a developmental perspective is at the core of each of these endeavours, allowing researchers a strategy for capturing the dynamic interplay that shapes developmental trajectories and eventual outcomes.

Acknowledgements

Preparation of this chapter was supported, in part, by grants to Koraly Pérez-Edgar from the National Institutes of Health (MH 073569) and NARSAD (Blowitz-Ridgeway Young Investigator Award), and to Yair Bar-Haim from The Israeli Science Foundation (grant 964/08).

References

Amin, Z., Constable, R.T. and Canli, T. (2004) Attentional bias for valenced stimuli as a function of personality in the dot-probe task. *Journal of Research in Personality*, **38**, 15–23.

Amso, D. and Casey, B.J. (2006) Beyond what develops: when neuroimaging may inform how cognition changes with development. *Current Directions in Psychological Science*, **15**, 24–29.

Angold, A., Costello, E.J. and Worthman, C.M. (1998) Puberty and depression: the roles of age, pubertal status and pubertal timing. *Psychological Medicine*, **28**, 51–61.

Bar-Haim, Y., Lamy, D. and Glickman, S. (2005) Attentional bias in anxiety: a behavioral and ERP study. *Brain and Cognition*, **59**, 11–22.

Bar-Haim, Y., Lamy, D., Pergamin, L. *et al.* (2007) Threat-related attentional bias in anxious and nonanxious individuals: a meta-analytic study. *Psychological Bulletin*, **133**, 1–24.

Beck, A. (1976) *Cognitive Therapy and the Emotional Disorders*, International Universities Press, New York.

Beck, A. and Clark, D. (1997) An information processing model of anxiety: automatic and strategic processes. *Behaviour Research and Therapy*, **35**, 49–58.

Beck, A.T., Emery, G. and Greenberg, R.L. (1985) *Anxiety Disorders and Phobias: A Cognitive Perspective*, Basic Books, New York.

Beesdo, K., Bittner, A., Pine, D.S. *et al.* (2007) Incidence of social anxiety disorder and the consistent risk for secondary depression in the first three decades of life. *Archives of General Psychiatry*, **64**, 903–912.

Bishop, S.J., Duncan, J. and Lawrence, A.D. (2004) State anxiety modulation of the amygdala response to unattended threat-related stimuli. *The Journal of Neuroscience*, **24**, 10364–10368.

Blair, R.J.R., Morris, J.S., Frith, C.D. *et al.* (1999) Dissociable neural responses to facial expressions of sadness and anger. *Brain and Cognition*, **122**, 883–893.

Bower, G.H. (1981) Mood and memory. *American Psychologist*, **36**, 129–148.

Bower, G.H. (1987) Commentary on mood and memory. *Behaviour Research and Therapy*, **25**, 443–455.

Casey, B.J., Davidson, M. and Rosen, B. (2002) Functional magnetic resonance imaging: basic principles of and application to developmental science. *Developmental Science*, **5**, 301–309.

Davidson, M.C., Thomas, K. and Casey, B.J. (2003) Imaging the developing brain with fMRI. *Mental Retardation and Developmental Disabilities Research Reviews*, **9**, 161–167.

De Bellis, M.D., Casey, B.J., Dahl, R.E. *et al.* (2000) A pilot study of amygdala volumes in pediatric generalized anxiety disorder. *Society of Biological Psychiatry*, **48**, 51–57.

Diamond, A., Kirkham, N.Z. and Amso, D. (2002) Conditions under which young children can hold two rules in mind and inhibit a prepotent response. *Developmental Psychology*, **38**, 352–362.

Durston, S., Davidson, M., Tottenham, N. *et al.* (2006) A shift from diffuse to focal cortical activity with development. *Developmental Science*, **9**, 1–8.

Durston, S., Thomas, K.M., Worden, M.S. *et al.* (2002) An fMRI study of the effect of preceding context on inhibition. *Neuroimage*, **16**, 449–453.

Eriksen, C. (1995) The flankers task and response competition: a useful tool for investigating a variety of cognitive problems, in *Visual Selective Attention* (eds

C. Bundesen and H. Shibuya), Lawrence Erlbaum Associates, Inc, Hillsdale, NJ, pp. 101–118.

Eysenck, M.W., Derakshan, N., Santos, R. and Calvo, M.G. (2007) Anxiety and cognitive performance: attentional control theory. *Emotion*, **7**, 336–353.

Foa, E.B. and Kozak, M.J. (1986) Emotional processing of fear: exposure to corrective information. *Psychological Bulletin*, **99**, 20–35.

Fox, N.A., Hane, A.A. and Pérez-Edgar, K. (2006) Psychophysiological methods for the study of developmental psychopathology, in *Developmental Psychopathology* (eds D. Cicchetti and D.J. Cohen), John Wiley & Sons, Hoboken, NJ, pp. 381–426.

Fox, N.A., Hane, A.A. and Pine, D.S. (2007) Plasticity for affective neurocircuitry: how the environment affects gene expression. *Current Directions in Psychological Science*, **16**, 1–5.

Fox, N.A., Henderson, H.A., Rubin, K.H. *et al.* (2001a) Continuity and discontinuity of behavioral inhibition and exuberance: psychophysiological and behavioral influences across the first four years of life. *Child Development*, **72**, 1–21.

Fox, E., Russo, R., Bowles, R. and Dutton, K. (2001b) Do threatening stimuli draw or hold visual attention in subclinical anxiety. *Journal of Experimental Psychology: General*, **130**, 681–700.

Fox, N.A., Schmidt, L.A. and Henderson, H.A. (2000) Developmental psychophysiology: conceptual and methodological perspectives, in *Handbook of Psychophysiology* (eds L.G.T.J.T. Cacioppo and G.G. Berntson), Cambridge University Press, Cambridge, pp. 665–686.

Gerstadt, C.L., Hong, Y.H. and Diamond, A. (1994) The relationship between cognition and action: performance of children 31/2 -7 years old on a Stroop-like day-night test. *Cognition*, **53**, 129–153.

Guyer, A., Lau, J.Y.F., McClure-Tone, E.B. *et al.* (2008) Amygdala and ventrolateral prefrontal cortex function during anticipated peer evaluation in pediatric social anxiety. *Archives of General Psychiatry*, **65**, 1303–1312.

Guyer, A.E., Nelson, E.E., Perez-Edgar, K. *et al.* (2006) Striatal functional alteration in adolescents characterized by early childhood behavioral inhibition. *Journal of Neuroscience*, **26**, 6399–6405.

Hariri, A., Mattay, V., Tessitore, A. *et al.* (2003) Neocortical modulation of the amygdala response to fearful stimuli. *Biological Psychiatry*, **53**, 494–501.

Hayward, C. and Sanborn, K. (2002) Puberty and the emergence of gender differences in psychopathology. *Journal of Adolescent Health*, **305**, 49–58

Hillyard, S. and Anllo-Vento, L. (1998) Event-related brain potentials in the study of visual selective attention. Proceedings of the National Academy of Sciences of the United States of America, **95**, 781–787.

Hillyard, S.A., Luck, S.J. and Mangun, G.R. (1994) The cuing of attention to the visual field locat analysis with ERP recordings, in *Cognitive Electrophysiology: Event-related Brain Potentials in Basic and Clinical Research* (eds H.J. Heinze, T.F. Muente and G.R. Mangun), Birkhauser, Boston, pp. 1–25.

Keller, J., Hicks, B.D. and Miller, G.A. (2000) Psychophysiology in the study of psychopathology, in *Handbook of Psychophysiology* (eds L.G.T.J.T. Cacioppo and G.G. Berntson), Cambridge University Press, New York, pp. 719–750.

Kostandov, E. and Azumanov, Y. (1977) Averaged cortical evoked potentials to recognized and non-recognized verbal stimuli. *Acta Neurobiologiae Experimentalis*, **37**, 311–324.

Ladouceur, C., Dahl, R., Birmaher, B. *et al.* (2006) Increased error-related negativity (ERN) in childhood anxiety disorders: ERP and source localization. *Journal of Child Psychology and Psychiatry*, **47**, 1073–1082.

LeDoux, J.E. (1995) Emotion: clues from the brain. *Annual Review of Psychology*, **46**, 209–235.

McClure, E.B., Monk, C.S., Nelson, E.E. *et al.* (2004) A developmental examination of gender differences in brain engagement during evaluation of threat. *Biological Psychiatry*, **55**, 1047–1055.

McClure, E.B., Monk, C.S., Nelson, E.E. *et al.* (2007) Abnormal attention modulation of fear circuit function in pediatric generalized anxiety disorder. *Archives of General Psychiatry*, **64**, 109–116.

McClure, E. and Pine, D.S. (2006) Social anxiety and emotion regulation: a model for developmental psychopathology perspectives on anxiety disorders, in *Developmental Psychopathology* (eds D. Cicchetti and D.J. Cohen), John Wiley & Sons, Hoboken, NJ, pp. 470–502.

McDermott, J.M., Pérez-Edgar, K. and Fox, N.A. (2007) Variations of the flanker paradigm: assessing selective attention in young children. *Behavior Research Methods*, **39**, 62–70.

McNally, R.J. (1998) Information-processing abnormalities in anxiety disorders: implications for cognitive neuroscience. *Cognition and Emotion*, **12**, 479–495

Mogg, K. and Bradley, B. (1998) A cognitive-motivational analysis of anxiety. *Behaviour Research And Therapy*, **36**, 809–848.

Mogg, K., Bradley, B.P., De Bono, J. and Painter, M. (1997) Time course of attentional bias for threat information in non-clinical anxiety. *Behaviour Research and Therapy*, **35**, 297–303.

Mogg, K., Holmes, A., Garner, M. and Bradley, B. (2008) Effects of threat cues on attentional shifting, disengagement and response slowing in anxious individuals. *Behaviour Research and Therapy*, **46**, 656–667.

Monk, C.S., McClure, E.B., Nelson, E.E. *et al.* (2003) Adolescent immaturity in attention-related brain engagement to emotional facial expressions. *NeuroImage*, **20**, 420–428.

Monk, C.S., Nelson, E.E., McClure, E.B. *et al.* (2006) Ventrolateral prefrontal cortex activation and attention bias in responsive to angry faces in adolescents with generalized anxiety disorder. *American Journal of Psychiatry*, **163**, 1091–1097.

Monk, C.S., Nelson, E.E., Woldehawariat, G. *et al.* (2004) Experience-dependent plasticity for attention to threat: behavioral and neurophysical evidence in humans. *Biological Psychiatry*, **56**, 607–610.

Monk, C.S., Telzer, E.H., Mogg, K. *et al.* (2008) Amygdala and ventrolateral prefrontal cortex activation to masked angry faces in children and adolescents with generalized anxiety disorder. *Archives of General Psychiatry*, **65**, 568–576.

Morris, J.S., Ohman, A. and Dolan, R.J. (1998) Conscious and unconscious emotional learning in the human amygdala. *Nature*, **393**, 467–470.

Munakata, Y., Casey, B.J. and Diamond, A. (2004) Developmental cognitive neuroscience: progress and potential. *Trends in Cognitive Sciences*, **8**, 122–127.

Navon, D. and Margalit, B. (1983) Allocation of attention according to informativeness in visual recognition. *The Quarterly Journal Of Experimental Psychology. A, Human Experimental Psychology*, **35**, 497–512.

Nelson, E., Leibenluft, E., McClure, E. and Pine, D. (2005) The social re-orientation of adolescence: a neuroscience perspective on the process and its relation to psychopathology. *Psychological Medicine*, **35**, 163–174.

Nelson, E.E., McClure, E.B., Monk, C.S. *et al.* (2003) Developmental differences in neuronal engagement during implicit encoding of emotional faces: an event-related fMRI study. *Journal of Child Psychology and Psychiatry*, **44**, 1015–1024.

Ochsner, K. and Gross, J. (2008) Cognitive emotion regulation: insights from social cognitive and affective neuroscience. *Current Directions in Psychological Science*, **17**, 153–158.

Overy, K., Norton, A., Cronin, K. *et al.* (2005) Examining rhythm and melody processing in young children using fMRI. *Annals of the New York Academy of Sciences*, **1060**, 210–218.

Paus, T. (2005) Mapping brain maturation and cognitive development during adolescence. *Trends in Cognitive Sciences*, **9**, 60–68.

Pérez-Edgar, K. and Fox, N.A. (2005a) A behavioral and electrophysiological study of children's selective attention under neutral and affective conditions. *Journal of Cognition and Development*, **6**, 89–118.

Pérez-Edgar, K. and Fox, N.A. (2005b) Temperament and anxiety disorders. *Child and Adolescent Psychiatric Clinics of North America*, **14**, 681–706.

Pérez-Edgar, K., Fox, N.A., Cohn, J.F and Kovacs, M. (2006) Behavioral and electrophysiological markers of selective attention in children of parents with a history of depression. *Biological Psychiatry*, **60**, 1131–1138.

Pine, D. (2007) Research review: a neuroscience framework for pediatric anxiety disorders. *Journal of Child Psychology and Psychiatry*, **48**, 631–648.

Pine, D.S., Cohen, P., Gurley, D. *et al.* (1998) The risk for early-adulthood anxiety and depressive disorders in adolescents with anxiety and depressive disorders. *Archives of General Psychiatry*, **55**, 56–64.

Pine, D.S., Helfinstein, S.M., Bar-Haim, Y. *et al.* (2009) Challenges in developing novel treatments for childhood disorders: lessons from research on anxiety. *Neuropsychopharmacology*, **34**, 213–228.

Pourtois, G., Grandjean, D., Sander, D. and Vuilleumier, P. (2004) Electrophysiological correlates of rapid spatial orienting towards fearful faces. *Cerebral Cortex*, **14**, 619–633.

Pourtois, G., Schwartz, S., Seghier, M. *et al.* (2006) Neural systems for orienting attention to the location of threat signals: an event-related fMRI study. *NeuroImage*, **31**, 920–933.

Rapee, R. and Heimberg, R. (1997) A cognitive-behavioral model of anxiety in social phobia. *Behaviour Research and Therapy*, **35**, 741–756.

Rauch, S.L., Shin, L.M. and Wright, C.I. (2003) Neuroimaging studies of amygdala function in anxiety disorders. *Annals of the New York Academy of Sciences*, **985**, 389–410.

Reynolds, G.D. and Richards, J.E. (2005) Familiarization, attention, and recognition memory in infancy: an event-related potential and cortical source localization study. *Developmental Psychology*, **41**, 598–615.

Richards, J.E. (2003) Attention affects the recognition of briefly presented visual stimuli in infants: an ERP study. *Developmental Science*, **6**, 312–328.

Riera, J., Aubert, E., Iwata, K. *et al.* (2005) Fusing EEG and fMRI based on a bottom-up model: inferring activation and effective connectivity in neural masses. *Philosophical Transactions of the Royal Society B*, **360**, 1025–1041.

Rothbart, M.K., Ellis, L.K., Rueda, M.R. and Posner, M.I. (2003) Developing mechanisms of temperamental effortful control. *Journal of Personality*, **71**, 1113–1143.

Santesso, D., Meuret, A., Hofmann, S. *et al.* (2008) Electrophysiological correlates of spatial orienting towards angry faces: a source localization study. *Neuropsychologia*, **46**, 1338–1348.

Szeszko, P.R., Robinson, D., Jose Ma, J. *et al.* (1999) Orbital frontal and amygdala volume reductions in obsessive-compulsive disorder. *Archives of General Psychiatry*, **56**, 913–919.

Taylor, M.J. (1988) Developmental changes in ERPs to visual language stimuli. *Biological Psychology*, **26**, 321–339.

Telzer, E.H., Mogg, K., Bradley, B.P. *et al.* (2008) Relationship between trait anxiety, prefrontal cortex, and attention bias to angry faces in children and adolescents. *Biological Psychology*, **79**, 216–222.

Vasey, M.W., Dalgleish, T. and Silverman, W.K. (2003) Research on information-processing factors in child and adolescent psychopathology: a critical commentary. *Journal of Clinical Child and Adolescent Psychology*, **32**, 81–93.

Williams, J., Watt, F., MacLeod, C. and Mathews, A. (1988) *Cognitive Psychology and Emotional Disorders*, John Wiley & Sons, Chichester, England.

The Origin and Treatment
of Information Processing Biases
in Child Anxiety

9

Genetics

Thalia C. Eley and Helena M.S. Zavos
thalia.eley@kcl.ac.uk

Anxiety disorders affect 25% of individuals at some point during their childhood and adolescence (Costello, Egger and Angold, 2005; Meltzer *et al.*, 2000) and commonly continue into adulthood (Gregory *et al.*, 2007). Adult anxiety disorders often begin in childhood and these show the poorest prognosis (Otto *et al.*, 2001). The mean onset age across all anxiety disorders is 11 years (Kessler *et al.*, 2005), highlighting the importance of understanding the development of paediatric anxiety. These disorders are associated with wide-ranging difficulties from academic attainments (Van Ameringen, Mancini and Farvolden, 2003) to interpersonal relationships (Morris and March, 2004) and with a heavy financial burden to society in general and the health services in particular (Meltzer *et al.*, 2000). Anxiety disorders frequently co-occur with one another and with depression (Angold, Costello and Erkanli, 1999). These complex disorders are associated with a wide array of risk factors; here, we explore links between two groups not commonly considered together: genetic influences and information processing biases.

It has been clear for centuries that anxiety and related conditions run in families. Patient's front sheets at the Bethlem Royal Hospital at the beginning of the nineteenth century contained a section 'Whether hereditary' with entries such as 'brother' or 'both parents'. More formal family studies over the past three decades have confirmed this observation (for a review see Eley, Collier and McGuffin, 2002). The beauty of family studies lies in their simplicity – if family members resemble one another for a trait this indicates a possible role for genetic factors. However, as family members tend also to live together, this simplicity is also the weakness of the design – it is unable to disentangle the role of the family environment from that of genetic influences. For this twin or adoption studies are needed, and in the field of anxiety extant data come from twin studies.

Information Processing Biases and Anxiety: A Developmental Perspective Edited by Julie A. Hadwin and Andy P. Field
© 2010 John Wiley & Sons, Ltd.

Twin Analyses

Twin studies make use of the natural experiment provided by the existence of two types of twins: monozygotic (MZ) twins who share all their genes and dizygotic (DZ) twins who share on average half their segregating genes. Variance in the phenotype is divided into three latent factors: heritability or additive genetics (A); aspects of the environment that make twins (and other family members) resemble one another, defined as shared environment (C); and aspects of the environment (including family and non-family influences) that make family members different from one another, termed non-shared environment (E). MZ twins share all their genes and all their shared environment (i.e. $rMZ = A + C$). In contrast, DZ twins share just half their genes, but again all of the effects of shared environment (i.e. $rDZ = \frac{1}{2}A + C$). The difference in correlation between a group of MZ and DZ twins, therefore, provides a rough estimate of heritability (i.e. $A = 2(rMZ - rDZ)$). Shared environment is the difference between MZ resemblance and heritability ($C = rMZ - A$). Non-shared environment or E is calculated as the difference between the MZ twin correlation and 1 ($E = 1 - rMZ$). It is important to point out that this term also includes any error variance. This is particularly important when considering experimental tasks, as these tend to be less reliable than data from questionnaires; the E term is, therefore, inflated owing to larger error, resulting in lower heritability and shared environment estimates than might be expected. In sum, this approach allows the variance in a trait to be divided into that due to each of these three factors. Model-fitting analyses estimate precise variance components, i.e. the contribution to variance in the measure of genes, shared environment and non-shared environment, along with confidence intervals. Furthermore, such models can be extended to examine more sophisticated hypotheses such as the role of genes, shared environment and non-shared environment on the covariation between two measures or on continuity over time.

However, there are limitations to the twin design, and these include the equal environments assumption, chorionicity, assortative mating and generalizability. The equal environment assumption states that both MZ and DZ twin pairs experience shared environment to the same degree. However, some authors question this assumption on the basis that twins who resemble one another more closely physically are more likely to be treated alike, inflating their experience of shared environment. In fact, studies exploring the equal environments assumption have found that for most aspects of psychopathology it holds true. For example, although MZ twins are treated more similarly to one another than twins within DZ pairs, this is because they behave in a more similar fashion and thus elicit more similar responses from others, an effect that is thus due to their genes (and therefore accurately modelled as such), rather than the environment (Martin, Boomsma and Machin, 1997). Chorionicity refers to the number of chorions, the sack within which, in singletons, the foetus develops. In all DZ twins there are two chorions, but in two-thirds of MZ twins there is just one chorion, leading to the possibility that increased MZ resemblance may be due to chorion-sharing. There is little data on this issue as determining chorionicity requires skilled work, but that which there is indicates that monochorionic MZ twins may be a little more similar to one another than dichorionic MZ twins, an effect which would slightly inflate heritability estimates (Plomin *et al.*, 2001; Martin, Boomsma and Machin, 1997). Assortative mating refers to the well-replicated finding that 'birds of a feather flock together' or that individuals mate with those similar to themselves. This leads to an increase in genetic variance in the population, and in increased genetic resemblance in DZ twin pairs which results in a decrease in genetic estimates (Plomin *et al.*, 2001). Finally, there is the question of the degree to which twins are representative of the non-twin population, i.e. the extent to which findings from these studies are generalizable. Extant data indicate that with the exception of a slight initial delay in language development, which disappears by school-age, twins are largely indistinguishable from non-twins (Rutter and Redshaw, 1991). These limitations mean that parameter estimates such as the level of genetic influence (heritability) or shared environmental influence from twin studies should not be regarded as absolute, but as an indication of the approximate role of genes on the measured trait. We turn now to a brief summary of extant findings.

Twin studies of anxiety, like almost all complex traits, have identified a moderate genetic component. However, there is huge variation across studies, because heritability estimates are population statistics, and vary depending on the population being studied. Overall, in adults the majority of estimates falls within the 35–70% range for heritability, with the remaining variance due to non-shared environment (Eley, Collier and McGuffin, 2002). In children and adolescents, the genetic influence may be somewhat lower, and appears to be influenced by a number of factors including age, sex, rater as well as phenotypic definition (Gregory and Eley, 2007). A review of this literature is beyond the scope of this chapter, which has a more specific focus on cognitive processing within anxiety, but a few patterns of effects that may prove relevant are as follows. First, there is some evidence for an overall increase in genetic influence on anxiety as children move from childhood into adolescence (e.g. Feigon *et al.*, 2001), although it should be noted that other studies have found the reverse (e.g. Bartels, 2007). Second, heritability estimates for anxiety are generally higher in females than males, where sex effects are found (e.g. Eaves *et al.*, 1997). Third, parent-reported (vs. child-reported) anxiety generally shows higher heritability (e.g. Thapar and McGuffin, 1995). Fourth, heritability estimates differ depending on whether anxiety is being considered as a trait, symptom, syndrome or disorder. Thus, for example, in one study, separation anxiety disorder (SAD) in children was highly heritable, with no shared environmental influence (Bolton *et al.*, 2006), in contrast to modest heritability and moderate shared environment estimates for separation anxiety *syndrome* (Bolton *et al.*, 2006), a pattern more similar to previous analyses of separation anxiety *symptoms* (e.g. Feigon *et al.*, 2001). Heritability is also likely to vary as a function of disorder type, though the literature is perhaps too small as yet to see clear patterns here. However, there is some evidence, for example, that obsessive-compulsive behaviours are more heritable than other aspects of anxiety (Eley *et al.*, 2003). In sum, in spite of the wide variability in heritability estimates for child and adolescent anxiety, it is clear that there are significant genetic influences.

Research has more recently moved on to answering more complex questions about the role of genes in the development of anxiety. Thus, twin analyses have been able to shed light on two particularly marked features of anxiety: (i) the high co-morbidity both with depression and across anxiety disorders and (ii) the strong continuity seen across time. Twin studies consistently show that genes are the most important influence on the high co-morbidity seen between child anxiety and depression symptoms (Eley and Stevenson, 1999) and disorders (Silberg, Rutter and Eaves, 2001) as in adults (Kendler *et al.*, 1987, 1992a; Kendler, 1996), whereas environmental influences are largely specific to either anxiety or depression. Genes also account for the majority of the association between anxiety sub-types in children (Eley *et al.*, 2003; Silberg, Rutter and Eaves, 2001) and between anxiety and depressive disorders and neuroticism in adults (Kendler *et al.*, 1992b, 2001; Hettema *et al.*, 2005; Fanous *et al.*, 2002; Sham *et al.*, 2000). Environmental influences again tend to be more symptom specific. Similarly, continuity over time for these phenotypes is largely genetically influenced, whereas the environment is more time specific (Lau and Eley, 2006). Whilst there are exceptions to these patterns, overall, genes have a general effect, whereas environmental influences are relatively time and symptom specific. These findings are consistent with a diathesis-stress model of a shared genetic diathesis to childhood anxiety and depression, the specific manifestation and timing of which depends on environmental experiences. Precisely, how such a genetic influence takes its effect is not yet clear, but one approach is to begin to identify specific genes, for which we turn to molecular genetics.

Association Analyses

In comparison to single-gene disorders, complex traits such as anxiety are known to be influenced by multiple risk factors. Variants within individual genes, or loci, thought to influence such complex traits are, therefore, described by the term 'quantitative trait loci' (QTL). QTLs are very hard to identify, because the effect of any one loci on a trait is likely to be very small (e.g. less than 1% of the variance). Whilst the traditional within-family method known as linkage worked well for single-gene disorders, for QTLs a more powerful statistical approach called association analysis is generally used (Plomin, Owen and McGuffin, 1994; Risch and Merikangas, 1996). The basis of this method is that allele frequencies are compared between cases and controls, with a significant difference implying that the genotype is related to the disorder differentiating the cases and controls. The approach, however, is neither comprehensive nor systematic, meaning that some neurobiological pathways involved may yet be identified. Genome-wide association studies will act as a starting point in the identification of new potential sites of interest.

Association studies have provided data exploring the relationship between specific genes and anxiety. The major focus of molecular genetic association studies in anxiety has been markers in the serotonin (5HT) system, due to its contribution to variation in many physiological functions such as fc sleep, motor activity and reproductive activity, in addition to emotiu... including mood and anxiety. This system is also the target of uptake-inhibiting antidepressant and anti-anxiety drugs. The first major result in this area utilized a trait approach to anxiety, and found an association between a marker within the serotonin transporter promoter gene (*SCL6A4*) and anxiety-related personality traits including neuroticism and harm avoidance (Lesch *et al.*, 1996). The marker used, *5-HTTLPR*, has a common 44 base pair insertion/deletion polymorphism (i.e. there is a section that varies; in some chromosomes there is a segment of DNA 44 base pairs long missing, which is present in other chromosomes). The short-form allele (S) reduces transcriptional efficiency of the promoter and results in decreased serotonin transporter expression. In two samples, individuals with one or two copies of the S allele had higher anxiety-related personality trait scores than individuals homozygous for the long-form (L) allele. This finding has been the subject of considerable attempts at replication, some of which have been positive (e.g. Katsuragi *et al.*, 1999; Osher, Hamer and Benjamin, 2000), others of which have not (Ball *et al.*, 1997; Jorm *et al.*, 1998). A meta-analysis on this topic concluded that the results appear to be specific to neuroticism, rather than some of the other anxiety-related traits examined (Sen *et al.*, 2004). Interestingly, associations with the S allele have been demonstrated with anxiety-related traits in *younger* samples, such as infant anxious temperament (Auerbach *et al.*, 1999; Ebstein *et al.*, 1998). However, other studies have found associations with the long (L) allele and shyness in school children (Arbelle *et al.*, 2003) and anxiety-related temperament in the mid-teens (Jorm *et al.*, 2000).

One source of non-replication in molecular genetics is sample heterogeneity, including gene–environment (G × E) interactions. In G × E interaction genetic and environmental risks do not add up independently. For example, a specific genetic risk might only have an effect when the individual experiences a particular environmental stress. Thus, in one high-profile study, the *5-HTTLPR* was associated with adult depressive disorder only in individuals exposed to serious negative life events (Caspi *et al.*, 2003). With regard to younger samples, this finding has been replicated for behavioural inhibition (BI) or shyness in *children* (Fox *et al.*, 2005), parent-rated shyness and nervousness during experimental tasks in a laboratory in *children* (Hayden *et al.*, 2007), and for *female adolescent* depression (Eley *et al.*, 2004b). Note, however, that in spite of positive replications in the adult literature too, there are also other replication studies for adult depression that are negative (Surtees *et al.*, 2006; Gillespie *et al.*, 2005).

In spite of the somewhat inconsistent findings, this marker is by far the most thoroughly explored with regard to anxiety-related phenotypes. Furthermore, this inconsistency leads some to advocate that it is now more important than ever to identify intermediate phenotypes which might be mediating any genetic effects. In Figure 9.1, we outline a basic model of genetic influence on child anxiety via intermediate phenotypes including brain function and information processing. We show how genetic risk has a general influence on all types of emotional symptom, which, via interaction with the environment, leads to distortions at both the brain and information processing level. We propose that more often than not, the

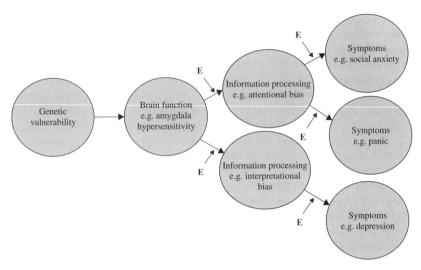

Figure 9.1 Model of genetic risk on emotional disorders with possible mediators (brain function and information processing) and moderators (environmental stimuli: E).

environment acts to increase the specificity of threat reactivity to one type of stimuli (e.g. social vs. physical threats) leading to specificity of symptoms or outcome.

Genes, Information Processing Biases and Anxiety

Information processing biases have long been associated with anxiety in adults. Work in younger samples is, as always, a newer field, and many of the exciting results are reviewed in other chapters of this book. Here, we focus on studies that combine both an information processing perspective *and* a genetically informative design. This research is perhaps best described as an emerging literature, as there are relatively few relevant publications. Pertinent studies fall into those using one of two major approaches: cognitive psychological assessment and neuropsychological assessment.

Cognitive Approaches

Cognitive models of anxiety emphasize hypersensitivity to threat as the key cognitive component of these disorders. There are three levels of bias described in cognitive models of anxiety: attention, interpretation and memory (reviewed by Muris and Field, 2008). In the sections below, studies that have assessed each of these three types of bias in child anxiety in the context of a genetically informative design are described.

Attentional biases

One of the core cognitive biases seen across all types of anxiety is biases of attention. For example, a leading theory of panic disorder (PD) emphasizes hypersensitivity and enhanced allocation of attention to internal bodily sensations (Clark, 1999). The construct anxiety sensitivity (AS) specifically refers to sensitivity to the physical and emotional symptoms of anxiety (an attentional bias) and the belief that these are harmful (an interpretational bias; Reiss, 1986). For example, fear of palpitations or a 'racing-heart' accompanied by the belief that these may indicate the onset of a heart attack. There is a considerable body of evidence supporting an association between AS and both anxiety in general and panic in particular in both adults (Taylor, 1999) and children (Silverman, 1999). More recently, interest has turned to considering whether AS may mediate genetic risk for anxiety disorders. The first twin study of AS used a large population-based sample of adults and produced a heritability estimate of around 50% (Stein, Jang and Livesley, 1999), with the remaining variance due to non-shared environment. Our team has extended these findings to both child and adolescent samples. First, in our sample of over 1300 adolescent twin and sibling pairs, heritability of AS was estimated at 47%, with the remaining variance due to non-shared environment (Zavos *et al.*, 2009). In a multivariate genetic analysis of anxiety ratings, depression ratings, AS and attributional style, the genetic correlation (extent of genetic over-lap) between AS and anxiety ratings was very high (e.g. 86 at wave 2), almost as high as that seen between anxiety and depression in this sample (.77, also wave 2). This finding indicates that AS largely reflects genetic vulnerability to anxiety. Of note, the genetic correlation between AS and depression ratings was also very high (.70 at wave 2), raising the possibility that AS reflects part of the shared genetic vulnerability to anxiety and depression, giving rise to their high levels of covariation. However, we caution that this measure is just a self-report questionnaire and so in terms of the model outlined earlier, is rather close to 'outcome', and indeed is considered by some simply to be another measure of anxiety.

In order to get further back towards the 'processing' end of this attentional bias, we assessed 300 pairs of 8-year-old twins, not just for AS, but also by using an experimental task designed to assess heart rate awareness. Studies of the internal focus of attention in PD have mainly focused on heartbeat perception (HBP), as palpitations (racing and/or pounding heart) are among the most prominent symptoms in PD patients. One method of assessing sensitivity to this phenomenon is a task called the *Mental Tracking Paradigm* in which subjects are asked to count their heartbeats during a signalled period of time without taking their pulse (Schandry, 1981). There have been several associations reported between increased heart rate awareness (i.e. good HBP) and panic-related phenotypes in both adults (e.g. Ehlers and Breuer, 1992; Ehlers, 1995; Van der Does *et al.*, 2000) and children (Eley *et al.*, 2004a). Our analyses revealed heritability estimates of 37% and 30–36% for AS and HBP, respectively, with the remaining variance largely due to non-shared environment. There was very wide variance in the HBP task reflecting the difficulty it held for the children and associated poor reliability, and as a result, only non-shared environmental influence was significant. With

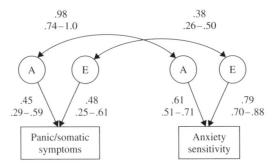

Figure 9.2 Genetic and environmental influences on panic/somatic symptoms and anxiety sensitivity and their association in 8-year-old twins.

regard to multivariate analyses, there was a high genetic correlation between AS and panic/somatic symptoms (.98, Figure 9.2) and a moderate (though non-significant) genetic correlation between HBP and panic/somatic symptoms (.47). These findings indicate that from a genetic perspective AS and our measure of panic/somatic symptoms were almost identical, in spite of removing any items that were similar on both from one measure. The genetic link between HBP and panic/somatic ratings was rather lower and non-significant, reflecting the lower reliability of this task, indicating a need to repeat this study with a larger sample.

Finally, there is evidence of an association between *5-HTTLPR* genotype and AS in adults (Stein *et al.*, 2008), in the context of a G × E interaction. Specifically, in a sample of 150 young adult subjects, those with the SS genotype *and* higher levels of maltreatment had significantly higher levels of AS than subjects with other genotypes. To our knowledge, molecular genetic analyses of AS in younger samples have yet to be published, but it seems highly likely that AS in younger samples will be associated with this marker, possibly in conjunction with life stress.

Whilst internal bodily symptoms are a particularly pertinent set of stimuli in PD, for other anxiety disorders, social phobia in particular, social interaction in general and emotional expressions in particular are the key threat. In adults, there are a number of papers supporting an association between attentional deployment with regard to facial expressions and anxiety (Mansell, 1999; Mogg and Bradley, 1999), although it is not entirely clear whether there is vigilance towards or avoidance of negative emotional expressions. In a sample of school children (*N* = 79), we found evidence for avoidance of both angry and fearful faces using a face dot-probe task (Stirling, Eley and Clark, 2006a, 2006b). With regard to genetic risk, one study examined attentional biases to fear facial expressions in children of parents with PD (Pine *et al.*, 2005). At-risk children (*N* = 65) reported significantly more fear and had significantly slower reaction times when rating fear than control children (*N* = 79), even after controlling for current anxiety level. Of note, child social phobia also predicted slower reaction times to fear faces, independently of parental PD indicating a role for current symptom level independent of familial genetic risk. Finally, in our twin study (at 10 years), using a matched cues task, anxious children again showed avoidance of angry faces, but there were no significant genetic effects on this trait (Lau *et al.*, 2008). Face-emotion recognition has also been associated with anxiety in both children (Richards *et al.*, 2007) and infants (Creswell *et al.*, 2008). We therefore tested ability to recognize specific facial expressions in our sample of child twin pairs and identified only modest non-significant genetic influence on recognition of each face type (Lau *et al.*, 2009a). However, in a multivariate model, we found evidence for a common genetic factor influencing ability to identify all 5 core facial expressions presented (angry, fearful, sad, disgusted and happy), which was highly heritable (75%; note this common factor would also be error-free) with the environmental influences in general being specific to identification of each face type (Lau *et al.*, 2009a).

Interpretation biases

One of the most well-established cognitive biases related to anxiety states is the interpretation of ambiguous information as threatening. Interpretive biases are thought to be important in both the origin and maintenance of anxiety (Williams *et al.*, 1997) and have been shown to be associated with anxiety in adults (e.g. Butler and Mathews, 1983; Clark *et al.*, 1997) and children (Barrett *et al.*, 1996; Taghavi *et al.*, 2000; Creswell, Schniering and Rapee, 2005). Whilst the majority of the literature has focused on anxiety, theories of depression also implicate interpretative biases (e.g. Beck, 1967), which have been demonstrated in depressed adults (Nunn, Mathews and Trower, 1997).

Interpretive biases have been examined in children using two main approaches. The most widely used approach has been to present ambiguous scenarios in which the child has to decide between threatening and neutral interpretations, with results tending to show an association between number of threat interpretations and anxiety and sometimes also depression (Barrett *et al.*, 1996; Creswell, Schniering and Rapee, 2005; Bogels and Zigterman, 2000; Dineen and Hadwin, 2004). A less widely used experimental approach utilizes simple homophone word tasks in which the subjects are asked to interpret words or make up sentences using homophones, words which have two or more meanings, of which at least two of the meanings differ such that one is negative and the other neutral/positive. The sentences are then coded for use of threat versus neutral meaning, which has been shown to differ between children with clinical anxiety and normal controls (Hadwin *et al.*, 1997; Taghavi *et al.*, 2000). Results are fairly consistent across these differing methodologies and support the hypothesis that emotional symptoms are associated with a tendency to interpret ambiguous information in a negative or threatening way. We used both approaches with our 8-year-old twin sample, in order to consider the heritability of the interpretation of ambiguous stimuli as threatening and to look at the origins of the association between this bias, and anxiety and depression symptoms (Eley *et al.*, 2007). Interpretational biases were moderate heritability (30% for the scenarios and 24% for the homophone word task), with the remaining variance due to non-shared environment. Notably, whilst both interpretational measures were associated with both anxiety and depression ratings, once partial correlations were estimated regressing out the other type of rating (e.g. association between anxiety and interpretational biases regressing out depression), there was no longer any association with anxiety ratings, revealing that the association was primarily with depression. Both genetic and environmental influences contributed to the association between threat interpretations and depression ratings.

Memory

There are only a handful of studies looking at memory deficits in child and adolescent anxiety, as this aspect of information processing has, in general, been linked more with depression than anxiety (Williams *et al.*, 1997). Two early studies found evidence for verbal memory deficits in anxiety disorders. The first showed that memory deficits predicted SAD and over-anxious disorder (OAD) in prepubertal boys at risk for delinquency (Pine *et al.*, 1999), whilst the second showed concurrent associations between memory deficits and both SAD and OAD in 6- to 18-year-olds (Toren *et al.*, 2000). A subsequent study showed memory deficits only in children with depressive disorders, but not in those with anxiety disorders (Gunther *et al.*, 2004), and indeed there are other studies showing memory deficits in child depression (e.g. Neshat-Doost *et al.*, 1998). Thus it may be that the associations seen between anxiety disorders and memory distortions are due to concurrent depressive symptoms. One study has looked at memory function in child anxiety using a genetically informative design. The study compared memory function in children at risk for anxiety disorders [by virtue of parental PD or major depressive disorder (MDD)] and normal controls (Vasa *et al.*, 2007). Interestingly, whilst social phobia was associated with visual (but not verbal) memory deficits, risk for anxiety disorder (i.e. parental diagnosis) had no association with memory function. Of note, whilst the link with social phobia in children controlled for separation and general anxiety disorder, it did not control for depression; thus the extent to which memory deficits in child anxiety are driven by associated depression symptoms remains unclear.

Neuropsychological Approaches

As outlined above, the other major approach to studying information processing is to use neuropsychological tests to assess aspects of brain function. With regard to understanding the development of child anxiety in the context of genetic risk, three main groups of studies have emerged thus far. The first group of studies looks at brain reactivity to processing of emotional facial expressions, generally using functional magnetic resonance imaging (fMRI). The second group uses skin conductance and startle reflex to assess stress reactivity. Finally, a small number of studies have explored the carbon dioxide challenge test and its association with panic.

Emotional face processing

The first paper to link a specific genetic marker to emotion-related brain processes came out in *Science* in 2002, indicating not only the importance but also the novelty of this approach (Hariri *et al.*, 2002). Specifically, the *5-HTTLPR* genotype was examined with respect to amygdala response to fearful stimuli. It is clear that the amygdala plays a central role in the perception of threat and danger, and in eliciting the emotions associated with these stimuli, that is, anxiety, fear and anger. In this study, two samples ($N = 14$ in each) were divided into those with one or more of the short (S) allele and those with only the long (L) alleles. The two groups were matched for age, gender and IQ in each of the two cohorts. During fMRI, subjects had to match the affect (angry or afraid) of one of two faces to that of a simultaneously presented target face. In both cohorts, as expected, this task led to significant amygdala activity. Furthermore, amygdala activity in the right hemisphere was significantly greater in the group with at least one S allele. These findings were not influenced by gender, and no such differences between the groups were identified for a working memory task, indicating a specific association between *5-HTTLPR* genotype and amygdala activity in response to processing emotional facial expressions. Furthermore, the two groups did not differ in their performance of this task, indicating no differences in core cognitive skills such as attention. There were also no differences in anxiety between the S carrier group and the L group. However, in the initial study associating this gene with anxiety-related traits (Lesch *et al.*, 1996), it accounted for only 3–4% of the variance, and in subsequent meta-analyses this figure has dropped to about 1%. Given the small size of the groups ($N = 14$) in the initial study this is not surprising. In sum, the findings implicate a genetic link between serotonin function and the response of brain regions that are known to be important for processing emotional cues. The authors then went on to extend their findings to examining the effects of *5-HTTLPR* on amygdala reactivity to a new set of emotional cues in a larger sample ($N = 94$), who had been screened for absence of psychiatric illness (Hariri *et al.*, 2005). Again they found greater right amygdala activity in response to angry and fearful faces in the matching task in the S as compared to L group. In this second study, the personality trait harm avoidance was also assessed, but no association was found between this and either genotype or amygdala activity. This study has been the subject of considerable attempts at replication, most of which have been positive. A recent meta-analysis of 14 studies including the initial publication found evidence for a significant association between *5-HTTLPR* genotype and amygdala activation, with an overall effect size of 0.63 (Munafo *et al.*, 2008). It is worth noting that this meta-analysis estimated that, assuming equal numbers of long and short alleles, any given study would require a sample size of at least 70 in order to have the power to detect an association with amygdala activation – only one of the studies had sufficiently large sample size. This also points to the general need for larger sample sizes to achieve more accurate estimates of effect and that the majority of studies in this field are underpowered.

As discussed above, continuity of anxiety and depression over time during childhood, adolescence and into adulthood is largely due to ongoing influences of genes with environmental influences tending to be more time specific (Lau and Eley, 2006). Thus, a particularly exciting recent paper presents results extending this association to adolescence (Lau *et al.*, 2009b). In this study, 33 psychiatrically well adolescents and 31 unmedicated adolescents with a current diagnosis of an anxiety disorder or MDD or both underwent a face-emotion paradigm, one component of which was to rate level of fear felt on seeing sets of emotional facial expressions. The *5-HTTLPR* was also genotyped, and divided not just into S versus L alleles, but also on the basis of a more recently identified single nucleotide polymorphism (A–G substitution) within the L allele resulting in L_A and L_G alleles, the latter being functionally similar to the S allele. There was a substantial and significant difference in right amygdala activation in response to the fearful faces as a function of *5-HTTLPR* genotype in both the healthy adolescents and in the patients. In the healthy adolescents, as in adults, activation was greater in those with at least one copy of the S or L_G alleles (Figure 9.3). In contrast, in the patients with anxiety or depressive disorder, the result was in the reverse direction, i.e. greater amygdala activation in response to fearful faces in those with two copies of the L_A allele. Interestingly, there was a similar, though weaker, association in the psychiatric patients with regard to happy faces. This difference in direction of findings between the healthy adolescents and the psychiatric patients is hard to explain, and further studies will be necessary. However, it is exciting to see the findings from healthy adults extended to a younger sample. Another study from the same group used familial risk rather than a specific gene to reflect genetic risk (Monk *et al.*, 2008). Specifically, adolescent offspring ($N = 17$) of adults with MDD showed greater amygdala activation to fearful faces in comparison with control adolescents ($N = 22$). Once again, this provides support for a role for the amygdala in mediating genetic risk on emotional disorders.

Finally, one group (Battaglia *et al.*, 2005) took a somewhat different approach to studying brain function by assessing cerebral visual event-related potentials (ERPs). ERPs are scalp potentials that occur within a few hundred milliseconds of

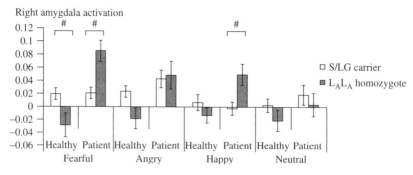

Figure 9.3 Bar graphs of activation in the right amygdala for the 'how afraid' condition relative to the task null-event baseline in various face emotions for patient and healthy adolescents across combined genotype groups (S/L_G carriers and $L_A L_A$ homozygotes).

the presentation of a visual stimulus. These are divided into earlier, 'exogenous' potentials (determined by the physical properties of the stimuli) and later, 'endogenous' potentials (which are more reflective of the interaction between the subject and the stimuli). Twin studies of ERPs in adults reveal significant heritability of later potentials (e.g. P300 and N400 waveforms) (Van Beijsterveldt and van Baal, 2002), indicating a heritable component to individual responses to stimuli. Children from around 10 years, like adults, show a characteristic ERP response when shown pictures of emotional facial expressions. Specifically, a negative wave-form that occurs at around 400 milliseconds (N400) is thought to reflect processing of human facial information. Indeed, some claim that the N400 reflects a temporal correlate of a corticoamygdala pathway to emotional processing (Williams *et al.*, 2004). In a highly novel study, an Italian group analysed links between N400 visual ERP responses to emotional facial expressions (of children), shyness/BI and *5-HTTLPR* genotype in a sample of 49 school children (Battaglia *et al.*, 2005). Not only did shyness/BI predict a reduction in the N400 amplitude for anger and neutral expressions, but the association for anger expressions was also driven by the children with the SS genotype (Figure 9.4).

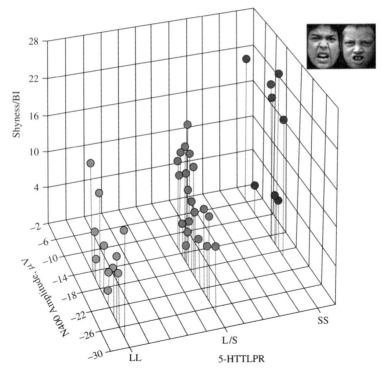

Figure 9.4 Scatterplot of subjects in the experiment ordered by serotonin transporter promoter polymorphism (*5-HTTLPR*) genotype. The graph shows the degree of shyness or behavioural inhibition (BI) and the N400 amplitude evoked by anger at the Pz electrode for each subject.

In sum, there is a growing body of evidence indicating that neural circuitry associated with threat processing is associated with *5-HTTLPR* genotype, not just in adults but in children too. Studies are beginning to examine the mechanisms of this association (Pezawas *et al.*, 2005).

There are also a small number of studies examining other genetic markers with regard to emotion-related brain processes. For example, in a study of adults, the gene encoding the regulator of G protein signalling 2 (*Rgs2*) was found to be associated with amygdala activation to emotional faces (Smoller *et al.*, 2008). Of note, a significant association between *Rgs2* and childhood behavioural inhibition was reported in the same paper, indicating that this gene may be relevant to anxiety-related information processing in younger samples. The field is moving fast that within a year there are likely to be many more such examples.

Skin conductance and startle response

Fear conditioning is a well-established risk factor for anxiety in both adults and children (Field, 2006). Aversive conditioning tasks consist of two phases: acquisition, where one of the stimuli is paired with an aversive noise (CS+) and the others have no associated aversive stimuli (CS−), followed by an extinction phase without the pairing. There is clear evidence for a larger conditioned response (generally using skin conductance) in adults with anxiety disorders (Lissek *et al.*, 2005) and in child anxiety (Liberman *et al.*, 2006; Waters *et al.*, 2008b) as compared to controls. For example, whilst skin conductance response (SCR) showed that neither anxiety disordered nor control children discriminated between CS+ and CS− stimuli during acquisition, during the extinction phase of the experiment, anxious children showed greater SCR and larger startle eye blink, both indicating greater emotional response (Liberman *et al.*, 2006). Startle response has also been investigated in children at risk of anxiety disorder (i.e. children of anxious parents) using a number of approaches. In the first, at-risk children were found to show greater startle response when anticipating an aversive stimuli (air puff) than children of healthy parents (Merikangas *et al.*, 1999). More recently, at-risk children ($N = 15$) were found to show greater SCR to aversive conditioned stimuli relative to the controls during each phase of the experiment (Craske *et al.*, 2008). Finally, in another recent study 7- to 12-year-old children who were either anxious ($N = 21$), at risk of anxiety (by virtue of parental anxiety disorder, $N = 16$) or non-anxious controls ($N = 13$) (Waters *et al.*, 2008a) were compared for startle response following a mildly stressful procedure. Children in the anxious group showed a stronger response compared to controls, and in the at-risk group there was an age-related association with the stronger response seen as the children got older. This suggests that this phenomenon develops in at-risk children over the middle childhood period, whereas it was already present in early childhood in those exhibiting a current anxiety disorder. With regard to specific genes, in adults, *acoustic* startle response to aversive stimuli has been shown to be associated with both *5-HTTLPR* (Brocke *et al.*, 2006) *COMT* (Montag *et al.*, 2008) genotypes, but this combination of risks has yet to be considered in a child sample.

Carbon dioxide challenge

In addition to sensitivity to heart rate acceleration and fear of cardiac arrest, patients with PD are also hypersensitive to fear of suffocation, most frequently tested with a carbon dioxide (CO_2) challenge. In this test, subjects wear a face-mask through which they breath, initially air and then CO_2 (the challenge). Several studies have now shown in adults that the CO_2 challenge test is associated with increased levels of panic response in PD patients and in their first-degree relatives (Coryell *et al.*, 2006). Of note, children and adolescents with anxiety disorders also show a heightened response to CO_2 challenge (Pine *et al.*, 1998; Coplan *et al.*, 2002). However, to date, the only study we are aware of that has examined CO_2 challenge in children at risk of anxiety disorders (i.e. children of adults with PD) showed no difference from children of healthy parents or parents with major depression (Terleph *et al.*, 2006). This may be due to the fact that of all the anxiety disorders, PD is the one that tends to develop latest (Ollendick and March, 2004), and rarely before late adolescence, so sufficient vulnerability to the disorder may not yet have built up in a young sample that is still anxiety disorder free.

In summary, there is a relatively small but growing body of evidence from studies using cognitive psychological or neuropsychological tasks within genetically sensitive designs. To date, these generally provide support for the hypothesis that aspects of brain and cognitive functioning mediate genetic influences on the development and maintenance of child anxiety. Two further issues to be considered are (i) methodological concerns and (ii) future directions.

Methodological Concerns

There are two particularly pertinent methodological concerns in this field of work: reliability and sample size. First, reliability is of course a key issue in any field, but it is particularly important in anything incorporating an experimental approach as the results from such tasks are almost always less reliable than questionnaire or interview data. The implications of this are considerable. For example, if there is 30% genetic influence on a phenotype, but this phenotype has a test–retest reliability of only 60%, then the genetic influence will be reduced to 18%, which will be much more difficult to detect, and will be more likely to result in a non-significant parameter estimate. With regard to molecular genetic work, it is even more daunting because the effect sizes are so small, usually less than 1% of the variance, so any reduction in reliability has a huge impact on power of the study. In addition to test–retest reliability being a useful tool here, cross-measure correlations can also be highly informative. Thus, of concern, a recent twin analysis revealed only very modest and negative genetic correlations between fear conditioning and self-report fear (Hettema *et al.*, 2008), indicating that when searching for endophenotypes, the method of assessment is crucial. One approach that is likely to be useful in countering such problems is to use a latent variable that combines reliable variance from two or more measures and to search for genetic influence on or associations with that latent construct. For example, as noted above, we identified only modest non-significant genetic influence on recognition of individual emotion expression types, but in a multivariate model found that a latent factor combining variance across all face types had a heritability of 75% (Lau et al., 2009a).

The second area of concern is to do with sample size and statistical power. Both quantitative and molecular genetic studies require sample sizes of a totally different magnitude from that generally seen in experimental work, where sample sizes are usually in the tens or low hundreds. Thus, for example, genetic association studies are currently expected to have a minimum of 2000 cases and 2000 controls to be published in the leading journals, but even that is regarded as small by many investigators. There are also other issues that influence the power of this type of analysis. For example, true associations may be masked by hidden population stratification (Aitchison and Gill, 2002). Furthermore, the power to detect gene–gene and G × E interactions is necessarily lower than that to detect main effects, resulting in a need for a further increase in sample size. In order to combine genetic and experimental approaches there will need to be methodological advances such that experimental data can be collected more cheaply and more practically on larger numbers, or greater use will need to be made of sub-samples, for example, by identifying subgroups of a set of cases who have a particular mixture of genetic risks on whom to conduct experimental work.

Future Directions

This field has achieved much in a short space of time. Clearly, however, there is still much work to be done. Many aspects of cognitive processing have yet to be considered within a twin design, and with regard to molecular genetics, there are virtually no studies of child anxiety-related cognitive processes that consider any genetic marker other than the 5-HTTLPR. However, there are also new avenues altogether that will hopefully be pursued, perhaps the most exciting of which is to consider treatment response as another relevant phenotype. Genetic factors are beginning to be explored with regard to treatment outcome in adults (Lesch and Gutknecht, 2005). Response to medication is likely to result not only from a number of genetic factors but also environmental ones, and it will also be important to consider the interplay between them (Rutter, Moffitt and Caspi, 2006). There have been interesting findings regarding the pharmacogenetics of antidepressant response (see Uher and McGuffin, 2008 for an example of the methodology used to investigate genetic and environmental factors and the interplay between them in predicting antidepressant response). Less research has been conducted with regard to anxiety and particularly pediatric anxiety. A recent review identified a mean positive response rate of around 60% to cognitive behavioural therapy (CBT) for child anxiety disorders (Cartwright-Hatton et al., 2004); thus for a substantial minority (~40%) it is ineffective. Studies examining potential predictors of treatment response identify three broad factors (Hudson, 2005): age, case severity and history of parental psychopathology. Generally, it has been found that adolescents rather than children, more severe cases and those with a history of parental psychopathology respond less well. These latter two factors implicate a possible role for genetic influence in treatment response. Notably, whilst anxious children show reductions in attention to threat and threat interpretations following CBT, they remain higher than control children on such tasks (Waters *et al.*, 2008c) indicating that (i) biases with a partial genetic influence are malleable to environmental treatments but that (ii) such biases remain present to some extent after treatment, indicating that they could be suitable targets for an endophenotype approach. To date, there have been no genetic studies of treatment response in child anxiety. One study of a pharmacological treatment for paediactric anxiety depression has been reported. The study found the S allele of the *5-HTTLPR* is associated with poorer response to citalopram in children and adolescents (Kronenberg *et al.*, 2007). Although the mechanism would be quite different, it is plausible that there could be a similar role for genetic factors in response to CBT. It is our hope that this chapter may inspire further people to undertake work in this exciting field, and, perhaps more importantly, that funding bodies may be inclined to promote this type of research! The translational impact of these findings will come when we are able to use them not only to improve treatment but perhaps also to get closer to being able to prevent the occurrence of these debilitating disorders.

References

Aitchison, K.J. and Gill, M. (2002) Pharmacogenetics in the postgenomic era, in *Behavioural Genetics in the Postgenomic Era* (eds R. Plomin and J.C. DeFries), American Psychological Association, Washington, DC, pp. 335–361.

Angold, A., Costello, E.J. and Erkanli, A. (1999) Comorbidity. *Journal of Child Psychology and Psychiatry*, **40**, 57–87.

Arbelle, S., Benjamin, J., Golin, M. *et al.* (2003) Relation of shyness in grade school children to the genotype for the long form of the serotonin transporter promoter region polymorphism. *American Journal of Psychiatry*, **160**, 671–676.

Auerbach, J., Geller, V., Lezer, S. *et al.* (1999) Dopamine D4 receptor (D4DR) and serotonin transporter promoter (5-HTTLPR) polymorphisms in the determination of temperament in 2-month-old infants. *Molecular Psychiatry*, **4**, 369–373.

Ball, D.M., Hill, L., Freeman, B. *et al.* (1997) The serotonin transporter gene and peer-rated neuroticism. *NeuroReport*, **8**, 1301–1304.

Barrett, P.M., Rapee, R.M., Dadds, M.M. and Ryan, S.M. (1996) Family enhancement of cognitive style in anxious and aggressive children. *Journal of Abnormal Child Psychology*, **24**, 187–203.

Bartels, M. (2007) An update on longitudinal twin and family studies. *Twin Research and Human Genetics*, **10**, 1–2.

Battaglia, M., Ogliari, A., Zanoni, A. *et al.* (2005) Influence of the serotonin transporter promoter gene and shyness on children's cerebral responses to facial expressions. *Archives of General Psychiatry*, **62**, 85–94.

Beck, A.T. (1967) *Depression: Causes and Treatment*, University of Pennsylvania Press, Philadelphia.

Bogels, S.M. and Zigterman, D. (2000) Dysfunctional cognitions in children with social phobia, separation anxiety disorder, and generalized anxiety disorder. *Journal of Abnormal Child Psychology*, **28**, 205–211.

Bolton, D., Eley, T.C., O'Connor, T.G. *et al.* (2006) Prevalence and genetic and environmental influences on anxiety disorders in 6-year-old twins. *Psychological Medicine*, **36**, 335–344.

Brocke, B., Armbruster, D., Muller, J. *et al.* (2006) Serotonin transporter gene variation impacts innate fear processing: acoustic startle response and emotional startle. *Molecular Psychiatry*, **11**, 1106–1112.

Butler, G. and Mathews, A. (1983) Cognitive processes in anxiety. *Advances in Behaviour Research and Therapy*, **5**, 51–62.

Cartwright-Hatton, S., Roberts, C., Chitsabesan, P. *et al.* (2004) Systematic review of the efficacy of cognitive behaviour therapies for childhood and adolescent anxiety disorders. *British Journal of Clinical Psychology*, **43**, 421–436.

Caspi, A., Sugden, K., Moffitt, T.E. *et al.* (2003) Influence of life stress on depression: moderation by a polymorphism in the 5-HTT gene. *Science*, **301**, 386–389.

Clark, D.M. (1999) Anxiety disorders: why they persist and how to treat them. *Behaviour Research and Therapy*, **37** (Suppl. 1), S5–S27.

Clark, D.M., Salkovskis, P.M., Ost, L.G. *et al.* (1997) Misinterpretation of body sensations in panic disorder. *Journal of Consulting & Clinical Psychology*, **65**, 203–213.

Coplan, J.D., Moreau, D., Chaput, F. *et al.* (2002) Salivary cortisol concentrations before and after carbon-dioxide inhalations in children. *Biological Psychiatry*, **51**, 326–333.

Coryell, W., Pine, D., Fyer, A. *et al.* (2006) Anxiety responses to CO2 inhalation in subjects at high-risk for panic disorder. *Journal of Affective Disorders*, **92**, 63–70.

Costello, E.J., Egger, H.L. and Angold, A. (2005) The developmental epidemiology of anxiety disorders: phenomenology, prevalence, and comorbidity. *Child and Adolescent Psychiatric Clinics of North America*, **14**, 631–648.

Craske, M.G., Waters, A.M., Lindsey, B.R. *et al.* (2008) Is aversive learning a marker of risk for anxiety disorders in children? *Behaviour Research and Therapy*, **46**, 954–967.

Creswell, C., Schniering, C.A. and Rapee, R.M. (2005) Threat interpretation in anxious children and their mothers: comparison with nonclinical children and the effects of treatment. *Behaviour Research and Therapy*, **43**, 1375–1381.

Creswell, C., Woolgar, M., Cooper, P.J. *et al.* (2008) Processing of faces and emotional expressions in infants at risk of social phobia. *Cognition and Emotion*, **22**, 437–458.

Dineen, K.A. and Hadwin, J.A. (2004) Anxious and depressive symptoms and children's judgements of their own and others' interpretation of ambiguous social scenarios. *Journal of Anxiety Disorders*, **18**, 499–513.

Eaves, L.J., Silberg, J.L., Meyer, J.M. *et al.* (1997) Genetics and developmental psychopathology: 2. The main effects of genes and environment on behavioral problems in the Virginia Twin Study of Adolescent Behavioral Development. *Journal of Child Psychology and Psychiatry*, **38**, 965–980.

Ebstein, R., Levine, J., Geller, V. *et al.* (1998) Dopamine D4 receptor and serotonin transporter promoter in the determination of neonatal temperament. *Molecular Psychiatry*, **3**, 238–246.

Ehlers, A. (1995) A 1-year prospective study of panic attacks: clinical course and factors associated with maintenance. *Journal of Abnormal Psychology*, **104**, 164–172.

Ehlers, A. and Breuer, P. (1992) Increased cardiac awareness in panic disorder. *Journal of Abnormal Psychology*, **101**, 371–382.

Eley, T.C., Bolton, D., O'Connor, T.G. *et al.* (2003) A twin study of anxiety-related behaviours in pre-school children. *Journal of Child Psychology and Psychiatry*, **44**, 945–960.

Eley, T.C., Collier, D. and McGuffin, P. (2002) Anxiety and eating disorders, in *Psychiatric Genetics and Genomics* (eds P. McGuffin, M.J. Owen and I.I. Gottesman), Oxford University Press, Oxford, pp. 303–340.

Eley, T.C., Gregory, A.M., Lau, J.Y.F. *et al.* (2007) In the face of uncertainty: a genetic analysis of ambiguous information, anxiety and depression in children. *Journal of Abnormal Child Psychology*, **48**, 1184.

Eley, T.C. and Stevenson, J. (1999) Exploring the covariation between anxiety and depression symptoms: a genetic analysis of the effects of age and sex. *Journal of Child Psychology and Psychiatry*, **40**, 1273–1284.

Eley, T.C., Stirling, L., Ehlers, A. *et al.* (2004a) Heart-beat perception, panic/somatic symptoms and anxiety sensitivity in children. *Behaviour Research and Therapy*, **42**, 439–448.

Eley, T.C., Sugden, K., Gregory, A.M. *et al.* (2004b) Gene–environment interaction analysis of serotonin system markers with adolescent depression. *Molecular Psychiatry*, **9**, 908–915.

Fanous, A., Gardner, C.O., Prescott, C.A. *et al.* (2002) Neuroticism, major depression and gender: a population-based twin study. *Psychological Medicine*, **32**, 719–728.

Feigon, S.A., Waldman, I.D., Levy, F. and Hay, D.A. (2001) Genetic and environmental influences on separation anxiety disorder symptoms and their moderation by age and sex. *Behavior Genetics*, **31**, 403–411.

Field, A.P. (2006) Is conditioning a useful framework for understanding the development and treatment of phobias? *Clinical Psychology Review*, **26**, 857–875.

Fox, N.A., Nichols, K.E., Henderson, H.A. *et al.* (2005) Evidence for a gene-environment interaction in predicting behavioral inhibition in middle childhood. *Psychological Science*, **16**, 921–926.

Gillespie, N.A., Whitfield, J.B., Williams, B. *et al.* (2005) The relationship between stressful life events, the serotonin transporter (5-HTTLPR) genotype and major depression. *Psychological Medicine*, **35**, 101–111.

Gregory, A.M., Caspi, A., Moffitt, T.E. *et al.* (2007) Juvenile mental health histories of adults with anxiety disorders. *American Journal of Psychiatry*, **164**, 301–308.

Gregory, A.M. and Eley, T.C. (2007) Genetic influences on anxiety in children: what we've learned and where we're heading. *Clinical Child and Family Psychology Review*, **10**, 199–212.

Gunther, T., Holtkamp, K., Jolles, J. *et al.* (2004) Verbal memory and aspects of attentional control in children and adolescents with anxiety disorders or depressive disorders. *Journal of Affective Disorders*, **82**, 265–269.

Hadwin, J., Frost, S., French, C.C. and Richards, A. (1997) Cognitive processing and trait anxiety in typically developing children: evidence for an interpretation bias. *Journal of Abnormal Psychology*, **106**, 486–490.

Hariri, A.R., Drabant, E.M., Munoz, K.E. *et al.* (2005) A susceptibility gene for affective disorders and the response of the human amygdala. *Archives of General Psychiatry*, **62**, 146–152.

Hariri, A.R., Mattay, V.S., Tessitore, A. *et al.* (2002) Serotonin transporter genetic variation and the response of the human amygdala. *Science*, **297**, 400–403.

Hayden, E.P., Dougherty, L.R., Maloney, B. *et al.* (2007) Temperamental fearfulness in childhood and the serotonin transporter promoter region polymorphism: a multimethod association study. *Psychiatric Genetics*, **17**, 135–142.

Hettema, J.M., Annas, P., Neale, M.C. *et al.* (2008) The genetic covariation between fear conditioning and self-report fears. *Biological Psychiatry*, **63**, 587–593.

Hettema, J.M., Prescott, C.A., Myers, J.M. *et al.* (2005) The structure of genetic and environmental risk factors for anxiety disorders in men and women. *Archives of General Psychiatry*, **62**, 182–189.

Hudson, J.L. (2005) Efficacy of cognitive-behavioural therapy for children and adolescents with anxiety disorders. *Behaviour Change*, **22**, 55–70.

Jorm, A.F., Henderson, A.S., Jacomb, P.A. *et al.* (1998) An association study of a functional polymorphism of the serotonin transporter gene with personality and psychiatric symptoms. *Molecular Psychiatry*, **3**, 449–451.

Jorm, A.F., Prior, M., Sanson, A. *et al.* (2000) Association of functional polymorphism of the serotonin transporter gene with anxiety-related temperament and behavior problems in children: a longitudinal study from infancy to the mid-teens. *Molecular Psychiatry*, **5**, 542–547.

Katsuragi, S., Kunugi, H., Sano, A. *et al.* (1999) Association between serotonin transporter gene polymorphism and anxiety-related traits. *Biological Psychiatry*, **45**, 368–370.

Kendler, K.S. (1996) Major depression and generalised anxiety disorder. Same genes, (partly)different environments – revisited. *British Journal of Psychiatry Supplement*, 68–75.

Kendler, K.S., Heath, A.C., Martin, N.G. and Eaves, L.J. (1987) Symptoms of anxiety and depression: same genes, different environments? *Archives of General Psychiatry*, **44**, 451–457.

Kendler, K.S., Myers, J., Prescott, C.A. and Neale, M.C. (2001) The genetic epidemiology of irrational fears and phobias in men. *Archives of General Psychiatry*, **58**, 257–265.

Kendler, K.S., Neale, M.C., Kessler, R.C. *et al.* (1992a) Major depression and generalized anxiety disorder. Same genes, (partly) different environments? *Archives of General Psychiatry*, **49**, 716–722.

Kendler, K.S., Neale, M.C., Kessler, R.C. *et al.* (1992b) The genetic epidemiology of phobias in women: the interrelationship of agoraphobia, social phobia, situational phobia, and simple phobia. *Archives of General Psychiatry*, **49**, 273–281.

Kessler, R.C., Berglund, P., Demler, O. *et al.* (2005) Lifetime prevalence and age-of-onset distributions of DSM-IV disorders in the National Comorbidity Survey Replication. *Archives of General Psychiatry*, **62**, 593–602.

Kronenberg, S., Apter, A., Brent, D. *et al.* (2007) Serotonin transporter polymorphism (5-HTTLPR) and citalopram effectiveness and side effects in children with depression and/or anxiety disorders. *Journal of Child and Adolescent Psychopharmacology*, **17**, 741–750.

Lau, J.Y.F., Burt, M., Leibenluft, E. *et al.* (2009a) Individual differences in children's facial expression recognition ability: The role of genetic and environmental influences. *Developmental Neuropsychology*, **34**, 37–51.

Lau, J.Y.F., Goldman, D., Buzas, B. *et al.* (2009b) Amygdala function and 5-HTT gene variants in adolescent anxiety and major depressive disorder. *Biological Psychiatry*, **65**, 349–355.

Lau, J.Y.F. and Eley, T.C. (2006) Changes in genetic and environmental influences on depressive symptoms across adolescence: a twin and sibling study. *British Journal of Psychiatry*, **189**, 422–427.

Lau, J.Y.F., Gregory, A.M., Viding, E. *et al.* (2008) Developmental origins of anxiety-related biases in threat recognition, interpretation and avoidance. *Journal of Clinical Child and Adolescent Psychology*. Submitted for publication.

Lesch, K.P., Bengel, D., Heils, A. *et al.* (1996) Association of anxiety-related traits with a polymorphism in the serotonin transporter gene regulatory region. *Science*, **274**, 1527–1531.

Lesch, K.P. and Gutknecht, L. (2005) Pharmacogenetics of the serotonin transporter. *Progress in Neuro-Psychopharmacology and Biological Psychiatry*, **29**, 1062–1073.

Liberman, L.C., Lipp, O.V., Spence, S.H. *et al.* (2006) Evidence for retarded extinction of aversive learning in anxious children. *Behaviour Research and Therapy*, **44**, 1491–1502.

Lissek, S., Powers, A.S., McClure, E.B. *et al.* (2005) Classical fear conditioning in the anxiety disorders: a meta-analysis. *Behaviour Research and Therapy*, **43**, 1391–1424.

Mansell, W. (1999) Social anxiety and attention away from emotional faces. *Cognition and Emotion*, **13**, 673–690.

Martin, N., Boomsma, D.I. and Machin, G. (1997) A twin-pronged attack on complex trait. *Nature Genetics*, **17**, 387–392.

Meltzer, H., Gatward, R., Goodman, R. and Ford, T. (2000) *Mental Health of Children and Adolescents in Great Britain*, The Stationary Office, London.

Merikangas, K.R., Avenevoli, S., Dierker, L. *et al.* (1999) Vulnerability factors among children at risk for anxiety disorders. *Biological Psychiatry*, **46**, 1523–1535.

Mogg, K. and Bradley, B.P. (1999) Some methodological issues in assessing attentional biases for threatening faces in anxiety: a replication study using a modified version of the probe detection task. *Behaviour Research and Therapy*, **37**, 595–604.

Monk, C.S., Klein, R.G., Telzer, E.H. *et al.* (2008) Amygdala and nucleus accumbens activation to emotional facial expressions in children and adolescents at risk for major depression. *American Journal of Psychiatry*, **165**, 90–98.

Montag, C., Buckholtz, J.W., Hartmann, P. *et al.* (2008) COMT genetic variation affects fear processing: psychophysiological evidence. *Behavioral Neuroscience*, **122**, 901–909.

Morris, T.L. and March, J.S. (2004) *Anxiety Disorders in Children and Adolescents*, Guilford Press, New York.

Munafo, M.R., Brown, S.M., Hariri, A.R. *et al.* (2008) Serotonin transporter (5-HTTLPR) genotype and amygdala activation: a meta-analysis. *Biological Psychiatry*, **63**, 852–857.

Muris, P. and Field, A.P. (2008) Distorted cognition and pathological anxiety in children and adolescents. *Cognition and Emotion*, **22**, 395–421.

Neshat-Doost, H.T., Taghavi, M.R., Moradi, A.R. *et al.* (1998) Memory for emotional trait adjectives in clinically depressed youth. *Journal of Abnormal Psychology*, **107**, 642–650.

Nunn, J.D., Mathews, A. and Trower, P. (1997) Selective processing of concern-related information in depression. *British Journal of Clinical Psychology*, **36**, 489–503.

Ollendick, T.H. and March, J.S. (2004) Phobic and anxiety disorders in children and adolescents: a clinician's guide to effective psychosocial and pharmacological interventions .

Osher, Y., Hamer, D. and Benjamin, J. (2000) Association and linkage of anxiety-related traits with a functionall polymorphism of the serotonin transporter gene regulatory region in Israeli sibling pairs. *Molecular Psychiatry*, **5**, 216–219.

Otto, M.W., Pollack, M.H., Maki, K.M. *et al.* (2001) Childhood history of anxiety disorders among adults with social phobia: rates, correlates, and comparisons with patients with panic disorder. *Depression and Anxiety*, **14**, 209–213.

Pezawas, L., Meyer-Lindenberg, A., Drabant, E.M. *et al.* (2005) 5-HTTLPR polymorphism impacts human cingulate-amygdala interactions: a genetic susceptibility mechanism for depression [see comment]. *Nature Neuroscience*, **8**, 828–834.

Pine, D.S., Coplan, J.D., Papp, L.A. *et al.* (1998) Ventilatory physiology of children and adolescents with anxiety disorders. *Archives of General Psychiatry*, **55**, 123–129.

Pine, D.S., Klein, R.G., Mannuzza, S. *et al.* (2005) Face-emotion processing in offspring at risk for panic disorder. *Journal of the American Academy of Child and Adolescent Psychiatry*, **44**, 664–672.

Pine, D.S., Wasserman, G.A., Workman, S.B. *et al.* (1999) Memory and anxiety in prepubertal boys at risk for delinquency. *Journal of the American Academy of Child and Adolescent Psychiatry*, **38**, 1024–1031.

Plomin, R., DeFries, J.C., McClearn, G.E. and McGuffin, P. (2001) *Behavioral Genetics*, 4th edn, Worth Publishers, New York.

Plomin, R., Owen, M.J. and McGuffin, P. (1994) The genetic basis of complex human behaviors. *Science*, **264**, 1733–1739.

Reiss, S. (1986) Anxiety sensitivity, anxiety frequency and the predictions of fearfulness. *Behaviour Research and Therapy*, **24**, 1–8.

Richards, A., French, C.C., Nash, G. *et al.* (2007) A comparison of selective attention and facial processing biases in typically developing children who are high and low in self-reported trait anxiety. *Development and Psychopathology*, **19**, 481–495.

Risch, N. and Merikangas, K. (1996) The future of genetic studies of complex human diseases. *Science*, **273**, 1516–1517.

Rutter, M., Moffitt, T.E. and Caspi, A. (2006) Gene-environment interplay and psychopathology: multiple varieties but real effects. *Journal of Child Psychology and Psychiatry*, **47**, 226–261.

Rutter, M. and Redshaw, J. (1991) Annotation: growing up as a twin: twin-singleton differences in psychological development. *Journal of Child Psychology and Psychiatry*, **32**, 885–895.

Schandry, R. (1981) Heart beat perception and emotional experiences. *Psychophysiology*, **18**, 483–488.

Sen, S., Burmeister, M., Ghosh, D. *et al.* (2004) Meta-analysis of the association between a serotonin transporter promoter polymorphism (5-HTTLPR) and anxiety-related personality traits. *American Journal of Medical Genetics, Part B, Neuropsychiatric Genetics*, **127B**, 85–89.

Sham, P.C., Sterne, A., Purcell, S. *et al.* (2000) GENESiS: creating a composite index of the vulnerability to anxiety and depression in a community-based sample of siblings. *Twin Research*, **3**, 316–322.

Silberg, J.L., Rutter, M. and Eaves, L. (2001) Genetic and environmental influences on the temporal association between earlier anxiety and later depression in girls [Erratum appears in *Biological Psychiatry* 2001;**50**(5), 393]. *Biological Psychiatry*, **49**, 1040–1049.

Silverman, W.K. (1999) Anxiety sensitivity in children, in *Anxiety Sensitivity* (ed. S. Taylor), Lawrence Erlbaum Associates, Mahwah, NJ, pp. 269–286.

Smoller, J.W., Paulus, M.P., Fagerness, J.A. *et al.* (2008) Influence of RGS2 on anxiety-related temperament, personality, and brain function. *Archives of General Psychiatry*, **65**, 298–308.

Stein, M.B., Jang, K.L. and Livesley, W.J. (1999) Heritability of anxiety sensitivity: a twin study. *American Journal of Psychiatry*, **156**, 246–251.

Stein, M.B., Schork, N.J., Gelernter, J. *et al.* (2008) Gene-by-environment (serotonin transporter and childhood maltreatment) interaction for anxiety sensitivity, an intermediate phenotype for anxiety disorders. *Neuropsychopharmacology*, **33**, 312–319.

Stirling, L., Eley, T.C. and Clark, D.M. (2006a) Avoidance of negative faces and social anxiety in children. *Journal of Clinical Child and Adolescent Psychology*, **35**, 440–445.

Stirling, L., Eley, T.C. and Clark, D.M. (2006b) Preliminary evidence for an association between social anxiety symptoms and avoidance of negative faces in school-age children. *Journal of Clinical Child and Adolescent Psychology*, **35**, 440–445.

Surtees, P.G., Wainwright, N.W., Willis-Owen, S.A. *et al.* (2006) Social adversity, the serotonin transporter (5-HTTLPR) polymorphism and major depressive disorder. *Biological Psychiatry*, **59**, 224–229.

Taghavi, M.R., Moradi, A.R., Neshat-Doost, H.T. *et al.* (2000) Interpretation of ambiguous emotional information in clinically anxious children and adolescents. *Cognition and Emotion*, **14**, 822.

Taylor, S. (1999) *Anxiety Sensitivity*, Lawrence Erlbaum Associates, Mahwah, NJ.

Terleph, T.A., Klein, R.G., Roberson-Nay, R. *et al.* (2006) Stress responsivity and HPA axis activity in juveniles: results from a home-based CO2 inhalation study. *American Journal of Psychiatry*, **163**, 738–740.

Thapar, A. and McGuffin, P. (1995) Are anxiety symptoms in childhood heritable? *Journal of Child Psychology and Psychiatry*, **36**, 439–447.

Toren, P., Sadeh, M., Wolmer, L. *et al.* (2000) Neurocognitive correlates of anxiety disorders in children: a preliminary report. *Journal of Anxiety Disorders*, **14**, 239–247.

Uher, R. and McGuffin, P. (2008) The moderation by the serotonin transporter gene of environmental adversity in the aetiology of mental illness: review and methodological analysis. *Molecular Psychiatry*, **13**, 131–146.

Van Ameringen, M., Mancini, C. and Farvolden, P. (2003) The impact of anxiety disorders on educational achievement. *Journal of Anxiety Disorders*, **17**, 561–571.

Van Beijsterveldt, C.E. and van Baal, G.C. (2002) Twin and family studies of the human electroencephalogram: a review and a meta-analysis. *Biological Psychology*, **61**, 111–138.

Van der Does, A.J.W., Antony, M.M., Ehlers, A. and Barsky, A.J. (2000) Heartbeat perception in panic disorder: a reanalysis. *Behaviour Research and Therapy*, **38**, 47–62.

Vasa, R.A., Roberson-Nay, R., Klein, R.G. *et al.* (2007) Memory deficits in children with and at risk for anxiety disorders. *Depression and Anxiety*, **24**, 85–94.

Waters, A.M., Craske, M.G., Bergman, R.L. *et al.* (2008a) Developmental changes in startle reactivity in school-age children at risk for and with actual anxiety disorder. *International Journal of Psychophysiology*, **70**, 158–164.

Waters, A.M., Neumann, D.L., Henry, J. *et al.* (2008b) Baseline and affective startle modulation by angry and neutral faces in 4–8-year-old anxious and non-anxious children. *Biological Psychology*, **78**, 10–19.

Waters, A.M., Wharton, T.A., Zimmer-Gembeck, M.J. *et al.* (2008c) Threat-based cognitive biases in anxious children: comparison with non-anxious children before and after cognitive behavioural treatment. *Behaviour Research and Therapy*, **46**, 358–374.

Williams, L.M., Liddell, B.J., Rathjen, J. *et al.* (2004) Mapping the time course of nonconscious and conscious perception of fear: an integration of central and peripheral measures. *Human Brain Mapping*, **21**, 64–74.

Williams, J.M.G., Watts, F.N., MacLeod, C. and Mathews, A. (1997) *Cognitive Psychology and Emotional Disorders*, 2nd edn., John Wiley & Sons, Guilford.

Zavos, H.M.S., Rijsdijk, F.V., Gregory, A.M. and Eley, T.C. (2009) Genetic influences on the cognitive biases associated with anxiety and depression symptoms in adolescents. *Journal of Affective Disorders*. (Epub ahead of print. PMID:19945751).

10

Temperamental Factors Associated with the Acquisition of Information Processing Biases and Anxiety

Lauren K. White, Sarah M. Helfinstein and Nathan A. Fox
Lwhite5@umd.edu

Between 5% and 10% of individuals are diagnosed with an anxiety disorder in childhood or adolescence, making anxiety disorders one of the most prevalent childhood psychiatric disorders (Albano, Chorpita and Barlow, 1996). Anxiety disorders cause significant detriments to children's social and academic functioning (Pine, 1997), and puts them at increased risk for developing additional psychiatric disorders during adolescence (Bittner *et al.*, 2007) and adulthood (Pérez-Edgar and Fox, 2005; Pine, 2007). Given the negative impact childhood anxiety has on quality of life and the increased risk it creates for the development of subsequent psychiatric disorders throughout life, the early identification and effective treatment of childhood anxiety is of vital importance. In order to effectively identify and treat childhood anxiety, understanding the aetiology of the disorder and examining possible precursors or risk factors for its development are critical goals.

Child temperament is an early emerging and observable marker that has been theoretically and empirically linked to the development of anxiety (Pérez-Edgar and Fox, 2005; Rothbart and Posner, 2006; Thomas and Chess, 1977). While there are many different theoretical approaches to the study of temperament (e.g. Kagan *et al.*, 1984; Rothbart and Derryberry, 1981; Thomas and Chess, 1977), this construct has generally been viewed as a reflection of innate individual differences in the manner in which one reacts to environmental stimuli and how one regulates or responds to this reactivity. Certain variations in a child's temperament, in terms of both their reactive and regulative tendencies, are thought

Information Processing Biases and Anxiety: A Developmental Perspective Edited by Julie A. Hadwin and Andy P. Field
© 2010 John Wiley & Sons, Ltd.

to put a child at risk for the development of psychopathology (Muris, Meesters and Blijlevens, 2007; Pérez-Edgar and Fox, 2005). Children with highly reactive temperaments that leave them prone to respond with fear to new or unfamiliar events, who are hyper-vigilant and hyper-sensitive to possible sources of threat in the environment and who have an inclination to withdraw during unfamiliar social situations have heightened rates of anxiety disorders throughout their life (Biederman *et al.*, 1990; Chronis-Tuscano *et al.*, 2009; Prior *et al.*, 2000). Young children who display this pattern of temperamental reactivity and response, referred to as behavioural inhibition (BI) (Kagan *et al.*, 1984), often continue to show this pattern of fearful reactivity throughout their childhood and adolescence (Degnan and Fox, 2007; Kagan *et al.*, 1988). Moreover, many of the defining characteristics of BI, such as hyper-vigilance towards threat, elevated stress response, neural hyper-responsivity, social withdrawal and avoidant coping style correspond to the defining characteristics of anxiety (Pérez-Edgar and Fox, 2005), suggesting that specific traits associated with BI in early childhood are likely antecedents of this form of psychopathology.

Despite the strong link between BI and the development of anxiety disorders, the majority of behaviourally inhibited children do not go on to develop a psychiatric disorder (Biederman *et al.*, 1990; Chronis-Tuscano *et al.*, 2009; Prior *et al.*, 2000). Thus, there are likely specific factors associated with BI that put a child at increased risk for the development of anxiety and/or serve as protective mechanisms against the development of anxiety (Degnan and Fox, 2007). Examining both the risk and protective factors is critical to understanding developmental trajectories of BI. In the present chapter, we discuss the literature demonstrating a link between childhood BI and the development of anxiety disorders in adolescence. We then discuss two domains of information processing biases: first, those that characterize both behaviourally inhibited children and individuals with anxiety, which may be risk factors, and, second, those that may serve as protective factors, decreasing the risk for the development of anxiety disorders in behaviourally inhibited children. Finally, we discuss how the environment may interact with a young child's temperament in the development and maintenance of anxiety.

Behavioural Inhibition and Anxiety

Children are classified as behaviourally inhibited based on their negative emotional and motor reactivity to novel situations and unfamiliar objects, contexts and people (Fox *et al.*, 2005; Kagan *et al.*, 1984). Behaviourally inhibited children tend to avoid unfamiliar toys, withdraw during interactions with unfamiliar peers, and are often labelled as 'slow to warm up,' or shy (Fox *et al.*, 2005). BI is also associated with a specific biological profile including higher baseline cortisol levels (Kagan, Reznick and Snidman, 1987; Schmidt *et al.*, 1997, 1999), greater potentiated startle response to threat (Schmidt and Fox, 1998), increased heart rate and beat-to-beat variability (Marshall and Stevenson-Hinde, 1998) and greater right frontal electroencephalogram (EEG) asymmetry (Fox *et al.*, 2001). This constellation of characteristics shows moderate stability over development (Fox *et al.*, 2001; Kagan,

Reznick and Snidman, 1988; Sanson *et al.*, 1996); while many children continue to show steady levels of BI over the course of their development, other children show considerable increases or decreases in their level of BI.

Several longitudinal studies examining developmental outcomes associated with temperament have found elevated levels of anxiety disorders in children who were identified as behaviourally inhibited during their childhood (Chronis-Tuscano *et al.*, 2009; Schwartz, Snidman and Kagan, 1999). Schwartz *et al.* (2003), for example, found that 15% of young adults characterized as BI in early childhood had been diagnosed with social anxiety disorder. Similarly, in a recent study examining how stability of BI over time relates to anxiety, Chronis-Tuscano *et al.* (2009) found that adolescents who demonstrated early stable BI were 3.8 times more likely to have a diagnosis of social anxiety disorder sometime over their lifespan than adolescents who did not. Although these studies suggest that a significant subset of behaviourally inhibited children go on to develop an anxiety disorder, the majority do not, indicating that other biological or cognitive processes associated with BI may lead to the development of anxiety disorders. For example, children with BI may have specific endophenotypes – characteristic distinctions in physiological processes that lead to different approaches to processing information or interacting with the world that can elevate that child's risk for the development of anxiety, if coupled with other biological and environmental factors. Conversely, there are likely other factors, such as high levels of attention control, that may buffer the detrimental interaction between these cognitive and biological markers and outside factors, making a behaviourally inhibited child less vulnerable to the development of psychopathology.

Processing Biases in Behaviourally Inhibited Children

At present, it remains unclear as to what causal mechanisms underlie the increased risk for the development of anxiety in behaviourally inhibited children. BI and anxiety in children are both associated with perturbations in the way social and emotional cues are encoded and interpreted, which can be linked to poor social and emotional outcomes (Lemerise, Gregory and Fredstrom, 2005; Mathews and MacLeod, 2002). These biases, when left unchecked and amplified by environmental factors, may increase behaviourally inhibited children's risk of developing anxiety disorders.

The perturbations in information processing that have been identified in behaviourally inhibited children include augmented neural responses to novel and threatening stimuli, greater allocation of attention to these stimuli, and overgeneralization of fear learning, all of which have also been documented in anxious children and adults (Hogan *et al.*, 2007; Pérez-Edgar and Fox, 2005), raising the possibility that these processing biases are risk factors or commonly shared processes that increase emotional vulnerability in both BI and anxiety. Given that BI is an early emerging trait, with distinct patterns of response to novelty found as early as 4 and 9 months of age (Fox *et al.*, 2001; Marshall, Reeb and Fox, 2009), it is possible that the early biases associated with BI lead to the development of more severe processing biases over time, which, in the presence of certain environmental conditions, result in the development of anxiety. We highlight specific research examining processing biases that may underlie the BI–anxiety link in children, focusing on three specific biases: hyper-responsive amygdala activation to threatening and unfamiliar stimuli, greater allocation of attention to these stimuli and overgeneralization of fear learning.

Amygdala hyper-responsivity to novelty and threat

The amygdala, a brain structure associated with fearful or anxious states (Ledoux, 1996), has been implicated in fear learning (Morris, Öhman and Dolan, 1998) and is thought to underlie biased information processing of threat (Bishop, Duncan and Lawrence, 2004; Monk *et al.*, 2008). Amygdala activation increases as a function of perceived threat (Aggleton, 2000) and subjective experience of fear (Monk *et al.*, 2003). Considerable neuroimaging work has revealed that anxiety is associated with a hyper-sensitive amygdala (Bishop, Duncan and Lawrence, 2004; Etkin *et al.*, 2004). Studies have shown that the level of an individual's anxiety is positively related to amygdala activation during the subliminal presentation of fearful faces (Etkin *et al.*, 2004) and when fearful faces are presented outside of attentional focus (Bishop, Duncan and Lawrence, 2004). Thus, even when potential threat is outside of attentional focus or awareness, anxious individuals show more amygdala activation compared to non-anxious individuals (although this effect may disappear when attentional demands are extremely high – see Bishop, Jenkins and Lawrence, 2007). Such hyper-responsivity of amygdala activation in anxious individuals is also seen when viewing neutral or ambiguous information (Somerville *et al.*, 2004).

Amygdala hyper-responsivity is also characteristic of behaviourally inhibited individuals (Fox *et al.*, 2008). Young adults identified as behaviourally inhibited in childhood showed greater amygdala activation when viewing novel neutral faces, compared to familiar neutral faces (Schwartz *et al.*, 2003). Similarly, Pérez-Edgar and Fox (2007) found that adolescents identified as temperamentally BI in infancy showed decreased amygdala activation when passively viewing emotionally evocative faces and increased activation when asked to rate their level of fear while viewing the faces. Moreover, increased amygdala activation was found in behaviourally inhibited individuals during unexpected or novel situations (e.g. rating their level of fear while viewing a happy face). Given the moderate stability of BI (Fox *et al.*, 2001), this pattern of amygdala hyper-responsivity is likely present throughout development, making behaviourally inhibited children susceptible to frequent experiences of fear and information processing biases associated with amygdala activation (Bishop, 2008; Bishop, Duncan and Lawrence, 2004; LeDoux, 2000). Amygdala sensitivity may therefore put a behaviourally inhibited child at increased risk for the development of anxiety.

Attention bias to threat

Anxious adults tend to allocate their attention towards threat (MacLeod, Mathews and Tata, 1986) and often interpret neutral or ambiguous information as a source of threat (Eysenck *et al.*, 1991). These patterns of attention are indexed by a difficulty in disengaging attention away from the source of threat and are found even towards mild or ambiguous sources of threat (Frenkel *et al.*, 2008; Richards *et al.*, 2002). For example, when simultaneously presented with a threat-related and a neutral stimuli (e.g. a neutral and a threatening facial expression), anxious individuals will orient their attention towards the threatening stimuli and keep their attention engaged towards the threat source (see Bar-Haim *et al.*, 2007 for review), a pattern typically not seen in non-anxious individuals.

Attention bias towards threat is not only detected in clinically anxious individuals, but also in individuals high in trait anxiety (Mogg, Bradley and Hallowell, 1994), and it has recently been found in child populations shown to be at risk for the development of anxiety disorders (Lonigan *et al.*, 2004; Pérez-Edgar *et al.*, in press). Pérez-Edgar *et al.* conducted two studies examining the allocation of attention towards threat in shy and behaviourally inhibited children and adolescents using the emotional Stroop and a dot-probe task. In the emotional Stroop paradigm (Perez-Edgar and Fox, 2003), a sample of 4-, 7-, and 11-year-olds were presented with a series of neutral and emotional words printed in a variety of colours. As each word was presented, the children were asked to name the colour of ink in which the word is written, while ignoring the meaning of the word. Those children who showed greater colour-naming interference on emotion words had higher temperament ratings of shyness and anxiety, and tended to be rated by their parents as more socially withdrawn compared to children who did not show emotional interference. Similar results were found in a study using a dot-probe task in a group of adolescents identified as behaviourally inhibited during their childhood (Perez-Edgar *et al.*, in press). Participants were asked to make a response to a probe that appeared subsequent to a pair of previously viewed threatening and neutral stimuli (i.e. angry and neutral facial expressions) presented for either 500 or 1500 milliseconds. Adolescents who had been identified as behaviourally inhibited showed an attention bias towards threat on the dot-probe task with short stimulus presentations, a pattern not found in the adolescents who had not been classified as inhibited. Additionally, the low behaviourally inhibited adolescents, but not the high BI adolescents, showed an attention bias towards happy faces at short stimulus presentations. No significant attention bias effects were detected at longer stimulus presentations. The result from this study suggests that high levels of behaviourally inhibited may be associated not only with the enhancement of maladaptive attention biases but also with the dampening of adaptive attention biases as well.

Attention bias towards threat has also been detected in children with temperaments that share many features with BI. In a study looking at fear acquisition and fear behaviour in children, children scoring high on the child version of Carver and White's (1994) BI System scale showed facilitated attention bias towards newly acquired threatening information (Field, 2006). Children high in the temperament construct negative affect coupled with low effortful control (an interaction discussed in detail later in this chapter) also showed increased attention bias towards threat in a dot-probe task (Lonigan and Vasey, 2009). Although only a handful of studies have specifically examined the link between temperament and attention bias towards threat, initial studies suggest that children with fearful temperaments tend to allocate their attention towards threat in a manner similar to individuals with high levels of anxiety, both in clinical and subclinical populations. If behaviourally inhibited children show an attention bias towards threat, then (given the causal link between attention biases and anxiety; see Mathews and MacLeod, 2002) this processing bias may increase vulnerability to develop anxiety. Interestingly, Pérez-Edgar et al. (in press) found that an adolescent's attention bias towards threat was only related to concurrent levels of social withdrawal if they were behaviourally inhibited in childhood. Consistently directing attention to threatening stimuli in the environment results in more frequent and sustained experiences of the anxiety that these stimuli produce. Thus, the presence of an attention bias towards threat over the entirety of a child's development, as is the case with many behaviourally inhibited children, likely enhances the risk of developing an anxiety disorder.

Overgeneralization of fear learning

In addition to their tendency to direct attention to fear-provoking stimuli in the environment, anxious individuals are also characterized by their predisposition to consider a larger number of stimuli and situations fear provoking. This trait may be linked to differences in the neural circuitry involved in the basic elements of fear learning and specifically in a type of fear conditioning known as context conditioning (Grillon, 2002).

In classical conditioning paradigms, also known as cue conditioning, a neutral stimulus is presented immediately prior to an aversive stimulus, such as a shock. When trained in such a paradigm, animals very rapidly come to display fear behaviours in response to the originally neutral stimulus when it is presented in isolation (e.g. Blanchard and Blanchard, 1969). In context conditioning, by contrast, the animal learns a fear response to the location in which the aversive event occurred. Because the stimuli in the environment predict the aversive event less precisely – the animals know that something bad could happen to them, but do not know exactly when – context conditioning leads to more sustained displays of fear than the brief, immediate fear responses seen in cue conditioning.

Since anxiety is characterized by more frequent displays of the sustained fear seen in context conditioning, rather than heightened fear to discrete aversive stimuli, researchers have hypothesized that anxious individuals are characterized by differences in their patterns of context fear conditioning (e.g. Grillon, 2002). One possible distinction between anxious and non-anxious individuals is that anxious individuals overgeneralize their context conditioning, showing fear responses not only to the aversively conditioned contexts themselves but also to other environments that share some features with the aversive environment.

This theory of anxiety has been supported by research on the serotonin 1A receptor knockout (5-HT1ARKO) mouse. The serotonin 1A receptor has been associated with trait anxiety in humans (Strobel et al., 2003), and mice lacking this receptor are considered a model for human anxiety. They display anxiety typical behaviours such as reduced locomotion in open-field tests (Parks et al., 1998), increased latency to feed in a novel environment (Gross *et al.*, 2002) and enhanced autonomic reactivity to novelty (Pattij *et al.*, 2002). These mice also demonstrate an overgeneralized context conditioning response (Tsetsenis *et al.*, 2007). They respond to discrete aversive cues in a manner similar to control rats, and show typical levels of fear behaviour when returned to a context where they were previously aversively conditioned. However, they show a heightened response to partial context conditioning when they are placed in an environment that shares some cues, but not others, with an aversive context. In these similar contexts, control mice display a muted fear response, but 5HT1ARKO mice display as many fear behaviours in the similar context as they do in contexts identical to the one where they actually received the shock. Interestingly, it appears that the anxiety phenotype of 5HT1ARKO mice is the result of changes in the development of the hippocampus (which plays a key role in context conditioning) during a quite narrow developmental window (between 5 and 21 days after birth) (Gross *et al.*, 2002; Tsetsenis *et al.*, 2007).

The pattern of behaviour seen in 5HT1ARKO mice parallels both our intuitions about the behaviour of anxious individuals and empirical research in humans. For example, a bad experience with a certain type of test turns into an anxiety in all testing situations or a negative encounter with certain individuals turns into anxiety in all social situations. In morphed face paradigms, individuals high in trait social anxiety will identify more ambiguous faces (one that shares fewer features with a full fear face) as fearful than non-socially anxious individuals (Richards *et al.*, 2002). The behaviour of anxious humans thus reflects a tendency to treat a much broader range of contexts as being threatening than just those contexts where a bad experience actually occurred.

Another line of research that examines the generalization of the fear response in anxious individuals involves a paradigm known as the *fear-potentiated startle*. In the fear-potentiated startle paradigm, the blink that occurs in response to an unexpected burst of white noise is measured by recording an electromyogram (EMG) signal from the orbicularis oculi muscle. Just as we startle more upon hearing an unexpected noise when already in a state of high anxiety, EMG in the eye muscles in response to a burst of noise is related to the physiological arousal of the subject, and individuals show larger startle responses when they are expecting an aversive event. Consistent with the role for enhanced responsivity to ambiguous predictors of threat, in a recent study, Grillon *et al.* (2008) demonstrated that when shown a cue that reliably predicts an aversive stimulus, controls and individuals with panic disorder showed comparable increases in startle amplitude, but individuals with panic disorder showed much greater increases in startle amplitude than did controls when placed in a context where aversive stimuli were unpredictably administered.

Similarly, alprazolam, an anxiolytic drug, reduces startle in contexts with unpredictable shocks, but not when the shock is predicted by a cue (Grillon *et al.*, 2006), as does 2-week treatment with a selective serotonin reuptake inhibitor (SSRI) (Grillon *et al.*, 2009). Several studies have shown that, when presented both with a threat context (when aversive stimuli sometimes occur) and a safety context (where aversive stimuli never occur), patients with post-traumatic stress disorder (PTSD) and panic disorder will show enhanced startle to the safety context (Lissek *et al.*, 2008; Morgan *et al.*, 1995). This pattern of responding has been interpreted as an overgeneralization of the threat response or an inability to distinguish between threatening and non-threatening environments.

Although there have only been a limited number of startle studies done with behaviourally inhibited individuals, initial results suggest that behaviourally inhibited individuals show some patterns of overgeneralization of threat. In a study with 9-month-old infants selected at 4 months of age for their response to novelty (thought to be a precursor of BI), startle was measured when a stranger approached the infant. The high negative high reactive infants showed greater stranger-potentiated startle than the high positive high reactive infants, suggesting a greater fear response (Schmidt and Fox, 1998). Whether this fear response was due to overgeneralization of fear learning, or greater fear of strangers, remains unclear. In a similar task, 7-year-olds recruited from the same longitudinal sample had their startle response measured while preparing to give a speech about their most embarrassing moment. In this paradigm, no group differences were seen between more and less shy children (Schmidt *et al.*, 1999). In addition, startle did not increase overall between baseline and speech preparation in either group, suggesting that this may not be an effective paradigm to elicit potentiated startle.

A recent study examining fear-potentiated startle in behaviourally inhibited adolescents examined the relation between BI, clinical anxiety diagnosis and potentiated startle (Reeb-Sutherland *et al.*, 2009). In this study, startle reflex was measured at baseline and during cues associated with safety and threat. Neither BI nor anxiety diagnosis by themselves related to startle during threat cues, but those individuals who were both behaviourally inhibited and had a lifetime diagnosis of anxiety had greater potentiated startle to safety cues than did the other adolescents. In combination with the data indicating that overgeneralization of fear learning is a commonly found deficit in adults with anxiety disorders, this finding suggests that a tendency to overgeneralize fear learning could be a critical processing bias for the development of anxiety.

Regulative Temperament Factors in Behaviourally Inhibited Children

The findings discussed above highlight automatic or reactive processes that are found more frequently in behaviourally inhibited children than their peers, and, when present, increase the likelihood of developing anxiety disorders. However, it appears that certain higher level cognitive regulative mechanisms can help to mitigate this relation, and, indeed, may play a key preventative role in the development of anxiety. For example, research has shown that attention control, inhibitory control and cognitive and behavioural monitoring can all significantly influence a behaviourally inhibited child's emotional vulnerability. Although there is significant maturation of these functions across the board in early childhood as the frontal cortex matures (Fox *et al.*, 2008), individual differences in these executive skills have been shown to influence both information processing biases and anxious symptomology.

Recent neuroimaging research has highlighted the importance of the prefrontal cortex (PFC) in the regulation of involuntary processing biases and anxious states (Bishop, 2008; Davidson, 2002). Particularly important in this regulation is the inverse coupling between the PFC and the amygdala. Under certain circumstances, PFC activation produces inhibition of the amygdala, facilitating a reduction in the processing of goal-irrelevant threatening information and extinction of fear and negative affect (Bishop *et al.*, 2004; Phan *et al.*, 2005; Phelps and LeDoux, 2005). This coupling between the PFC and the amygdala is less robust in anxious individuals (Bishop, 2007; Hare *et al.*, 2008; Monk *et al.*, 2008), suggesting poor or improper recruitment of the cognitive mechanisms necessary to regulate fear or excessive threat processing. For example, in a group of healthy adults, when frequent threat-related distracters were present, self-reported anxiety was associated with reduced recruitment of PFC (Bishop, Duncan and Lawrence, 2004). A similar decrease in amygdala–PFC coupling was found in anxious youth between the ages of 11 and 18 relative to non-anxious youth in a dot-probe paradigm (Monk *et al.*, 2008). In a group of healthy adolescents, decreased amygdala habituation on an emotional go/no-go task was related to decreased PFC–amygalda connectivity, which in turn was related to the adolescent's level of anxiety (Hare *et al.*, 2008).

Taken together, the neuroimaging studies reveal that prefrontal circuitry is critical for the down-regulation of the amygdala, and a failure to properly recruit PFC leads to continued activation of the amygdala. The findings also illustrate that the amygdala–PFC coupling is reduced in anxious individuals, even when anxiety levels are in the non-clinical range. Thus, given that behaviourally inhibited children appear to show greater amygdala responsivity, deficits in the proper recruitment of cognitive mechanisms associated with the PFC could result in increased experience of anxiety and biased information processing.

Consistent with the relations between PFC functionality and amygdala activation in the neuroimaging literature, there is a great deal of research in the behavioural literature suggesting that a cognitive function mediated by the PFC – voluntary attention control – moderates fear, shyness, anxiety symptoms and attention biases. Poor attention control is linked to increases in internalizing behaviours such as shyness or anxiety (Calkins and Fox, 2002; Derryberry and Rothbart, 1997; Muris *et al.*, 2008), where such an association is higher in children with fearful temperaments or negative affectivity (Muris, Meesters and Blijlevens, 2007). For example, temperamentally shy adolescents who report high levels of attention control have lower levels of social anxiety compared to shy adolescents with poor attention control (Henderson *et al.*, 2005). The two mechanisms that comprise voluntary attention control – attention focusing and attention shifting – appear to both be particularly important in the regulation of anxiety. Attention focusing, which reflects the ability to select certain relevant information from the environment and keep attention focused on such information while filtering out or ignoring irrelevant information, and attention shifting, which involves voluntarily shifting attention focus away from irrelevant information (Rothbart *et al.*, 2003), both appear to be compromised in anxious adults and children (Bishop, Jenkins and

Lawrence, 2007; Muris, Meesters and Rompelberg, 2007). In fact, attention biases to threat, which result in part from the inability to voluntarily shift attention away from threat and from the failure to ignore irrelevant threatening information, are causally linked to anxiety (Bishop, Jenkins and Lawrence, 2007; Eldar, Ricon and Bar-Haim, 2008; Georgiou *et al.*, 2005; Mathews and MacLeod, 2002).

Experimental paradigms have illustrated the significant influence that voluntary control of attention (i.e. voluntary attention shifting and attention focusing) can have on the biased processing of threatening stimuli seen in behaviourally inhibited children (Derryberry and Reed, 2002; Lonigan *et al.*, 2004; Muris, Meesters and Rompelberg, 2007; Reinholdt-Dunne, Mogg and Bradley, 2009). Using a dot-probe task with short (250 milliseconds) and long (500 milliseconds) stimulus presentations, Derryberry and Reed (2002) found that during long stimulus presentations an individual's self-reported level of attention control moderated the link between anxiety and attention bias to threat; high anxious individuals with poor attention control showed an attention bias to threat whereas high anxious individuals with good voluntary attention control showed no bias. During short stimulus presentations, where there was presumably insufficient time to voluntarily control attention, high anxious individuals showed a greater attention bias to threat than non-anxious individuals, regardless of their level of attention control. In a recent study, Reinholdt-Dunne, Mogg and Bradley (2009) found similar effects when attention control was measured objectively using the attention network task (ANT) (Fan *et al.*, 2002). Anxious individuals who were more distracted by the irrelevant flanker stimuli on the ANT, an index of poor attention control, showed biased processing of emotional faces on a pictorial emotional Stroop. However, the study found no relation between anxiety and attention control on the processing of emotion words on a linguistic emotional Stroop.

A similar influence of attention control has been found in children high in negative affect (Lonigan and Vasey, 2009) such that children with high negative affect and high attention control did not show an attention bias to threatening stimuli, while children with high negative affect and low attention control did show this bias. In a recent study examining attention bias in behaviourally inhibited adolescents using a dot-probe task, a significant attention bias towards threat was seen for short stimulus durations, but not for long stimulus durations (Pérez-Edgar *et al.*, in press). Although attention control was not measured in the study, the finding suggests that when given sufficient time to exert voluntary attention control, behaviourally inhibited adolescents were able to shift their attention away from the threatening stimuli. Efficient attention control processes may serve as a protective factor decreasing the association between BI and the development of anxiety by reducing an individual's attention biases towards threat and resulting anxiety (Lonigan *et al.*, 2004; Muris, Meesters and Rompelberg, 2007).

Although high levels of voluntary attention control have been found to decrease a behaviourally inhibited child's vulnerability for anxiety and related information processing biases, evidence does exist that other aspects of regulative temperament factors – specifically, the ability to inhibit dominant behaviours and override inappropriate prepotent responses in favour of more appropriate responses (e.g. inhibitory control: Rothbart *et al.*, 2003), and cognitive and behavioural monitoring – may actually serve to increase the risk of developing anxiety disorders. Recent research indicates that high behaviourally inhibited children who have high levels of inhibitory control as assessed with performance-based measures (Osher *et al.*, 2007; White *et al.*, 2009b) have more anxiety problems than high behaviourally inhibited children with lower levels of inhibitory control. For example, in a group of toddlers selected for their level of reactivity to novelty at 4 months of age, BI was significantly related to their level of anxiety at 4 and 5 years. However, a child's level of inhibitory control, as assessed by his or her interference scores on a non-emotional Stroop at 4 years, moderated this association. Specifically, children with high BI and high inhibitory control had significantly higher levels of anxiety (White *et al.*, 2009b). Similarly, Thorell, Bohlin and Rydell (2004) found that in a group of 5-year-olds, those with a combination of high BI and high inhibitory control as assessed by performance on a go/no-go task were significantly more likely to have high levels of social anxiety 3 years later. One explanation for this finding is that the high levels of fear associated with BI serve as one form of reactive control, leading to inhibition, avoidance and withdrawal in many situations (Rothbart and Sheese, 2007). When this reactive inhibition is coupled with high levels of inhibitory control, reflecting increased inhibition of prepotent responses, it can lead to overcontrol and inflexibility of behaviours, resulting in more withdrawal, avoidance and anxiety. Thus, aspects of voluntary attention control appear to reduce the risk of anxiety by helping behaviourally inhibited children direct their attention away from threat and ignore irrelevant threat distracters. Conversely, high levels of inhibitory control likely lead to increased inhibition of approach behaviours, increasing avoidant behaviours and anxiety.

High levels of cognitive monitoring may also be a risk factor for the development of anxiety in behaviourally inhibited individuals. Much of the research examining this relation has focused on an event-related potential (ERP) component known as the error-related negativity (ERN), a fronto-central component that appears within 150 milliseconds of the commission of an error. The neural source of the ERN is believed to be the anterior cingulate cortex (ACC), a brain region involved in cognitive control and emotional processing. Enlarged ERN amplitude after committing an error has been linked to both adult and child anxiety disorders (Gehring, Himle and Nisenson, 2000; Ladouceur *et al.*, 2006). For example, in a group of 8- to 14-year-old children, Ladouceur *et al.* (2006) found that children with a range of anxiety disorders showed larger ERNs than their non-anxious peers. Such heightened error monitoring is also associated with trait anxiety and worry (Hajcak, McDonald and Simons, 2003). Thus, it appears the neurophysiological processing of error is related to anxiety, and the alteration in neurophysiological processing that is indexed by the ERN is an early appearing characteristic of anxious individuals.

Recent temperamental research examining cognitive monitoring has also detected enhanced ERN amplitude in individuals high in negative affect and BI (Hajcak, McDonald and Simons, 2004; McDermott *et al.*, 2009). Adolescents who had been assessed for levels of BI at several points in infancy and early childhood performed a simple button-press task designed to elicit an ERN. Results revealed that high behaviourally inhibited adolescents had greater ERN amplitudes than the low behaviourally inhibited adolescents. Moreover, in the high BI group, ERN amplitude predicted the likelihood of an anxiety diagnosis, with behaviourally inhibited individuals with the largest ERN amplitudes being most likely to be diagnosed with an anxiety disorder. In the low BI group, however, there was no relation between ERN amplitude and anxiety diagnosis. This suggests that a high level of monitoring, indexed by the ERN, could increase the risk that behaviourally inhibited children will develop an anxiety disorder in childhood or adolescence. Although the data do not provide a causal relation, given that the ERN was measured concurrently with assessment of anxiety disorders, it is possible that high levels of monitoring one's actions is a potential risk factor for behaviourally inhibited children, leaving them more likely to develop anxiety disorders.

Childcare Environment

In the sections above, we have discussed a number of intrinsic factors that place behaviourally inhibited children at risk for the development of child and adolescent anxiety disorders. This information is most useful, however, when coupled with an understanding of how these biases can be fostered or mitigated by environmental factors (e.g. Hadwin, Garner and Perez-Olivas, 2006; Hudson and Rapee, 2004; see also Chapters 11 and 12 in the current book). A behaviourally inhibited child's caregiving environment appears to have a powerful influence on his or her developmental outcomes. In particular, parental personality, parenting style and childcare history have all been shown to significantly influence outcomes of behaviourally inhibited children (Degnan and Fox, 2007; Degnan et al., 2008).

In a recent study, Degnan et al. (2008) found that temperamentally fearful infants whose mothers self-reported heightened symptoms of depression or neuroticism displayed stable BI over childhood. Conversely, positive maternal personality traits, such as extraversion, have been linked to decreased internalizing behaviours in children (Rosenbaum et al., 1988). Thus, behaviourally inhibited children with mothers displaying negative emotionality appear to be at increased risk for negative outcomes, whereas positive maternal traits may protect against this risk.

Parenting behaviours have also been shown to significantly influence the continuation of inhibited behaviours across development. For example, while sensitive parenting has been shown to be associated with positive child outcomes (Park et al., 1997), for behaviourally inhibited children sensitive parenting, such as over-attentive responsivity and excessive warmth, may enhance a child's fears leading to stability of BI over childhood (Degnan and Fox, 2007; Degnan et al., 2008; Kagan, 1994). Hane et al. (2008) have also shown that temperamentally fearful children whose mothers display high levels of hostility and negative control show increases in social withdrawal during early childhood.

The type and context of non-parental caregiving has also been shown to influence the continuation of BI. Behaviourally inhibited children who have a history of non-parental caregiving with peers show a reduction in inhibition over time compared to behaviourally inhibited children with no history of such caregiving (Fox et al., 2001). Non-parental childcare likely provides the child with increased exposure to situations involving interactions with unfamiliar peers and decreases in overly sensitive parenting that the child may otherwise have been exposed to. Thus, in non-parental childcare behaviourally inhibited children may learn strategies through which to approach unfamiliar social situations and interactions (Degnan and Fox, 2007) that likely decrease their level of social withdrawal and inhibition over time. However, two studies have failed to show a relation between non-parental childcare and decreases in BI over time (Broberg, 1993; Degnan *et al.*, 2008), suggesting that issues of quality of care and other contextual characteristics and initial level of BI of the child may influence this relation.

Taken together, the childcare environment that a behaviourally inhibited child is exposed to across development significantly influences his or her level of inhibition throughout childhood. Maternal personality and behaviours likely provide the children a model in which they learn how to navigate through the world and respond to their environment. If parents are overprotective and highlight uncertainty, ambiguity or mild threat in the environment, this may enhance temperamental dispositions towards fear and withdrawal (Fox, Hane and Pine, 2007) and increase a child's level of anxiety (Perez-Olivas, Stevenson and Hadwin, 2008). But if the mother encourages interaction with unfamiliar peers or exposes the child to new and sometimes novel contexts this may decrease dispositions to withdraw or avoid novel situations. For this reason, maternal behaviour and personality may play a particularly important role in exacerbating or diminishing specific processing biases of a behaviourally inhibited child. A child's experience plays a significant role in how he or she processes threat (LoBue, in press), with anxious children showing facilitation in threat learning (Fulcher, Mathews and Hammerl, 2008) and facilitated attention bias towards recently acquired threat information (Field, 2006). Thus, the experiences that children are exposed to in their childcare environment likely influence how they perceive, weigh and process threat (see Hadwin, Garner and Perez-Olivas, 2006 for a review). This influence may prove to be particularly critical for children with high levels of fear at the outset, such as a behaviourally inhibited child. Parental behaviours that foster a child's fear may inadvertently strengthen many of the threat associations the child has already created, leading to more concrete biases. Moreover, mothers high in depression or anxiety may tend to highlight negative and threatening events in the environment from which the behaviourally inhibited child may quickly learn to process a source of threat.

Conclusions

The constellation of characteristics that make up a behaviourally inhibited child strongly echo those of anxious children. Nevertheless, while a significant proportion of behaviourally inhibited children develop anxiety disorders over the lifespan, the majority of these children do not, and instead show steady or dwindling levels of inhibition with age. We suggest that the causal pathway between temperamental factors and anxiety involves a complex interplay between automatic processing biases, effortful cognitive abilities and a child's environment.

Augmented neural responses to novel and threatening stimuli, greater allocation of attention to these stimuli or an overgeneralization of fear learning will likely all, under appropriate circumstances, increase an individual's risk for anxiety.

Further, each bias will also likely lead to a cascade of subsequent maladaptive information processing biases (White *et al.*, 2009a), exacerbating the risk for anxiety by introducing the child to additional stages of perturbed information processing. Given that similar neural circuitry underlies these initial information processing biases (Bishop, 2008; Morris, Öhman and Dolan, 1998), it is likely that a behaviourally inhibited child will have a combination of these biases, and the confluence of these processing biases may substantially increase the risk for psychopathology. Therefore, determining the factors that may reduce this risk is vital. Enhanced attention control abilities, the absence of overcontrol and monitoring, and a positive caregiving environment all appear to dampen the link between BI and anxiety. Thus, future developmental research examining the link between temperamental factors and anxiety should utilize multiple levels of analysis to examine the complex interplay of these factors over both the time course of development and in variable contexts.

References

Aggleton, J.P. (2000) *The Amygdala: A Functional Analysis*, Oxford University Press, Oxford.

Albano, A.M., Chorpita, B.F. and Barlow, D.H. (1996) Childhood anxiety disorders, in *Child Psychopathology* (eds E.J. Mash and R.A. Barkley), Guilford Press.

Bar-Haim, Y., Lamy, D., Pergamin, L. *et al.* (2007) Threat-related attentional bias in anxious and nonanxious individuals: a meta-analytic study. *Psychological Bulletin*, **133** (1), 1–24.

Biederman, J., Rosenbaum, J.F., Hirshfeld, D.R. *et al.* (1990) Psychiatric correlates of behavioral inhibition in young children of parents with and without psychiatric disorders. *Archives of General Psychiatry*, **47** (1), 21–26.

Bishop, S.J. (2007) Neurocognitive mechanisms of anxiety: an integrative account. *Trends in Cognitive Sciences*, **11** (7), 307–316.

Bishop, S.J. (2008) Neural mechanisms underlying selective attention to threat. *Annals of the New York Academy of Sciences*, **1129**, 141–152.

Bishop, S.J., Duncan, J. and Lawrence, A.D. (2004) State anxiety modulation of the amygdala response to unattended threat-related stimuli. *Journal of Neuroscience*, **24**, 10364–10368.

Bishop, S.J., Jenkins, R. and Lawrence, A.D. (2007) Neural processing of fearful faces: effects of anxiety are gated by perceptual capacity limitations. *Cerebral Cortex*, **17**, 1595–1603.

Bittner, A., Egger, H.L., Erkanli, A. *et al.* (2007) What do childhood anxiety disorders predict? *Journal of Child Psychology and Psychiatry*, **48** (12), 1174–1183.

Blanchard, R.J. and Blanchard, D.C., (1969) Crouching as an index of fear. *Journal of Comparative Physiological Psychology*, **67** (3), 370–375.

Broberg, A.G. (1993) Inhibition and children's experience of out-of-home care, in *Social Withdrawal, Inhibition, and Shyness in Childhood* (eds K.H. Rubin and J.B. Asendorf), University of Chicago Press, Chicago.

Calkins, S.D. and Fox, N.A. (2002) Self-regulatory processes in early personality development: a multilevel approach to the study of childhood social withdrawal and aggression. *Development and Psychopathology*, **14**, 477–498.

Carver, C.S. and White, T.L. (1994) Behavioral inhibition, behavioral activation, and affective responses to impending reward and punishment: the BIS/BAS scales. *Journal of Personality and Social Psychology*, **67**, 319–333.

Chronis-Tuscano, A., Degnan, K.A., Pine, D.S. *et al.* (2009) Stable, early behavioral inhibition predicts the development of social anxiety disorder in adolescence. *Journal of the American Academy of Child and Adolescent Psychiatry.* **49**, 928–935.

Davidson, R.J. (2002) Anxiety and affective style: role of prefrontal cortex and amygdala. *Biological Psychiatry*, **51**, 68–80.

Degnan, K.A. and Fox, N.A. (2007) Behavioral inhibition and anxiety disorders: multiple levels of a resilience process. *Development and Psychopathology*, **19** (3), 729–746.

Degnan, K.A., Henderson, H.A., Fox, N.A. and Rubin, K.H. (2008) Predicting social wariness in middle childhood: the moderating roles of child care history, maternal personality, and maternal behavior. *Social Development*, **71** (3), 471–487.

Derryberry, D. and Reed, M.A. (2002) Anxiety-related attentional biases and their regulation by attentional control. *Journal of Abnormal Psychology*, **111**, 225–236.

Derryberry, D. and Rothbart, M.K. (1997) Reactive and effortful processes in the organization of temperament. *Development and Psychopathology*, **9** (4), 633–652.

Eldar, S., Ricon, T. and Bar-Haim, Y. (2008) Plasticity in attention: implications for stress response in children. *Behaviour Research and Therapy*, **46**, 450–461.

Etkin, A., Klemenhagen, K.C., Dudman, J.T. *et al.* (2004) Individual differences in trait anxiety predict the response of the basolateral amygdala to unconsciously processed fearful faces. *Neuron*, **44**, 1043–1055.

Eysenck, M., Mogg, K., May, J. *et al.* (1991) Bias in interpretation of ambiguous sentences related to threat in anxiety. *Journal of Abnormal Psychology*, **100** (2), 144–150.

Fan, J., McCandliss, B.D., Sommer, T. *et al.* (2002) Testing the efficiency and independence of attentional networks. *Journal of Cognitive Neuroscience*, **14**, 340–347.

Field, A.P. (2006) The behavioral inhibition system and the verbal information pathway to children's fears. *Journal of Abnormal Psychology*, **115** (4), 742–752.

Fox, N.A., Hane, A.A. and Pine, D.S. (2007) Plasticity for affective neurocircuitry: how the environment affects gene expression. *Current Directions in Psychological Science*, **16** (1), 1–5.

Fox, N.A., Henderson, H.A., Marshall, P.J. *et al.* (2005) Behavioral inhibition: linking biology and behavior within a developmental framework. *Annual Review of Psychology*, **56**, 235–262.

Fox, N.A., Henderson, H.A., Pérez-Edgar, K. and White, L.K. (2008) The biology of temperament: an integrative approach, in *Handbook of Developmental Cognitive Neuroscience*, 2nd edn (eds C.A. Nelson and M. Luciana), MIT Press, Cambridge, pp. 839–854.

Fox, N.A., Henderson, H.A., Rubin, K.H. *et al.* (2001) Continuity and discontinuity of behavioral inhibition and exuberance: psychophysiological and behavioral influences across the first four years of life. *Child Development*, **72**, 1–21.

Frenkel, T.I., Lamy, D., Alogom, D. and Bar-Haim, Y. (2008) Individual differences in perceptual sensitivity and response bias in anxiety: evidence from emotional faces. *Cognition and Emotion*, **23** (4) 688–700.

Fulcher, E.P., Mathews, A. and Hammerl, M. (2008) Rapid acquisition of emotional information and attentional bias in anxious children. *Journal of Behavior Therapy and Experimental Psychiatry*, **39** (3), 321–339.

Gehring, W.J., Himle, J. and Nisenson, L.G. (2000) Action-monitoring dysfunction in obsessive–compulsive disorder. *Psychological Science*, **11** (1), 1–6.

Georgiou, G.A., Bleakley, C., Hayward, J. *et al.* (2005) Focusing on fear: attentional disengagement from emotional faces. *Visual Cognition*, **12**, 145–158.

Grillon, C. (2002) Startle reactivity and anxiety disorders: aversive conditioning, context, and neurobiology. *Biological Psychiatry*, **52** (10), 958–975.

Grillon, C., Baas, J.M., Cornwell, B. and Johnson, L. (2006) Context conditioning and behavioral avoidance in a virtual reality environment: effect of predictability. *Biological Psychiatry*, **60** (7), 752–759.

Grillon, C., Chavis, C., Covington, M.F. and Pine, D.S. (2009) Two-week treatment with the selective serotonin reuptake inhibitor citalopram reduces contextual anxiety but not cued fear in healthy volunteers: a fear-potentiated startle study. *Neuropsychopharmacology*, **34** (4), 964–971.

Grillon, C., Lissek, S., Rabin, S. *et al.* (2008) Increased anxiety during anticipation of unpredictable but not predictable aversive stimuli as a psychophysiologic marker of panic disorder. *The American Journal of Psychiatry*, **165** (7), 898–904.

Gross, C., Zhuang, X., Stark, K. *et al.* (2002) Serotonin 1A receptor acts during development to establish normal anxiety-like behaviour in the adult. *Nature*, **416**, 396–400.

Hadwin, J.A., Garner, M. and Perez-Olivas, G. (2006) The development of information processing biases in childhood anxiety: a review and exploration of its origin in parenting. *Clinical Psychology Review*, **26**, 876–894.

Hajcak, G., McDonald, N. and Simons, R.F. (2003) Anxiety and error-related brain activity. *Biological Psychology*, **64** (1–2), 77–90.

Hajcak, G., McDonald, N. and Simons, R.F. (2004) Error-related psychophysiology and negative affect. *Brain and Cognition*, **56** (2), 189–197.

Hane, A.A., Fox, N.A., Henderson, H.A. and Marshall, P.J. (2008) Behavioral reactivity and approach-withdrawal bias in infancy. *Developmental Psychology*, **44** (5), 1491–1496.

Hare, T.A., Tottenham, N., Galvan, A. *et al.* (2008) Biological substrates of emotional reactivity and regulation in adolescence during an emotional go–nogo task. *Biological Psychiatry*, **63** (10), 927–934.

Henderson, H.A., Schwartz, C.E., Mejia, E. and Moas, O. (2005) Attentional Control and the Regulation of Approach/Withdrawal Tendencies in Children. Paper presented at the SRCD Temperament/Personality Preconference, Atlanta, GA.

Hogan, A.M., Butterfield, E.L., Phillips, L. and Hadwin, J.A. (2007) Brain response to unexpected novel noises in children with low and high trait anxiety. *Journal of Cognitive Neuroscience*, **19** (1), 25–31.

Hudson, J.L. and Rapee, R.M. (2004) From anxious temperament to disorder: an etiological model of generalized anxiety disorder, in *Generalized Anxiety Disorder: Advances in Research and Practice* (eds R.G. Heimberg, C.L. Turk and D.S. Mennin), Guilford Press, New York, pp. 51–74.

Kagan, J. (1994) On the nature of emotion. *Monographs of the Society for Research in Child Development*, **59** (2–3), 7–24.

Kagan, J., Reznick, J.S., Clarke, C. *et al.* (1984) Behavioral inhibition to the unfamiliar. *Child Development*, **55**, 2212–2225.

Kagan, J., Reznick, J.S. and Snidman, N. (1987) The physiology and psychology of behavioral inhibition in children. *Child Development*, **58**, 1459–1473.

Kagan, J., Reznick, J.S. and Snidman, N. (1988) Biological bases of childhood shyness. *Science*, **240**, 167–171.

Kagan, J., Reznick, J.S., Snidman, N. *et al.* (1988) Childhood derivatives of inhibition and lack of inhibition to the unfamiliar. *Child Development*, **59**, 1580–1589.

Ladouceur, C.D., Dahl, R.E., Birmaher, B. *et al.* (2006) Increased error-related negativity (ERN) in childhood anxiety disorders: ERP and source localization. *Journal of Child Psychology and Psychiatry, and Allied Disciplines*, **47** (10), 1073–1082.

Ledoux, J. (1996) Emotional networks and motor control: a fearful view. *Progress in Brain Research*, **107**, 437–446.

LeDoux, J.E. (2000) Emotion circuits in the brain. *Annual Review of Neuroscience*, **23**, 155–184.

Lemerise, E.A., Gregory, D.S. and Fredstrom, B. (2005) The influence of provocateurs' emotion displays on the social information processing of children varying in social adjustment and age. *Journal of Experimental Child Psychology*, **90**, 344–366.

Lissek, S., Biggs, A.L., Rabin, S.J. *et al.* (2008) Generalization of conditioned fear-potentiated startle in humans: experimental validation and clinical relevance. *Behaviour Research and Therapy*, **46** (5), 678–687.

LoBue, V. (in press) What's so scary about needles and knives? Examining the role of experience in threat detection. *Cognition and Emotion*.

Lonigan, C.J. and Vasey, M.W. (2009) Negative affectivity, effortful control, and attention to threat-relevant stimuli. *Journal of Abnormal Child Psychology*, **37** (3) 387–399.

Lonigan, C.J., Vasey, M.W., Phillips, B.M. and Hazen, R.A. (2004) Temperament, anxiety, and the processing of threat-relevant stimuli. *Journal of Clinical Child and Adolescent Psychology*, **33**, 8–20.

MacLeod, C., Mathews, A. and Tata, P. (1986) Attentional bias in emotional disorders. *Journal of Abnormal Psychology*, **95**, 15–20.

Marshall, P.J., Reeb, B.C. and Fox, N.A. (2009) Electrophysiological responses to auditory novelty in temperamentally different 9-month-old infants. *Developmental Science*, **12** (4) 568–582.

Marshall, P.J. and Stevenson-Hinde, J. (1998) Behaviorally inhibition, heart period, and respiratory sinus arrythmia in young children. *Developmental Psychobiology*, **33**, 283–292.

Mathews, A. and MacLeod, C. (2002) Induced processing biases have causal effects on anxiety. *Cognition and Emotion*, **16** (3), 331–354.

McDermott, J.M., Pérez-Edgar, K., Henderson, H.A. *et al.* (2009) A history of childhood behavioral inhibition and enhanced response monitoring in adolescence are linked to clinical anxiety. *Biological Psychiatry*, **65** (5) 445–448.

Mogg, K., Bradley, B.P. and Hallowell, N. (1994) Attentional bias to threat: roles of trait anxiety, stressful events, and awareness. *Quarterly Journal of Experimental Psychology*, **47**, 841–864.

Monk, C.S., Grillon, C., Baas, J.M. *et al.* (2003) A neuroimaging method for the study of threat in adolescents. *Developmental Psychobiology*, **43** (4), 359–366.

Monk, C.S., Telzer, E.H., Mogg, K. *et al.* (2008) Amygdala and ventrolateral prefrontal cortex activation to masked angry faces in children and adolescents with generalized anxiety disorders. *Archives of General Psychiatry*, **65**, 568–576.

Morgan, C.A.III, Grillon, C., Southwick, S.M. *et al.* (1995) Fear-potentiated startle in posttraumatic stress disorder. *Biological Psychiatry*, **38** (6), 378–385.

Morris, J.S., Öhman, A. and Dolan, R.J. (1998) Conscious and unconscious emotional learning in the human amygdala. *Nature*, **393**, 467–470.

Muris, P., Mayer, B., van Lint, C. and Hofman, S. (2008) Attentional control and psychopathological symptoms in children. *Personality and Individual Differences*, **44**, 1495–1505.

Muris, P., Meesters, C. and Blijlevens, P. (2007) Self-reported reactive and regulative temperament in early adolescence: relations to internalizing and externalizing problem behavior and 'Big Three' personality factors. *Journal of Adolescence*, **30**, 1035–1049.

Muris, P., Meesters, C. and Rompelberg, L. (2007) Attention control in middle childhood: relations to psychopathological symptoms and threat perception distortions. *Behaviour Research and Therapy*, **45** (5), 997–1010.

Osher, J.E., McDermott, J.N.M., Degnan, K.A. *et al.* (2007) The Interactive Effects of Temperament and Inhibitory Control on Maladaptive Preschool Behavior. Poster Presented at the Society for Research in Child Development, Boston, MA.

Park, S., Belsky, J., Putnam, S. and Crnic, K. (1997) Infant emotionality, parenting, and 3-year inhibition: exploring stability and lawful discontinuity in a male sample. *Developmental Psychology*, **33**, 218–227.

Parks, C.L., Robinson, P.S., Sibille, E. *et al.* (1998) Increased anxiety of mice lacking the serotonin 1A receptor. *Proceedings of the National Academy of Sciences*, **95**, 10734–10739.

Pattij, T., Groenink, L., Hijzen, T.H. *et al.* (2002) Autonomic changes associated with enhanced anxiety in 5-HT(1A) receptor knockout mice. *Neuropsychopharmacology*, **27** (3), 380–390.

Pérez-Edgar, K. and Fox, N.A. (2003) Individual differences in children's performance during an emotional stroop task: a behavioral and electrophysiological study. *Brain and Cognition*, **52**, 33–51.

Pérez-Edgar, K. and Fox, N.A. (2005) Temperament and anxiety disorders. *Child and Adolescent Psychiatric Clinics of North America*, **14**, 681–706.

Pérez-Edgar, K. and Fox, N.A. (2007) Temperamental contributions to children's performance in an emotion-word processing task: a behavioral and electrophysiological study. *Brain and Cognition*, **65**, 22–35.

Pérez-Edgar, K., Fox, N.A., Bar-Haim, Y. *et al.* (in press) Attention bias to threat link behavioral inhibition in early childhood to adolescent social withdrawal. *Emotion*.

Perez-Olivas, G., Stevenson, J. and Hadwin, J.A. (2008) Do anxiety-related attentional biases mediate the link between maternal over involvement and separation anxiety in children? *Cognition and Emotion*, **22** (3), 509–521.

Phan, K.L., Fitzgerald, D.A., Nathan, P.J. *et al.* (2005) Neural substrates for voluntary suppression of negative affect: a function magnetic resonance imaging study. *Biological Psychiatry*, **57**, 210–219.

Phelps, E.A. and LeDoux, J.E. (2005) Contributions of the amygdala to emotion processing: from animal models to human behavior. *Neuron*, **48**, 175–187.

Pine, D.S. (1997) Childhood anxiety disorders. *Current Opinion in Pediatrics*, **9**, 329–338.

Pine, D.S. (2007) Research review: a neuroscience framework for pediatric anxiety disorders. *Journal of Child Psychology*, **48** (7), 631–648.

Prior, M., Smart, D., Sanson, A. and Oberklaid, F. (2000) Does shy-inhibited temperament in childhood lead to anxiety problems in adolescence? *Journal of the American Academy of Child and Adolescent Psychiatry*, **39** (4), 461–468.

Reeb-Sutherland, B.C., Helfinstein, S.M., Pérez-Edgar, K. *et al.* (2009) Startle modulation in behaviorally inhibited adolescents with a lifetime occurrence of anxiety disorders. *Journal of the American Academy of Child and Adolescent Psychiatry*, **48**, 610–617.

Reinholdt-Dunne, M.L., Mogg, K. and Bradley, B. (2009) Effects of anxiety and attention control on processing pictorial and linguistic emotional information. *Behaviour Research and Therapy*, **47** (5), 410–417.

Richards, A., French, C.C., Calder, A.J. *et al.* (2002) Anxiety-related bias in the classification of emotionally ambiguous facial expressions. *Emotion*, **2**, 273–287.

Rosenbaum, J.F., Biederman, J., Gersten, M. *et al.* (1988) Behavioral inhibition in children of parents with panic disorder and agoraphobia. A controlled study. *Archives of General Psychiatry*, **45** (5), 463–470.

Rothbart, M.K. and Derryberry, D. (1981) Development of individual differences in temperament, in *Advances in Developmental Psychology*, vol. 1 (eds M.E. Lamb and A.L. Brown), Erlbaum, Hillsdale, NJ, pp. 37–86.

Rothbart, M.K., Ellis, L.K., Rueda, M.R. and Posner, M.I. (2003) Developing mechanisms of temperamental effortful control. *Journal of Personality*, **71** (6), 1113–1143.

Rothbart, M.K. and Posner, M.I. (2006) Temperament, attention, and developmental psychopathology, in *Developmental Psychopathology: Developmental Neuroscience*, 2nd edn, vol. 2 (eds D. Cicchetti and D.J. Cohen), John Wiley & Sons, Inc., Hoboken, NJ, pp. 465–501.

Rothbart, M.K. and Sheese, B.E. (2007) Temperament and emotion regulation, in *Handbook of Emotion Regulation* (ed. J.J. Gross), Guilford Press, New York.

Sanson, A., Pedlow, R., Cann, W. *et al.* (1996) Shyness ratings: stability and correlates in early childhood. *International Journal of Behavioral Development*, **19**, 705–724.

Schmidt, L.A. and Fox, N.A. (1998) Fear-potentiated startle responses in temperamentally different human infants. *Developmental Psychobiology*, **32** (2), 113–120.

Schmidt, L.A., Fox, N.A., Rubin, K.H. *et al.* (1997) Behavioral and neuroendocrine responses in shy children. *Developmental Psychobiology*, **30**, 127–140.

Schmidt, L.A., Fox, N.A., Sternberg, E.M. *et al.* (1999) Adrenocortical reactivity and social competence in seven year-olds. *Personality and Individual Differences*, **26** (6), 977–985.

Schwartz, C.E., Snidman, N. and Kagan, J. (1999) Adolescent social anxiety as an outcome of inhibited temperament in childhood. *Journal of the American Academy of Child and Adolescent Psychiatry*, **38** (8), 1008–1015.

Schwartz, C.E., Wright, C.I., Shin, L.M. *et al.* (2003) Differential amygdalar response to novel versus newly familiar neutral faces: a functional MRI probe developed for studying inhibited temperament. *Biological Psychiatry*, **53**, 854–862.

Somerville, L.H., Kim, H., Johnstone, T. *et al.* (2004) Human amygdala responses during presentation of happy and neutral faces: correlations with state anxiety. *Biological Psychiatry*, **55** (9), 897–903.

Strobel, A., Gutknecht, L., Rothe, C. *et al.* (2003) Allelic variation in 5-HT1A receptor expression is associated with anxiety- and depression-related personality traits. *Journal of Neural Transmission*, **110** (12), 1445–1453.

Thomas, A. and Chess, S. (1977) *Temperament and Development*, Brunner/Mazel, New York.

Thorell, L.B., Bohlin, G. and Rydell, A. (2004) Two types of inhibitory control: predictive relations to social functioning. *International Journal of Behavioral Development*, **28** (3), 193–203.

Tsetsenis, T., Ma, X.H., Lo Iacono, L. *et al.* (2007) Suppression of conditioning to ambiguous cue by pharmacogenetic inhibition of the dentate gyrus. *Nature Neuroscience*, **10**, 896–902.

White, L.K., Bar-Haim, Y., Fox, E. *et al.* (2009a) The relation between attention bias to threat and interpretive bias. Poster presented at the Society for Research in Child Development, Denver, CO.

White, L.K., Martin McDermott, J., Osher, J.E. and Fox, N.A. (2009b) Reactivity, regulation, and anxiety: contributions of attentional flexibility and inhibitory control. Poster presented at the Society for Research in Child Development, Denver, CO.

11

Learning of Information Processing Biases in Anxious Children and Adolescents

Andy P. Field and Kathryn J. Lester
andyf@sussex.ac.uk

Learning Cognitive Biases

We have seen throughout this book that there is compelling evidence that anxiety vulnerability is associated with distinctive patterns of attentional and interpretive bias. Clinical and experimental theories assume that these processing biases represent a causal substrate that operates to influence cognitive representation in such a way as to directly mediate anxiety vulnerability (see Beck and Clark, 1997 for a review; Williams *et al.*, 1997). In Chapter 9, we saw that genetic studies show that 30–40% of the variance in cognitive biases is heritable, leaving environmental factors to explain the remaining two-thirds of the variance. In an extensive review exploring the mechanisms that underpin the development of cognitive distortions in childhood, Muris and Field (2008) concluded that although learning undoubtedly plays an important causal role, there is a distinct lack of research into (i) whether verbal information, vicarious learning and direct traumatic incidents create specific cognitive distortions in children; (ii) the mechanism through which these pathways achieve this change in the cognitive processing of threat material; and (iii) the role of parents in providing anxiogenic learning environments through which children acquire distorted cognitive processes.

This chapter will be a speculative journey through the processes and mechanisms that might underlie the acquisition of information processing biases in childhood. The dearth of research in children that attempts to address the important question of from where information processing biases come permits us the luxuries of speculation and indulging our own theoretical whims in the hope of laying a

Information Processing Biases and Anxiety: A Developmental Perspective Edited by Julie A. Hadwin and Andy P. Field
© 2010 John Wiley & Sons, Ltd.

foundation for research in the coming years. We will use recent research on cognitive bias modification paradigms in adults as a foundation on which to put forward ideas about how children acquire these biases. We will propose that trials in these paradigms mirror experiences that a child has in which external agents such as parents act as feedback. We will argue that both attentional and interpretational biases are driven by associations between a stimulus or situation and an outcome, which could be a traumatic event or visual, verbal or behavioural feedback from a parent or other external agent. These associations can form habitually or result from cognitive processes. In both cases, we suggest that cognition will affect the strength of the association and how it is expressed. We will then look at what cognitive capacities a child might need to learn information processing biases. We ∗ suggest that 4–7 years might be an important developmental period for learning interpretational biases to threat but that attentional biases can develop much earlier (i.e. in infancy). We hope that, although speculative, this chapter might provide inspiration for future research that might support or refute our ideas.

Cognitive Bias Modification and Training in Adults

Recently, experimental methods have been developed permitting attentional and interpretive biases to be simulated in the laboratory. Referred to variously as bias training, bias induction or cognitive bias modification, these procedures are designed to modify directly each class of processing bias and have produced evidence suggesting that biased interpretive and attentional processing are causally implicated in anxiety vulnerability (Hoppitt *et al.*, 2009; Mackintosh *et al.*, 2006; MacLeod *et al.*, 2002a; Murphy *et al.*, 2007; See, MacLeod and Bridle, 2009; Wilson *et al.*, 2006). The ability of these procedures to emulate anxiety-linked processing biases may make cognitive bias modification a potentially useful means of thinking about the mechanisms by which processing biases are acquired.

Interpretive and attentional bias modification procedures have been created by introducing contingencies into experimental tasks previously used only to assess these biases (Hirsch and Mathews, 1997; MacLeod, Mathews and Tata, 1986). During the most widely used variant of cognitive bias modification for interpretation,[1] participants read a series of emotionally ambiguous descriptions (often approximately 100 trials) configured to yield one of two bias modification conditions depending upon participant randomization (Mathews and Mackintosh, 2000). Each description ends with a word fragment and comprehension question. Completion of the fragment resolves the ambiguity in the description in either a negative or a positive direction. In one condition, designed to induce an interpretive

---

[1]An alternative method of cognitive bias modification for interpretation involves presenting a series of ambiguous threat/neutral homographs, for example, 'Batter' followed by a word fragment for completion. Completion of the word fragment consistently constrains the meaning of the homograph in a non-threatening (e.g. p-nc-ke, pancake) or threatening direction (as-au-t, assault) (Grey and Mathews, 2000).

bias towards threat, completion of the fragment consistently produces a threatening interpretation of the description whereas in the other condition, completion of the fragment resolves the ambiguity in the description in a non-threatening manner. Correctly responding to the comprehension question requires reference to and further reinforces the to-be-modified interpretation.

The most common test of the effects of interpretation bias modification has been a modified form of the ambiguous sentence task developed by Eysenck *et al.* (1991). In this test, participants read novel ambiguous descriptions where the ambiguity is preserved and are later asked to rate four different sentences for their similarity to the original description. Two of these sentences, referred to as targets, reflect plausible interpretations of the description, one being positive and the other negative. The remaining two sentences, referred to as foils (one positive, one negative) do not reflect legitimate interpretations, because they are not factually correct or relevant in the context of the original passage. Any systematic tendency to rate one valence of target sentence (positive or negative) as more similar than the other is considered evidence of a bias in interpretation.

A consistent finding across numerous research studies is that interpretation bias modification leads to congruent and spontaneous biases in interpretation of similar, but novel material (Mackintosh *et al.*, 2006; Mathews and Mackintosh, 2000; Murphy *et al.*, 2007; Salemink, van den Hout and Kindt, 2007a, 2007b; Teachman and Addison, 2008; Yiend, Mackintosh and Mathews, 2005). Following non-threat modification, participants endorse non-threatening interpretations as more similar, while following threat modification participants endorse threat interpretations as more similar. In a small number of studies, the numerical advantage for non-threatening interpretations remains following threat modification; however, it is clearly reduced compared to that after non-threat modification.

During the most widely used variant of cognitive bias modification for attention,[2] participants perform a dot-probe task (see Chapters 4 and 13) where systematic contingencies are introduced between the emotional stimuli (emotional words or faces) and probe positions to induce a biased attentional response either towards or away from threat (MacLeod *et al.*, 2002b; Mathews and MacLeod, 2002). Each modification trial begins with the presentation of a word pair consisting of an emotionally negative and an emotionally neutral word. A probe, consisting of a single pixel (.) or two adjacent pixels (..) then replaces the word pair and can appear in the location previously occupied by either of the words. Participants are required to discriminate the probe identity (. or ..), and their relative discrimination latencies for probes appearing in the location previously occupied by the neutral and negative word provide a measure of their attentional bias.

In the modification condition designed to induce an attentional bias towards threat, the probe is consistently presented in the location previously occupied by the threat member of the word pair. In the condition designed to induce an attentional bias away from threat, the probe is consistently presented in the location previously occupied by the neutral word. The attentional effect of the modification procedure is assessed using catch trials distributed across the dot-probe task or in blocks pre- and post-modification phase. Here, the probe is presented with equal frequency in the location previously occupied by the negative or neutral word. Where the modification procedure is effective in inducing a systematic preference to attend to stimuli of one valence, threat trained participants are faster to discriminate the identity of probes presented in the location of negative words compared to neutral words, with the reverse observed following non-threat attentional bias modification.

While still in its infancy, there is an increasing body of evidence indicating that cognitive bias modification procedures are effective in modifying processing biases both towards and away from threatening stimuli. However, many questions remain unanswered regarding the mechanisms involved in specific modification techniques and in mapping the boundaries of any effects, in particular regarding the generalizability and durability of any biases induced. Evidence regarding the generalization of induced interpretive biases remains somewhat mixed and as yet it is not known what features are critical for provoking modification-congruent effects on subsequent assessments of cognitive processing. A small number of studies have reported modification-congruent interpretive bias effects on test tasks, other than the ambiguous sentences rating task described previously (Hirsch, Mathews and Clark, 2007; Mathews et al., 2007b). For example, Hirsch et al. (2007) demonstrated that following negative interpretation modification participant's images of themselves that were generated in response to hearing an ambiguous description were rated as significantly more unpleasant by themselves and by an independent assessor compared to image perceptions following a benign modification procedure. However, there have also been failures to observe generalization of modification-congruent effects. For example, Salemink et al. (2007a), while observing generalization to the ambiguous sentences rating task failed to observe modification-congruent effects to the Ambiguous Social Situations Interpretation Questionnaire (Stopa and Clark, 2000) and a modified version of the Extrinsic Affective Simon Task (De Houwer, 2003) using ambiguous homographs.

Further promising research suggests that induced interpretive biases are not context dependent and are capable of enduring changes in testing location, experimenter, testing context (e.g. group vs. individual) and modality of presentation (visual vs. aural) between the modification phase and subsequent testing of any modification effects (Mackintosh et al., 2006). However, it remains to be established whether induced biases would be resistant to the type of context changes that may be experienced in the real world. It also remains to be determined whether the biases induced using these procedures are in fact the same as those occurring naturally in high trait and clinically anxious individuals. It could be argued, for example, that the biases induced using current bias modification procedures are likely to be relatively transient compared to those occurring naturally. Existing evidence suggests that the biases induced following a single session of interpretive bias modification remain stable for a duration of up to 24 hours (Yiend, Mackintosh and Mathews, 2005).

(Of course, the transience of induced biases could be because bias modification procedures are brief relative to years of lifetime experience.)

By manipulating processing biases using cognitive bias modification procedures, it is possible to test directly the hypothesis that selective processing contributes causally to anxiety vulnerability. Several experiments have exposed participants to experimental stressors, such as the solving of difficult and insoluble anagrams and the viewing of real-life accident footage following bias modification (e.g. images of fire rescues and car accidents). Typically, this research has shown that induced processing biases appear to reduce or enhance vulnerability to stressors in a manner similar to naturally occurring variations in emotional reactivity. Negative emotional responses are reduced in those participants trained to avoid threatening stimuli compared to those participants trained to attend towards threat or to make threatening interpretations (Amir *et al.*, 2008; Hirsch, Mathews and Clark, 2007; Mackintosh *et al.*, 2006; MacLeod *et al.*, 2002b; Murphy *et al.*, 2007; See, MacLeod and Bridle, 2009; Wilson *et al.*, 2006). Mathews and MacLeod (2002) suggest that it is not the bias modification procedures themselves that alter anxiety responses directly. Instead, effects on anxiety reactivity are observed only when the bias induced is actively deployed to process ambiguous aspects of personally significant emotional events.

Recent research has begun to investigate whether stable attentional and inter-pretive change can be achieved through more extensive exposure to cognitive bias modification procedures. In these experiments an increased number of modifi-cation trials are presented over multiple sessions scheduled over several weeks (Amir *et al.*, 2009; Beard and Amir, 2008; Mathews *et al.*, 2007a; Schmidt *et al.*, 2009; See, MacLeod and Bridle, 2009) with the focus on reducing, rather than increasing, selective processing towards threatening information and attenuating associated anxiety vulnerability. Research of this nature highlights the possibility that the amelioration of anxiety-related cognitive biases in high anxious individuals may reduce vulnerability to experience excessive, negative emotional reactions to subsequent real-life stressful experiences (see Chapter 13). Multiple sessions of an interpretation or attention modification procedure have been shown to lead to a subsequent reduction in attentional (Amir *et al.*, 2009; See, MacLeod and Bridle, 2009) and interpretation biases towards threat (Beard and Amir, 2008; Mathews *et al.*, 2007a), reductions in trait and social anxiety (Amir *et al.*, 2009; Beard and Amir, 2008; Mathews *et al.*, 2007a; Schmidt *et al.*, 2009; See, MacLeod and Bridle, 2009) and reductions in the proportion of participants who continued to meet diagnostic criteria for social anxiety disorder (Schmidt *et al.*, 2009) and generalized anxiety disorder (Amir *et al.*, 2009) compared to no-modification control groups. See, MacLeod and Bridle (2009) also demonstrated that the extent to which a sam-ple of students responded with increases in trait and state anxiety to a naturalistic stressful life event (moving country to attend tertiary education) was mediated by the extent to which the attentional modification procedure was effective in inducing an attentional bias away from threat. As such, those participants who evidenced the greatest increase in attentional avoidance of threat also reported the greatest reductions in trait anxiety across the 17-day period of the study and also evidenced the smallest increases in state anxiety in the immediate hours after the stressful event occurred. This study directly supports the hypothesis that selective processing of threatening stimuli can causally contribute to naturalistic anxiety vulnerability.

It has been proposed that the effects of cognitive bias modification can be attributed to two mechanisms (Hoppitt *et al.*, 2009; Mathews and MacLeod, 2002): a learned production rule involving selection of one competing meaning, where consistently attending to or selecting valenced meanings during the modification phase strengthens the processes required to make similar selections subsequently. Alternatively, they can be attributed to a priming mechanism where repeated processing of words or texts from a valenced category (threat or non-threat) during the modification phase may prime access to a whole domain of meanings consistent with that valence. Shared associative links may then facilitate activation of subsequent related novel exemplars, increasing their chances of being accessed. At present, there is insufficient evidence to choose one explanation above the other and, in fact, there is some evidence to suggest that both mechanisms may contribute to the observed effects of bias modification procedures (Hoppitt *et al.*, 2009; Mathews and MacLeod, 2002). A general enhancement of priming favouring a specific valence may be sufficient to explain performance on some test tasks, where both ambiguous and unambiguous cues facilitate preferential access to positive and negative meanings. However, previous research suggests that the transfer of an implicit production rule where participants have learned to select threatening or non-threatening meanings during the modification phase when encountering a subsequent potentially emotional event may be critical for observing emotional effects of cognitive bias modification (Hoppitt *et al.*, 2009; Mathews and MacLeod, 2002).

Bias Training in Children

There is compelling evidence that childhood anxiety is associated with similar information processing biases to those experienced by anxious adults (reviews by Hadwin, Garner and Perez-Olivas, 2006; Muris and Field, 2008). However, there is a noticeable paucity of research investigating the genesis of processing biases in childhood anxiety. Two recent studies have used an innovative analogue of the adult bias modification studies previously mentioned to train interpretation biases in children (Muris *et al.*, 2008, 2009). In their 'space odyssey' paradigm, children play a computer game in which they imagine taking a journey to an unknown planet where they must discover the living conditions. They are presented with a series of ambiguous scenarios (e.g. 'On the street, you encounter a spaceman. He has a sort of toy handgun and he fires at you...') that are accompanied by a positive ('you are laughing: it is a water pistol and the weather is fine anyway') and negative ('Oops, this hurts! The pistol produces a red beam which burns your skin!') outcome. Children select an outcome and are told whether their decision is correct or wrong. By consistently reinforcing either the positive or the negative outcome for each scenario, the child is 'trained' to interpret ambiguous situations positively or negatively. Following the modification phase, children are asked to rate the level of threat associated with various ambiguous scenarios describing everyday situations that could occur on Earth (e.g. going to school, encountering unfamiliar people). The first study to use this procedure showed that non-clinical children aged 8–12 years successfully learned to select either positive or negative outcomes (depending on the condition to which they were assigned), but most importantly, their subsequent interpretation bias scores were affected by the bias modification procedure: children reported higher threat interpretations after negative modification than after positive modification. Furthermore, trait anxiety moderated these effects, with the impact of the negative modification condition particularly pronounced in those children with pre-existing high levels of anxiety symptoms (Muris *et al.*, 2008).

In a second study, Muris *et al.* used a pre–post design to look for *changes* in interpretational biases due to the space odyssey procedure and they measured changes in anxiety and avoidance (Muris *et al.*, 2009). They broadly replicated the finding that children's interpretations of ambiguity could be trained to be positive or negative. However, they did not replicate the finding that trait anxiety influenced this effect. In addition, they also failed to show a significant association between the induced bias and avoidance tendencies. This latter finding contradicts adult research that has shown that an induced bias causally affects anxiety (e.g. Mathews and Mackintosh, 2000). These studies do, however, demonstrate that (like adults) interpretational biases can be modified in children using simple feedback-learning paradigms.

In terms of attentional biases, there is currently little work to show that children can be trained to attend to threat. Two studies partially support the idea that children can learn attentional biases using verbal information to induce this bias (Field, 2006c). In the first experiment, children between 7 and 9 years were given positive information about one novel animal, negative information about another and no information about a third. This manipulation has been shown to change children's fear cognitions over 6 months, encourage avoidance behaviour and increase heart rate during an approach task (e.g. Field and Lawson, 2003; Field, Lawson and Banerjee, 2008; Field and Schorah, 2007). An immediate or 24-hour delayed pictorial dot-probe task revealed that children acquired an attentional bias in the left visual field[3] towards the animal about which they held negative beliefs compared to the control animal. The change in fear cognitions created by the threat information mediated the attentional bias towards that animal.

A second study replicated the basic finding that verbal information created an attentional bias to threat. In addition, it further showed that the acquisition of this bias was mediated by trait anxiety (Field, 2006a). Neither of these studies trained a bias as such (at least not in the sense that MacLeod *et al.* have done by consistently reinforcing attentional deployment to stimuli of a particular emotional valence). Instead, Field's studies were designed to explore the possibility

---

[3]The fact that the bias was found only in the left visual field is consistent with some attentional bias research in adults (e.g. Mogg and Bradley, 1999, 2002) and probably reflects the involvement of the right hemisphere of the brain in processing emotional stimuli.

that children categorize stimuli in their environment as positive or negative because of the information they hear. The studies demonstrate that once categorized as threatening, the neurological systems geared to attend to threat (see Chapter 8) take effect when presented with pictures of these animals. Field's studies, therefore, tell us how learning interacts with existing attentional systems; however, they say little about how a general attentional system learns to be over-sensitive to threat.

What Do Bias Modification Paradigms Tell Us about How Children Learn in the Real World?

In the real world, children do not sit for hours in front of computerized tasks that reinforce specific interpretational or attentional styles. However, bias modification tasks could be a close analogue of naturally occurring events. One way in which children are likely to acquire cognitive processing biases is through learning from parents and other influential individuals (e.g. teachers, older siblings) – in other words, environmental transmission.[4] The way in which this transmission of cognitive biases between parents[5] and children might occur could be thought of rather like the bias modification tasks described previously. Anxious parents may transmit anxiety-related cognitive biases to their children through the provision of cues to threat and feedback on their cognitions and behaviours that act in a manner similar to cognitive bias modification (see Chapter 12).

During childhood, children experience an ongoing stream of novel, often ambiguous situations and stimuli. One means by which they may seek to resolve ambiguity and uncertainty and to learn appropriate emotional and behavioural responses to novel stimuli is through parental guidance. How a parent responds to novel experiences involving their child may act to change the learning experiences to which the child is exposed. The parents could resolve novel experiences for their child in a relatively benign manner or in a more threatening manner, thus providing their child with an array of anxiogenic learning experiences. Each experience is rather like a 'trial' in a bias modification procedure: the child is faced with an ambiguous situation/stimulus, and the parent offers (i.e. reinforces) either a threat interpretation or draws the child's attention to some threatening aspect of the situation. This could be through verbal information (Field, Lawson and Banerjee, 2008), gestures such as pointing, or even more subtle behavioural reactions to the situation (Murray *et al.*, 2007). In this way, anxious parents represent an analogue of bias modification conditions that attempt to induce an interpretative or attentional bias towards threatening stimuli or situations. Similar to bias modification procedures (although extended over many more potential learning experiences), repeated exposure to novel, ambiguous situations where

---

[4]There will, of course, be gene–environment interactions also (see Muris and Field, 2008, for a discussion within a relevant context).
[5]Although parents are probably the primary source of environmental transmission, when we use the term 'parents' we mean it to include any significant person in the child's life.

their parents resolve that ambiguity for them in a threatening manner may increase the likelihood of the child acquiring similar threat-related cognitive biases (or at least developmental antecedents of these biases).

This theory assumes several things. First, we would need to show that parents' and children's threat-related cognitions and interpretational biases are associated. There is good evidence that parent and child threat-related cognitions in particular often correlate (Barrett *et al.*, 1996; see the next chapter for a thorough review, and Creswell and O'Connor, 2006; Creswell, O'Connor and Brewin, 2006; but see Gifford *et al.*, 2008, for conflicting results). Second, for parents to disambiguate situations involving their children in a threatening way, they must interpret those situations as threatening or negative. As parental anxiety increases, only if their own cognitive biases towards threat extend to influence how they process aspects of their child's world will they be more likely to selectively evoke threat interpretations or attend to threatening aspects of an ambiguous situation in their child's environment. If the anxious parents' cognitive processing bias towards threat does not generalize to influence the way in which they process ambiguous or novel stimuli and situations in their child's environment, then it is unlikely that they will disambiguate situations for their children in a threatening way. Lester *et al.* (2009a) tested the hypothesis that anxious parents would not only demonstrate threat interpretation biases regarding ambiguous situations involving themselves but that they would also interpret ambiguous stimuli and situations involving their children in a similar threatening way. They found that as trait anxiety increased in parents so did their tendency to interpret ambiguous child-related situations as threatening. For example, anxious parents rated the threat interpretation 'The doctor says your child's tumour has changed little since the last visit' as more similar in meaning to the ambiguous statement 'The doctor examined your child's growth' than the alternative non-threatening interpretation 'The doctor says your child's height is normal for their age'. The relationship between parental trait anxiety and threat interpretation bias towards child-related situations were weaker than the relationship between parental trait anxiety and threat interpretation bias for self-referent situations. Mediation analyses indicated that parental trait anxiety drives a self-referent interpretation bias in the parent, which in turn drives a bias for interpreting ambiguous situations involving their child in a threatening way.

The hypothesis that parents 'train' their anxious children to attend to threat or interpret ambiguity in a threatening way relies on an empirical demonstration that when children are faced with an ambiguous situation in the presence of their anxious parent, their parent does actually guide attention to threat or disambiguate the situation for them in a more threatening (or less positive) way than a parent low on trait anxiety. There is some tentative evidence that this could be the case. In a recent study in our own laboratory (Lester *et al.*, 2006), we presented children with several ambiguous scenarios (e.g. 'You and your mum/dad are walking down a street when you see a dog on its own a little way in front of you. You are not sure if the dog is friendly') based on Barrett *et al.* (1996). We asked children how they thought their mother and father would react in each situation in an open-ended way ('What do you think your dad will do?') and by selecting either a positive ('Let you pat the dog on the way past') or negative ('Cross the road so the dog doesn't bite either of you') interpretation. This measure was intended as a proxy of the children's past experiences of ambiguity with their parents. There was a significant relationship between what children reported their parents would do and the children's interpretation of different ambiguous situations. Children who interpreted ambiguous situations in a threatening way also anticipated that their parents would interpret or react in a threatening way to similar ambiguous situations involving them. Although it could be the case that children's existing interpretation biases drove their responses about how they anticipated their parents would react to ambiguous situations, this evidence could also suggest that a child's interpretation bias develops as a function of how their parents have disambiguated situations for them in the past. That is, children whose parents have disambiguated situations for them in a negative way in the past may learn to interpret ambiguity in their own environment in a similarly threatening manner. Ongoing research is seeking to test whether trait anxious mothers do disambiguate novel situations in a less positive way compared with non-anxious parents. There is evidence that parenting behaviours affect attentional biases too. The tendency to find threat in the child's environment that we have previously described is likely to express itself in over-involved parenting practices. Maternal over-involvement has been shown to contribute to children's vigilance for angry (threat) faces, which in turn augmented the child's separation anxiety (Perez-Olivas, Stevenson and Hadwin, 2008). This finding supports our notion that the tendency of parents to see threat in their child's environment translates into a processing bias in the child, although further work is needed to verify or refute our notion that this transfer happens through the parents' behaviour acting as 'training'.

We have tried to argue that the cognitive bias modification procedures used in adults are a useful analogue of the learning experiences a child has from parents and other significant people in their environment. Further research is needed to elaborate this process of transmission and to see whether this proposition bears up to empirical scrutiny. In addition, the little research that has tried to look at whether parenting practices act as 'training' have focused on interpretational biases. A parallel line of research needs to be developed to look at whether a similar intergenerational transmission process could explain how attentional biases develop in children. In this context, shared attention paradigms including social referencing will be invaluable in determining how attentional biases could be transmitted (Murray *et al.*, 2007, and see Chapter 12).

Despite the infancy of research supporting our ideas, we propose that bias modification is a useful framework in which to conceptualize the development of interpretational and attentional biases in childhood. One limitation of this paradigm as a proxy to the developmental experiences that might shape cognitive processing biases in children is that bias modification studies typically induce processing biases using situations and stimuli that already have emotional meanings attached to them. This is because the ambiguous stimuli used often depict highly familiar events (e.g. buying clothes) and situations about which people are likely to hold existing attitudes, beliefs and experiences. Presumably, in the early formation of cognitive processing biases children will experience situations and stimuli that are entirely novel. Therefore, the bias modification paradigms used to date may be relatively limited in what they can say regarding the development of processing biases towards completely novel stimuli. Another useful line of research might be to look at how processing biases for novel stimuli can be trained (it may be pragmatically easier to study attentional biases in this context).

Mechanisms of Learning

So far, we have suggested that when faced with ambiguity or potential threat, external agents (such as parents and siblings) direct attention or disambiguate the situation through verbal information and gestures (their own reactions). In this section, we discuss the underlying mechanism through which this training might work. Field (2006b) has suggested that associative learning provides a useful framework for understanding the development of anxiety generally, and we believe that it also has something to offer as an underlying mechanism through which information processing biases may develop and interact with aspects of cognitive development – especially given that some theories of bias modification are based on the formation of associative connections (see earlier).

A full review of associative learning models is beyond the scope of this chapter (see Dickinson, 1980; Field, 2006b; Pearce and Bouton, 2001 for reviews), and instead we will highlight some features of prominent theories that could provide a framework for thinking about the acquisition of attentional and interpretational biases. Attentional bias modification presumably works via operant learning principles in which a response (attention to a threat stimulus) is reinforced. Theories of goal-directed behaviour assume a two-process system in which a stimulus (S) is associated with an outcome (O) through Pavlovian learning principles (S → O). An instrumental learning process then generates an association between the outcome and the animal's response (R). As such, performance is controlled by an S → O → R associative chain. For example, when faced with a threat stimulus, a child thinks of the outcome (reward) which then activates thoughts of what behaviour elicited that reward (i.e. directed attention). A different model of operant conditioning suggests that a direct stimulus–response (S → R) association is formed through the pairing of a stimulus with a response. The associative chain would, therefore, be S → R → O; the threat stimulus evokes a representation of the response, which in turn activates a representation of the outcome of that response.

However, arguably, attentional bias modification is not goal directed. In this context, it might be useful to adopt Dickinson *et al.*'s distinction between goal-directed and habitual instrumental learning (Dickinson *et al.*, 1995). Dickinson argues that goal-directed instrumental learning requires two separate learning systems: the habitual learning system does not encode details of the outcome and is used for stimulus–response learning only, whereas a separate system learns goal-directed action and so does encode information about the outcome. The existence of two systems is well-supported by a variety of studies and there is evidence too that goal-directed instrumental learning becomes easier in humans aged over 2 years (Klossek, Russell and Dickinson, 2008). If the habitual learning system functions more prominently than the goal-directed system in infants then attentional biases to threat might be acquired through the habitual system because they have been shown in 5-month-old infants (Rakison and Derringer, 2008). The idea that attentional biases develop earlier than interpretational biases is also supported by our earlier observation that attention can be directed by parents and other external agents through gestures, whereas interpretations of situations require linguistic feedback to the child. Furthermore, unlike interpretational biases attentional biases do not require any understanding of the implicational meaning of a response and, therefore, might take advantage of the habitual learning system.

Although an instrumental learning account of attentional bias modification paradigms seems plausible, in the real world children are probably not reinforced for directing attention to threat (there is no 'correct' response). Instead, in the face of a threat stimulus they pick up on other people's attention (through social referencing) or the consequences (an external agent removes them from the situation). As such, it might also be reasonable to assume that a stimulus–outcome association is learned through Pavlovian associative learning.

In contrast to attentional biases, interpretational biases require an understanding of the implicational meaning of responses. As such they should not only take advantage of the more complex learning system that drives goal-directed operant learning, but also be more influenced by cognitive development (see the next section). However, as with attentional biases, it may not be realistic to think in terms of stimulus–response learning; although interpretation biases could be learnt over successive trials through an association between an ambiguous cue and a threat response (interpretation). However, in reality, children probably learn a simple stimulus–outcome association. In colloquial terms, children learn that 'when faced with ambiguity the outcome will be bad'. Whether they experience actual bad outcomes or are simply told that the outcome will be bad probably has little effect on the underlying association that is formed (Dickinson, 2001; Field, 2006b). It is also worth noting that when we talk about 'outcomes', these need not be real because imagined outcomes are sufficient to sustain the formation of associative connections (see Field, 2006b, for a review). As such, although a parent/external agent's response to a stimulus/situation might not in itself be traumatic or negative, if their reaction triggers imagery or cognitions that are traumatic in the child then these mental representations can act as a powerful negative outcome.

Regardless of whether attentional and interpretational biases develop through operant (stimulus–response) or classical (stimulus–stimulus) associations, the underlying mechanism is association between stimuli in memory. As such, models of associative learning might prove useful tools in understanding the underlying process of how information processing biases are learned (but see De Houwer, 2009; Mitchell, De Houwer and Lovibond, 2009, for an alternative view of associative learning). One such model devised by Rescorla and Wagner (1972) is based on the idea that associations are formed between cues and surprising outcomes:

$$\Delta V_A = \alpha_A \beta \left(\lambda - \sum V \right)$$

This equation means that the change in associative strength of a given cue (ΔV_A) is a function of the intensity or salience of the cue itself (α_A), known as its *associability*, and the intensity of the outcome (β). The crucial part of the equation is the part in parenthesis, which reflects the difference between the maximum associative strength that the outcome can support (i.e. the maximum amount of conditioning possible with a given outcome, λ) and the sum of the associative strengths of *all cues* presented on the trial (ΣV). In bias modification paradigms, we might expect cues (in attentional paradigms the threat stimuli and in interpretation paradigms the ambiguous situation) and also the outcome (the parent removing the child, looking scared or providing a threatening interpretation) to be fairly salient (α_A and β would be relatively high). In essence, the change in associative strength on a given trial will be quite strong.

Mackintosh (1975) extended the Rescorla–Wagner model to suggest that the attention devoted to a given cue is a function of its importance in predicting an outcome: that is, organisms attend to relevant stimuli at the expense of not attending to irrelevant ones. Unlike Rescorla–Wagner, the emphasis is on processing the cue rather than the outcome:

$$\Delta V_A = \alpha_A \beta \left(\lambda - V_A \right)$$

in which V_A is the existing associative strength of the cue. The associability of the cue (α_A) is not constant as in the Rescorla–Wagner model, but updates as a function of the degree to which that cue predicts the outcome relative to any other cues presented on the same trial. If the cue is better than all other predictors then α_A will remain high, but if there are better predictors within the environment then α_A will decrease. These ideas are formalized as follows:

$$\Delta \alpha_A^n > 0 \quad \text{If} \quad \left| \lambda^n - V_A^{n-1} \right| < \left| \lambda^n - V_X^{n-1} \right|$$

$$\Delta \alpha_A^n < 0 \quad \text{If} \quad \left| \lambda^n - V_A^{n-1} \right| \geq \left| \lambda^n - V_X^{n-1} \right|$$

The first equation simply means that for a given trial, n, the salience of the conditioned stimulus (CS) on that trial, $\Delta \alpha_A^n$, will be positive if the discrepancy between the maximum amount of conditioning possible (λ^n) and the associative strength of the cue on the previous trial (V_A^{n-1}) is smaller than the discrepancy between the maximum amount of conditioning possible and the associative strength of all other cues on the previous trial (V_X^{n-1}). So, as the associative strength of the cue approaches the maximum (or is closer to the maximum for that cue than any other cues) then the salience of that cue increases. The second of the two equations means that for a given trial, n, the salience of the cue on that trial, $\Delta \alpha_A^n$, will be negative if the discrepancy between the maximum amount of conditioning possible (λ^n) and the associative strength of the cue on the previous trial (V_A^{n-1}) is greater than or equal to the discrepancy between the maximum amount of conditioning possible and the associative strength of all other cues on the previous trial (V_X^{n-1}). Therefore, when the associative strength of the other cues is as close or closer to the maximum possible, then the salience of the cue will decrease.

Kruschke (2001), in extending this model, suggests that learning involves an attentional system that aims to implement the assumption that any cue should receive some attention, and to decide how attention should be distributed over multiple cues. Finite attentional resources are assumed so increased attention to one cue necessarily implies less attention to another. The system receives feedback and shifts attention in such a way as to reduce error; these shifts in attention lead to changes in the association weights (of the cues), which themselves act to reduce the error in learning. In the case of learning about threat, cues that reliably (i.e. result in less error) predict unpleasant outcomes will garner more attention (or associability). As such, processing biases to threat can be learnt associatively through experiences early on in life in which a stimulus/situation (or feature of that stimulus/situation) accurately predicts negative (not necessarily traumatic) outcomes. In effect, this learnt attentional pull of a stimulus/situation can be viewed as part of a conditioned anxiety response, the strength of which depends upon the severity of the negative outcomes (parents' physical or verbal responses, verbal information about the likely outcome, the parent taking the child from the situation) with which it has been associated.

Pearce and Hall's (1980) model is also based on cue processing, but in direct contradiction to Mackintosh's model they argue that attention would not be placed on cues that reliably predict an outcome but on cues that do not reliably predict an outcome. The rationale is that because it is costly to expend resources on stimuli already known to predict an outcome, those resources will be allocated to establishing the significance of the 'unknowns' in the environment. In Pearce and Hall's model, different equations determine the change in associative strength depending on whether the trial is excitatory (in anxiety terms, cue → threat outcome) or inhibitory (in anxiety terms, cue → no threat outcome). For excitatory trials, when a threat outcome (a threat response from a parent or a direct traumatic experience) is present, the change in associative strength is determined by a function of a learning rate parameter related to the intensity of the outcome (β_E), the maximum possible conditioning (λ^n) and the associative strength of the cue on the previous trial (α_A^{n-1}):

$$\Delta V_A^n = \beta_E \alpha_A^{n-1} \lambda^n$$

In other words, consistent with other attention-based associative models, the change in 'attentional pull' of the cue will depend on the intensity of the threat outcome or parental behaviour (β_E). It will depend also on whether the cue has, in the past, predicted a similar threat outcome/parental behaviour (α_A^{n-1}).

In inhibitory trials, where no threat outcome occurs (no one is there to provide verbal or vicarious threat information or nothing bad happens), the change in associative strength is determined by a function of a learning rate parameter related to the outcome intensity (β_I), the associative strength of the cue on the previous trial (α_A^{n-1}), and the discrepancy between the maximum possible conditioning (λ^n) and the extent to which an outcome is predicted by all stimuli presented on that trial ($\sum V_{NET}^{n-1}$).

$$\Delta \bar{V}_A^n = \beta_E \alpha_A^{n-1} \left(\lambda^n - \sum V_{NET}^{n-1} \right)$$

In other words, when no threat feedback is present, the change in 'attentional pull' of the cue is governed by what happens (β_1) instead of threat that has happened in the past (α_A^{n-1}), and what other stimuli are present and how well they predict what has happened ($\sum V_{NET}^{n-1}$).

Having determined the change in associative strengths on a given trial, the associability (attentional pull) of a given cue is determined by

$$\alpha_A^n = \gamma \left| \lambda^n - \sum V_{NET}^{n-1} \right| + (1 - \gamma)\alpha^{n-1}$$

in which γ is a parameter lying between 0 and 1 that defines the degree to which associability is governed by the preceding trial ($\gamma = 1$ when the previous trial is solely responsible for the salience of the cue) or by earlier trials ($\gamma = 0$ when the salience of the cue is solely determined by earlier trials and not the directly preceding one). To put it very simply, the attentional pull of a cue depends on past experience with that cue (α_A^{n-1}), how important that past experience is (γ), whether other cues predict the threat outcome/parental feedback ($\sum V_{NET}^{n-1}$) and the maximum amount of learning that the cue can support (λ^n).

The potential advantage of the attentional models over that of Rescorla–Wagner is that they address the issue of multiple cues predicting an outcome (as may well be the case when a child learns an attentional bias to threat). Also, the emphasis in these models is on the salience of the cue rather than the salience of the outcome (and in our conceptualization of how a child might learn a cognitive bias through associatively learning, these outcomes might be relatively innocuous). A hybrid model exists too that combines features of the Rescorla–Wagner, Mackintosh's and Pearce–Hall's models (e.g. Le Pelley, 2004). This model has at its core both cue (as in Mackintosh's and Pearce–Hall's models) and outcome processing (as in Rescorla–Wagner).

Clear predictions from these models can be made, such as that as a cue becomes more frequently associated with some threat-related outcome or parental behaviour, the bias to that cue will increase at the expense of a bias to other cues in the environment. In other words, as certain cues reliably predict threat-related outcomes (either by experience or verbal information), the information processing bias to that cue becomes stronger. Also, the change in associative strength (i.e. the degree to which a cognitive bias is learned) will depend on (i) the intensity of the outcome – more traumatic experiences should support greater bias learning; (ii) the salience of the cue (i.e. the stimulus or situation about which the child is learning) itself, which could be influenced by any number of factors such as novelty and prior information; and (iii) the extent to which the threat stimulus is presented with other cues that already have some associative connection to the outcome (cue competition effects). These offer three directly testable predictions about bias acquisition. The limitation of our conceptualization of bias learning as an associative process, however, is that information processing biases generalize beyond the specific learning environment to novel situations and it is not clear how these associative models explain this generalization.

Cognitive Development and Information Processing Biases

Associative learning provides a framework for understanding how a child forms associations between certain cues (stimuli or situations) and certain outcomes (parental reactions or information, or directly traumatic experiences). However, it is now well accepted that basic associative learning in humans can be influenced by a person's cognition (Field and Davey, 2001; Mitchell, De Houwer and Lovibond, 2009). Many theorists have pointed out that children might need certain cognitive abilities before they acquire information processing biases (see Alfano, Beidel and Turner, 2002; Muris, 2007, for reviews). However, we believe that the issues might be rather different for attentional and interpretation biases. Arguably, attentional biases are automatic and are activated with little or no explicit cognition. As mentioned earlier, they might, therefore, begin to develop through a habitual learning system at a rather younger age than interpretational biases. Attentional biases may well, therefore, begin as normal developmental phenomena over which children gradually gain control as they become older (see Chapter 3). Children with anxiety disorders may fail to control or inhibit these biases, or a failure to inhibit these biases may create anxiety. This is not to say that attentional biases cannot develop later in a child's life, just that the learning process can begin younger than for interpretational biases, which presumably require language and some understanding of what ambiguity is before they manifest.

The role of cognitive development in learning cognitive biases is probably, therefore, quite different for attentional and interpretational biases. Associations between cues and threat can be formed without higher level cognitive structures being in place. We will call these *habitual associations*. Cognition might affect habitual associations later inlife, but they are formed in a relatively pure way. Habitual associations probably underlie attentional biases: they are formed without the need for higher order thought, but can be influenced by such thoughts as the child develops. Other associations rely on cognition to be formed; we will call these *cognition-based associations*. For example, a child probably needs to understand what ambiguity is before they can form an association of the kind 'ambiguity → threat'. These are the associations on which interpretation biases are based. Habitual and cognition-based associations differ only in the time in life at which they are formed; we are not claiming that they behave in different ways. Cognition can affect both types of association, but habitual ones are formed very early in life and without the need for complex thought. Attentional biases could be based on both habitual and cognition-based associations whereas interpretation biases will be based only on cognition-based associations. As such, interpretation biases should develop later in life than attentional biases.

Cognitive development may have a role not only in the formation of associations, but also in altering and maintaining those associations. Regardless of whether threat associations are formed habitually or as a result of cognitive activity, they will be influenced by the children's growing understanding of the world. For example, the implicational meaning that the children attribute to the verbal and vicarious threat information that their parents provide to a given cue will change as a function of their cognitive abilities. This implicational meaning could affect both the strength of existing (attentional or interpretational) associations and the formation of new associations. Therefore, higher order cognitions might be important in maintaining learned associative responses to ambiguous situations or in creating associated feelings of anxiety through an understanding of the implicational meaning of a threat outcome. It is also possible that if children develop threat-related biases at a young age, then they will not go on to develop the flexibility of thought (about threat) that typically emerges with age (Davidson *et al.*, 2006; Deak, Ray and Pick, 2004). Effectively, the child's early experience places him or her on to a different developmental pathway compared to a child who has not had similar negative early experiences and formed corresponding threat associations.

To explore the contribution of cognitive development in forming and maintaining threat associations, we need to think about what a child needs to have cognitively to have an attentional or interpretational bias. Various researchers have tried to look at how cognitive development affects anxiety responses. This research may give us some clues about how cognition interacts with learning to create information processing biases. Banerjee and Henderson (2001) looked at the link between children's understanding of mental states in social anxiety. They measured social anxiety, theory of mind using a standard second-order false belief task, children's understanding of scenarios involving a faux pas and children's understanding of deceptive presentational displays (such as not crying after getting hurt because the child does not want to be perceived as a wimp). They found that theory of mind did not significantly correlate with social anxiety, but that understanding of faux pas and deceptive self-presentation was inversely related to social anxiety in children who scored high (but not low) on shyness. In other words, in highly shy children, social anxiety was not linked to general deficiencies in mental state understanding; but it was associated with a relatively poor insight into how self-presentational motives can create effective emotional displays and a poorer appreciation of the unintentional emotional consequences of faux pas. Although Banerjee and Henderson's findings show a relationship between social anxiety and general social cognitive development, they do not tell us directly about what cognitive precursors might be necessary to support information processing biases.

Muris *et al.* have made most of the attempts to systematically link cognitive development to information processing biases. In an early study, (Muris *et al.*, 2004) children were presented with brief scenarios in which the main character experienced an anxiety-related physical symptom (e.g. heart beating very fast). They indicated whether the character in the story was happy, sad, angry, anxious or in pain. They found that from the age of 7, children were increasingly able to link physical symptoms to anxiety, suggesting a cognitive shift occurring at this age. In a later study, Muris, Vermeer and Horselenberg (2008) measured children's cognitive development using several Piagetian conservation tasks. These children were interviewed after listening to vignettes across which the presence of anxiety-related physical symptoms was systematically varied. Like his earlier study, Muris found that from 7 years on, children were increasingly able to relate physical symptoms to the anxiety emotion. In addition, cognitive development enhanced this understanding of anxiety-related physical symptoms. Most recently, Muris *et al.* (2007) measured children's performance on conservation tasks and on a theory of mind test. They found that both tasks predicted anxious interpretations and emotional reasoning scores. These findings support the idea that interpretation and reasoning biases are influenced by (and perhaps depend upon) cognitive development.

The dearth of research linking cognitive development and anxiety-related cognitive processing biases creates an important challenge for researchers in terms of unpicking which cognitive factors underpin processing biases and whether these cognitive abilities develop with the biases in parallel or in sequential (in which case the bias is acquired only after certain cognitive building blocks are in place). These issues are not easy to unpick, not least of all because of the theoretical issues surrounding which cognitive abilities might or might not be important. For example, Muris *et al.*'s decision to measure Piagetian conservation and theory of mind was entirely sensible given that they are cornerstones of cognitive development. However, how these tasks relate specifically to the cognitive abilities necessary and sufficient for information processing biases is less clear.

Piagetian conservation tasks typically involve a child seeing two objects that are the same (for example, balls of clay, beakers of liquid, etc.), one of which is then transformed (the liquid is poured into a taller, thinner beaker; the clay ball is rolled into a sausage shape). The child is then asked a question to assess whether he or she realizes that the two objects are still the same even though a transformation has occurred (e.g. 'Is there the same amount of liquid in the two beakers?' 'Which object has more clay?'). To pass the task correctly, the child responds that the objects are the same; a child would fail the task by responding, for example, that the taller beaker contains more liquid, or that the sausage shape contains more clay. This test was traditionally used to assess whether a child had reached Piaget's *concrete operational stage* of development (which typically occurs around age 7). This stage represents a time when a child begins to be able to perform mental operations on actual or imagined concrete objects. The conservation task, for example, tests a child's ability to mentally reverse the transformation of one of the objects to understand that although its visual appearance has changed, its critical properties have not. There are various abilities associated with this stage other than conservation. Perhaps the most pertinent is *decentering*, which is a child's ability to entertain multiple aspects of a problem to solve it. Arguably, an appreciation of ambiguity requires an ability to hold multiple potential outcomes in mind. However, during this developmental stage a child's thinking is proposed to be based on concrete reality and it is not, until the *formal operational stage*, that the child becomes more able to consider abstract ideas. This stage starts at approximately 11 years of age.

An understanding of ambiguity arguably would involve an appreciation of abstract ideas and an ability to entertain multiple perspectives on a problem, and we might reasonably expect that children under the age of 11 do not (in Piagetian terms) have the cognitive skills to misinterpret ambiguity. However, Piaget's developmental stages are entrenched in logical reasoning and, so perhaps it is not the best framework to think about children's emerging cognitive understanding of ambiguity and interpretation. Research into children's understandings of social and emotional knowledge has focused to a large extent on their developing understanding of mental states or their theory of mind. One view is that by about the age of 4–5 years, a child begins to understand knowledge as representation and with that starts to appreciate characteristics associated with representation (Perner, 1991). The most crucial characteristic to the current argument is 'interpretation'. Arguably, success on false belief tasks and other measures of theory of mind depend on a child's appreciation that the same object can be represented in different and seemingly contradictory ways (Flavell, Green and Flavell, 1993, 1995). For example, in the classic theory of mind task, a character believes that an object (usually a ball or sweet) is in one location, but this object is moved to another location without the character's knowledge. The child has to say where the character thinks the object is. To do this successfully, the child needs to know that in reality the object is in one location but that the character has a representation of that object being in a different location. As such, a child needs an interpretational understanding of representation to pass the task (Wellman and Hickling, 1993). If this view of the development of a child's understanding of mental states is adopted, then theory of mind probably is a necessary condition for understanding ambiguity, but not necessarily a sufficient one.

Like the Piagetian developmental framework, there is a sense in which theory of mind can tell us only so much about cognitive abilities that might relate to interpretational biases. An alternative view to the above is that theory of mind tasks do not tap an interpretive theory of mind (Carpendale and Chandler, 1996). Carpendale and Chandler argue that the complex process of understanding the interpretative nature of knowledge does not develop at the age of 4–5 years (as theory of mind tasks suggest) but begins to emerge only at the age of 6–8 years and is by no means complete at this age. They review a body of evidence and suggest that only at 7- to 8-year-old children begin to understand that an object or message can have multiple meanings. This observation has direct implications for interpretational biases, which presumably require a child to understand multiple consequences of a situation. In two experiments, Carpendale and Chandler gave children a standard false belief task and also several tasks involving (i) lexical ambiguity (e.g. two characters are waiting for a 'ring', where it is not clear if they are waiting for a diamond ring or a phone call); (ii) ambiguous communication (e.g. a penny is hidden under one of three cards, two of which depict a red block, and a puppet is told that the penny is hidden under a card with a red block); and (iii) visual ambiguity (e.g. Jastrow's (1900) 'duck-rabbit'). The results showed that although children aged 5 routinely passed the false belief task, they generally did not have competence in the interpretation tests until several years later. It was only at 7–8 years of age that, when discussing matters of interpretation, children could explain differences in opinion in terms of the ambiguity of the original situation. Children's understanding of the distinction between facts and opinions also develops with age. When justifying matters of personal taste in ambiguous situations, 56% of 5-year-olds will refer to the 'truth' of the matter, whereas only 6% of 9-year-old children will do this and the remaining 94% will show an appreciation of subjectivity (Wainryb et al., 2004).

Although it seems clear from this literature that children's explicit reasoning about ambiguity does not develop until around the age of 7, learning a behavioural response pattern in the face of ambiguity does not necessarily require such reasoning. Arguably, if, as we propose, children acquire interpretational biases through feedback (from parents and other people) in the face of ambiguity then all that is required of the child is the ability to respond to ambiguous input. In a particularly interesting study by Beck and Robinson (2001), children were shown four cards depicting animals, and they were asked to select which card was being discussed based on different levels of information: ambiguous information referred to all cards ('it's an animal'), partially informative information referred to two cards ('it's black and white') and informative information referred to only one card ('it goes "moo"'). The most relevant findings were that 7- to 8-year-old children when faced with ambiguous input were able to seek clarification. Younger children, however, seemed unable to identify the best strategies for gathering this further information. Beck and Robinson conclude that even quite young children (5- to 6-year-olds) have an impulsive need to respond to ambiguity, but do lack the skills to search for appropriate clarifying information. One implication is that older children have formed pro-active strategies for getting clarification about ambiguous situations. This ability could weaken the impact of information from parents in ambiguous situations because, rather than blindly accepting their parents' interpretation, they will proactively guide the information that they receive. Conversely, children under 7 years might be more vulnerable to information about ambiguous situations because they have yet to develop skills that enable them to question their parents' interpretation. Finally, there is also some evidence that 3- to 4-year-olds are limited in their thinking about future hypothetical outcomes (Beck et al., 2006), which might suggest that if external feedback points towards a threatening outcome when faced with ambiguity, young children will struggle to entertain other possible outcomes.

To sum up, the developmental issues in learning interpretational biases are complex. Although some research has shown that general measures of cognitive competence, such as conservation and theory of mind, relate to information processing biases, there has been little research looking at the specific cognitive abilities necessary for children's understanding or responses to ambiguity in the context of anxiety (see Chapter 2). Based on the developmental research, 3- to 4-year-olds can perform on tasks involving ambiguous input, but they lack good strategies for disambiguating those situations for themselves. This may make them particularly vulnerable to accepting and not questioning the kind of threatening interpretations offered to them by anxious parents. These children also have limitations in their cognitive ability to consider different future outcomes. This pattern of results suggest that early childhood (4–7 years) might be a prime time during which entrenched behavioural responses can be reinforced because the children lack the cognitive capacity to steer the feedback they receive in a constructive direction. As children get older, they become better able to grapple with multiple future possibilities and to actively gather information to disambiguate the situation. From 7 years upwards, children start to develop an ability to reflect on subjectivity and (presumably) that the likely outcome of an ambiguous situation is subjective. At present, studies showing threat-related interpretational biases in children have used children aged 6 years or above, which supports our claim that they do not develop at younger ages, but new methodologies need to be developed to enable these biases to be tested in younger children who are just beginning to grapple with understanding future hypotheticals.

Summary

Although the clear message is that there is not nearly enough research to warrant a coherent summary of how learning contributes to information processing biases, we believe that children might acquire these biases rather like adults do in cognitive bias modification paradigms. We believe that both attentional and interpretational biases are driven by associations between a stimulus or situation and an outcome, which could be a traumatic event or visual, verbal or behavioural feedback from a parent or other external agent. These associations can form habitually but might also result from cognitive processes; in both cases cognition will affect the strength of the association and how it is expressed. Attentional biases have the potential to be based on both types of association whereas some cognitive abilities are probably necessary to form the associations that drive interpretational biases. Finally, we suggest that 4–7 years might be an important developmental period for learning interpretational biases to threat but that attentional biases can develop much earlier (i.e. in infancy).

Acknowledgements

Economic and Social Research Council Grant number RES-062-23-0406 awarded to Andy Field and Sam Cartwright-Hatton enabled us to write this chapter.

The authors would like to thank Robin Banerjee for some very helpful and inspiring conversations about children's development of an understanding of ambiguity. This chapter was greatly improved as a result of picking his brains!

References

Alfano, C.A., Beidel, D.C. and Turner, S.M. (2002) Cognition in childhood anxiety: conceptual, methodological, and developmental issues. *Clinical Psychology Review*, **22**, 1209–1238.

Amir, N., Beard, C., Burns, M. and Bomyea, J. (2009) Attention modification program in individuals with generalized anxiety disorder. *Journal of Abnormal Psychology*, **118** (1), 28–33.

Amir, N., Weber, G., Beard, C. *et al.* (2008) The effect of a single-session attention modification program on response to a public-speaking challenge in socially anxious individuals. *Journal of Abnormal Psychology*, **117** (4), 860–868.

Banerjee, R. and Henderson, L. (2001) Social-cognitive factors in childhood social anxiety: a preliminary investigation. *Social Development*, **10** (4), 558–572.

Barrett, P.M., Rapee, R.M., Dadds, M.M. and Ryan, S.M. (1996) Family enhancement of cognitive style in anxious and aggressive children. *Journal of Abnormal Child Psychology*, **24** (2), 187–203.

Beard, C. and Amir, N. (2008) A multi-session interpretation modification program: changes in interpretation and social anxiety symptoms. *Behaviour Research and Therapy*, **46** (10), 1135–1141.

Beck, A.T. and Clark, D.A. (1997) An information processing model of anxiety: automatic and strategic processes. *Behaviour Research and Therapy*, **35** (1), 49–58.

Beck, S.R. and Robinson, E.J. (2001) Children's ability to make tentative interpretations of ambiguous messages. *Journal of Experimental Child Psychology*, **79** (1), 95–114.

Beck, S.R., Robinson, E.J., Carroll, D.J. and Apperly, I.A. (2006) Children's thinking about counterfactuals and future hypotheticals as possibilities. *Child Development*, **77** (2), 413–426.

Carpendale, J.I. and Chandler, M.J. (1996) On the distinction between false belief understanding and subscribing to an interpretive theory of mind. *Child Development*, **67** (4), 1686–1706.

Creswell, C. and O'Connor, T.G. (2006) 'Anxious cognitions' in children: an exploration of associations and mediators. *British Journal of Developmental Psychology*, **24**, 761–766.

Creswell, C., O'Connor, T.G. and Brewin, C.R. (2006) A longitudinal investigation of maternal and child 'anxious cognitions'. *Cognitive Therapy and Research*, **30** (2), 135–147.

Dandeneau, S.D. and Baldwin, M.W. (2004) The inhibition of socially rejecting information among people with high versus low self-esteem: the role of attentional bias and the effects of bias reduction training. *Journal of Social and Clinical Psychology*, **23** (4), 584–602.

Dandeneau, S.D., Baldwin, M.W., Baccus, J.R. *et al.* (2007) Cutting stress off at the pass: reducing vigilance and responsiveness to social threat by manipulating attention. *Journal of Personality and Social Psychology*, **93** (4), 651–666.

Davidson, M.C., Amso, D., Anderson, L.C. and Diamond, A. (2006) Development of cognitive control and executive functions from 4 to 13 years: evidence from manipulations of memory, inhibition, and task switching. *Neuropsychologia*, **44** (11), 2037–2078.

De Houwer, J. (2003) The extrinsic affective Simon task. *Experimental Psychology*, **50** (2), 77–85.

De Houwer, J. (2009) The propositional approach to associative learning as an alternative for association formation models. *Learning & Behavior*, **37**, 1–20.

Deak, G.O., Ray, S.D. and Pick, A.D. (2004) Effects of age, reminders, and task difficulty on young children's rule-switching flexibility. *Cognitive Development*, **19** (3), 385–400.

Dickinson, A. (1980) *Contemporary Animal Learning Theory*, Cambridge University Press, Cambridge, UK.

Dickinson, A. (2001) Causal learning: an associative analysis. *Quarterly Journal of Experimental Psychology Section B – Comparative and Physiological Psychology*, **54** (1), 3–25.

Dickinson, A., Balleine, B., Watt, A. *et al.* (1995) Motivational control after extended instrumental training. *Animal Learning and Behavior*, **23** (2), 197–206.

Eysenck, M.W., Mogg, K., May, J. *et al.* (1991) Bias in interpretation of ambiguous sentences related to threat in anxiety. *Journal of Abnormal Psychology*, **100** (2), 144–150.

Field, A.P. (2006a) The behavioral inhibition system and the verbal information pathway to children's fears. *Journal of Abnormal Psychology*, **115** (4), 742–752.

Field, A.P. (2006b) Is conditioning a useful framework for understanding the development and treatment of phobias? *Clinical Psychology Review*, **26** (7), 857–875.

Field, A.P. (2006c) Watch out for the beast: fear information and attentional bias in children. *Journal of Clinical Child and Adolescent Psychology*, **35** (3), 431–439.

Field, A.P. and Davey, G.C.L. (2001)Conditioning models of childhood anxiety, in *Anxiety Disorders in Children and Adolescents: Research, Assessment and Intervention* (eds W.K. Silverman and P.A. Treffers), Cambridge University Press, Cambridge, pp. 187–211.

Field, A.P. and Lawson, J. (2003) Fear information and the development of fears during childhood: effects on implicit fear responses and behavioural avoidance. *Behaviour Research and Therapy*, **41** (11), 1277–1293.

Field, A.P., Lawson, J. and Banerjee, R. (2008) The verbal information pathway to fear in children: the longitudinal effects on fear cognitions and the immediate effects on avoidance behavior. *Journal of Abnormal Psychology*, **117** (1), 214–224.

Field, A.P. and Schorah, H. (2007) The negative information pathway to fear and heart rate changes in children. *Journal of Child Psychology and Psychiatry*, **48** (11), 1088–1093.

Flavell, J.H., Green, F.L. and Flavell, E.R. (1993) Children's understanding of the stream-of-consciousness. *Child Development*, **64** (2), 387–398.

Flavell, J.H., Green, F.L. and Flavell, E.R. (1995) Young children's knowledge about thinking. *Monographs of the Society for Research in Child Development*, **60** (1), R5–R95.

Gifford, S., Reynolds, S., Bell, S. and Wilson, C. (2008) Threat interpretation bias in anxious children and their mothers. *Cognition and Emotion*, **22** (3), 497–508.

Grey, S. and Mathews, A. (2000) Effects of training on interpretation of emotional ambiguity. *Quarterly Journal of Experimental Psychology Section A – Human Experimental Psychology*, **53** (4), 1143–1162.

Hadwin, J.A., Garner, M. and Perez-Olivas, G. (2006) The development of information processing biases in childhood anxiety: a review and exploration of its origins in parenting. *Clinical Psychology Review*, **26** (7), 876–894.

Hirsch, C.R. and Mathews, A. (1997) Interpretative inferences when reading about emotional events. *Behaviour Research and Therapy*, **35** (12), 1123–1132.

Hirsch, C.R., Mathews, A. and Clark, D.M. (2007) Inducing an interpretation bias changes self-imagery: a preliminary investigation. *Behaviour Research and Therapy*, **45** (9), 2173–2181.

Hoppitt, L., Mathews, A., Yiend, J. and Mackintosh, B. (2009) Cognitive Bias Modification: The critical role of active training in modifying emotional responses. *Behaviour Therapy*, advance online publication.

Jastrow, J. (1900) *Fact and Fable in Psychology*, Houghton-Mifflin, Boston.

Klossek, U.M.H., Russell, J. and Dickinson, A. (2008) The control of instrumental action following outcome devaluation in young children aged between 1 and 4 years. *Journal of Experimental Psychology – General*, **137** (1), 39–51.

Kruschke, J.K. (2001) Toward a unified model of attention in associative learning. *Journal of Mathematical Psychology*, **45**, 812–863.

Le Pelley, M.E. (2004) The role of associative history in models of associative learning: a selective review and a hybrid model. *Quarterly Journal of Experimental Psychology Section B – Comparative and Physiological Psychology*, **57** (3), 193–243.

Lester, K.J., Field, A.P., Oliver, S. and Cartwright-Hatton, S. (2009a) Do anxious parents interpretive biases towards threat extend into their child's environment? *Behaviour Research and Therapy*, **47** (2), 170–174.

Lester, K.J., Seal, K., Nightingale, Z.C. and Field, A.P. (2009b) Are children's own interpretations of ambiguous situations based on how they perceive their mothers have interpreted ambiguous situations for them in the past? *Journal of Anxiety Disorders*. Advanced online publication.

Mackintosh, N.J. (1975) Theory of attention – variations in associability of stimuli with reinforcement. *Psychological Review*, **82** (4), 276–298.

Mackintosh, B., Mathews, A., Yiend, J. *et al.* (2006) Induced biases in emotional interpretation influence stress vulnerability and endure despite changes in context. *Behavior Therapy*, **37** (3), 209–222.

MacLeod, C., Mathews, A. and Tata, P. (1986) Attentional bias in emotional disorders. *Journal of Abnormal Psychology*, **95**, 15–20.

MacLeod, C., Rutherford, E., Campbell, L. *et al.* (2002a) Selective attention and emotional vulnerability: assessing the causal basis of their association through the experimental manipulation of attentional bias. *Journal of Abnormal Psychology*, **111** (1), 107–123.

MacLeod, C., Rutherford, E., Campbell, L. *et al.* (2002b) Selective attention and emotional vulnerability: assessing the causal basis of their association through the experimental manipulation of attentional bias. *Journal of Abnormal Psychology*, **111** (1), 107–123.

Mathews, A. and Mackintosh, B. (2000) Induced emotional interpretation bias and anxiety. *Journal of Abnormal Psychology*, **109** (4), 602–615.

Mathews, A. and MacLeod, C. (2002) Induced processing biases have causal effects on anxiety. *Cognition and Emotion*, **16** (3), 331–354.

Mathews, A., Ridgeway, V., Cook, E. and Yiend, J. (2007a) Inducing a benign interpretational bias reduces trait anxiety. *Journal of Behavior Therapy and Experimental Psychiatry*, **38** (2), 225–236.

Mathews, A., Ridgeway, V., Cook, E. and Yiend, J. (2007b) Inducing a benign interpretational bias reduces trait anxiety. *Journal of Behaviour Therapy and Experimental Psychiatry*, **38** (2), 225–236.

Mitchell, C.J., De Houwer, J. and Lovibond, P.F. (2009) The propositional nature of human associative learning. *Behavioral and Brain Sciences*, **32**, 183–198.

Mogg, K. and Bradley, B.P. (1999) Orienting of attention to threatening facial expressions presented under conditions of restricted awareness. *Cognition and Emotion*, **13** (6), 713–740.

Mogg, K. and Bradley, B.P. (2002) Selective orienting of attention to masked threat faces in social anxiety. *Behaviour Research and Therapy*, **40** (12), 1403–1414.

Muris, P. (2007) *Normal and Abnormal Fear and Anxiety in Children and Adolescents*, Elsevier Science, Oxford.

Muris, P. and Field, A.P. (2008) Distorted cognition and pathological anxiety in children and adolescents. *Cognition and Emotion*, **22** (3), 395–421.

Muris, P., Hoeve, I., Meesters, C. and Mayer, B. (2004) Children's conception and interpretation of anxiety-related physical symptoms. *Journal of Behavior Therapy and Experimental Psychiatry*, **35**, 233–244.

Muris, P., Huijding, J., Mayer, B. and Hameetman, M. (2008) A space odyssey: experimental manipulation of threat perception and anxiety-related interpretation bias in children. *Child Psychiatry and Human Development*, **39** (4), 469–480.

Muris, P., Huijding, J., Mayer, B. *et al.* (2009). Ground control to Major Tom: experimental manipulation of anxiety-related interpretation bias by means of the "space odyssey" paradigm and effects on avoidance tendencies in children. *Journal of Anxiety Disorders*, **23** (3), 333–340.

Muris, P., Mayer, B., Vermeulen, L. and Hiemstra, H. (2007) Theory-of-mind, cognitive development, and children's interpretation of anxiety-related physical symptoms. *Behaviour Research and Therapy*, **45** (9), 2121–2132.

Muris, P., Vermeer, E. and Horselenberg, R. (2008) Cognitive development and the interpretation of anxiety-related physical symptoms in 4- to 12-year-old non-clinical children. *Journal of Behavior Therapy and Experimental Psychiatry*, **39**, 73–86.

Murphy, R., Hirsch, C.R., Mathews, A. *et al.* (2007) Facilitating a benign interpretation bias in a high socially anxious population. *Behaviour Research and Therapy*, **45** (7), 1517–1529.

Murray, L., Cooper, P., Creswell, C. *et al.* (2007) The effects of maternal social phobia on mother–infant interactions and infant social responsiveness. *Journal of Child Psychology and Psychiatry*, **48** (1), 45–52.

Pearce, J.M. and Bouton, M.E. (2001) Theories of associative learning in animals. *Annual Review of Psychology*, **52**, 111–139.

Pearce, J.M. and Hall, G. (1980) A model for Pavlovian learning: variations in the effectiveness of conditioned but not unconditioned stimuli. *Psychological Review*, **87**, 532–552.

Perez-Olivas, G., Stevenson, J. and Hadwin, J.A. (2008) Do anxiety-related attentional biases mediate the link between maternal over involvement and separation anxiety in children? *Cognition and Emotion*, **22** (3), 509–521.

Perner, J. (1991) *Understanding the Representational Mind*, MIT Press, Cambridge, MA.

Rakison, D.H. and Derringer, J.L. (2008) Do infants possess an evolved spider-detection mechanism? *Cognition and Emotion*, **107**, 381–393.

Rescorla, R.A. and Wagner, A.R. (1972)A theory of Pavlovian conditioning: variations in the effectiveness of reinforcement and onreinforcement, in *Classical Conditioning II: Current Research and Theory* (eds A.H. Black and W.F. Prokasy), Appleton-Century-Crofts, New York, pp. 64–99.

Salemink, E., van den Hout, M. and Kindt, M. (2007a) Trained interpretive bias and anxiety. *Behaviour Research and Therapy*, **45** (2), 329–340.

Salemink, E., van den Hout, M. and Kindt, M. (2007b) Trained interpretive bias: validity and effects on anxiety. *Journal of Behavior Therapy and Experimental Psychiatry*, **38** (2), 212–224.

Schmidt, N.B., Richey, J.A., Buckner, J.D. and Timpano, K.R. (2009) Attention training for generalized social anxiety disorder. *Journal of Abnormal Psychology*, **118** (1), 5–14.

See, J., MacLeod, C. and Bridle, R. (2009) The reduction of anxiety vulnerability through the modification of attentional bias: a real-world study using a home-based cognitive bias modification procedure. *Journal of Abnormal Psychology*, **118** (1), 65–75.

Stopa, L. and Clark, D.M. (2000) Social phobia and interpretation of social events. *Behaviour Research and Therapy*, **38** (3), 273–283.

Teachman, B.A. and Addison, L.M. (2008) Training non-threatening interpretations in spider fear. *Cognitive Therapy and Research*, **32** (3), 448–459.

Wainryb, C., Shaw, L.A., Langley, M. *et al.* (2004) Children's thinking about diversity of belief in the early school years: judgments of relativism, tolerance, and disagreeing persons. *Child Development*, **75** (3), 687–703.

Wellman, H.M. and Hickling, A.K. (1993) The mind's "I": children's conception of the mind as an active agent. *Child Development*, **65**, 1564–1580.

Williams, J.M.G., MacLeod, C., Watts, F. and Mathews, A. (1997) *Cognitive Psychology and Emotional Disorders*, 2nd edn, John Wiley & Sons, Chichester.

Wilson, E.J., MacLeod, C., Mathews, A. and Rutherford, E.M. (2006) The causal role of interpretive bias in anxiety reactivity. *Journal of Abnormal Psychology*, **115** (1), 103–111.

Yiend, J., Mackintosh, B. and Mathews, A. (2005) Enduring consequences of experimentally induced biases in interpretation. *Behaviour Research and Therapy*, **43** (6), 779–797.

12

Intergenerational Transmission of Anxious Information Processing Biases

Cathy Creswell, Peter Cooper and Lynne Murray
c.creswell@reading.ac.uk

The question of the process of intergenerational transmission of anxiety has received increasing research attention in recent years. The aim of this chapter is to review the evidence that relates to one aspect of this process, namely, the intergenerational transmission of an anxious information processing style, and to consider the mechanisms by which this may occur. Research in this field is at an early stage and conclusions remain speculative; however, there is a sufficient empirical basis to outline a tentative cognitive-behavioural model of the intergenerational transmission of anxious information processing biases, which we hope will guide research in this area and ultimately inform developments in clinical practice.

The Intergenerational Transmission of Anxiety

There is strong evidence for the familiality of anxiety disorders from studies of mixed generations (e.g. Noyes *et al.*, 1987) and those which examine cross-generational associations (Chapter 16). Thus, 'top-down' studies have consistently revealed that children of adults with an anxiety disorder are more likely to exhibit an anxiety disorder in comparison to children of non-anxious adults (Weissman *et al.*, 1984; Turner, Biedel and Costello, 1987; Biederman *et al.*, 1991; Warner, Mufson and Weissman, 1995). Similarly, 'bottom-up' studies have found that parents of children with anxiety disorders (particularly mothers) have a raised prevalence of anxiety disorders compared to parents of non-anxious children (Last *et al.*, 1987, 1991;

Information Processing Biases and Anxiety: A Developmental Perspective Edited by Julie A. Hadwin and Andy P. Field
© 2010 John Wiley & Sons, Ltd.

Cooper *et al.*, 2006). For example, Cooper *et al.* (2006) reported that mothers of a clinic sample of children with a range of anxiety disorders were almost three times more likely to be diagnosed with a current anxiety disorder compared with mothers of non-anxious control children.

The intergenerational transmission of anxiety disorders is likely to be accounted for by a range of factors including (i) inherited vulnerability, (ii) adverse life events and lifestyle factors, and (iii) learning from others through their behaviour and information transfer (see Murray, Creswell and Cooper, 2009 for a review). While the majority of studies have focused on the intergenerational transmission of anxiety as a general construct (e.g. as a diagnostic category), there are reasons for believing that specific cognitions associated with anxiety may be important in the transmission process. Thus, some theoretical accounts suggest that familial influences on the development of anxiety may operate by influencing children's developing perceptions of threat and coping (e.g., Hadwin, Garner and Perez-Olivas, 2006; Krohne, 1980; Hudson and Rapee, 2004; Murray *et al.*, 2008; Rapee, 2001). This issue is discussed in particular depth by Hudson and Rapee (2004). They suggest that one pathway by which parental anxiety influences the development of generalized anxiety disorder (GAD) in a vulnerable child is by its association with parental behaviours that increase the child's perception of threat and reduce the child's perceived control over threat. For example, parents who engage in over-involved or controlling behaviours in an attempt to protect their child from perceived danger may give a message that the world is a dangerous place that is out of the child's control and from which the child must be protected. Such parents may also provide threat information by modelling an anxious response in an ambiguous situation. Hudson and Rapee suggest that these processes are exaggerated in parents who are highly anxious, and who will, themselves, exhibit a cognitive bias towards threat, and hence be more likely to perceive danger in their child's environment and be more sensitive to their child's distress.

This theory leads to a number of hypotheses regarding the intergenerational transmission of anxious information processing biases. Four of these appear to be of particular importance: (i) parents and children will show similarities in how they process information regarding threat and coping; (ii) parents' information processing style will extend to judgements they make regarding threat to their child and their child's coping potential; (iii) parents' information processing style will be associated with particular parental behaviours and (iv) these parental behaviours, will be associated with how the child processes information regarding threat and coping. This chapter will consider each of these hypotheses in turn.

Do Parents and Children Share a Common Information Processing Style for Threat and Coping Information?

Studies using ambiguous scenarios to assess threat interpretation have reported a positive association between parent and child information processing. For example,

Creswell, Schniering and Rapee (2005) presented 60 clinic and non-clinic Australian children, aged 7–15 years, and their mothers with ambiguous situations (adapted from Barrett *et al.*, 1996) that could be interpreted as either threatening or non-threatening. Children were presented with 12 ambiguous situations (e.g. 'You notice at school one day that a favourite book of yours is missing') and were asked to indicate which of a choice of explanations was most likely (e.g. 'Someone has stolen the book' or 'You left your book at home'). The same procedure was used for adults, with adult-appropriate scenarios (e.g. 'You have organized a dinner party for 7.00 pm and at 7.25 pm, no one is there'. Your first thought would be: 'No one will turn up' or 'They are all running late'). In this study, although self-reported trait anxiety of the mother and child were not significantly correlated, the level of their threat interpretation was significantly associated. The same pattern of results was found by Creswell and O'Connor (2006), reporting on a community sample of 10- to 11-year-old British children and their mothers.

These findings support the notion that threat cognitions may be a proximal index of what is transmitted from parent to child concerning potentially anxiety-provoking situations. There have, however, been some conflicting findings. Gifford *et al.* (2008), for example, studying clinically anxious and non-clinic children aged 7–12 years, failed to find a significant association between threat interpretation of children and their mothers using a homophone task (Chapter 2). They did, however, report intriguing associations between maternal threat interpretation and child anxiety. The authors proposed that there are likely to be a complex set of interactions between information processing and anxiety symptoms within mother–child dyads; for example, children may be exposed to anxiety-enhancing environments within their family, even if their parents do not experience anxiety symptoms. The extent to which differences in the findings outlined above relate to methodological or sample characteristics is unclear. For example, it is possible that associations between parent and child information processing vary at different points in the development. This notion is consistent with the finding that the mediating influence of children's processing bias on the association between parenting and child anxiety was more evident in older than younger children (Perez-Olivas, Stevenson and Hadwin, 2008; see later). If there were a 'sensitive period' for parental influence on children's developing cognitions, it would have clear clinical implications and hence is worthy of further investigation.

To date, studies of information processing in parents and children have been limited to the interpretation of threat information, rather than threat detection or perception (Chapters 4–6). However, it is notable that the presence of anxiety disorders in parents has been found to be associated with these latter cognitive variables in children. Thus, in a comparison of children of parents with post-traumatic stress disorder (PTSD) with children of parents without PTSD, Moradi *et al.* (1999) found information processing differences in response to a Stroop test (Chapter 3) which included trauma-related words. Similarly, Pine *et al.* (2005) reported differences in attentional allocation to emotional faces for children of parents diagnosed with panic disorder or major depressive disorder compared to children of non-clinic adults. Whether these findings are accounted for by shared attentional biases has not been directly tested, but clearly warrants further research.

Does a Parent's Information Processing Style Extend to Expectations about Their Child?

A number of studies have reported that parents of anxious children hold characteristic expectations of their children, which have been attributed to both their own tendency to process information in an anxious manner and their experience of their anxious child. Barrett *et al.* (1996), for example, found that parents of anxious children predicted that their children would interpret ambiguous scenarios as threatening and would choose an avoidant solution. The authors conclude that 'Parents of anxious children seem to expect their children to "see" threat and to respond to difficult situations with avoidance' (Barrett *et al.*, 1996; p. 197), however the role of parental anxiety in contributing to parental expectations over and above child anxiety is unclear. Research concerning this proposition has produced somewhat conflicting results. Kortlander, Kendall and Panichelli-Mindel (1997) found that mothers of anxious children did not report a higher number of threat-related thoughts. Their task (giving a 5 minute videotaped speech), however, involved little ambiguity and both mothers of anxious children and the comparison group reported more negative than positive thoughts. In contrast, mothers of children with anxiety disorders (compared with mothers of non-anxious children) did expect their child to be more distressed, less able to comfort themselves, and less able to perform task-related behaviours. In both of these studies, the parental predictions seemed accurately to reflect children's responses. Nevertheless, where this has been assessed, studies have suggested that the interpretations and expectations of parents in relation to their child's world are also influenced by the parents' own anxiety and information processing style. Cobham, Dadds and Spence (1999), for example, using a naturalistic stressful public speaking task, reported differences in the expectations of high versus low anxious parents, but not high versus low anxious children. Thus, parents who were highly anxious were more likely to predict that their child would be more anxious and more likely to choose an avoidant solution than less anxious parents regardless of actual child anxiety (Cobham, Dadds and Spence, 1999). Parental anxiety also appears to be associated with parental expectations of their potential to alter their child's response. In a community study, parents of 104 children aged 3–5 years completed questionnaires regarding their own anxiety level, their child's anxiety level and expectations about their child's and their own responses to a series of age-appropriate child-relevant ambiguous scenarios. Higher parental anxiety was found to be associated with lower expectations of their own control of their child's behaviour, independently of the association with child anxiety (Wheatcroft and Creswell, 2007).

In order to assess parents' own interpretation biases, authors have asked parents to report on their view of how a typical child would respond to ambiguous scenarios (Bögels, van Dongen and Muris, 2003; Micco and Ehrenreich, 2008). Like Barrett *et al.* (1996), Bögels van Dongen and Muris (2003) found that the negative interpretations that parents attributed to children in general were related to their children's negative interpretations. Micco and Ehrenreich (2008), however, reported that, although mothers of anxious children, compared to mothers of non-anxious children, expected their own child to interpret events in a more threatening way, they made significantly lower threat interpretation than mothers of non-clinic children when asked about a 'typical child'. In other words, assessment of mothers' interpretation biases that were independent of their expectations for their own children, did not correlate with their expectations for their children's. The authors highlighted how their method of assessment may have, however, encouraged mothers to highlight the discrepancy between their own child's atypical threat perception and other children's more typical interpretations.

An alternative approach to that adopted by Micco and Ehrenreich is to assess parental interpretations using adult-relevant ambiguous materials, as described above (Creswell, Schniering and Rapee, 2005; Creswell and O'Connor, 2006; Gifford *et al.*, 2008). Where mothers' own interpretation bias and their expectations about their children's response have been assessed, significant correlations have been found for both interpretation of threat and expectations of distress in response to the ambiguous scenario (Creswell and O'Connor, 2006). In other words, mothers who were themselves more inclined to see danger in the world and feel unable to cope with it, expected their children to respond in a similar way. Furthermore, mothers' expectations of their children's response partially mediated the association between mother and child threat interpretation, accounting for 25% of the association. More recently, Lester *et al.* (2008) used a recognition memory test to assess parents' interpretation bias in relation to threat to themselves and threat to their child. A significant association was found between parental interpretations in relation to themselves and their children. Furthermore, the interpretive biases were modified by parental anxiety (i.e. higher parental anxiety was associated with more negative interpretive biases in their own and their child's environment). The suggestion that parents' expectations are not only informed by their experience of their child but also by their own way of interpreting the world is consistent with findings from other areas of developmental psychopathology. For example, when under stress, parents have been found to make more negatively biased attributions for their child's behaviour, even when their child's behaviour is observed to be no different from that of comparison children (Mash and Johnston, 1983).

In summary, it appears that parents and their children hold similar levels of anxious interpretational biases, at least when it comes to interpreting ambiguity. Future research is required to assess whether a similar pattern exists for parent and child attentional biases. While evidence for the direction of effects is lacking, the evidence is consistent with the view that how parents interpret the world in general is associated with the expectations they hold for their child. These findings raise the possibility that parental expectations may influence the developmental course of children's anxious cognitions. Preliminary support comes from a longitudinal study, following 10–11-year-old children over a 1-year period. Here, it was found that maternal expectations about their children's coping (specifically, how distressed they would be in response to ambiguous scenarios) predicted change in children's anxious cognitions over time, that is, children of mothers who anticipated that their children would be more highly distressed evidenced a greater increase in anxious cognitions over time (Creswell, O'Connor and Brewin, 2006).

Are Parents' Information Processing Styles Associated with Particular Parental Behaviours?

A possible mechanism by which parental expectations may influence children's developing cognitions is proposed by Rubin, Cheah and Fox (2001), who suggested that parental beliefs centred around child vulnerability in a dangerous world may lead to parenting behaviours which strengthen the relationship between child temperament and behaviour. In other words, parents' beliefs, and their consequent behaviour, may determine whether an inhibited child temperament becomes expressed as anxiety. Specifically, lower expectations for child coping have been hypothesized to lead to 'over-solicitous' (Rubin, Cheah and Fox, 2001) or over-involved parenting (Kortlander, Kendall and Panichelli-Mindel, 1997).

The broader field of developmental psychopathology provides numerous examples of how parents' beliefs and expectations influence parenting behaviour. For example, a number of studies have supported a tendency for mothers of children with challenging behaviour (e.g. conduct disorder, attention-deficit and hyperactivity disorder) to make global and stable negative attributions concerning their children's behaviour (e.g. Bugental and Johnston, 2000), and for these blame-oriented attributions to be associated in turn with harsh parental strategies (e.g. Smith and O'Leary, 1995). An interesting study which has successfully shed light on the direction of these effects was conducted by Smith-Slep and O'Leary (1998), who conducted an experimental manipulation in which parents were led to believe that their child either was, or was not, to blame in a challenging situation. Parents who believed that their child was to blame (despite no initial differences in the child's behaviour) were more likely to feel anger and to discipline the child more strongly. Consequently, these children subsequently experienced greater negative affect and behaviours.

Few studies have examined the association between parental cognitions and behaviours in relation to child anxiety, although a recent experimental study has provided evidence for such a link. Creswell, O'Connor and Brewin (2008) allocated parents of 52 children aged 7–11 years to either a 'positive' or 'negative' expectations' group. All parents were informed that their children would be given a set of difficult word puzzles to do. The positive expectation group was told that 'the puzzles we are giving your child are tricky, but we expect s/he will find them fun to do and enjoy the challenge' and the negative expectation group was told 'the puzzles we are giving your child are tricky. We expect s/he might struggle with the task, which may be upsetting for him/her at some point during the task'. Parents and children in both groups were then given the same anagram task to complete and blind coders observed and rated parental behaviour on scales of parental involvement and negativity. The results showed that parents who were given negative expectations displayed increased levels of involvement during the task, suggesting that parental expectations about children's vulnerability are associated with more involved parenting behaviours.

Based on this set of studies, one can speculate that parental cognitions may be a suitable target for interventions which aim to improve child anxiety by changing parental behaviour. The application of this model to other parenting behaviours associated with child anxiety is clearly warranted.

Are Parental Behaviours Associated with How Children Process Information?

The majority of studies to date have examined parenting variables in relation to the general construct of child anxiety, with no attention paid to specific associations with cognitions, behaviour or affect, and so these are only briefly reviewed here (see Murray *et al.* (2008) for a more complete review). The focus is on studies that have addressed the hypothesis that parental behaviours influence the development of children's anxious thoughts and beliefs. In Chapter 11, various learning pathways were suggested that could 'train' children to have information processing biases and it was suggested that parents would be a particularly rich source of these experiences. Parenting variables associated with child anxiety can be categorized as vicarious learning, information transfer, parental involvement (vs. autonomy granting) and negativity (vs. warmth), and these are discussed in turn.

Vicarious learning

Following a series of non-human primate studies which demonstrated that persistent fears may develop after observing others' fearful responses (Mineka *et al.*, 1984; Cook and Mineka, 1987), similar effects have been found in experimental studies with young children (see Askew and Field (2008) for a review). These studies found infants to evidence increased fear and avoidance in relation to potentially fear-provoking objects (Gerull and Rapee, 2002) and social interactions (De Rosnay *et al.*, 2006) following a fearful maternal modelling episode. Recently, Murray *et al.* (2008) have also shown that the extent to which mothers with social phobia or no history of anxiety disorder expressed anxiety in a social interaction when their infants were 10 months of age predicted increased infant stranger avoidance 4 months later. As these studies have been limited to young children, they have focused on behavioural indices of child anxiety. The extent to which behavioural modelling influences cognitive processes is yet to be established.

Information transfer

In a series of studies (e.g. Field *et al.* (2003), Field, Lawson and Banerjee (2008), Field and Lawson (2003) and Lawson, Banerjee and Field (2007) have demonstrated that the information that children are given in relation to threat influences both avoidant behaviours and fear beliefs, measured both directly and indirectly (Chapter 7). Parents may be particularly important sources of information transfer through tuition and spontaneous conversations, including recall of the past and planning for the future (Fivush, 1991; Nelson, 1993; Denham, Zoller and ırd, 1994). A seminal study in relation to child anxiety was conducted by Barrett *et al.* (1996) who reported that, following discussions with their parents, anxious children were increasingly likely to propose avoidant solutions to ambiguous scenarios. The authors labelled this the 'FEAR effect': Family Enhancement of Avoidant Responses. Although this study did not establish whether the parent–child discussions influenced children's *interpretations* of the ambiguous scenarios, the authors suggested that 'the microprocesses of family interaction has the potential to clarify the developmental course of these cognitive vulnerabilities' (Dadds and Barrett, 1996, p. 733). Consistent with this view were the findings of Chorpita, Albano and Barlow (1996) that anxious children made more threat interpretations and more avoidant plans following family discussions.

Furthermore, a recent experimental study offers preliminary evidence that the effects of family discussions generalize to novel scenarios and apply to non-clinical populations (i.e. the discursive style has not arisen purely as a result of parenting an anxious child but may indeed play a role in the development of child anxiety). Murray (2008) administered an ambiguous scenarios questionnaire to 30 non-clinical children aged 7–8 years. She then trained mothers to either mimic the FEAR effect or act in a contrasting manner. For example, the FEAR group were instructed to agree with a threatening interpretation or avoidant plan, show enthusiasm for it and/or respond with a reciprocal interpretation or plan. If their children made an unthreatening interpretation or a non-avoidant plan, they were asked to respond neutrally, giving a minimal response and not providing any reciprocal responses. In contrast, the non-FEAR group were instructed to agree with a non-threat interpretation or active (non-avoidant) plan, show enthusiasm for it and/or respond with a reciprocal interpretation or plan. If the child made a threat interpretation, they were asked to respond neutrally and to ask a prompt question. Following a training period, the children and their mothers discussed two ambiguous scenarios. The children were then assessed on their interpretation of the scenarios that had been discussed as well as a novel set of ambiguous scenarios. While the non-FEAR group exhibited a reduction in threat interpretation to both the discussed scenarios and novel scenarios, the FEAR group maintained their initial level of threat interpretation. In other words, family discussions that reinforced adaptive interpretations led children to adopt and generalize a more adaptive style, whereas discussions that reinforced anxious interpretations maintained this processing style.

Parental involvement

As discussed above, parental over-involvement has been implicated in the development of anxiety. It is hypothesized that such a parenting style, firstly, teaches the child that the world is a dangerous place that the child is not able to control, and from which they must be protected (Hudson and Rapee, 2004); and, secondly, by discouraging independence, it limits the child's sense of competence and mastery (Parker, 1983; Chorpita and Barlow, 1998). Despite differences in definitions of the construct of parental involvement (varying in the extent of protection, control and intrusiveness), Wood *et al.* (2003) in their review of the relevant research literature concluded that there is broadly consistent support for an association between parental over-involvement and child anxiety. McLeod, Wood and Weisz (2007), in a quantitative meta-analysis of parenting predictors of child anxiety, found an overall effect size of 0.25 for control behaviours; however, this was significantly moderated by the source of information, the measure of child anxiety and the subtype of parenting considered, with the effect size rising to 0.42 when the more specific construct of autonomy granting (i.e. the converse of involvement) was considered.

The suggestion that parental involvement may influence child anxiety by cognitive mechanisms is supported by Chorpita, Brown and Barlow (1998), who found in a study of 93 clinic and non-clinic children aged 6–15 years, that children's perceived control mediated the association between a measure of control in the family environment and child negative affect (anxiety and depression). While this study was limited by its reliance on child self-report questionnaires, an observational study by Gordon, Nowicki and Wichern (1981) provides support for an association between parental over-involvement and children's cognitive style. These researchers administered a difficult puzzle task to children who were accompanied by their mothers, and found that offspring of mothers who tended to help more, give more directions and generally interfere more had a more external locus of control.

An association between involved parenting and children's beliefs about competence and mastery has also been supported by a recent experimental study. Using a repeated measures design, Thirlwall (2008) trained mothers to work with their 4- to 5-year-old children, in either a child-led autonomy granting manner or a more involved, directive manner, to prepare them to talk to an experimenter filming them with a video camera. Where mothers were more involved, children predicted that they would be less able to perform well when it came to doing the task. This difference in children's performance beliefs was particularly sensitive to differences in parenting, showing larger effects than either self-ratings or independent observations of anxious affect and behaviour during the task.

As mentioned earlier, the majority of work concerning the role of parenting in the development of information processing biases has focused on the interpretation stage of information processing. A recent study by Perez-Olivas, Stevenson and Hadwin (2008), however, suggests that the association between maternal over-involvement and separation anxiety may be related to an earlier stage of information processing, specifically increased vigilance to threat. In this study, 129 non-referred children (6–14 years) and their mothers participated. Children completed a visual search task to assess attentional bias to angry faces, and a 5-minute speech sample was used with mothers to assess emotional over-involvement. The latter involves asking mothers to speak about their children (with minimal prompting) for 5 minutes, and ratings are then made on the basis of the content and tone of the narratives. The results provided evidence for a cognitively mediated pathway in which maternal over-involvement contributed to the child's vigilance for angry faces, which in turn augmented the degree of separation anxiety in the child. These results are important as they emphasize the potential utility of extending research in this area to explore attentional processing biases for threat in children whose parents show particular parenting styles.

Parental warmth/negativity

Lack of parental warmth has also been considered important for its effect on children's developing cognitive style. Specifically, lack of warmth may lead the child to believe that the environment is hostile and threatening, that she or he will experience negative outcomes and, hence, to a sense of low self-worth and competence (Parker, 1983; Bögels and Tarrier, 2004). However, Wood *et al.* (2003) concluded that the evidence for lack of parental warmth being associated with child anxiety is weak and inconsistent. Indeed, Rapee (1997) suggests that the association between parental lack of warmth and child anxiety may be a function of the relationship between lack of parental warmth and children's low mood, which in many cases will be associated with child anxiety. In fact, there is an extensive literature examining lack of parental warmth, children's negative affect and associated cognitions such as attribution style and perceived self-worth (e.g. Garber and Flynn, 2001; Koestner, Zuroff and Powers, 1991), however, few studies have examined associations between parental warmth and anxious cognitions. Recent exceptions are two studies by Field and colleagues (Field *et al.*, 2007; Price-Evans and Field, 2008) which suggest that negative parenting may interact with other pathways in the development of children's fear beliefs. They reported in a study of 6–10-year-old children that both a punitive maternal style and a greater number of negative father–child interactions interacted with the effect of threat information (Field *et al.*, 2007). Specifically, where children reported negative parental behaviours, they appeared to be increasingly sensitive to what they were told about a novel animal. In the case of negative interactions with fathers, fear beliefs also increased when no information was given about the animals. These effects were not found for children's reported maternal warmth, neglect, monitoring or overprotection. The authors suggest that a negative parenting style may be a particular influence on fear beliefs as it may prime children to expect negative outcomes. These results provide preliminary support for the proposition that negative parenting practices are not, in themselves, mechanisms through which fears are acquired but augment established pathways to fear, such as verbal information, vicarious learning and, in some cases, direct traumatic experiences (Chapter 11).

Summary

The studies reviewed above broadly support a cognitive-behavioural model of the intergenerational transmission of anxious information processing, as illustrated in Figure 12.1. This model is not intended to stand alone as an explanation of the development of cognitive biases or childhood anxiety, as other factors are clearly of importance, including both genetic (Chapter 16) and broader socialization factors (e.g. see Murray *et al.*, 2009). Instead, it is intended to clarify how parental factors may contribute to similarities in the cognitive style of children and parents.

The model suggests that parents' own interpretive biases may influence their behaviour with their child either directly (for example, by modelling an anxious

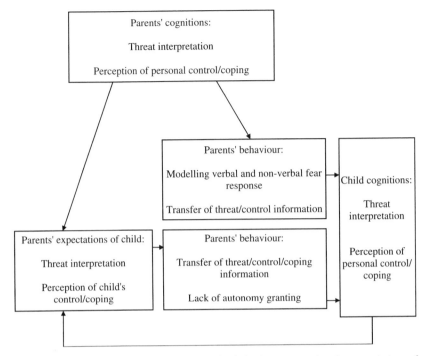

Figure 12.1 A cognitive-behavioural model of the intergenerational transmission of anxious interpretation biases. Based on Murray, Creswell and Cooper (2009).

response, conveying or reinforcing threat information or low perceived control) or indirectly by influencing expectations about how the child is likely to respond (e.g. by conveying expectations about poor coping, or restricting autonomy), and that these behaviours will promote the development and maintenance of child anxious cognitions. A feedback cycle is hypothesized in which parents' expectations will be enhanced by their experience of parenting an anxious child. This latter element is important because parents' expectations are known to be influenced by factors such as child temperament and age (e.g. Teti and Gelfand, 1991). Furthermore, in their longitudinal study, Creswell, O'Connor and Brewin (2006) found that daughter's anxious cognitions predicted change in maternal expectations over time.

Limitations and Implications for Future Research

The current available evidence supports the general hypotheses that (i) parents and children show similarities in how they process information regarding threat and coping; (ii) parents' information processing style extends to judgements they make regarding threat to their children and their children's coping potential;

(iii) parents' information processing style is associated with particular parental behaviours; and (iv) these parental behaviours are associated with how the child processes information regarding threat and coping. Specific associations between types of parental cognitions and expectations and particular behaviours, however, warrant further examination. The model is also, currently, limited to anxious interpretation and ignores earlier stages of processing because of the lack of investigation into intergenerational patterns of attentional processes relating to threat. There is some evidence, however, for similarities in how information is processed at different stages of processing. Richards *et al.* (2007), for example, found that responses to an ambiguous face task was associated with performance on a more implicit attentional Stroop task in late childhood (Chapter 2) . There are also various limitations that run across the research presented which future research should attempt to overcome. In particular is the restriction of many studies to data from mothers only. Studies also tend to include children either from a single narrow age band or from a broad age band, but with insufficient numbers of participants to take developmental factors into account (but see Perez-Olivas, Stevenson and Hadwin, 2008). This is an important limitation because studies of the association between cognitions and symptoms of depression have suggested that, with age, cognitions become more stable and more influential in the development of depression (Nolen-Hoeksema, Girgus and Seligman, 1992).

Conclusions about the direction of effects are also limited by the reliance on cross-sectional studies, although increasingly experimental and longitudinal studies are being reported in the field which are better able to clarify the nature of the relationship between parental and child cognitions and behaviours. In addition, the field has benefited from increasing use of observational assessments of parenting. Nevertheless, cognitive variables are commonly assessed by pen and paper measures that may lack ecological validity and fail to create a context that will activate the expression of maladaptive cognitions. An example of a methodology that overcomes these limitations is the SNAP task (Murray *et al.*, 2001). In this task, 5-year-old children who had been exposed to maternal depression, spontaneously expressed negative cognitions (expressions of hopelessness or low self-worth) only when negative mood was induced by experimentally manipulating winning or losing a card game. The application of similarly ecologically valid assessment procedures is likely to be necessary to elucidate the relationship between parental and child cognition in the context of the development of anxiety disorders.

Implications for Clinical Practice

Cognitive-behavioural interventions for childhood anxiety by definition include, as a key component, measures to modify children's anxious cognitions. The model proposed here suggests that, where parental cognitions and behaviours which reinforce children's anxious cognitions exist, addressing these parental factors will maximize the possibility of bringing about and maintaining change in children's anxious cognitions. The findings of the treatment trial of

Barrett, Rapee and Dadds (1996) are consistent with this suggestion. In their study, children's threatening interpretations of ambiguous scenarios were significantly reduced following cognitive-behaviour therapy (CBT) with a family component, compared to both CBT with no family component and a wait-list condition. Recent research has introduced paradigms which are highly transportable from the laboratory to the clinic, both for assessment (e.g. the use of ambiguous scenarios to assess parental cognitions and expectations; see Barrett *et al.*, 1996) and treatment (e.g. the use of training videos to modify parental behaviour and explicitly track resultant changes in children's responses; e.g. Thirlwall 2008).

Currently, findings are mixed with regard to the clinical benefits of including parents in treatments for child anxiety (Creswell and Cartwright-Hatton, 2007). A clearer understanding of the cognitive and behavioural processes that promote the development and maintenance of children's anxious cognitions offers the potential to improve family treatments for childhood anxiety and to identify who would be most likely to benefit from this form of treatment.

References

Askew, C. and Field, A.P. (2008) The vicarious learning pathway to fear 40 years on. *Clinical Psychology Review*, **28**, 1249–1265.

Barrett, P.M., Rapee, R.M. and Dadds, M.R. (1996) Family treatment of childhood anxiety: a controlled trial. *Journal of Consulting and Clinical Psychology*, **64**, 333–342.

Barrett, P.M., Rapee, R.M., Dadds, M.M. and Ryan, S.M. (1996) Family enhancement of cognitive style in anxious and aggressive children. *Journal of Abnormal Child Psychology*, **24**, 187–203.

Biederman, J., Rosenbaum, J.F., Bolduc, E.A. *et al.* (1991) A high risk study of young children of parents with panic disorder and agoraphobia with and without comorbid major depression. *Psychiatry Research*, **37**, 333–348.

Bögels, S.M. and Tarrier, N. (2004) Unexplored issues and future directions in social phobia research. *Clinical Psychology Review*, **24**, 731–736.

Bögels, S.M., van Dongen, L. and Muris, P. (2003) Family influences on dysfunctional thinking in anxious children. *Infant and Child Development*, **12**, 243–252.

Bugental, D.B. and Johnston, C. (2000) Parental and child cognitions in the context of the family. *Annual Review of Psychology*, **51**, 315–344.

Chorpita, B.F., Albano, A.M. and Barlow, D.H. (1996) Cognitive processing in children: relationship to anxiety and family influences. *Journal of Clinical Child Psychology*, **25**, 170–176.

Chorpita, B.F. and Barlow, D.H. (1998) The development of anxiety: the role of control in the early environment. *Psychological Bulletin*, **124**, 3–21.

Chorpita, B.F., Brown, T.A. and Barlow, D.H. (1998) Perceived control as a mediator of family environment in etiological models of childhood anxiety. *Behavior Therapy*, **29**, 457–476.

Cobham, V.E., Dadds, M.M. and Spence, S.H. (1999) Anxious children and their parents: what do they expect? *Journal of Clinical Child Psychology*, **28**, 220–231.

Cook, M. and Mineka, S. (1987) Second-order conditioning and overshadowing in the observational conditioning of fear in monkeys. *Behavior Research and Therapy*, **25**, 349–364.

Cooper, P.J., Fearn, V., Willetts, L. *et al.* (2006) Affective disorder in the parents of a clinic sample of children with anxiety disorders. *Journal of Affective Disorder*, **93**, 205–212.

Creswell, C. and Cartwright-Hatton, S. (2007) Family treatment of child anxiety: outcomes, limitations and future directions. *Child and Family Clinical Psychology Review*, **10**, 232–252.

Creswell, C. and O'Connor, T. (2006) 'Anxious cognitions' in children: an exploration of associations and mediators. *British Journal of Developmental Psychology*, **24** (4), 761–766.

Creswell, C., O'Connor, T. and Brewin, C. (2006) A longitudinal investigation of maternal and child 'Anxious Cognitions'. *Cognitive Therapy and Research*, **30**, 135–147.

Creswell, C., O'Connor, T. and Brewin, C. (2008) The impact of parents' expectations on parenting behaviour: an experimental investigation. *Behavioural and Cognitive Psychotherapy*, **36**, 483–490.

Creswell, C., Schniering, C. and Rapee, R. (2005) Threat interpretation in anxious children and their mothers: group and treatment effects. *Behavior Research and Therapy*, **43**, 1375–1381.

Dadds, M.R. and Barrett, P.M. (1996) Family processes in child and adolescent anxiety and depression. *Behavior Change*, **13**, 231–239.

De Rosnay, M., Cooper, P.J., Tsigaras, N. and Murray, L. (2006) Transmission of social anxiety from mother to infant: an experimental study using a social referencing paradigm. *Behavior Research and Therapy*, **44**, 1165–1175

Denham, S., Zoller, D. and Couchard, E. (1994) Socialisation of pre-schoolers emotion understanding. *Developmental Psychology*, **30**, 928–936.

Field, A.P., Ball, J.E., Kawycz, N.J. and Moore, H. (2007) Parent-child relationships and the verbal information pathway to fear in children: two preliminary experiments. *Behavioural and Cognitive Psychotherapy*, **35**, 473–486.

Field, A.P., Hamilton, S.J., Knowles, K.A. and Plews, E.L. (2003) Fear information and social phobic beliefs in children: a prospective paradigm and preliminary results. *Behaviour Research and Therapy*, **41**, 113–123.

Field, A.P. and Lawson, J. (2003) Fear information and the development of fears during childhood: effects on implicit fear responses and behavioural avoidance. *Behaviour Research and Therapy*, **41**, 1277–1293.

Field, A.P., Lawson, J. and Banerjee, R. (2008) The verbal threat information pathway to fear in children: the longitudinal effects on fear cognitions and the immediate effects on avoidance behavior. *Journal of Abnormal Psychology*, **117** (1), 214–224.

Fivush, R. (1991) The social construction of personal narratives. *Merrill Palmer Quarterly*, **37**, 59–82.

Garber, J. and Flynn, C. (2001) Predictors of depressive cognitions in young adolescents. *Cognitive Therapy and Research*, **25**, 353–376

Gerull, F.C. and Rapee, R.M. (2002) Mother knows best: effects of maternal modelling on the acquisition of fear and avoidance behavior in toddlers. *Behavior Research and Therapy*, **40**, 279–287.

Gifford, S., Reynolds, S., Bell, S. and Wilson, C. (2008) Threat interpretation bias in anxious children and their mothers. *Cognition and Emotion*, **22**, 497–508.

Gordon, D., Nowicki, S. and Wichern, F. (1981) Observed maternal behaviors in a dependency producing task as a function of children's locus of control orientation. *Merrill-Palmer Quarterly*, **27**, 43–51.

Hadwin, J.A., Garner, M. and Perez-Olivas, G. (2006) The development of information processing biases in childhood anxiety: a review and exploration of its origin in parenting. *Clinical Psychology Review*, **26**, 876–894.

Hudson, J.L. and Rapee, R.M. (2004) From anxious temperament to disorder: an etiological model of generalized anxiety disorder, in *Generalized Anxiety Disorder: Advances in Research and Practice* (eds R.G. Heimberg, C.L. Turk and D.S. Mennin), Guilford Press, New York, pp. 51–74.

Koestner, R., Zuroff, D.C. and Powers, T.A. (1991) Family origins of adolescent self-criticism and its continuity into adulthood. *Journal of Abnormal Psychology*, **100**, 191–197.

Kortlander, E., Kendall, P.C. and Panichelli-Mindel, S.M. (1997) Maternal expectations and attributions about coping in anxious children. *Journal of Anxiety Disorders*, **11**, 297–315.

Krohne, H.W. (1980) Parental child rearing behaviour and the development of anxiety and coping strategies in children, in *Stress and Anxiety* (eds I.G. Sarason and C.D. Spielberger), Hemisphere Publishing Corporation, Washington, DC, pp. 233–245.

Last, C.G., Hersen, M., Kazdin, A.E. *et al.* (1987) Psychiatric illness in the mothers of anxious children. *American Journal of Psychiatry*, **144**, 1580–1583.

Last, C.G., Hersen, M., Kazdin, A.E. *et al.* (1991) Anxiety disorders in children and their families. *Archives of General Psychiatry*, **48**, 928–939.

Lawson, J., Banerjee, R. and Field, A.P. (2007) The effects of verbal information on children's fear beliefs about social situations. *Behaviour Research and Therapy*, **45**, 21–37.

Lester, K.J., Field, A.P., Oliver, S. and Cartwright-Hatton, S. (2008) Do anxious parents interpretive biases towards threat extend into their child's environment? *Behaviour Research and Therapy*, **47** (2), 170–174.

Mash, E.J. and Johnston, C. (1983) Parental perceptions of child behavior problems, parenting self-esteem, and mothers' reported stress in younger and older hyperactive and normal children. *Journal of Consulting and Clinical Psychology*, **51**, 86–99.

McLeod, B.D., Wood, J.J. and Weisz, J.R. (2007) Examining the association between parenting and childhood anxiety: a meta-analysis. *Clinical Psychology Review*, **27**, 155–172.

Micco, J.A. and Ehrenreich, J.T. (2008) Children's interpretation and avoidant response biases in response to non-salient and salient situations: relationships with mothers' threat perception and coping expectations. *Journal of Anxiety Disorders*, **22**, 371–385.

Mineka, S., Davidson, M., Cook, M. and Kein, R. (1984) Observational conditioning of snake fear in rhesus monkeys. *Journal of Abnormal Psychology*, **93**, 355–372.

Moradi, A., Neshat-Doost, H.T., Taghavi, R. *et al.* (1999) Performance of children of adults with PTSD on the Stroop color-naming task: a preliminary study. *Journal of Traumatic Stress*, **12**, 663–671.

Murray, L., Creswell, C. and Cooper, P.J. (2009) The development of anxiety disorders in childhood: an integrative review. *Psychological Medicine*, **39**, 1413–1423.

Murray, L., DeRosnay, M., Pearson, J. *et al.* (2008) Intergenerational transmission of maternal social anxiety: the role of the social referencing process. *Child Development*, **79** (4), 1049–1064.

Murray, H. (2008) An experimental investigation of the FEAR effect in non-clinical children and their mothers. Doctoral thesis, University College London, London, UK.

Murray, L., Woolgar, M., Cooper, P. and Hipwell, A. (2001) Cognitive vulnerability to depression in 5 year old children of depressed mothers. *Journal of Child Psychology and Psychiatry*, **42**, 891–899.

Nelson, K. (1993) The psychological and social origins of autobiographic memory. *Psychological Science*, **4**, 1–8.

Nolen-Hoeksema, S., Girgus, J.S. and Seligman, M.E.P. (1992) Predictors and consequences of childhood depressive symptoms: a 5-year longitudinal study. *Journal of Abnormal Psychology*, **101**, 405–422.

Noyes, R., Clarkson, C., Crowe, R.R. *et al.* (1987) A family study of generalized anxiety disorder. *American Journal of Psychiatry*, **144**, 1019–1024.

Parker, G. (1983) *Parental Overprotection: A Risk Factor in Psychosocial Development*, Grune and Stratton, New York.

Perez-Olivas, G., Stevenson, J. and Hadwin, J. (2008) Do anxiety-related attentional biases mediate the link between maternal over involvement and separation anxiety in children? *Cognition and Emotion*, **22**, 509–521.

Pine, D.S., Klein, R.G., Mannuzza, S. *et al.* (2005) Face-emotion processing in offspring at risk for panic disorder. *Journal of the American Academy of Child and Adolescent Psychiatry*, **44**, 664–672.

Price-Evans, K. and Field, A.P. (2008) A neglectful parenting style moderates the effect of the verbal threat information pathway on children's heart rate responses to novel animals. *Behavioural and Cognitive Psychotherapy*, **36**, 473–482.

Rapee, R.M. (1997) Potential role of childrearing practices in the development of anxiety and depression. *Clinical Psychology Review*, **17**, 47–67.

Rapee, R.M. (2001) The development of generalized anxiety disorder, in *The Developmental Psychopathology of Anxiety* (eds M.W. Vasey and M.R. Dadds), Oxford University Press, New York, pp. 481–504.

Richards, A., French, C.C., Nash, G. *et al.* (2007) A comparison of selective attention and facial processing biases in typically developing children who are high and low in self-reported trait anxiety. *Development and Psychopathology*, **19**, 481–495.

Rubin, K.H., Cheah, C.S.L. and Fox, N. (2001) Emotion regulation, parenting and display of social reticence in preschoolers. *Early Education and Development*, **12** (1), 97–115.

Smith, A.M. and O'Leary, S.G. (1995) Attributions and arousal as predictors of maternal discipline. *Cognitive Therapy and Research*, **19**, 345–357.

Smith-Slep, A.M. and O'Leary, S.G. (1998) The effects of maternal attributions on parenting: an experimental analysis. *Journal of Family Psychology*, **12**, 234–243.

Teti, D.M. and Gelfand, D.M. (1991) Behavioural competence among mothers of infants in the first year: the mediational role of maternal self-efficacy. *Child Development*, **62**, 918–929.

Thirlwall, K. (2008) The impact of maternal control on children's anxious cognitions, behaviour and affect: an experimental study. Doctoral thesis, University of Oxford, Oxford, UK.

Turner, S.M., Biedel, D.C. and Costello, A. (1987) Psychopathology in the offspring of anxiety disordered patients. *Journal of Consulting and Clinical Psychology*, **55**, 229–235.

Warner, V., Mufson, L. and Weissman, M.M. (1995) Offspring at low and high risk for depression and anxiety: mechanisms of psychiatric disorder. *Journal of the Academy of Child and Adolescent Psychiatry*, **34**, 786–797.

Weissman, M.M., Leckman, J.F., Merikangas, K.R. *et al.* (1984) Depression and anxiety disorders in parents and children. *Archives of General Psychiatry*, **41**, 845–852.

Wheatcroft, R. and Creswell, C. (2007) Parental cognitions and expectations of their preschool children: the contribution of parental anxiety and child anxiety. *British Journal of Developmental Psychology*, **25**, 435–441.

Wood, J.J., McLeod, B.D., Sigman, M. *et al.* (2003) Parenting and childhood anxiety: theory, empirical findings, and future directions. *Journal of Child Psychology and Psychiatry*, **44**, 134–151.

13

Attentional Biases in Children: Implications for Treatment

Maria J.W. Cowart and Thomas H. Ollendick

mjw@vt.edu

A large body of evidence has established a relationship between anxiety and informational biases, more broadly, and attentional biases to threat, more specifically, in both adults and children. However, the direction of causality is not always clear. The anxiety vulnerability hypothesis proposed some years ago by MacLeod and Rutherford (1992) argued that these biases serve as a diathesis predisposing individuals to anxiety. Recent research, primarily with adults, has provided strong support for this hypothesis (Bar-Haim *et al.*, 2007).

These findings have inspired interest in designing treatment paradigms that directly address anxiety-related biases. Cognitive-behavioural treatment (CBT) has been shown to be effective in 50–90% of adults (Barlow, 2001) and 60–70% of children (Kendall *et al.*, 2005; Ollendick, King and Chorpita, 2006) with anxiety disorders. Although CBT addresses some cognitive features of anxiety such as overestimation of danger, it does not typically address directly the attentional biases to threat associated with these disorders. Some researchers have suggested that the failure of CBT to directly address these biases may be responsible for treatment failures associated with this approach (Lavy, van den Hout and Arntz, 1993; Watts *et al.*, 1986; Ollendick, King and Chorpita, 2006). In an attempt to address this treatment need, researchers have begun to develop approaches based on attention retraining techniques (ATT). Thus far, these treatments have been applied largely to adults, with some researchers beginning to extend these treatments to children. These protocols involve the modification of current experimental paradigms used to identify information processing biases (e.g. emotional Stroop, dot-probe tasks). In brief, ATT trains anxious individuals to attend to neutral stimuli rather than the threatening stimuli that would generally draw their attention in the natural environment. The treatment requires less time and resources than

Information Processing Biases and Anxiety: A Developmental Perspective Edited by Julie A. Hadwin and Andy P. Field
© 2010 John Wiley & Sons, Ltd.

traditional treatments, and it seems to be as effective in addressing attentional biases and anxiety as more traditional procedures. In fact, early research with adults suggests that direct treatment of attentional biases alone using ATT mitigates not only attentional biases, but also associated anxious symptoms (Papageorgiou and Wells, 1998).

The present chapter will explore the suitability of ATT in treating anxious children. Given that attentional biases have been shown to serve as a diathesis for anxiety in adults, it is reasonable to assume that such biases are also important to the development of anxiety in children, and that children could benefit from treatments such as ATT as well. Because ATT requires individuals to learn to shift their attention from negative to neutral stimuli, the development of attentional shifting mechanisms will be described in some detail. As such, an examination of the developmental literature regarding effortful control will be highlighted as one explanatory mechanism that underlies the possible success of ATT. Other factors that might uniquely influence the ability of children to participate in attention retraining will also be considered. Finally, implications of ATT for both adults and children will be considered, and recommendations will be made for use of ATT in the treatment of anxiety disorders in child and adolescent populations.

Current Treatments and Attention

If information and attentional biases to threat serve a causal function in the development and maintenance of anxiety disorders, then treatments should directly address these biases. As noted, the treatment of choice for anxiety disorders in children is CBT. One of the primary goals of CBT is to reduce or eliminate anxiety-related cognitive biases. Often, this goal is accomplished through cognitive restructuring, as well as the challenging of those cognitions with competing evidence and the facilitation of more accurate cognitions (cf. Barlow, 2001; Prins and Ollendick, 2003; Woody and Ollendick, 2006). Although these strategies aid in the treatment of anxiety, Papageorgiou and Wells (1998) argued they are not sufficient to address the attentional biases that are a distinctive feature of these disorders.

Results regarding the mitigation of attentional biases using CBT with adults have been mixed. In one of the earliest studies of treatment effects on attentional biases, Foa and McNally (1986) successfully treated individuals with obsessive-compulsive disorder using imaginal flooding and in vivo exposure with response prevention. At the end of treatment, participants were tested using a dichotic listening task. The participants no longer evidenced attentional biases towards threat stimuli after undergoing the exposure-based treatments.

In another early study, Watts and colleagues (1986) treated spider-phobic adults with four sessions of 'desensitization in vivo' in small groups over 6–8 weeks. Treatment included an emphasis on handling spiders as much as possible and allowing the least phobic group members to serve as models for the more highly phobic individuals. Although participants evidenced an elimination of attentional bias towards spiders, a behavioural approach test did not show significant improvement in approach to spiders. This finding suggests that the attentional bias and behavioural avoidance may be independent of one another. Thus, counter to expectations, observed changes in attentional bias were not associated with changes in avoidance behaviour.

In another early study with spider-phobic adults, Lavy, van den Hout and Arntz (1993) examined attentional bias reduction following treatment. They employed one-session treatment (OST) as designed by Öst (1989). Following OST, which included both behavioural and cognitive components, attentional biases were reduced but not eliminated, suggesting that some attentional biases remained following treatment. Moreover, the relations between attentional bias and behavioural avoidance were not evident – some patients changed on both measures but others on only one or the other measure.

More recently, Mathews and colleagues (Mathews *et al.*, 1990, 1995) reported two studies with adults having generalized anxiety disorder (GAD). In the first study, they showed that vigilance effects remained among recovered patients with GAD who had received anxiety management training. In the second study, however, it was demonstrated that GAD patients, following 7 weeks of treatment, were not distinguishable from non-clinical controls on an attentional bias task.

With regard to children, Waters *et al.* (2008) recently examined the effect of CBT on a sample of anxious children. Following 10 sessions of group CBT, as well as 6 parent sessions and a booster session, results regarding attentional biases were mixed. Although the children evidenced elimination of abnormal attentional biases on a stories task, they continued to demonstrate an attentional bias towards threat on a dot-probe task. Thus, further research is needed to examine the effectiveness of CBT in reducing attentional biases in children and adolescents and, in particular, in determining which types of biases might be affected.

In short, while these findings suggest that behavioural and cognitive treatments can be effective at reducing and potentially eliminating attentional biases in adults and children, there is need for caution. These mixed results leave room for new treatment strategies to either supplement or replace CBT in the treatment of information processing biases. It seems clear that these biases are important to the development and maintenance of anxiety disorders. Thus, at least hypothetically, elimination of these biases should be quite powerful in the treatment of these disorders.

Attention Retraining with Adults

Given the role of attentional biases in anxiety disorders (Mathews and MacLeod, 2002), new treatment strategies that specifically target these biases in anxious populations are in process (see Mohlman, 2004, for a review). ATT utilizes modified versions of experimental tasks, most commonly dot-probe tasks, in attempts to manipulate attentional biases to directly decrease anxiety, in the absence of traditional psychotherapeutic treatment modalities.

Although methodological differences exist across studies (e.g. number of training sessions, length of sessions), some basic strategies are evident across the various ATT protocols (Mohlman, 2004). Typically, sessions are brief (e.g. 15–30 minutes) and involve experimental tasks designed with neutral stimuli as targets, and anxiety-related stimuli as distracters. This approach is the opposite of some experimental measurement paradigms, which include anxiety-related stimuli as targets with neutral distracters (e.g. dot probe). The goal of training is to learn to disengage attention from anxiety-related stimuli in the environment in favour of attention to neutral stimuli.

ATT is based on the Self-Regulatory Executive Function (S-REF) model of psychopathology developed by Wells and Mathews (1996). The S-REF model, in turn, is based on three interacting levels of cognition, including automatic and reflexive units, attentionally demanding controlled processing, and stored meta-knowledge including beliefs about the self. According to Wells and Mathews (1996), emotional disorders are the result of increased self-focused attention, decreased cognitive efficiency, attentional bias, and activation of appraisal and self-beliefs. Thus, resources for processing competing positive and corrective information in the environment are reduced. In addition, individuals experiencing psychopathology may be unaware that their cognitive abilities, including attentional biases, are within voluntary control.

On the basis of the S-REF model, Wells (2000) developed attention retraining to address the proposed deficits. Early studies did not include modified experimental tasks but involved therapist-led training in attentional skills. One of the first studies of ATT attempted to train the redirection of attention from internal physiological cues to the external environment in a single patient with panic disorder and relaxation difficulties (Wells, 1990). An ABCB design was implemented, with autogenic relaxation as the comparator treatment. ATT consisted of 15-minute treatment sessions, once per week for 7 weeks, along with 15 minutes of home practice daily. Treatment began with training the patient to focus on external sounds, using auditory cues from the therapist. For example, the patient was first directed to focus on sounds in the room, then outside the room, then outside the building. Following that, the patient was directed in attention-shifting exercises. Finally, training in divided attention was employed. After this phase of treatment, the patient received five sessions of autogenic relaxation training, which were designed to increase attention to bodily cues. This, of course, is in direct contrast to ATT which trained the client to direct attention away from internal sensations in favour of external sounds. After 5 weeks of autogenic training, Wells (1990) reported that the patient requested discontinuation due to discomfort. At that time, ATT was reintroduced for another 6 weeks. Results indicated that panic attacks and neck tension were absent during ATT treatment periods and increased during relaxation training periods. At 3- and 12-month follow-up, panic attacks continued to be absent, suggesting that ATT was effective in treating this particular case of panic disorder, over an extended period of time.

Wells, White and Carter (1997) applied ATT to three patients with anxiety disorders, two with panic disorder and one with social phobia. ATT intervention in each case lasted for 2 weeks, with sessions of 30–40 minutes duration. Ten minutes of each session were devoted specifically to ATT. As in the first study, the patients were trained in selective attention and attention switching. Training utilized sounds such as those found in the consulting room as targets, rather than anxious thoughts identified by the individual patients (e.g. 'I'm losing control'). Attentional practice at home was also recommended for 10–15 minutes per day. Results indicated reductions in panic attacks, general anxiety levels, and maladaptive beliefs for all participants. Treatment effects were maintained at 3- and 6-months follow-up.

Similarly, Papageorgiou and Wells (1998) applied ATT to three cases of hypochondriasis. In this study, a 13-week treatment was utilized. Sessions were approximately 30-minutes long, with approximately 15-minutes of ATT practice. ATT training methods were similar to those used in the 1997 study (Wells, White and Carter, 1997). As in that study, patients were also encouraged to practice for 10–15 minutes per day at home. All participants displayed improvement in self-rated affect, and illness-related behaviour and cognition. These effects were maintained at 6-month follow-up.

Interestingly, Papageorgiou and Wells (2000) have also applied their ATT paradigm to treating adults with major depressive disorder. In this multiple baseline study, four patients were provided eight sessions of ATT using identical procedures to those used in their previous studies with anxious adults. As part of their ATT training, the patients were encouraged to engage in at-home practice sessions. Patients in this trial displayed improvement in depression, self-focused attention and maladaptive cognitions. While this study was designed to address depression, it is interesting to note that treated participants displayed reductions in anxiety as well as other symptoms. As in the other studies, improvements were maintained over time, at 3-, 6- and 12-month follow-ups. Overall, these uncontrolled single-case studies provide suggestive clinical support for ATT training.

Clinicians and researchers have also used ATT in a computer-based format, employing modified versions of experimental paradigms such as dot-probe and Stroop tasks. As in the earlier experimental studies, these tasks are designed to train the participants to attend to neutral rather than threat cues. For example, Hazen and colleagues designed Attentional Retraining for Threat Stimuli (ARTS) for use with pathological adult worriers (R. Hazen, M.W. Vasey and N.B. Schmidt, (1996) unpublished manuscript available from authors). In an initial study, adults reporting high levels of worry were treated with five 30-minute sessions of ARTS, with an average 6-day interval between sessions. ARTS consisted of a modified dot-probe paradigm, in which probes followed neutral rather than threat words on 94.4% of the trials. A control group received a placebo procedure (Sham-ARTS), which was identical to the ARTS procedure, except that probes followed neutral and threat words with equal frequency. At 1-week post-treatment, participants in the ARTS condition showed reduced attentional biases, as well as reductions in both anxiety and depression. Those in the placebo condition did not evidence such improvements. While no long-term follow-up was reported, the fact that symptom reductions persisted for even 1 week suggests that the effects of attentional retraining on symptoms endured beyond the immediate treatment. In fact, Amir (2006) reports successful replication of the work of Hazen and colleagues with GAD patients. Similarly, Mohlman (2004) described a study by Rutherford, MacLeod and Campbell (2002) which applied ATT to a sample of high trait anxious individuals. ATT again consisted of a modified dot-probe task, with probes following neutral rather than threat cues in 100% of trials. ATT was administered in 8–10 sessions over the course of 3 weeks. Treated participants displayed subliminal and supraliminal benefits and a reduction in trait anxiety as compared to a control group completing a placebo task.

In an attempt to extend attention retraining to other anxious populations, Amir (2006) has presented evidence that an attention retraining paradigm, termed the Attention Disengagement Task (ADT), shows promise for the treatment of social phobia. In an initial study, socially phobic individuals received one session of either active ADT or a placebo condition. Active ADT was similar to ARTS. It comprised a modified dot-probe paradigm in which the probes followed neutral facial stimuli on 80% of trials. In the placebo condition, probes followed neutral and threatening facial stimuli with equal probability. Following treatment, participants were asked to complete a speech task. Individuals who had received ADT reported significantly less anxiety during the speech task than those in the placebo condition. In addition, those who had received ADT exhibited reductions in attentional bias on a Posner task. In a replication study, Amir (2006) reported similar results.

Amir (2006) reported a third study to test the efficacy of more long-term ADT treatment in individuals with social phobia. In this study, patients received ADT or placebo sessions twice per week for 4 weeks for a total of eight sessions. The methodology was similar to that used in the previous trials. Participants who received ADT showed greater reductions in social anxiety, both fear and avoidance, than those in the placebo group. Further, Amir was able to demonstrate that ADT produced greater reductions in social anxiety than did the gold-standard CBT treatment for social anxiety (Heimberg, Liebowitz and Hope, 1998).

Richey and Schmidt (2006) have also utilized attention retraining in adults with social phobia. Their attention training paradigm included eight twice-weekly attention retraining sessions, with each session lasting approximately 12 minutes. As in other studies, a modified dot-probe task was used with probes replacing neutral facial stimuli in 90% of trials. In a placebo condition, participants also completed a modified dot-probe task, but probes followed neutral or threatening facial stimuli with equal frequency. Those individuals with social phobia who received ATT evidenced significant decreases on a number of measures of anxiety and depression, compared to those in the placebo group. In addition, 75% of those adults who received treatment no longer met diagnostic criteria for social anxiety disorder, compared to only 25% of those in the placebo group who displayed remittance of symptoms.

MacLeod and Bridle (2006) also report an ongoing programme of research implementing ATT in a home-based, internet-delivered programme. Like other studies, this ATT programme consists of a modified dot-probe paradigm. In the training phase, probes appear only in the location of the neutral probe. Meanwhile, in the control and assessment paradigms, probes are presented equally often after neutral or threatening stimuli. The programme requires 15 daily treatment sessions, with each session lasting approximately 10 minutes. In an initial study, participants were a non-referred group of Singaporean high school students about to undergo a stressful life event (moving to Australia to begin university studies). While attentional bias towards threat increased in control participants as the stressful event approached, the opposite pattern was observed for those in the treatment group. That is, over the course of treatment, these participants developed an attentional avoidance of threatening stimuli. In addition, these participants evidenced significant declines in both state and trait anxiety.

Like others, MacLeod and Bridle (2006) went on to test their ATT paradigm with a sample of socially anxious individuals. Before treatment, patients in both the treatment and control groups displayed an attentional bias towards threat. Those in the control group continued to display such a bias throughout the study. However, those who received the ATT treatment displayed a reversal of their initial bias, such that they displayed an attentional bias away from threat and towards neutral stimuli. In addition, treated subjects displayed 35–40% reductions in scores on several measures of social anxiety.

In summary, ATT has been applied to a number of adults with high trait anxiety and with either social or generalized anxiety disorders. The method has demonstrated success in alleviating both attentional biases and anxiety in these populations.

Attention Retraining in Children and Adolescents

Attentional biases in children

As in anxious adults, a considerable amount of research has shown that anxious children display an attentional bias towards threat (see reviews by Puliafico and Kendall (2006); Vasey and MacLeod (2001)). Studies of attentional bias in children, like those with adults, typically employ modified Stroop and dot-probe paradigms (Chapters 3 and 4). For example, the first study to employ a modified Stroop task with children used a card format to assess attentional bias in spider-fearful children ranging in age from 6 to 13 years (Martin, Horder and Jones, 1992). The spider-fearful children displayed the expected Stroop interference, with delayed colour-naming of spider-related words as compared to non-fearful children. Similar results were found in the first dot-probe study with children (Vasey et al., 1995). When clinically anxious children were compared with non-anxious children, anxious children displayed evidence of attentional bias towards threat-related words. Similar results have been found among anxious children in other studies as well (e.g., Vasey, El-Hag and Daleiden, 1996).

However, information processing research with children is not as straightforward as similar research with adults, and findings have been more mixed (see Muris and Field, 2008 for a recent review). Indeed, some researchers have failed to find attentional biases to threat among children (e.g, Kindt, Bierman and Brosschot, 1997; Kindt, Brosschot and Everaerd, 1997). When appropriate methodological and developmental concerns are considered, however, attentional biases seem to emerge as an important factor in childhood anxiety, as they do in adult anxiety. Given the success of attention retraining in attenuating such biases and accompanying anxiety in adult samples, it is reasonable to assume such treatment could be beneficial for anxious children. It is difficult, however, to simply import adult treatments directly to child populations (Ollendick and Vasey, 2001; Ollendick and Cerny, 1981). In the following section, developmental considerations for the possible implementation of ATT in children are examined.

Effortful control

The most relevant developmental process to consider with regard to the use of attentional bias paradigms with children is effortful control. At its core, effortful control involves executive functioning processes supporting the engagement and allocation of attention (Lonigan *et al.*, 2004). It is defined as the 'ability to inhibit a dominant response to perform a subdominant response' (Rothbart and Bates, 1998, p. 137). Effortful control is thought to have two dimensions, including self-regulation of attention (attentional control) and the ability to regulate and inhibit behaviour when necessary to do so (inhibitory control; Rothbart, Ellis and Posner, 2004). Therefore, effortful control is closely related to behaviour and especially, to emotional regulation (see Muris and Ollendick, 2005). Indeed, a lack of effortful control is associated with the development of diverse emotional problems in children and adolescents (Lonigan *et al.*, 2004; Muris and Ollendick, 2005).

Effortful control is generally considered to be an aspect of temperament (Poggi Davis, Bruce and Gunnar, 2002). Relative stability in effortful control has been demonstrated from toddlerhood through preschool and into school age (Kochanska and Knaack, 2003; Kochanska, Murray and Coy, 1997). Given the importance of this temperament-like feature to attention and behaviour, it may also need to be considered in attentional research and treatment.

Development of effortful control

Attention is generally conceptualized as coming under increasing voluntary control with development (Ruff and Rothbart, 1996). The behavioural development of attention is accompanied by the neurological development of three separate systems. First, general arousal is controlled by the alerting network, which arises in the midbrain (Posner and Rothbart, 2006). This network is active in early infancy, controlling sleep/wake states and levels of alertness. The functions of this system mature within the first few months of life. Next, a spatial orienting network involving the parietal and temporal cortices contributes to aligning attention to specific locations and objects in the environment. This system becomes fully functional within the first year of life (Ruff and Rothbart, 1996). The third attentional network to emerge is the executive network, which provides the basis for voluntary behaviour and conflict resolution (Posner and Rothbart, 2006). It is this network that is most important for effortful control, and thus will be discussed in more detail.

The development of the executive network likely begins as a result of factors in the external environment. For example, caregivers' efforts to soothe the infant likely help to train regulation of emotion (Posner and Rothbart, 2006, p. 80). Effortful control emerges between 6 and 12 months of age, with the development of the anterior attention network (Rothbart, Derryberry and Posner, 1994). The anterior attention network serves both cognitive and affective functions, and this network is believed to primarily serve a conflict-resolution function. That is, the development of this system is thought to support the ability to exercise voluntary control in choosing between competing cognitive and emotional stimuli present at a given moment (Rothbart, Ahadi and Evans, 2000). Thus, studies of its development employ conflict tasks, such as Stroop tasks, flanker tasks, or spatial location versus identity tasks. For our purposes, it is interesting to note that these tasks are very similar and sometimes identical to those used to identify and retrain attentional biases.

Research suggests that the period from 9 to 12 months is important in the development of such conflict-resolution skills. For example, in early research, Diamond (1991) showed that 9-month old infants have difficulty resolving the conflict between reaching for an object in the line of sight versus retrieving an object through the side of a transparent box. However, at 12 months, the infants were able to complete this conflict-resolution task with relative ease. Studies with slightly older children suggest that these skills continue to develop through toddlerhood. For example, Gerardi-Caulton (2000) devised a task in which children 24–36 months of age were required to identify an object while ignoring the relationship between the location of the object and the location of the appropriate response key. At every age tested, children responded more slowly and less accurately when there was a conflict between location and identity. However, at 30 and 36 months of age, performance on the conflict task was found to be related to parent-rated self-regulation ability. Using the same location-identity conflict task, Rothbart, Ellis and Rueda (2003) also found that children improved in accuracy on the task from 24 to 36 months. The first age at which children were able to perform the task better than chance level was 30 months. However, there was evidence at 24 months to suggest that effort to make anticipatory eye movements is a precursor to the development of effortful control. By 36 months, the task was performed so well that there was very little evidence of any interference effect.

Kochanska, Murray and Harlan (2000) used a multitask battery and parent ratings to track the development of effortful control in toddlers. As with the other researchers, they found that effortful control improved considerably between 22 and 33 months, became more coherent and stable, and was higher in girls. Interestingly, they also found that greater effortful control at 33 months was related to more well-regulated anger and joy, suggesting a link between attentional processes and adaptive emotional functioning.

Effortful control is often measured in young children using modifications of the common game 'Simon Says', which itself is a conflict-resolution task, with conflict between sources of instruction (Posner and Rothbart, 2006). Ability to perform this task does not develop fully until approximately 4 years of age. Similarly, the ability to perform an Attention Network Test (ANT; Fan et al., 2002) develops at approximately 4 years of age. The ANT is a modified flanker task in which children are required to respond to an incongruent stimulus in a field of congruent stimuli. Posner and Rothbart (2006) report that children continue to show improvement on this task from age 4 to age 7, with no additional improvement after that time. Indeed, 10-year-old children performed similarly to adults on this conflict-resolution task. Thus, aspects of the executive attention network and conflict resolution, in particular, appear to develop up to the age of 7 years. Because conflict resolution is correlated with effortful control (e.g., Gerardi-Caulton, 2000), the implications for the temperamental dimension of effortful control are evident. These results suggest that the substrate for effortful control is in place by 7 years of age. Although evidence suggests that effortful control is largely in place by age 7, other results suggest that this dimension continues to improve into early adolescence. For example, Kindt *et al.* (2000) examined attentional control in spider-phobic children ages 8–11. They found that attentional control was somewhat limited in the younger children, but gradually increased with age.

Although ATT has not yet been tested as an intervention for children with anxiety disorders, Posner and Rothbart (2006) reported that young children have successfully been trained in broad effortful control strategies. For purposes of their study, children between 4 and 6 years of age were selected, since these children should have been in the process of developing the executive attention network, as described above. It was believed that these children could benefit most from training in effortful control. The children were trained using a series of computer-based training exercises. For example, children were trained on the value of digits and instructed to move their joystick to the larger of two arrays. Conflict trials consisted of arrays in which more copies of the smaller digit appeared on one side of the screen, while fewer copies of the larger digit appeared on the other side. The presented conflict was between the value of the digits and the size of the arrays. The children received 5 days of training, with sessions lasting 30–40 minutes. This training was compared to 2 years of typical development, by calculating the percentage change between ages 4 and 6.

Over the 2 years of typical development, the children showed improvement in overall reaction time, conflict reaction time and error rates. Brief training also increased all of these variables, but the percentage of change was somewhat smaller. Posner and Rothbart (2006) attributed at least part of their success to the developmentally sensitive nature of their training task, which the children enjoyed and could complete successfully. These observations are critical to our purposes, as we consider the development of appropriate ATT paradigms for children. The suggestion that children will benefit most from treatment paradigms that they enjoy should not come as a surprise: quite simply, an ATT paradigm for children should employ stimuli and a design that children find pleasurable.

Effortful control and emotion regulation

The development of effortful control is important not only for attention, but particularly when considered in light of its impact on emotional regulation, as well as the potential development of psychopathology (Hannesdottir and Ollendick, 2007). The temperamental factors of emotionality/neuroticism and such lower order traits as fear, anger/frustration and sadness are involved in the aetiology and maintenance of several childhood disorders (Muris and Ollendick, 2005). However, Rothbart's and Bates (1998) temperament theory would argue that such temperamental factors do not lead to psychopathology for every child exposed to threat or stressful life events. Instead, Rothbart argues that effortful control serves a regulatory temperamental function. It has been suggested that it is the combination of high emotionality/neuroticism and low effortful control that leads to psychopathology (Lonigan and Phillips, 2001).

Indeed, research suggests that effortful control, and particularly the attentional control dimension, may play a protective role against many forms of emotional and behavioural disorder. For example, in a sample of non-referred preschool children, Liew, Eisenberg and Reiser (2004) found that effortful control was associated with minimization or masking of negative verbal and gestural reactions in the presence of a stranger. The researchers also found that children high (vs. those low) in effortful control recovered more quickly from disappointment. More specifically, children who were low in effortful control expressed negative emotion openly and in ways that violated social norms (e.g. complaining, acting out). More recently, Valiente and colleagues (2006) followed a normative sample of children longitudinally. At the start of the study, the children were 6.5–10 years old, and the children were reassessed after 2 years and again after 4 years. Maternal expressivity of emotion at the initial assessment was related to child behaviour problems at 4-year follow-up. However, this relationship was mediated by effortful control at 2-year follow-up. Thus, effortful control served as a protective factor against the development of behavioural problems over time.

With regard to clinical symptoms of psychopathology, Muris, De Jong and Engelen (2004) found that attentional control was negatively related to anxiety symptoms in children 8–13 years of age. In addition, attentional control has been shown to be negatively related to self-reported aggression, attention-deficit hyperactivity disorder (ADHD), depression and anxiety symptoms in a non-referred sample of children and adolescents (Muris, Meesters and Rompelberg, 2007; Meesters, Muris and van Rooijen, 2007) Together, these results suggest that effortful control, and attentional control in particular, may serve an emotion regulation function and prevent the development of a wide variety of pathological emotional and behavioural symptoms. Again, these findings suggest that interventions that address attentional processes may be critical to the prevention of a wide range of psychopathology. Indeed, interventions such as ATT may be particularly important in child samples, since effortful control is still developing and may be more malleable.

Effortful control and attentional biases

Lack of attention to the dimension of effortful control may have contributed to inconsistency in attentional bias findings in children (Lonigan et al., 2004). Attentional bias studies with anxious children are mixed in finding both attention towards and away from threat. Some studies have found that rather than displaying an attention bias towards threat, anxious children exhibit an opposite bias. That is, they avoid the processing of threat-related cues. Specifically, in studies employing the Stroop task to detect attentional biases, results have been mixed. Although several studies have found the expected bias towards threat in anxious children (e.g., Richards, Richards and McGeeney, 2000; Richards *et al.*, 2007; Taghavi *et al.*, 2003), a similar number of studies have failed to find such a bias among children (e.g., Dalgleish *et al.*, 2003). Indeed, one study (Morren *et al.*, 2003) found that anxious children responded faster to threat words than non-anxious children on a Stroop task, counter to expected threat bias effects. Heim-Dreger *et al.* (2006) argued that these results may be explained by avoidance of threat-related stimuli. Thus, the children are applying more effort to the processing of threat stimuli in order to avoid (i.e. read quickly) the threatening stimuli. Such effects have not typically been found with dot-probe paradigms (see Vasey and MacLeod, 2001 for review) presumably since such response patterns do not serve to allow avoidance in that paradigm.

Mogg *et al.* (1993) suggested an alternate explanation for such mixed findings. They argued that such findings could be the result of methodological differences between the studies with regard to stimulus presentation. Specifically, they suggested that the manner of stimulus presentation in some studies allows for the effortful control of attention, whereas in other studies, opportunities for effortful control are absent or at least greatly reduced. This hypothesis has been supported in the adult literature. For example, Derryberry and Reed (2002) compared dot-probe performance by trait anxious subjects with a 250 milliseconds versus 500 milliseconds delay between cue and target. They found a bias towards threat when the target appeared 250 milliseconds after the cue. However, when the target appeared 500 milliseconds after the cue, a bias towards the non-threatening 'safe' location was found. The authors found that effortful control moderated these effects. That is, at the 500 milliseconds delay, trait anxious participants with poor effortful control showed the same threat bias as was found at 250 milliseconds. However, if the anxious participants had high levels of effortful control, they were better able to shift from the threat location at 500 milliseconds delay. Thus, effortful control of attention allowed these anxious adults to limit the impact of the threatening information when given sufficient time.

Lonigan and others (2004) report similar results in anxious adolescents. In a sample of high trait anxious adolescents, anxiety was found to be related to attentional bias towards threat. However, anxiety significantly interacted with effortful control. Specifically, anxiety was related to attentional bias at low levels of effortful control; at high levels of effortful control, attentional bias scores for high and low anxious adolescents were not significantly different. Similarly, a recent study by Stirling, Eley and Clark (2006) suggested that socially anxious children displayed avoidance of threatening faces presented in a dot-probe paradigm, rather than a bias towards threat. However, the authors argue that their findings are the result of extended stimulus presentation (1000 milliseconds) which allowed for attentional shifting and avoidance.

In attempting to control for effortful control of attention, dot-probe presentation intervals as brief as 14 milliseconds have been implemented effectively with adults (e.g. Mogg *et al.*, 1993). However, it is unclear at this time whether such brief intervals are advisable for use with children, given their still-developing perceptual systems and slower reaction times.

Effortful control as a bias mechanism

Developmental evidence regarding effortful control suggests a viable mechanism by which attentional biases may become extreme and maladaptive. Specifically, individuals low in effortful control may have particular difficulty managing their attentional processes. Thus, the attentional bias that is natural in most individuals may be undercontrolled among those low in effortful control. These individuals might then have particular difficulty disengaging attention from sources of potential threat. This difficulty may, in fact, be the root of the attentional vulnerability that contributes to the development of anxiety disorders. Indeed, several researchers have recently argued that attentional biases to threat result from an inability to disengage attention from threatening stimuli, rather than a specific attraction to such stimuli. For example, in a sample of high trait anxious adults, Fox *et al.* (2001) found that threatening stimuli did not differentially attract the attention of individuals high in trait anxiety. However, such individuals had difficulty disengaging their attention from the threatening stimuli. Similarly, high trait anxious individuals have more difficulty than controls in identifying peripheral targets when a fearful facial expression is presented centrally (Georgiou *et al.*, 2005). Thus, high trait anxious individuals had difficulty disengaging attention from threatening facial stimuli in order to complete task demands.

Further evidence that anxiety-related attentional biases are fundamentally undercontrolled attentional processes is reflected in new evidence that biases do not occur preattentively. In two studies of performance on visual search tasks in anxious individuals, Batty, Cage and Pauli (2005) found no evidence of preattentive detection of threat-valence. Other researchers have found similar results with anxious adults, suggesting that attentional biases do not occur without some level of conscious awareness (e.g. Ohman, Flykt and Esteves, 2001). These findings are currently considered controversial but suggest a role for effortful control in attentional biases to threat (see Chapters 2 and 10, for a further discussion of these issues).

ATT as effortful control training

We propose that ATT may operate successfully through the training of effortful control. As noted above, Wells (1990) initially designed ATT based on the S-REF model, which posits that emotional disorders result from several attentional factors, including increased self-focused attention, decreased cognitive efficiency, and attentional bias. According to the S-REF model, these attentional factors lead to activation of appraisals and self-beliefs which in turn, contribute to emotional disorders. Thus, Wells (1990) designed ATT to address dysregulated, inefficient attention. Effortful control, again, is defined as the 'ability to inhibit a dominant response to perform a subdominant response' (Rothbart and Bates, 1998, p. 137). It can be argued that it is this skill that is addressed in attention training, which requires participants to learn to 'inhibit a dominant response' (attend to threat) 'to perform a subdominant response' (shift attention to a neutral stimulus in the presence of a threatening stimulus). When individuals are then able to shift attention from threat, they are able to take in information that contrasts with anxious cognitions and therefore stops the vicious cycle of anxiety itself. This process may account for the demonstrated link between effortful control and emotion regulation (e.g. Muris and Ollendick, 2005).

If ATT is successful through its effects on effortful control, then this link suggests that children may be particularly good candidates for such an intervention. The success of Posner and Rothbart (2006) in training effortful control in a normative sample of children suggests that such intervention is possible. In fact, the somewhat modest results reported by those researchers may have been attenuated by the use of a non-referred sample. That is, some of the children in their sample were likely to be more developmentally advanced, with some perhaps having already attained high levels of effortful control. If indeed effortful control deficits are at the heart of attentional biases that contribute to anxiety, there may be more room for improvement in children already showing signs of anxiety. ATT improves on the treatment programme used by Posner and Rothbart by training efficient attentional shifting in the presence of emotionally valenced stimuli. As noted, anxious children seem to have particular difficulty controlling their attention in the presence of potential environmental threats, perhaps due to concurrent neuroticism (Lonigan and Phillips, 2001). Thus, ATT for these children may generalize into improvements in attentional functioning outside of the treatment setting, when threat is encountered in the environment.

While it is exciting to think of ATT as potentially training the broader substrate of effortful control, there is need for caution. As noted above, effortful control is typically considered a temperamental characteristic (Poggi Davis, Bruce and Gunnar, 2002) and such trait-like characteristics are generally considered more difficult to change than later-developed and transitory phenomena (e.g. developmental problems or clinical disorders). Thus, ATT may not be addressing effortful control directly, but rather attentional shifting or distraction as a coping strategy for anxiety. On the other hand, Posner and Rothbart (2006) have recently reported success in training effortful control. This training was, of course, accomplished with children who were still developing effortful control, so it is difficult to determine if such training might also be possible in older children or adult samples.

Considerations and Recommendations

Given the demonstrated success of attention retraining with adults, as well as the malleability of childhood characteristics, it is reasonable to assume that attention retraining could be beneficial with anxious children. If indeed attention retraining is to be used with anxious children, however, ATT paradigms currently in use with adults need to be modified to ensure that they are developmentally and methodologically appropriate. Clearly, children present particular challenges not encountered in the treatment of adults. First, any treatment with children should be enjoyable and fun to aid in rapport-building and child engagement (Ollendick and Cerny, 1981). In the case of ATT, this could be accomplished in many ways. For example, ATT could include cartoon characters to give instructions, along with colourful stimuli, in order to mimic a computer game. In addition, stimuli used with children should be pictorial rather than lexical. This would also likely allow for children to be treated regardless of reading level.

Specificity is another important element to consider in ATT treatment of children, on several levels. First, instructions should be very specific to ensure that children understand task demands and are able to complete those demands reliably (Vasey and MacLeod, 2001). In addition, special care should be taken to ensure that the specific anxieties and fears of the treated population are addressed. Findings with adults suggest that attentional biases are very specific (e.g. Mathews and MacLeod, 1985). That is, what is attended to as threatening varies based on disorder type. Thus, treatment needs to be equally specific in addressing attentional biases. This may be particularly difficult in children, given developmental changes in fear and anxiety (Muris and Merkelbach, 2001; Ollendick, King and Chorpita, 2006; Vasey, Crnic and Carter, 1994).

In addition, given that children tire more quickly than adults, ATT sessions should be relatively brief. Since ATT has already been shown to be effective with adults in sessions as brief as 10–15 minutes, this particular paradigm lends itself well to use with children. Within the ATT protocol for children, stimulus presentation times should be carefully planned. In order to allow for appropriate perception, developmental findings suggest that presentation intervals should not be briefer than 100 milliseconds (Schul, Townsend and Stiles, 2003). However, children's perceptual development may allow for use of briefer presentation intervals among older rather than younger children. Findings also suggest that most children are able to volitionally shift attention with sufficiently long presentation intervals (Dalgleish *et al.*, 2003). Thus, if ATT is to be successful in making attentional shifting more efficient in children, it should employ presentation intervals that are sufficiently long to allow for perception (100 milliseconds) but brief enough to allow for progress in attentional shifting efficiency (e.g. less than 800 milliseconds). Indeed, presentation intervals could be gradually shortened over time, as children become more and more efficient in their attentional shifting.

In addition to these methodological concerns, several research questions need to be addressed. As is evident, ATT has not yet been tested in direct comparison to existing treatments (Mohlman, 2004). More generally, ATT needs to be tested on larger and more diverse samples to explore moderators of treatment outcomes and over longer periods of time to assess the durability of the treatment effects. Potential mediators such as effortful control also need to be measured with regard to ATT treatment paradigms in order to determine the mechanisms through which attention retraining influences anxiety and attention.

Recently, we conducted a pilot study examining the use of ATT with two children. Participants included two boys, ages 9 and 11, with diagnoses of social anxiety disorder. The boys were treated using the ADT developed by Amir (2006). In this preliminary study, the procedures closely followed those used with adults. The boys received 10 weekly sessions of attention retraining, with each session lasting approximately 15 minutes. Approximately 2 weeks post-treatment, both boys evidenced significant decreases in anxiety, as demonstrated by reductions in scores on the Social Phobia Subscale of the Spence Children's Anxiety Scale (Spence, 1998). In addition, neither boy met Anxiety Disorders Interview Schedule for Children (ADIS-C/P; Silverman and Albano, 1996) criteria for social anxiety disorder at follow-up. While current analyses are underway to determine the role of effortful control in these findings, these preliminary findings suggest that ATT could prove successful in the treatment of childhood anxiety disorders. However, it is clear that much more research is needed.

Once ATT has been further tested and examined with children and adolescents, it could be standardized and manualized for use either as a stand-alone treatment or in concert with CBT. Indeed, there has been some debate about the use of ATT alone versus as an adjunct to existing CBT paradigms (Mohlman, 2004). While researchers have demonstrated success in adults using ATT alone (e.g. MacLeod and Bridle, 2006), it may be even more successful in combination with CBT. In particular, as noted, ATT seems to train effortful control in the presence of threatening stimuli. Besides aiding in generalization and maintenance of skills outside of treatment, ATT could also aid in CBT treatment itself. In particular, ATT could supplement exposure therapy and allow clients to engage more appropriately with threatening stimuli. In addition, individuals treated with ATT may show improvements in other types of cognitive functioning, such as the ability to generate alternative explanations of events. On the other hand, children and adolescents treated with CBT who thus interpret situations less catastrophically may be more able to engage in ATT and thus receive more benefit (Mohlman, 2004).

One possible critique of attention retraining for both adults and children that has been offered is that the paradigm may train anxious individuals to distract themselves by directing attention away from sources of threat. This seems to be in direct contradiction to the principles underlying CBT and which have been shown to be effective in treating anxiety disorders (see Barlow, 2001; Woody and Ollendick, 2006) and which call for graduated and prolonged exposure to feared situations or stimuli. However, if we consider ATT as training in effortful control, it becomes a potentially useful element of exposure therapy. In fact, Wells (2000) argued that in anxious individuals with attentional biases, there is a tendency to become cognitively 'stuck' on threatening stimuli. Methods such as attention retraining may allow these individuals to become 'unstuck', and more appropriately control their own attentional processes. This process may allow the individuals to more fully experience exposures to threatening stimuli, and thus ATT may provide a useful adjunct to exposure-based therapy.

Another argument for the use of ATT in combination with CBT rather than as a stand-alone treatment stems from concern regarding therapist–client relationship.

Quality of the relationship between therapist and client has been found to be an important predictor of therapy outcome. Indeed, in an early meta-analysis, Horvath and Symonds (1991) indicated that the therapeutic relationship accounted for 9% of the variance in outcomes. Therapeutic relationships may also be particularly important to outcomes in children and adolescents (Karver *et al.*, 2005; Ollendick and Shirk, in press). Thus, if ATT is used in combination with traditional CBT, interaction between a therapist and client will be increased and may improve treatment outcomes as compared to ATT alone.

In addition to the use of ATT alone or in concert with CBT as an intervention for anxiety, it also shows promise as a potential preventative against anxiety in children. That is, if anxiety is caused by attentional biases (MacLeod and Hagan, 1992) and attentional biases can be changed, anxiety disorders may be prevented. As noted, this could be particularly successful in children who are still developing attentional biases and effortful control, as well as the anxiety disorders themselves.

Summary

A relationship between anxiety and attentional bias to threat has been strongly established both in adults and children. Recent research has suggested that attentional biases may, in fact, serve as a diathesis for anxiety disorders; however, current treatments (e.g. CBT) do not directly address these biases. Thus, researchers have begun to design ATT paradigms that directly address anxiety-related biases.

ATT is based on the S-REF model of psychopathology, which posits that emotional disorders are the result of executive function difficulties (e.g. attentional biases) which reduce available resources for processing competing corrective information from the environment. Original ATT paradigms involved therapist-led training in attentional skills. More recently, researchers have begun to develop computer-based ATT protocols based on experimental paradigms such as dot-probe tasks. These tasks are designed to train participants to attend to neutral rather than threat cues. Thus far, ATT has primarily been used with adults, and has shown success in treating a wide variety of anxiety disorders as well as the depressive disorders.

Given the success of ATT in treating adults, it is reasonable to assume that such treatment may be beneficial for anxious children, but developmental issues must be considered. The most relevant developmental process to consider with regard to ATT paradigms with children is effortful control, including attentional control and inhibitory control. Effortful control emerges between 6 and 12 months of age, and continues to develop throughout early childhood and possibly into adolescence. It has been implicated in the development of diverse child psychopathologies. Indeed, effortful control and attentional control, in particular, may serve emotion regulatory functions and serve as a protective factor against the development of emotional and behavioural problems. Evidence regarding effortful control suggests that it may be the mechanism by which attentional biases become maladaptive and, in turn, lead to the development of anxiety disorders.

We propose that ATT may operate successfully through the training of effortful control and thus children may prove to be particularly good candidates for this type of intervention. However, interventions with children need to take developmental considerations into account. For example, special care should be taken to design protocols that are engaging, specific to the anxieties of the treated population, and relatively brief. Research is desperately needed to determine if ATT can be successfully used to treat anxious children, to compare ATT to existing treatments, and to test it on larger and more diverse samples. Longitudinal outcome studies and examination of mediators and moderators of outcome area are also needed. Once ATT has been further examined with children and adolescents, it could be implemented as a stand-alone treatment or as a supplement to more traditional CBT treatment, as well as a preventative treatment for the anxiety disorders.

References

Amir, N. (2006) Modifications of attention bias: a novel treatment for anxiety disorders. Paper presented at the European Association for Behavioral and Cognitive Therapies. Paris, France.

Bar-Haim, Y., Lamy, D., Pergamin, L. *et al.* (2007) Threat-related attentional bias in anxious and non-anxious individuals: a meta-analytic study. *Psychological Bulletin*, **133**, 1–24.

Barlow, D.H. (2001) *Clinical Handbook of Psychological Disorders: A Step-by-Step Treatment Manual*, Guilford Press, New York.

Batty, M.J., Cage, K.R. and Pauli, P. (2005) Abstract stimuli associated with threat through conditioning cannot be detected preattentively. *Emotion*, **5**, 418–430.

Dalgleish, T., Taghavi, R., Neshat-Doost, H. *et al.* (2003) Patterns of processing bias for emotional information across clinical disorders: a comparison of attention, memory, and prospective cognition in children and adolescents with depression, anxiety, and post-traumatic stress disorder. *Journal of Clinical Child and Adolescent Psychology*, **32**, 10–21.

Derryberry, D. and Reed, M.A. (2002) Anxiety-related attentional biases and their regulation by attentional control. *Journal of Abnormal Psychology*, **111**, 225–236.

Diamond, A. (1991) Neuropsychological insights into the meaning of object concept development, in *The Epigenesis of Mind: Essays on Biology and Cognition* (eds S. Carey and R. Gelman), Lawrence Erlbaum Associates, Hillsdale, NJ, pp. 67–110.

Fan, J., McCandliss, B.D., Sommer, T. *et al.* (2002) Testing the efficiency and independence of attentional networks. *Journal of Cognitive Neuroscience*, **14**, 340–347.

Foa, E.G. and McNally, R.J. (1986) Sensitivity to feared stimuli in obsessive-compulsives: a dichotic listening analysis. *Cognitive Therapy and Research*, **10**, 477–485.

Fox, E., Russo, R., Bowles, R. and Dutton, K. (2001) Do threatening stimuli draw or hold attention in subclinical anxiety? *Journal of Experimental Psychology: General*, **130** (4), 681–700.

Georgiou, G.A., Bleakley, C., Hayward, J. *et al.* (2005) Focusing on fear: attentional disengagement from emotional faces. *Visual Cognition*, **12**, 145–158.

Gerardi-Caulton, G. (2000) Sensitivity to spatial conflict and the development of self-regulation in children 24-36 months of age. *Developmental Science*, **3**, 397–404.

Hannesdottir, D.K. and Ollendick, T.H. (2007) The role of emotion regulation in the treatment of child anxiety disorders. *Clinical Child and Family Psychology Review*, **10**, 275–293.

Heimberg, R.G., Liebowitz, M.R. and Hope, D.A. (1998) Cognitive behavioral group therapy vs phenelzine therapy for social phobia: 12-week outcome. *Archives of General Psychiatry*, **55** (12), 1133–1141.

Heim-Dreger, U., Kohlmann, C., Eschenbeck, H. and Burkhardt, U. (2006) Attentional biases for threatening faces in children: vigilant and avoidant processes. *Emotion*, **6**, 320–325.

Horvath, A.O. and Symonds, B.D. (1991) Relation between working alliance and outcome in psychotherapy: a meta-analysis. *Journal of Counseling Psychology*, **38**, 139–149.

Karver, M.S., Handelsman, J.B., Fields, S. and Bickman, L. (2005) A theoretical model of common process factors in youth and family therapy. *Mental Health Services Research*, **7**, 35–51.

Kendall, P.C., Hudson, J.L., Choudhury, M. *et al.* (2005) Cognitive-behavioral treatment for childhood anxiety disorders, in *Psychosocial Treatments for Child and Adolescent Disorders: Empirically Based Strategies for Clinical Practice*, 2nd edn (eds E.D. Hibbs and P.S. Jensen), APA, Washington, DC, pp. 47–73.

Kindt, M., Bierman, D. and Brosschot, J.F. (1997) Cognitive bias in spider fear and control children: assessment of emotional interference by a card format and a single-trial format of the Stroop task. *Journal of Experimental Child Psychology*, **66**, 163–179.

Kindt, M., Brosschot, J.F. and Everaerd, W. (1997) Cognitive processing bias of children in a real life stress situation and a neutral situation. *Journal of Experimental Child Psychology*, **64**, 79–97.

Kindt, M., Van den Hout, M., De Jong, P.J. and Hoeksema, B. (2000) Cognitive bias for pictoral and linguistic threat cues in children. *Journal of Psychopathology and Behavioral Assessment*, **22**, 201–219.

Kochanska, G. and Knaack, A. (2003) Effortful control as a personality characteristic of young children: antecendants, correlates, and consequences. *Journal of Personality*, **71**, 263–277.

Kochanska, G., Murray, K. and Coy, K.C. (1997) Inhibitory control as a contributor to conscience in childhood: from toddler to early school age. *Child Development*, **68**, 263–277.

Kochanska, G., Murray, K.T. and Harlan, E.T. (2000) Effortful control in early childhood: continuity and change, antecedents, and implications for social development. *Developmental Psychology*, **36**, 220–232.

Lavy, E., van den Hout, M. and Arntz, A. (1993) Attentional bias and spider phobia: conceptual and clinical issues. *Behaviour Research and Therapy*, **31**, 17–24.

Liew, J., Eisenberg, N. and Reiser, M. (2004) Preschoolers' effortful control and negative emotionality, immediate reactions to disappointment, and quality of social functioning. *Journal of Experimental Child Psychology*, **89**, 298–319.

Lonigan, C.J. and Phillips, B.M. (2001) Temperamental influences on the development of anxiety disorders, in *The Developmental Psychopathology of Anxiety* (eds M.W. Vasey and M.R. Dadds), Oxford University Press, New York.

Lonigan, C.J., Vasey, M.W., Phillips, B.M. and Hazen, R.A. (2004) Temperament, anxiety, and the processing of threat-relevant stimuli. *Journal of Clinical Child and Adolescent Psychology*, **33**, 8–20.

MacLeod, C. and Bridle, R. (2006) The modification of anxiety through the manipulation of attentional bias: evaluation of a 16 day on-line attentional training program. Paper presented at the convention of the European Association of Behavioral and Cognitive Therapies.

MacLeod, C. and Hagan, R. (1992) Individual differences in the selective processing of threatening information, and emotional responses to a stressful life event. *Behaviour Research and Therapy*, **30**, 151–161.

MacLeod, C. and Rutherford, E. (1992) Anxiety and the selective processing of emotional information: mediating roles of awareness, trait and state variable, and personal relevance of stimulus materials. *Behavior Research and Therapy*, **30**, 479–491.

Martin, M., Horder, P. and Jones, G.V. (1992) Integral bias in naming of phobia-related words. *Cognition and Emotion*, **6**, 479–486.

Mathews, A. and MacLeod, C. (1985) Selective processing of threat cues in anxiety states. *Behaviour Research and Therapy*, **23**, 563–569.

Mathews, A. and MacLeod, C. (2002) Induced processing biases have causal effects on anxiety. *Cognition and Emotion*, **16**, 331–354.

Mathews, A., May, J., Mogg, K. and Eysenck, M. (1990) Attentional bias in anxiety: selective search or defective filtering? *Journal of Abnormal Psychology*, **99**, 166–173.

Mathews, A., Mogg, K., Kentish, J. and Eysenck, M. (1995) Effect of psychological treatment on cognitive bias in generalized anxiety disorder. *Behaviour Research and Therapy*, **33**, 293–303.

Meesters, C., Muris, P. and van Rooijen, B. (2007) Relations of neuroticism and attentional control with symptoms of anxiety and aggression. *Journal of Psychopathology and Behavioral Assessment*, **29**, 149–158.

Mogg, K., Bradley, B.P., Williams, R. and Mathews, A. (1993) Subliminal processing of emotional information in anxiety and depression. *Journal of Abnormal Psychology*, **102**, 304–311.

Mohlman, J. (2004) Attention training as an intervention for anxiety: review and rationale. *The Behavior Therapist*, **27** (2), 37–41.

Morren, M., Kindt, M., van den Hout, M. and van Kasteren, H. (2003) Anxiety and the processing of threat in children: further examination of the of the of the cognitive inhibition hypothesis. *Behaviour Change*, **20**, 131–142.

Muris, P., De Jong, P.J. and Engelen, S. (2004) Relationships between neuroticism, attentional control, and anxiety disorder symptoms in non-clinical children. *Personality and Individual Differences*, **37**, 789–797.

Muris, P. and Field, A. (2008) Distorted cognition and pathological anxiety in children and adolescents. *Cognition and Emotion*, **22**, 395–421.

Muris, P., Meesters, C. and Rompelberg, L. (2007) Attention control in middle childhood: relations to psychopathological symptoms and threat perception distortions. *Behaviour Research and Therapy*, **45**, 997–1010.

Muris, P. and Merckelbach, H. (2001) The etiology of childhood specific phobia: a multifactorial model, in *The Developmental Psychopathology of Anxiety* (eds M.W. Vasey and M.R. Dadds), Oxford University Press, New York.

Muris, P. and Ollendick, T.H. (2005) The role of temperament in the etiology of child psychopathology. *Clinical Child and Family Psychology Review*, **8**, 271–289.

Ohman, A., Flykt, A. and Esteves, F. (2001) Emotion drives attention: detecting the snake in the grass. *Journal of Experiemental Psychology: General*, **130**, 466–478.

Ollendick, T.H. and Cerny, J.A. (1981) *Clinical Behavior Therapy with Children*, Plenum Press, New York.

Ollendick, T.H., King, N.J. and Chorpita, B.F. (2006) Empirically-supported treatments for children and adolescents, in *Child and Adolescent Therapy: Cognitive-Behavioral Procedures*, 3rd edn (ed. P.C. Kendall), Guilford Press, New York.

Ollendick, T.H. and Shirk, S.R. (in press) Clinical interventions with children and adolescents, in *Handbook of Clinical Psychology* (ed. D.H. Barlow), Oxford University Press, Oxford.

Ollendick, T.H. and Vasey, M.W. (2001) Operant conditioning influences in childhood anxiety, in *The Developmental Psychopathology of Anxiety* (eds M.W. Vasey and M.R. Dadds), Oxford University Press, New York.

Öst, L. (1989) One-session treatment for specific phobias. *Behaviour Research and Therapy*, **27**, 1–7

Papageorgiou, C. and Wells, A. (1998) Effects of attention training on hypochondriasis: a brief case series. *Psychological Medicine*, **28**, 193–200.

Papageorgiou, C. and Wells, A. (2000) Treatment of recurrent major depression with attention retraining. *Cognitive and Behavioral Practice*, **4**, 407–413.

Poggi Davis, E., Bruce, J. and Gunnar, M.R. (2002) The anterior attention network: associations with temperament and neuroendocrine activity in 6-year-old children. *Developmental Psychobiology*, **40**, 43–56.

Posner, M.I. and Rothbart, M.K. (2006) *Educating the Human Brain*, American Psychological Association, Washington, DC.

Prins, P. and Ollendick, T.H. (2003) Cognitive change and enhanced coping: missing meditational links in cognitive-behavior therapy with anxiety-disordered children. *Clinical Child and Family Psychology Review*, **6**, 87–105.

Puliafico, A.C. and Kendall, P.C. (2006) Threat-related attentional biases in anxious youth: a review. *Clinical Child and Family Psychology Review*, **9**, 162–180.

Richards, A., French, C.C., Nash, G. *et al.* (2007) A comparison of selective attention and facial processing biases in typically developing children who are high and low in self-reported trait anxiety. *Development and Psychopathology*, **19**, 481–495.

Richards, A., Richards, L.C. and McGeeney, A. (2000) Anxiety-related Stroop interference in adolescents. *The Journal of General Psychology*, **127**, 237–333.

Richey, J.A. and Schmidt, N.B. (2006) Attention retraining as a treatment for social anxiety disorder. Paper presented at the conference of the Association for Behavioral and Cognitive Therapies. Chicago, IL.

Rothbart, M.K., Ahadi, S.A. and Evans, D.E. (2000) Temperament and personality: origins and outcomes. *Journal of Personality and Social Psychology*, **7**, 122–135.

Rothbart, M.K. and Bates, J.E. (1998) Temperament, in *Handbook of Child Psychology*, 5th edn, vol. 3 (eds W. Damon and N. Eisenberg), *Social, Emotional, and Personality Development*, John Wiley and Sons, Inc, Hoboken, NJ.

Rothbart, M.K., Derryberry, D. and Posner, M.I. (1994) A psychobiological approach to the development of temperament, in *Temperament: Individual Differences at the Interface of Biology and Behavior* (eds J.E. Bates and T.D. Wachs), American Psychological Association, Washington, DC.

Rothbart, M.K., Ellis, L.K. and Posner, M.I. (2004) Temperament and self-regulation, in *Handbook of Self-Regulation: Research, Theory, and Applications* (eds R.F. Baumeister and K.D. Vohs), Guilford Press, New York.

Rothbart, M.K., Ellis, L.K. and Rueda, M.R. (2003) Developing mechanisms of temperamental effortful control. *Journal of Personality*, **7**, 1113–1143.

Ruff, H.A. and Rothbart, M.K. (1996) *Attention in Early Development: Themes and Variations*, Oxford University Press, New York.

Rutherford, E., MacLeod, C. and Campbell, L. (2002) Practice makes perfect: The reduction of trait anxiety through the extended retraining of attentional response to threat. Paper presented at the 36th annual meeting of the Association for Advancement of Behavior Therapy, Reno, Nov. 2000.

Schul, R., Townsend, J. and Stiles, J. (2003) The development of attentional orienting during the school-age years. *Developmental Science*, **6** (3), 262–272.

Silverman, W.K. and Albano, A.M. (1996) *Anxiety Disorders Interview Schedule for Children*, Psychological Corporation, San Antonio, TX.

Spence, S.H. (1998) A measure of anxiety symptoms among children. *Behaviour Research and Therapy*, **3**, 545–566.

Stirling, L.J., Eley, T.C. and Clark, D.M. (2006) Preliminary evidence for an association between social anxiety symptoms and avoidance of negative faces in school-age children. *Journal of Clinical Child and Adolescent Psychology*, **35**, 440–445.

Taghavi, M.R., Dalgleish, T., Moradi, A.R. *et al.* (2003) Selective processing of negative emotional information in children and adolescents with generalized anxiety disorder. *British Journal of Clinical Psychology*, **42**, 221–230.

Valiente, C., Eisenberg, N., Spinrad, T.L *et al.* (2006) Relations among mothers' expressivity, children's effortful control, and their problem behaviors: a four-year longitudinal study. *Emotion*, **6**, 459–472.

Vasey, M.W., Crnic, K.A. and Carter, W.G. (1994) Worry in childhood: a developmental perspective. *Cognitive Therapy and Research*, **18**, 529–549.

Vasey, M.W., Daleiden, E.L., Williams, L.L. and Brown, L. (1995) Biased attention in childhood anxiety: a preliminary study. *Journal of Abnormal Child Psychology*, **23**, 267–279.

Vasey, M.W., El-Hag, N. and Daleiden, E.L. (1996) Anxiety and the processing of emotionally threatening stimuli: distinctive patterns of selective attention among high- and low- test-anxious children. *Child Development*, **67**, 1173–1185.

Vasey, M.W. and MacLeod, C. (2001) Information-processing factors in childhood anxiety: a review and developmental perspective, in *The Developmental Psychopathology of Anxiety* (eds M.W. Vasey and M.R. Dadds), Oxford University Press, New York.

Waters, A.M., Wharton, T.A., Zimmer-Gembeck, M.J. and Craske, M.G. (2008) Threat-based cognitive biases in anxious children: comparison with non-anxious children before and after cognitive behavioural treatment. *Behaviour Research and Therapy*, **46**, 358–374.

Watts, F.N., McKenna, F.P., Sharrock, R. and Trezise, L. (1986) Colour naming of phobia-related words. *British Journal of Psychology*, **77**, 97–108.

Wells, A. (1990) Panic disorder in association with relaxation induced anxiety: an attentional training approach to treatment. *Behavior Therapy*, **21**, 273–280.

Wells, A. (2000) *Emotional Disorders and Metacognition: Innovative Cognitive Therapy*, John Wiley & Sons, Chichester.

Wells, A. and Matthews, G. (1996) Modeling cognition in emotional disorder: the S-REF model. *Behaviour Research and Therapy*, **34**, 881–888.

Wells, A., White, J. and Carter, K. (1997) Attention training: effects on anxiety and beliefs in panic and social phobia. *Clinical Psychology and Psychotherapy*, **4**, 226–232.

Woody, S.R. and Ollendick, T.H. (2006) Technique factors in treating anxiety disorders, in *Principles of Therapeutic Change that Work* (eds L. Castonguay and L.E. Beutler), Oxford University Press, New York, pp. 167–186.

Index

Information Processing Biases and Anxiety: A Developmental Perspective Edited by Julie A. Hadwin and Andy P. Field
© 2010 John Wiley & Sons, Ltd.